Human Resource and Personnel Management

The Irwin Series in Management and the Behavioral Sciences

L. L. Cummings and E. Kirby Warren *Consulting Editors*
John F. Mee *Advisory Editor*

Human Resource and Personnel Management

Lloyd L. Byars, Ph.D.

Department of Management
Atlanta University

Leslie W. Rue, Ph.D.

Department of Management
Georgia State University

1984
RICHARD D. IRWIN, INC.
Homewood, Illinois   60430

Some references appear on page of citation to fulfill
stipulation of the copyright holder.

ISBN 0-256-03013-8

Library of Congress Catalog Card No. 83–81766

Printed in the United States of America

1 2 3 4 5 6 7 8 9 0 V 1 0 9 8 7 6 5 4

To Susan, Elizabeth and Lee Byars
and
Elizabeth, Meggin and Leslie Rue

Preface

Human resource management has become a vital function in modern organizations. Changing governmental requirements, increasing demands for a more skilled and better motivated work force, and intensifying foreign competition are just a few of the factors that have contributed to the importance of human resource management in today's organizations.

This book is designed to emphasize both the theoretical and practical sides of human resource management. We feel this has been accomplished by the use of numerous examples scattered throughout the text and by the end-of-chapter materials. In addition to review questions, each chapter is accompanied by several in-depth discussion questions and two minicases, both of which require application of the concepts provided in the chapter. Each major section of the book contains a comprehensive case. The purpose of the section cases is to integrate the various concepts presented in the respective sections. A recent incident from a real organization has been added to each chapter to emphasize the practicality of the chapter material.

The book's content is arranged in five major sections. Section One, "Introduction," is designed to provide the student with the basic foundation necessary to embark on a study of the work of human resource management. Job analysis, job design, human resource planning, and equal employment opportunity are topics that impact on all areas of human resource management. Section Two, "Obtaining and Developing Employees," discusses the topics of employee recruitment, selection, orientation and training, management development, and organization development. Section Three, "Compensating Employees," describes basic wage and salary systems, incentive systems, benefits, pensions, and retirement programs. Section Four, "Guiding and Directing Employees," explores performance appraisal systems, career counseling, discipline, and grievance handling. Section Five, "Understanding Unions and Improving Employee Welfare," is concerned with understanding unions, the collective bargaining process, and employee health and safety matters.

In addition, five appendixes are provided to increase the practicality of the book. Appendix A, "Preemployment Inquiry Guide," provides a detailed description of questions that can and cannot be asked in an employment interview. Appendix B, "Finding a Job," presents a practical process for aiding the student in choosing a career and finding a job in that career. Appendix C, "Resume Writing," outlines how to prepare an effective resume. Appendix D provides a listing of journals in human resource management. Appendix E gives a listing of important organizations in human resource management.

Tom Chacko of Iowa State University, David Grigsby of Clemson University, and Dwight Norris of Auburn University provided valuable assistance through their insightful reviews of this material. Larry Cummings and Kirby Warren, as consulting editors, provided very helpful assistance. Thanks are extended to Johnnie L. Clark, dean, Graduate School of Business Administration; and to Kofi B. Bota, president, both of Atlanta University. Thanks are also due Noah Langdale, president; Bill Suttles, provost-executive vice president; Kenneth Black, Jr., dean, College of Business Administration; and Michael Mescon, chairman, Department of Management, all of Georgia State University. We also wish to thank Linda Byars for her invaluable assistance on this project. And final thanks are due Sylvia Wyatt, Betty Allen, and Ardalia Green for typing the manuscript.

Lloyd L. Byars
Leslie W. Rue

Contents

Affirmative action plans (AAP). Landmark court cases. Griggs *v.* Duke Power Company. Albemarle Paper *v.* Moody. Washington *v.* Davis. University of California Regents *v.* Bakke. United Steelworkers *v.* Weber. Uniform Guidelines on Employee Selection Procedures: *Adverse impact. Eliminating adverse impact.* Additional equal employment opportunity legislation: *Equal Pay Act. Education Amendments Act. Age Discrimination in Employment Act. Veterans Readjustment Act. Rehabilitation Act.* Current issues in equal employment opportunity: *Sexual harassment. Equal pay for work of comparable value.* Record-keeping and equal employment opportunity.

Section two
Obtaining and developing employees

5. Recruiting employees, 98

Recruitment—a two-way street. Sources of qualified personnel: *Internal sources. External sources.* Methods of recruitment: *Job posting. Advertising. Campus recruiting. Employment agencies. Employee referrals and walk-ins/write-ins. Effectiveness of recruitment methods.* Who does the recruiting? Organizational inducements. The recruitment interview. Equal employment opportunity and recruitment.

6. Selecting employees, 120

Validation of selection procedures: *Empirical validity. Content and construct validity.* Reliability. Uniform Guidelines on Employee Selection Procedures. The selection process: *The application form. Preliminary interview. Applicant testing. Diagnostic interview. Reference checking. Physical examination. Making the final selection decision.*

7. Orientation and employee training, 148

Orientation: *Shared responsibility. Company orientation. Departmental and job orientation. Orientation kit. Orientation length and timing. Follow-up and evaluation.* Training employees: *Determining training needs. Establishing training objectives. Evaluating training.* Methods of training: *On-the-job training and job rotation. Vestibule training. Apprenticeship training. Classroom training.* Principles of learning: *Motivation to achieve personal goals. Knowledge of results. Reinforcement. Flow of the training program. Practice and repetition. Spacing of sessions. Whole or part training.*

Section five
Understanding unions and improving employee welfare

SECTION ONE

Introduction

Chapter 1

Human resource management: Present and future

Objectives

1. To define human resource management.
2. To describe the functions of human resource management.
3. To discuss some common misconceptions about human resource management.
4. To explore job opportunities available in human resource management.

Outline

Human resource functions Those tasks and duties that human resource managers perform (e.g., determining the organization's human resource needs, recruiting, selecting, developing, counseling, and rewarding employees, acting as liaison with unions and government organizations, and handling other matters of employee well-being).

Human resource management The activities designed to provide for and coordinate the human resources of an organization.

Human resource planning Process by which the human resource needs of an organization are determined.

Operating manager Person who manages people directly involved with the production of an organization's products or services (e.g., a production manager in a manufacturing plant or a loan manager in a bank).

Human resource specialist Person who is specially trained in one or more areas of human resource management (e.g., labor relations specialist, wage and salary specialist).

Personnel management Term used synonymously with human resource management. Some authors view personnel management as much narrower and more clerically oriented than human resource management.

Every aspect of a firm's activities is determined by the competence, motivation, and general effectiveness of its human organization. Of all the tasks of management, managing the human component is the central and most important task, because all else depends upon how well it is done.

Rensis Likert *

Human resource management encompasses those activities designed to provide for and coordinate the human resources of an organization. The human resources of an organization represent one of its largest investments. In fact, government reports show that over 75 percent of national income is used to compensate employees.[1] The value of an organization's human resources frequently becomes evident when the organization is sold. Often the purchase price is greater than the total value of the physical and financial assets. This difference, sometimes called goodwill, partially reflects the value of an organization's human resources. In addition to wages and salaries, organizations often make other sizable investments in their human resources. Recruiting, hiring, and training represent some of the more obvious examples.

Human resource management is a modern term for what has traditionally been referred to as personnel administration or personnel management. Some authors view human resource management as being somewhat different from traditional personnel management.[2] These authors see personnel management as much narrower and more clerically oriented than human resource management. For the purposes of this book, the terms *human resource management* and *personnel management* will be used interchangeably.

HUMAN RESOURCE FUNCTIONS

Human resource functions refer to those tasks and duties performed in both large and small organizations to provide for and coordinate human resources. Human resource functions are concerned with a variety of activities that significantly influence all areas of an organization and include the following:

1. Conducting job analyses to establish the specific requirements of individual jobs within an organization.
2. Forecasting the personnel requirements necessary for the organization to achieve its objectives.
3. Developing and implementing a plan to meet these requirements.
4. Ensuring that the organization fulfills all of its equal employment opportunity and other government obligations.
5. Recruiting the personnel required by the organization to achieve its objectives.

---

*R. Likert, *The Human Organization* (New York: McGraw-Hill, 1967), p. 1.

6. Selecting (or hiring) personnel to fill specific jobs within an organization.
7. Orienting and training employees.
8. Designing and implementing management and organizational development programs.
9. Designing and implementing compensation systems for all employees.
10. Designing systems for appraising the performance of individual employees.
11. Assisting employees in developing career plans.
12. Designing discipline and grievance-handling systems.
13. Serving as an intermediary between an organization and its union(s).
14. Designing and implementing programs to ensure employee health and safety and providing assistance to employees with personal problems that influence their work performance.

This book has been organized into five major sections as a means of examining each of these functions in detail and showing how they interrelate. Section One serves as an introduction and examines topics that influence all areas of personnel management. Job design and job analysis, human resource planning, and equal employment opportunity are discussed. Section Two explores those personnel functions that are specifically concerned with obtaining and developing an organization's human resources. The topics of recruitment, selection, orientation and training, and development of both employees and managers are discussed in this section. Section Three is concerned with all aspects of employee compensation. Motivation theory, base wage and salary systems, incentive pay systems, and benefits are discussed. Section Four concentrates on those functions necessary to guide and direct employees. Performance appraisal, career planning, discipline, and grievance handling are covered here. Section Five is concerned with understanding unions and improving employee welfare. Labor unions, the collective bargaining process, and employee health and safety are topics included in this section. In addition to the five major sections, five appendixes are provided at the end of the book.

WHO PERFORMS THE HUMAN RESOURCE FUNCTIONS?

All managers are periodically involved in some human resource functions. For example, almost all managers, at one time or another, are involved in training, developing, and evaluating their employees. In small organizations, most personnel functions are performed by the owner or operating managers. Large organizations usually have a human resource or personnel department that is responsible for directing the human resource functions. Such a department is normally staffed by one or more human resource specialists. These specialists are trained in one or more areas of human resource management.

When a human resource department exists, many personnel functions are still performed by operating managers. Unfortunately, however, operating managers often try to divorce themselves from personnel-related matters. This rarely is successful because many personnel functions are directly linked with the functions performed by operating managers. It is simply not possible for operating managers to leave all personnel-related matters to the personnel department. Customarily, a human resource department organizes and coordinates hiring and training, maintains personnel records, acts as a liaison between management, labor, and government, coordinates safety programs, and advises operating managers on human resource matters.

Precisely how the personnel functions are divided between operating managers and the human resource department varies from organization to organization. For example, the human resource department may do all of the hiring below a certain level in one company. In another company all the hiring decisions may be made by operating managers, with the human resource department acting only in an advisory capacity.

It is helpful to look upon the human resource department as providing three types of assistance: (1) specific services, (2) advice, and (3) coordination. Thus, the human resource department might do the actual hiring in one company and yet in another it might only advise operating managers with regard to hiring matters. Figure 1–1 illus-

Figure 1–1   Three types of assistance provided by a human resource department

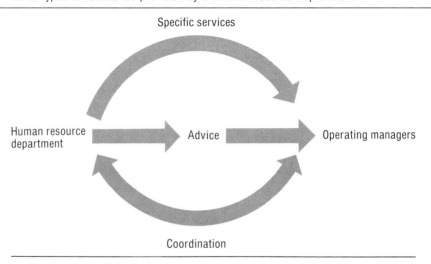

Figure 1–2 Examples of the different types of assistance provided by a human resource department

Specific services	Advice	Coordination
Maintaining employee records	Displinary matters	Performance appraisals
Initial phases of employee orientation	Equal employment opportunity matters	Compensation matters

trates the different roles that a human resource department might fill. Figure 1–2 presents some typical examples of each of these types of assistance.

When a human resource department does exist, it normally acts in an advisory capacity and does not have authority over operating managers. As a result, conflict can occur when operating managers appear to ignore the suggestions and recommendations of the human resource department. If the department is to be effective, it must continually cultivate good relations with operating managers.

MISCONCEPTIONS ABOUT HUMAN RESOURCE MANAGEMENT

Unfortunately, many top managers are guilty of holding a very narrow and often inaccurate view of human resource management. The human resource function is usually viewed by these people as being rather unimportant. In these situations, the human resource function is seen as encompassing primarily the staffing and employment activities that no one else really wants to do. These activities usually include such things as maintaining the vast array of records required by the government, directing employee recreation programs, and presiding at retirement parties.

It is precisely because of this view that the term *human resource* has emerged in place of *personnel.* The hope is that this term will get away from the negative connotation associated with the word *personnel.* It has been suggested that this inaccurate view of human resource management has been advanced in some organizations because of two major problems: an alleged lack of expertise on the part of human resource specialists, and disrespect for the human resource function, deserved or not, on the part of many top managers.[3]

Lack of expertise

Many managers criticize human resource people for having little interest in or knowledge of other areas of the organization. For example, one author, referring to a group of surveys, reported that "although they always knew without exception the number of employees, a majority of major corporation personnel directors couldn't state the dollar volume of sales for their company, didn't know the profit level, and had little idea of the rate of return."[4]

Top management often perceives human resource people as playing the role of humanists but believes that they cannot translate their concepts and programs into significant contributions to the organization's objectives. Human resource people are sometimes viewed as living in an idealistic world. In other words, they have good theories but lack a basic understanding of the business principles necessary to implement them.

A related problem is the opinion held by some operating managers that human resource people view themselves as do-gooders serving as the conscience of their respective organizations. Managers who have this attitude can become antagonistic, especially when personnel people talk about the poor working conditions and injustices that face employees. Even if the human resource people are right, it is often their approach that bothers operating managers. Some human resource people seem to think in terms of the company ("they") versus the employees and themselves ("we"). Such an attitude naturally alienates other managers in the organization. The point is not that these problems are unimportant, but that they could be handled in a much more effective and less abrasive manner than they sometimes are.

In addition, many operating managers think that human resource people become obsessed with promoting the latest fads in the human resource field.[5] In hopes of finding a "personnel cure-all," the human resource department sometimes enthusiastically endorses the latest personnel and training techniques, which promise to increase organizational performance. Unfortunately, many of these efforts fail simply because the human resource department did not completely explore the limitations and the appropriate applications of the technique in question.

Lack of respect

Another critical problem for human resource managers is a lack of respect for the human resource area on the part of many managers. This problem is closely allied to the perceived lack of expertise of human resource people. Often a move into the human resource area is viewed as a demotion or a dead-end job. Unfortunately, this attitude may be justified in organizations that follow a policy of moving unsuccessful operating managers into human resource positions. Staffing the human resource department with people who have little or no expertise in the field results in a continual downgrading of the department.

In addition, some human resource departments tend to deal with problems in a reactionary manner. In these situations, they do little to anticipate and prevent problems; they react only after the problem has emerged. Such actions can lead to top management lacking respect for the human resource department. As a result, human resource people are sometimes excluded from long-range planning and other key policy decision-making activities of the organization.

The preceding paragraphs represent a rather severe criticism of human resource departments as they allegedly have performed in some organizations. These problems have been pointed out with the hope that future human resource managers will be aware of them and actively work to resolve them. There is ample evidence that those organizations with such problems must change if they are to meet the challenges of the future.

THE EXPANDING ROLE OF HUMAN RESOURCE MANAGEMENT

There seems to be a growing awareness that human resource management has moved beyond mere administration of the traditional activities of employment, labor relations, compensation, and benefits.[6] The organizational environment has become much more complex. The deluge of government regulations and laws has placed a tremendous burden on human resource managers. New regulations are regularly issued in the areas of safety and health, equal employment opportunity, pension reform, environment, and quality of work life. For example, at the end of the 1970s, the United States had 100,980 federal government regulators—appointed not elected. In 1979, these appointees added 7,496 regulations to those that already filled 60,000 pages. Most of these new regulations were aimed at business, with many of them involving jail sentences for noncompliance.[7]

Along with the responsibility for interpreting and implementing the constantly changing government regulations, human resource departments also must deal with a work force that is becoming more demanding with regard to job satisfaction and the quality of work life.[8] In addition, important changes have occurred and are still occurring, in the composition of the work force. For example, females have increased from approximately 33 percent of the work force in 1960 to over 43 percent today.[9]

Computerization has also had an impact on the personnel field. In addition to their uses in performing the traditional functions of accounting and payroll calculations, computers are now being used to maintain easily accessible employee data that is valuable in job placement and labor utilization. This has naturally increased the responsibilities of the resource department. In fact, the personnel profession is fast becoming one of the largest customers of computer software and, to an increasing extent, hardware.[10]

The new corporate hero

During the past three years, a new and developing breed of management has evolved, in response to the discipline of corporate strategic planning.

The purpose of this new management is to apply the contemporary tools of planning to the problems facing the human resources manager and his or her organization as they deal with the increasingly complex tasks of managing for uncertainty.

Helped by the federal government's emphasis on regulating human resources (such as the Equal Employment Opportunity Commission, Occupational Safety and Health Administration, and Employment Retirement Income Security Act), the corporate human resources executive has emerged, according to a recent *Fortune* article, as "the new corporate hero"—a more critical person in the corporate decision-making structure, ensuring corporate compliance with the law and avoidance of the pitfalls of noncompliance. While finance, marketing, and other traditional and sometimes more visible executives in the corporation have generally been the highest paid in a company, today we are also seeing human resource executives compensated at commensurate levels.

Shift to strategic planning

The pressures to assure the maximum profit potential of their corporate assets encourages the development of a "strategic" frame of reference rather than a "transactional" one; that is, one that contributes to the shape of the business enterprise and environment, rather than merely reacts to the latest crisis or pressure.

The trend has been confirmed by a recent study which Kien Associates performed for a group of forest products companies.

The purpose of this study was twofold. It was designed, first, to provide fundamental comparative information regarding the organization and staffing necessary in order to meet the principal objectives of the human resources departments. Second, it was designed to provide a perspective on the role and performance of the senior human resource executives in these forest products companies.

The companies who participated in the program have total sales in excess of $26 billion and employ almost 300,000 people at over 1,400 facilities around the world. Their human resource departments must, therefore, be able to respond to a wide range of complex challenges.

Contributors to corporate management

We found that the senior human resource executives in these companies have become major contributors to the overall corporate management process.

Almost 20 percent to 25 percent of their time is spent in activities outside the company. These include trade association, governmental, or professional activities that are directly related to their role as the principal human resource executives of their companies. For example, from 25 percent to 40 percent of their time is spent in direct contact with the chief executive officer, chief operating officer, or group executive. This interaction is independent of specific functional review such as personnel planning, compensation, or labor relations.

With regard to the way in which human resource executives allocate their time among functional specialties, the traditional standby—labor relations—occupies fully 20 percent to 30 percent of their time. Next in importance was personnel development and human resource planning activities.

The final point in our survey suggests that major forest products companies have more human resources staff per employee than do large manufacturing companies in general.

It would appear, therefore, that other surveys of this type conducted by such groups as the American Society for Personnel Administration (ASPA) or the Bureau of National Affairs have essentially focused on smaller companies and service organizations (e.g., banks, retailers, utilities), with relatively few focusing on large industrial organizations.

Leaving aside the usual problems of definition and comparability, it would appear that the Kien Associates study provides the necessary "apples to apples" comparison of large industrial companies.

Source: *Pulp and Paper*, February 1982, p. 43, published by Miller Freeman Publications, 500 Howard St., San Francisco, Calif. 94105.

HUMAN RESOURCE MANAGEMENT TOMORROW

If these challenges are to be met, tomorrow's human resource departments must be much more sophisticated than their predecessors were. With the expanding role that the human resource department must fill, it is essential that human resource managers be integrally involved in the organization's long-range planning and policymaking activities.[11] This will require that the human resource manager play an active role in the top management of an organization. Fortunately, there are signs that many of these changes are currently taking place. For example, in almost every one of the Fortune 500 companies, the head of the human resource department is an officer—usually a vice president—answering to the chief executive officer. In a significant number of companies, the head of the human resource department sits on either the board of directors or the planning committee, or both. A recent survey conducted by the Opinion Research Corporation found that 69 percent of the top managers and 73 percent of the human resource managers surveyed expect the human resource function to increase in importance over the next few years.[12] This survey included 266 of the Fortune 1,000 companies. At least three other surveys have also revealed an expanding role for human resource management.[13]

If tomorrow's human resource managers are to earn the respect of their colleagues and of top management, they must work to overcome the previously discussed negative impressions and biases that are sometimes associated with human resource management. It has been suggested that this can be accomplished in several ways:

1. The human resource specialist should become a more well-rounded business person. This will help overcome the common feeling that human resource people "don't understand the real problems and issues facing the organization."
2. The human resource specialist should become a better human resource specialist. By becoming fully knowledgeable about present

and future trends and issues in personnel, the human resource specialist is less likely to become enamored of passing fads or ineffective techniques.

3. The human resource specialist should promote effective human resource utilization within his or her own organization. Rather than take a moralistic approach when dealing with operating managers, human resource specialists should stress the importance of achieving a return on organizational investment by effectively utilizing the organization's human resources (i.e., human resource specialists should sell their programs from the standpoint of how the programs can improve the organization's effectiveness).

4. The human resource specialist should help solve important organizational problems. Instead of "living in their own world," human resource specialists should make suggestions that are practical and useful in meeting current organizational objectives.[14]

In addition to performing the traditional personnel functions, human resource people should look for fresh and effective approaches to improving organizational performance. For example, it has been suggested that human resource people should develop or refine their expertise in the following areas: attitude surveys and other upward communication programs, issues related to changing working conditions, job humanization, career planning and development, pay and benefits, supplemental uses of the workplace, and flexible work schedules. While this list certainly is not exhaustive, it does point out some possibilities.

JOB OPPORTUNITIES IN HUMAN RESOURCE MANAGEMENT

What are the specific job opportunities in human resource management? In general, the size of the organization determines the number and types of human resource jobs available. Naturally, larger organizations offer more opportunity for specialization. Figure 1–3 lists some typical human resource jobs in large organizations.

Entering the field

Probably the most desirable path leading to human resource work is from operating management. By first obtaining some experience in the latter area, an individual moving into a human resource job can better understand the problems facing operating managers. If a human resource employee does not have this type of experience, he or she might be provided with at least occasional operating experience within the organization. This might be done through work on a project, through certain committee assignments, or through a temporary assignment in another department. Historically, many people have entered human resource management via promotion from a secretarial or clerical position within the human resource department.[15] However,

Figure 1–3 Typical human resource jobs in large organizations

Employee benefits supervisor—Coordinates and administers benefit programs relating to vacations, insurance, pensions, and other benefit plans.

Employee counselor—Assists employees in understanding and overcoming social and emotional problems; also helps employees appraise their interests, aptitudes, and abilities.

Employment interviewer—Interviews job applicants, records and evaluates such information as job experience, education and training, skills, knowledge and abilities, physical and personal qualifications, and other pertinent data for classification, selection, and referral.

Job analyst—Collects, analyzes, and develops occupational data concerning jobs, job qualifications, and worker characteristics required to perform jobs.

Labor relations director—Organizes, directs, and coordinates industrial relations functions; these activities include dealing with human resource problems relating to absenteeism, turnover, grievances, strikes, and demands made by labor.

Personnel recruiter—Travels to areas geographically distant from the organization's operations and interviews job applicants.

Test administrator—Administers tests and interprets the results; rates applicants and makes recommendations for employment based on the test results.

Training director—Organizes, administers, and conducts training and educational programs for purposes of employee development and improvement of employee performance.

Training representative—Evaluates training needs to develop educational materials for improving employee performance; prepares and conducts training for organization personnel.

Wage and salary administrator—Establishes and administers the wage and salary system in the organization to ensure that the pay system is equitable and that it conforms to government regulations, organization policy, and agreements with labor unions.

the expanding role of the human resource department now requires that new entrants have significantly more educational and business experience. Today, for example, approximately 95 percent of human resource management professionals have some college training.[16] The increasing professionalization of the field now requires that new entrants carefully plan their career development activities if they want to advance. As was not true in the past, today's human resource professional is not likely to be someone who could not handle "operating management responsibilities" and/or had a liberal arts degree and "liked working with people."[17] A recent college graduate entering directly into the human resource area without full-time experience usually will start as a job analyst, employment interviewer, test administrator, or training representative.

Advancement potential in human resource management

From an entry position, a person in human resource management has several possible advancement paths. As previously mentioned, more opportunities exist in larger organizations. Figure 1–4 outlines some paths that an individual might follow, depending on his or her interests and degree of expertise. The paths shown in Figure 1–4 are

Figure 1–4 Possible advancement paths in the human resource field.

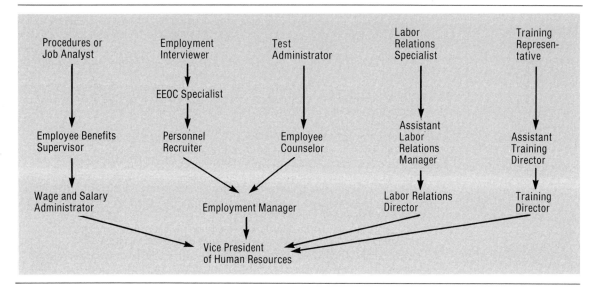

by no means the only possible ones that an individual might follow, but merely some of the more logical ones. For example, an employment interviewer might switch paths and become a wage and salary administrator.

The top management job in human resource management is given many different titles. Some of these include vice president of human resources, vice president of personnel, personnel manager, or personnel director. Presently, some organizations have people with human resource backgrounds serving as president or chief operating officer for the company. With the expanding role of human resource management, a greater opportunity now exists for human resource people to advance to these positions.

Employment outlook

It has been estimated that in the late 1970s there were more than 405,000 people engaged in human resource work throughout the United States. Nearly two out of every three of these people worked in private industry, and the remainder worked for federal, state, and local governments. The number of persons in human resource work is expected to grow about as fast as the average for all occupations through the 1980s. Table 1–1 presents the demand forecasts through 1990 for human resource employees. Most of this growth should occur in the private sector. The U.S. Department of Labor is forecasting that the majority of growth in the public sector will be at the state and local levels.[18]

Table 1–1   Forecast human resource jobs

Employment, 1978	405,000
Projected employment, 1990	473,000
Percent growth, 1978–90	16.8
Average annual openings, 1978–90	17,000
Growth	6,000
Replacement	11,000

Source: U.S. Department of Labor, *Occupational Projections and Training Data*, Bulletin No. 1918 (Washington, D.C.: U.S. Government Printing Office, 1980), p. 36.

On the other hand, the competition for jobs in the human resource area is also increasing. As mentioned earlier, increased education and experience are now required to enter the field. A 1980 U.S. Department of Labor bulletin states, "A bachelor's degree is the minimum educational background for a beginning job in personnel work."[19] The same source goes on to state that "graduate study in industrial relations, economics, business, or law usually is required for labor relations jobs."[20] Thus, higher qualifications will be required not only to perform effectively in the expanding role of human resource management but also to obtain a job in the human resource field. One positive impact of this increased competition for human resource jobs is that the numbers of highly qualified people in human resource work should increase.

Earnings in human resource management

Salary is of great interest to people when selecting a career. Starting pay and long-term salary potential are both important considerations. A 1982–83 U.S. Department of Labor publication indicated the following facts about salaries and working environment for human resource people as of 1980:[21]

Starting salaries for job analysts ranged from $14,800 to $21,900, with an average of $16,000.

Job analysts with more than five years experience had salaries in the $21,000 to $31,600 range, with an average of $25,000.

Starting salaries averaged $18,000 for benefit analysts and $19,00 for training specialists.

Benefits analysts and training specialists with over five years experience had salaries of $25,000 to $27,000, on the average.

Average annual salaries for personnel directors in private industry ranged from $27,719 to $49,730. Top personnel executives in large corporations earn considerably more.

Salaries for beginning personnel specialists employed by state governments ranged from $12,700 to $17,200. Personnel specialists with supervisory responsibilities averaged from $18,900 to $25,900. State directors of personnel earned average salaries ranging from $36,500 to $42,200.

In the federal government, new graduates with bachelor's degrees generally started at about $12,300; those with master's degrees started at about $18,600. The average federal salary for a personnel specialist was $27,374.

These data indicate that the starting pay in human resource work is competitive. Furthermore, as was briefly mentioned in the previous section, there are indications that the upward potential of human resource managers has expanded and will continue to expand with regard to both job responsibilities and pay. Thus, if the human resource role continues to expand as forecast, there is every reason to believe that this expansion will be accompanied by commensurate salary increases.

HUMAN RESOURCE MANAGEMENT AND ORGANIZATIONAL PERFORMANCE

The primary goal of human resource management in any organization is to facilitate organizational performance. One of the most effective ways of enhancing organizational performance is by increasing productivity. The American Productivity Center defines productivity as the efficiency with which an organization uses its labor, capital, material, and energy resources to produce its output. Human resource managers often can do little to influence the capital, material, and energy aspects of productivity. However, they can have a great impact on the labor component. Specifically, they can affect the commitment of employees and the management philosophy of the individual managers. Because of this, human resource managers have a unique opportunity to improve productivity.[22]

SUMMARY

Human resource management encompasses those activities designed to provide for and coordinate the human resources of an organization. Human resource management is a modern term for what has traditionally been referred to as personnel administration or personnel management. Some authors view human resource management as being much narrower and more clerically oriented than human resource management. This book uses the terms human resource management and personnel management interchangeably.

Human resource functions are those tasks and duties performed to provide for and coordinate an organization's human resources. These functions are many and varied and include such things as human resource planning, recruiting, selecting, training, and counseling employees, compensation management, and labor relations.

All managers are involved in human resource work. In small organizations, most human resource functions are performed by owners or operating managers. Large organizations usually have a human resource or personnel department that is responsible for coordinating and directing the human resource functions. Even when a human resource department exists, many human resource functions are performed by operating managers. Normally, a human resource department acts in an advisory capacity and does not have authority over operating managers.

Many have traditionally viewed human resource people as glorified clerks. However, as the organizational environment has become more complex, the prestige of human resource people has grown. In light of new challenges, there are indications that human resource people will play an increasingly important role in the future.

Probably the most desirable path to human resource work is from operating management. By first obtaining some experience in the latter area, an individual moving into a human resource job can better understand the problems facing operating managers. The recent college graduate entering directly into the human resource area without full-time experience will usually start as a job analyst, employment interviewer, test administrator, or training representative. From an entry position, an employee in a human resource department may advance along numerous paths.

The number of people in human resource work is expected to grow about as fast as the average for all occupations through the 1980s. Current data indicate that starting pay in human resource work is competitive with that for other jobs.

REVIEW QUESTIONS

1. What is human resource management?
2. What functions does a human resource or personnel department normally perform?
3. Describe some of the problems that have often been characteristic of human resource departments in the past.
4. Identify the steps that might be taken to overcome the negative impressions and biases that have sometimes been associated with human resource departments.
5. What are some potential human resource jobs that might be found in a typical large organization?
6. How does the future look for a career in human resource management?

DISCUSSION QUESTIONS

1. In many organizations, the general feeling is that human resource management is an area reserved for those "who can't do anything else." Why do you think this belief has emerged and is there any factual basis for it?

2. Describe some current trends that you feel will have an impact on human resource management in the next 10 years.

3. Many human resource managers claim to love their work because they like to work with people. Do you think that "liking people" is the most important ingredient in becoming a successful human resource manager?

4. Do you think that personnel work is in danger of becoming overly specialized to the point that the work of the average human resource specialist will become repetitive and boring?

REFERENCES AND ADDITIONAL READINGS

1. *Statistical Abstract of the United States,* 103d ed. (Washington, D.C.: U.S. Government Printing Office, 1982), p. 423.

2. L. B. Prewitt, "The Emerging Field of Human Resources Management," *Personnel Administrator,* May 1982, p. 82.

3. F. K. Faulkes, "The Expanding Role of the Personnel Function," *Harvard Business Review,* March–April 1975, p. 73.

4. Ibid.

5. E. S. Stanton, "Last Chance for Personnel to Come of Age," *Personnel Administrator,* November 1975, p. 15; and Faulkes, "Expanding Role of the Personnel Function."

6. For example, see: M. Zippo, "Managers See a Bright Future for the Human Resource Function," *Personnel,* March–April 1981, pp. 36–37; "Human Resources Professionals: The New Corporate Heroes," *Personnel,* January–February 1981, pp. 43–44; F. R. Edney, "The Greening of the Profession," *Personnel Administrator,* July 1980, pp. 27–30ff.; P. Pascarella, "Human Resources Rates Top-Management Status," *Industry Week,* 26 May 1980, p. 34.

7. Edney, "Greening of the Profession," p. 28.

8. *Work in America,* Report of Special Task Force to the Secretary of Health, Education, and Welfare (Cambridge, Mass.: M.I.T. Press, 1973); and D. L. Lunda, "Personnel Management: What's Ahead," *Personnel Administrator,* April 1981, pp. 52–53.

9. *Statistical Abstract,* 1982, p. 377.

10. Edney, "Greening of the Profession," p. 28.

11. Ibid.

12. Zippo, "Managers see a Bright Future," p. 36.

13. Pascarella, "Human Resources," p. 34.

14. Stanton, "Last Chance for Personnel," p. 16.

15. W. E. Hophe, ed., *The Encyclopedia of Careers and Vocational Guidance,* 3d ed. (Chicago: J. G. Ferguson, 1975), p. 211.

16. D. R. Hoyt and J. D. Lewis, "Planning for a Career in Human Resource Management," *Personel Administrator,* October 1980, p. 53.

17. Ibid.

18. U.S. Department of Labor, *Occupational Projections and Training Data,* Bulletin No. 1918 (Washington, D.C.: U.S. Government Printing Office, 1980), p. 36.

19. Ibid.

20. Ibid.

21. U.S. Department of Labor, *Occupational Outlook Handbook* (Washington, D.C.: U.S. Government Printing Office, 1982), p. 44.

22. E. K. Burton, "Productivity: A Plan for Personnel," *Personnel Administrator*, September 1981, p. 85.

Case 1–1 **HUMAN RESOURCE MANAGEMENT AND PROFESSIONALS**

You are a senior member of a national law firm in New York City; the managing partner of the firm has asked you to head up the southern branch in Birmingham, Alabama. This branch is one of 10 under the main office. On the whole, the firm has been successful since its establishment in the mid-1920s, but in the last five years many of the younger staff have elected to leave the organization. The managing partner is convinced that the problem is not salary because a recent survey indicated that the firm's salary structure is competitive with that of other major firms. However, he requests that you study this matter firsthand in your new assignment.

After getting settled in Birmingham, one of your first projects is to meet with the four senior managers to determine why the branch has had such a high attrition rate among the younger staff. Harding Smith, who is about 45, states that the younger staff lacks dedication, their hair is too long for the profession, and in general, they fail to appreciate the career opportunities provided by the firm. William Thompson, about 50, says that the younger staff members are always complaining about the lack of meaningful feedback on their performance and that many had mentioned that they would like to have a sponsor in the organization to assist with their development. Thompson further explains that the firm does provide performance ratings to staff and that the previous manager had always maintained an open-door policy. Brian Scott, about 40, says he has received complaints that training is not relevant and is generally dull and boring. He explains that various persons in the firm who worked with training from time to time acted mainly on guidance from New York. Dennis Rutherford, about 38, says he believes the root of the problem is the lack of a human resource department. However, he says that when the idea was mentioned to the managing partner in New York, he rejected it totally.

1. *What do you think about the idea of a human resource department in a professional office?*

2. *How would you sell the idea of a human resource department to the managing partner?*

3. *What type of organizational structure would you propose?*

Case 1–2   **CHOOSING A PROFESSION**

Tom Russell is a junior majoring in business administration at a large midwestern university. Tom, who is an honor student, hasn't fully decided what his major should be. He has considered majoring in management, but just can't get excited about the field. It seems to him that it is too general.

Tom's first course in management did appeal to him; however, this was largely because of the professor. Tom decided to talk to this professor about his dilemma. The following conversation occurred:

Tom: Professor, I would like your advice on selecting a major field of study. Right now I just don't know what to do.

Professor: Tom, just let me say that you are making an important decision and are justified in your concern. How many courses have you taken in the School of Business Administration?

Tom: Only your introductory course in management, a basic course in marketing, and a statistics course. I do know that I don't want to major in statistics!

Professor: How about majoring in human resource management?

Tom: I don't think so. That is basically a staff job that can't really lead anywhere.

Professor: Hold on, Tom, I think I had better tell you a little more about human resource management.

1. *If you were the professor, what would you tell Tom?*
2. *If Tom should choose human resource management as a major, what courses would you recommend that he take?*

Chapter 2

Job design and job analysis

Glossary of terms

Element The smallest step into which it is practicable to subdivide any work task without analyzing separate motions, movements, and the mental process involved.

Duties One or more tasks performed in carrying out a job responsibility.

Job A group of positions which are identical with respect to their major or significant tasks and responsibilities and sufficiently alike to justify their being covered by a single analysis. There may be one or many persons employed in the same job.

Job analysis The process of determining and reporting pertinent information relating to the nature of a specific job.

Job depth The freedom of jobholders to plan and organize their own work, to work at their own pace, and to move around and communicate as they desire.

Job description A written synopsis of the nature and requirements of a job.

Job design Defines the specific work activities of an individual or group of individuals.

Job enlargement Involves giving a jobholder more tasks of a similar nature to perform.

Job enrichment Involves upgrading the job by increasing both job scope and job depth.

Job rotation The practice of periodically rotating job assignments.

Job scope The number and variety of different tasks performed by the jobholder.

Job specification A description of the qualifications that a person holding a job must possess to perform the job successfully.

Motion study Technique that involves determining the basic motions and movements necessary to perform a job or task and then designing the most efficient method for putting these motions and movements together.

Occupation A grouping of jobs or job classes within a number of different organizations that involve similar skill, effort, and responsibility.

Organizing A process which involves the grouping of activities necessary to attain common objectives and the assignment of each grouping to a manager who has the authority necessary to supervise the people performing the activities.

Position A collection of tasks and responsibilities constituting the total work assignment of a single employee. There are as many positions as there are employees in the organization.

Process charts Graphical representation of the sequence of activities which occur when a job or task is performed.

Task May consist of one or more elements. A task is one of the distinct activities that constitute logical and necessary steps in the performance of work by an employee. A task is created whenever human effort, physical or mental, is exerted for a specific purpose.

Time study Procedure used to determine the average length of time required to perform a given task.

Work sampling A statistical technique for analyzing job methods based on random sampling.

I dare say that you think there is no science in shoveling dirt, that any one can shovel dirt. "Why," you say, "to shovel it you just shovel, that is all there is to it." Those who have had anything to do with Scientific Management realize, however, that there is a best way in doing everything.

Frederick W. Taylor *

Organizations provide the means for accomplishing work that could not be completed by individuals working separately. The process of organizing is the grouping of activities necessary to attain common objectives and the assignment of each grouping to a manager who has the authority necessary to supervise the people performing the activities.[1] Thus, organizing is basically a process of division of labor accompanied by appropriate delegation of authority. The manner and degree of division of labor define the jobs in an organization.

Labor can be divided either vertically or horizontally. Vertical division of labor is based on the establishment of lines of authority and defines the levels that make up the organizational structure. In addition to establishing the lines of authority, vertical division of labor facilitates the flow of communication within the organization.

Horizontal division of labor is based on specialization of work. The basic assumption underlying this division is that by making each worker's task specialized, more work can be produced with the same effort through increased efficiency and quality.

Jobs must be designed and analyzed before many of the other human resource functions can be performed. For example, effective recruitment cannot be accomplished unless the recruiter knows and can communicate the requirements of the job. Similarly, it is impossible to design base wage systems without having clearly defined jobs. The purpose of this chapter is to examine the methods and techniques used in designing and analyzing jobs.

BASIC TERMINOLOGY

Today, the word *job* has different meanings depending on how, when, or by whom it is used. It is often used interchangeably with the words *position* and *task*. To eliminate confusion and clarify terms, Figure 2–1 defines many of the words frequently encountered in job design and job analysis.

The simplest unit of work is the work *element*. A grouping of work elements makes up a work *task*. Related tasks comprise the *duties* of a job. Distinguishing between tasks and duties is not always easy. It is sometimes helpful to view tasks as a subset of duties. For example, suppose one duty of a receptionist is to handle all incoming correspondence. One task, as part of this duty, would be to respond to all

*F. W. Taylor, *Addresses and Discussions at the Conference on Scientific Management,* (Hanover, N.H.: Dartmouth College, 1913), p. 36.

Figure 2–1   Definitions of terms used in job design and job analysis

---

Element—The smallest step into which it is practicable to subdivide any work activity without analyzing separate motions and movements, and the mental processes involved.*

Task—Consists of one or more elements, and is one of the distinct activities that constitute logical and necessary steps in the performance of work by an employee. A task is created whenever human effort, physical or mental, is exerted for a specific purpose.*

Responsibilities—Obligations to perform certain tasks and assume certain duties.

Duties—One or more tasks performed in carrying out a job responsibility.†

Position—A collection of tasks and responsibilities constituting the total work assignment of a single employee. There are as many positions as there are employees in the organization.*

Job—A group of positions which are identical with respect to their major or significant tasks and sufficiently alike to justify their being covered by a single analysis. There may be one or many persons employed in the same job.

Occupation—Job of a general class within a number of different organizations. Examples of occupations include accountant, programmer, and carpenter.

---

*Definition adapted from U.S. Department of Labor, *Handbook for Analyzing Jobs* (Washington, D.C.: U.S. Government Printing Office, 1972), p. 3.
†Definition taken from Richard I. Henderson, *Compensation Management*, 3d ed. (Reston, Va.: Reston Publishing, 1979), p. 118. Reprinted with permission of Reston Publishing Co., a Prentice-Hall Co., 11480 Sunset Hills Road, Reston, VA 22090.

routine inquiries. Duties when combined with obligations to be performed (*responsibilities*) define a *position*. A group of positions which are identical with respect to their major tasks and responsibilities form a *job*. The difference between a position and a job is that a job may be held by more than one person, whereas a position cannot. For example, an organization may have two receptionists performing the same job. However, they occupy two separate positions. A group of similar jobs forms an *occupation*. Because the job of receptionist requires similar skill, effort, and responsibility in different organizations, being a receptionist may also be viewed as an occupation. Figure 2–2 graphically shows the relationships between elements, tasks, duties, responsibilities, positions, jobs, and occupations.

JOB DESIGN   Job design defines the specific work tasks of an individual or group of individuals. Job design answers the questions of how the job is to be performed, who is to perform it, and where it is to be performed. Figure 2–3 outlines the different components of the job design process. These different components all come together to form the job structure.

The job design process can generally be divided into three phases:

1. The specification of individual tasks.
2. The specification of the method of performing each task.

Figure 2–2 Relationships between different job components

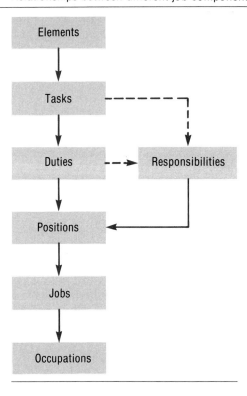

3. The combination of individual tasks into specific jobs to be assigned to individuals.[2]

Phases one and three determine the content of the job, while phase two indicates precisely how the job is to be performed.

Job content For many years, the prevailing practice in designing the content of jobs was to focus almost totally on the types of tasks utilized to do the job. This usually meant minimizing short-run costs by minimizing the unit operation time. The easiest and most convenient way of minimizing the unit operation time was usually to make jobs as specialized as possible.

Job specialization The basic idea behind specialization is to produce more work with the same effort through increased efficiency. Specifically, specialization can result in the following advantages:

Figure 2–3 Components of the job-design process

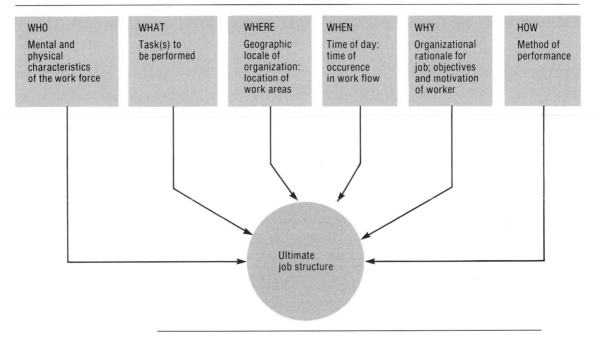

Source: Richard B. Chase and Nicholas J, Aquilano, *Production and Operations Management: A Life-Cycle Approach* (Homewood, Ill.: Richard D. Irwin, 1981), p. 329.

1. Fewer skills required per person.
2. Easier specification of the skills required for selection or training purposes.
3. Increased proficiency through repetition and practice of the same tasks.
4. More efficient use of skills by primarily utilizing each employee's best skills.
5. Concurrent operations.
6. More conformity in the final product or service.

The major problem with specialization is that it can result in boredom and even degradation of the employee. A vivid example of specialization is the automobile assembly line. It is not hard to imagine the behavioral problems associated with such an assembly line. The key is to specialize, but not to overdo it. Several approaches for accomplishing this are discussed later in this chapter.

Obviously, specialization is not more efficient or even desirable in all situations. At least two basic requirements must exist for the successful use of specialization. The first is a relatively large volume of work. Enough must be produced to allow for specialization and also to keep each worker busy. A second basic requirement is stability in the volume of work, worker attendance, quality of raw materials, product/service design, and production technology.

Job scope and job depth Job scope and job depth are two important dimensions of job content. Job scope refers to the number and variety of different tasks performed by the job holder. In performing a job with narrow scope, the jobholder would perform few different tasks and repeat these tasks frequently. The negative effects of jobs lacking in scope vary with the jobholder, but can result in more errors and lower quality.

Job depth refers to the freedom of jobholders to plan and organize their own work, to work at their own pace, and to move around and communicate as desired. A lack of job depth can result in job dissatisfaction which can, in turn, lead to tardiness, absenteeism, and even sabotage.

A job can be high in job scope and low in job depth or vice versa. For example, newspaper delivery involves the same few tasks each time, but there is considerable freedom in organizing and pacing the work. Therefore, the job is low in scope but high in depth. Of course, many jobs are low (or high) in both job scope and job depth.

Job rotation, job enlargement, and job enrichment Job rotation, job enlargement, and job enrichment are three terms which relate directly to job content and which are frequently confused. Job rotation is periodically rotating work assignments. For instance, an employee in a retail store might work one month as a salesperson, then one month as a cashier. Job enlargement involves adding more tasks of a similar nature to the job. In other words, enlarging a job means increasing the scope. The job of an assembly line worker might be enlarged by assigning the jobholder more assembly operations of a similar nature. Thus, the job is enlarged in the sense that the jobholder performs more different operations. Job enrichment involves upgrading the job by increasing both job scope and job depth. Adding responsibility is one of the most common ways of "enriching" a job. Job enrichment is discussed in more depth in Chapter 9.

Job methods Once job content has been established, the next step is to determine the precise methods that should be used to perform the job. The optimum method of performing a job is a function of the manner in which the human body is used, the arrangement of the workplace, and the design of the tools and equipment which are used.[3]

The overriding objective of job methods design is to find the one best way of performing a particular job.

Several techniques have been developed to assist in determining the methods to be used for performing a job.[4]

Process charts Process charts graphically represent the sequence of activities which occur when the tasks of a job are performed. Most process charts assign these activities to one of five classifications: operations, transportation, inspections, delays, and storage. Process charts chronologically present the job tasks so that any inefficiencies become obvious. Operation process charts, flow process charts, and multiple activity charts are all specialized types of process charts. An operation process chart shows only the operations and inspections performed during a task. It is designed to give a quick, overall understanding of the task. Flow process charts are similar to operation process charts, but they include material handling and storage activities. Multiple activity process charts graphically represent the coordinated working and idle time of two or more persons, machines, or any combination of the two.

Motion study Motion study is a technique that involves determining the basic motions and movements necessary to perform a task or job and then designing the most efficient method for putting these motions and movements together. Specifically, the task or job is reduced to its very basic elements such as reach, move, grasp, position, and so forth. After the task or job has been broken down into its basic elements, each element is analyzed to see whether it can be eliminated or made more efficient. The remaining elements are then put together to form an improved method for performing the task or job. The improved method is then carefully analyzed to determine whether further improvements can be made. This procedure is continued until no further improvements appear possible.

Time study Time study is a procedure used to determine the average length of time required to perform a given task. Although the exact method used in a time study may vary, it normally·involves the following basic steps:

1. Dividing the task into its elements, each of which is timed.
2. Determining those elements that are essential for completion of the task.
3. Determining an operation time for each element by selecting or correcting the original data.
4. Determining operation time for the total task by adding together the operation times of all elements.
5. Determining extra time allowances.
6. Determining the standard time for the task by adding together operation time and extra time allowances.[5]

Time study is similar to motion study except that it adds the dimension of time.

Work sampling Work sampling is a statistical technique for analyzing job methods based on random sampling. A number of random observations are made of an individual performing a task. The state of the individual is recorded for each observation, indicating what the individual was doing. By making an adequate number of observations, inferences can be drawn about the content of the job and the methods used.

Work sampling is most applicable for measuring noncyclical types of work where many different tasks are performed and where there is no set pattern or cycle. For example, most office and staff work lends itself to work-sampling methods.

The physical work environment

The physical work environment, which includes factors such as temperature, humidity, ventilation, noise, light, and color, can have an impact on the design of jobs. While there are studies which clearly show that adverse physical conditions do have a negative effect on performance, the degree of influence varies from individual to individual.

The importance of safety considerations in the design process was magnified by the implementation of the Occupational Safety and Health Act (OSHA) in 1970. Designed to reduce the incidence of job-related injuries and illnesses, the act outlines very specific federal safety guidelines which must be followed by all organizations in the United States. OSHA is discussed at length in Chapter 18.

In general, the work environment should allow for normal lighting, temperature, ventilation, and humidity. Baffles, acoustical wall materials, and sound absorbers should be used where necessary to reduce unpleasant noises. If employees must be exposed to less than ideal conditions, it is wise to limit these exposures to short periods of time to minimize the probability that the worker will suffer any permanent physical or psychological damage.[6]

Design guidelines

The risks of focusing solely on minimizing the tasks performed by a jobholder have already been outlined. Such an approach often results in jobs that are overly routine and repetitive and, hence, boring. The key to avoiding job boredom is to balance concern for specialization with a concern for human needs. Figure 2–4 presents some specific guidelines that can help achieve this balance without sacrificing technical efficiency.

Figure 2–4   Some practical guidelines for designing jobs

Elements of workers' jobs	Suggested design guidelines	Workers' needs affected
Workers' job tasks (The work itself— arrangement of machines, work-place layouts, work methods, and sequence of work tasks)	1. Avoid machine pacing of workers. Workers should determine, when possible, rates of output.	Self-control
	2. When practical, combine inspection tasks into jobs so that workers inspect their own output.	Self-control
	3. Work areas should be designed to allow open communication and visual contact with other workers in adjacent operations.	Socialization
	4. When economically feasible, and generally desired by workers, combine machine changeovers, new job layouts, setups, and other elements of immediate job planning into workers' jobs.	Self-direction/control
Immediate job setting (The management policies and procedures that directly impinge upon employees' jobs)	1. Rotate workers, where practical, between jobs that are repetitive, monotonous, boring, and short cycled.	Variety and relief from boredom and monotony
	2. Assign new workers to undesirable jobs for fixed periods of time, then transfer them to more preferred jobs.	Equity
	3. Provide workers with periodic rest periods away from repetitive jobs to relieve monotony.	Relief of boredom and socialization
	4. Set higher pay rates for undesirable jobs.	Physiological security, equity, and achievement

Source: Adapted from Norman Gaither, *Production and Operations Management: A Problem Solving and Decision Making Approach* (Hinsdale, III.: Dryden Press, 1980), p. 415. Copyright © 1980 by The Dryden Press, a division of Holt, Rinehart and Winston, Publishers. Reprinted by permission of Holt, Rinehart and Winston, CBS College Publishing.

Sociotechnical approach to job design

The thrust of the sociotechnical approach to job design is that both the technical system and the accompanying social system should be considered when designing jobs.[7] According to this concept, jobs should be designed by taking a "holistic" or "systems" view of the entire job situation, including its physical and social environment. The sociotechnical approach is situational because few jobs involve identical technical requirements and social surroundings. Specifically, the sociotechnical approach requires that the job designer carefully consider the role of the employee in the sociotechnical system, the nature of the tasks performed, and the autonomy of the work group. Using the sociotechnical approach, the following guidelines have been developed for designing jobs:

1. A job needs to be reasonably demanding for the individual in terms other than sheer endurance and yet provide some variety (not necessarily novelty).

Renault discovers what is wrong with manual work

Many companies automate or simply try to eliminate arduous and boring jobs. This is costly. And where companies cannot afford to do this, the jobs remain unchanged.

For this reason, Régie Nationale des Usines Renault in France four years ago devised a method to find out precisely what is bad about a job.

"We often find it is just one aspect of a job, feeding a machine, for example, that is particularly difficult or monotonous," says André Lucas, senior manager responsible for working conditions at the car manufacturer's 11 production plants in France. "If so, we then need to change only that part of the job. We can do so more quickly and at a much lower cost than if we tried to automate or change the entire job."

The company measures the disagreeable aspects of jobs using 27 criteria covering social and psychological as well as purely physical aspects. Senior managers, engineers, and others concerned with work organization now use this information together with economic and technological data when considering proposals for alternative working methods or arrangements. As a result, more consideration is being given to social and human aspects in making these decisions.

Several years ago, for example, Renault set up partitions around workers on grinding machines to reduce noise levels. Although the noise was cut down significantly, the workers felt themselves isolated. To make matters worse, the partitions behind them had windows through which visitors to the company could watch the men. The workers complained that they felt like animals in a zoo.

"We would never have erected these partitions had we considered social relationships," admits Pierre Tarrière, head of work restructuring at Renault. "We were so preoccupied with reducing the noise that we neglected the social and psychological factors." As a result of the workers' complaints, the partitions were reerected, without windows, around groups of three workers. Although this raised noise levels, the workers were happier.

So far, Renault has analysed some 250 jobs, affecting more than 2,000 workers, using this approach.

Several other major French firms, including PSA Peugeot-Citroën and SAVIEM, a Renault subsidiary, have adopted the analytical approach devised by Renault.

The Renault system is linked with a major exercise started four years ago to identify those jobs which did not meet norms or standards set by law or by the company regarding safety, temperature and lighting, for example. The aim was to establish priorities for allocating budgets and improving working conditions.

Having identified the worst jobs, the company is now analyzing them according to the 27 criteria. These are divided into nine categories: specifications, safety, environment, physical strain, mental stress, autonomy—the freedom of a jobholder to leave his post without disrupting production—relationships with other workers, job repetition and job content.

Each of the criteria is graded on a scale of one to five, using the theories and research findings of ergonomists, behavioral scientists, and others concerned with working conditions. A score of one is considered ideal, while five is highly unfavourable. Some criteria, such as mental stress, must be assessed subjectively. But others, such as autonomy, are measured quantitatively. The job of a worker who is able to leave his post for more than 30 minutes at a time gets a score of one, for example. Another job where the worker cannot leave his post when he wishes for more than a minute at a time would get a score of five.

The frequency with which a task is repeated

is measured to rate the job for repetition. A job where a worker repeats a task 120 times an hour, for example, would get a score of five.

All analyses are carried out by the same team of three specialists in each plant to help ensure the standards used are consistent.

The ratings given for each of the 27 criteria are recorded on a chart. A graph is drawn for each job by connecting the scores.

Any changes in working methods are also analyzed and profiles of proposed new job structures produced. The company has several times found that the impact of changes is not so evident without such analyses.

Similar profiles are also made for groups of jobs to show the effects of work reorganization.

The company now aims to involve workers themselves in the design of their work systems, using job profiles. At one Renault plant, workers in charge of safety have already been trained to do so, at their request.

Source: Adapted from Gerard Tavernier, "Renault Discovers What is Wrong with Manual Work," *International Management*, March 1979, pp. 33–35, published by McGraw-Hill International Publications, 34 Dover St., London, W1, England.

2. Employees need to be able to learn on the job and to go on learning.
3. Employees need some minimum area of decision making that they can call their own.
4. Employees need some minimal degree of social support and recognition at the workplace.
5. Employees need to be able to relate what they do and what they produce to their social life.

JOB ANALYSIS

Job analysis is defined as: "the process of determining and reporting pertinent information relating to the nature of a specific job. It is the determination of the tasks which comprise the job and of the skills, knowledges, abilities, and responsibilities required of the holder for successful job performance."[8]

When doing a job analysis, the job and its requirements, as opposed to the characteristics of the person currently holding the job, are studied. The tasks that comprise the job should be listed and a determination made concerning the skills, personality characteristics, educational background, and training necessary for successfully performing the job. A job analysis should "report the job as it exists at the time of the analysis, not as it should exist, not as it has existed in the past, and not as it exists in similar establishments."[9]

Products of a job analysis

Job analysis involves not only analyzing jobs but also reporting the results of the analysis. These results are normally presented in the form of a job description and a job specification. A job description concentrates on the job. It explains what the job is and what the duties, responsibilities, and general working conditions are. A job specification concentrates on the characteristics needed to perform the job. It describes the qualifications that the incumbent must possess to perform the job. Figure 2–5 outlines the general information obtained through a job analysis and included on a job description. Figure 2–6 summarizes the information normally contained in a job description and a job specification.

Uses of job analysis

Data obtained from a job analysis form the basis for a variety of human resource activities.[10] These include:

Job redesign Focusing attention on a job through a job analysis often indicates when a job needs to be redesigned.

Recruitment Regardless of whether a job that is to be filled has been in existence or is newly created, its requirements must be defined as precisely as possible for recruiting to be effective. A job analysis not only identifies the job requirements, but it also outlines the skills needed to perform the job. This information helps determine what type of people to recruit.

Selection and placement Selection is basically a matter of properly matching an individual with a job. To be successful in the process, the job and its requirements must be clearly and precisely known.

Orientation Effective job orientation cannot be accomplished without a clear understanding of the job reqirements. The duties and responsibilities of a job must be clearly defined before a new employee can be taught how to perform his or her job.

Figure 2–5   Information provided by job analysis

Job title and location.

Organizational relationship—a brief explanation of the number of persons supervised (if applicable) and the job title(s) of the position(s) supervised. A statement concerning supervision received.

Relation to other jobs—describes and outlines the coordination required by the job.

Job summary—condensed explanation of the content of the job.

Job tasks and duties—listing of tasks and duties with approximate time spent on each.

Information concerning job requirements—the content of this section varies greatly from job to job and from organization to organization. Typically, this section includes information on such topics as machines, tools, and materials; mental complexity and attention required; physical demands; working conditions.

Figure 2-6 Job descriptions and job specifications

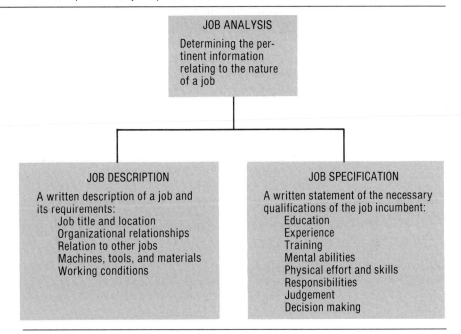

JOB ANALYSIS
Determining the pertinent information relating to the nature of a job

JOB DESCRIPTION
A written description of a job and its requirements:
Job title and location
Organizational relationships
Relation to other jobs
Machines, tools, and materials
Working conditions

JOB SPECIFICATION
A written statement of the necessary qualifications of the job incumbent:
Education
Experience
Training
Mental abilities
Physical effort and skills
Responsibilities
Judgement
Decision making

Training Many aspects of training are affected by job analysis. Whether or not a current or potential jobholder needs additional training can be decided only after the specific requirements of the job have been determined through a job analysis. Certainly the establishment of training objectives is dependent on a job analysis. Another training-related use of job analysis is in helping to determine whether a problem is occurring because of a training need or because of some other reason.

Vocational counseling Managers and human resource specialists are in a much better position to counsel employees about their careers when they have a complete understanding of the different jobs in the organization. Similarly, employees can better appreciate their career options when they understand the exact requirements of other jobs.

Employee safety A thorough job analysis often uncovers unsafe practices and/or environmental conditions associated with a job. By focusing precisely on how a job is done, any unsafe procedures usually become evident.

Performance appraisal The objective of performance appraisal is to evaluate an individual employee's performance on a job. A prerequisite is a thorough understanding of exactly what the employee is supposed to do. Then, and only then, can a fair evaluation be made of how an individual is performing.

Compensation A proper job analysis helps ensure that employees receive fair compensation for their jobs. Job analysis is the first step in determining the relative worth of a job by identifying its level of difficulty, its duties and responsibilities, and the skills and abilities required to perform the job. Once the worth of a job has been established, relative to other jobs, an equitable wage or salary schedule can be established.

JOB ANALYSIS METHODS

Several methods are available for conducting a job analysis. Four of the most frequently used methods are discussed below.

Observation

Observation is a method of analyzing jobs that is relatively simple and straightforward. Observation can be used independently or in conjunction with other methods of job analysis.

With observation, the person making the analysis observes the individual or individuals performing the job and takes pertinent notes describing the work. This information includes such things as what was done, how it was done, how long it took, what the job environment was like, and what equipment was used. A major drawback is that observation is somewhat limited to jobs involving short and repetitive cycles. Complicated jobs and jobs that do not have repetitive cycles require such a lengthy observation period that direct observation becomes impractical. For example, it would require a tremendous amount of time to observe the work of a traveling salesperson or a lawyer. On the other hand, direct observation can be used to "get a feel" for a particular job and then combined with another method for thoroughly analyzing the job. A second drawback is that the observer must be carefully trained to know what to look for and what to record. It is sometimes helpful to use a form with standard categories of information to be filled in as the job is observed. This helps ensure that certain basic information is not omitted.

Interviews

The interview method requires that the person conducting the job analysis meet with and interview the jobholder. Usually, the interview is held at the job site. These interviews can be either structured or unstructured. In a structured interview, a predesigned format is followed. Unstructured interviews have no definite checklist or preplanned format; the format that is followed develops as the interview unfolds. Structured interviews have the advantage of ensuring that all pertinent aspects of the job are covered. Also, the structured interview makes it easier to compare information obtained from different people holding the same job.

The major drawback to the interview method is that it can be extremely time-consuming because of the period required to schedule, get to, and actually conduct the interview. This problem is naturally compounded when several people are interviewed concerning the same job.

Functional job analysis

Functional job analysis (FJA) is a method for analyzing jobs developed by the United States Training and Employment Service (USTES) of the Department of Labor. FJA uses standardized statements and terminology to describe the content of jobs. The primary premises of FJA include the following:

1. A fundamental distinction must be made between what gets done and what employees do to get things done. For example, bus drivers do not carry passengers but rather they drive vehicles and collect fares.
2. Jobs are done in relation to data, people, and things.
3. In relation to things, employees draw on physical resources; in relation to data, employees draw on mental resources; and in relation to people, employees draw on interpersonal resources.
4. All jobs require employees to relate data, people, and things to some degree.
5. Although the behavior of employees and their tasks can be described in numerous ways, there are only a few definitive functions involved. For example, in interacting with machines, employees function to feed, tend, operate, or set up. Although each of these functions occurs over a wide range of difficulty and content, essentially, each draws on a relatively narrow and specific range of similar kinds and degrees of employee characteristics and qualifications.
6. The levels of difficulty required in dealing with data, people, and things are hierarchical and can be represented by an ordinal scale.[11]

Figure 2–7 defines the levels of difficulty a job requires in dealing with data, people, and things. The lower the number associated with a function, the more difficult the function is. For example, synthesizing data (0) is more difficult than compiling data (3).

After a job's difficulty has been described using the numerical scheme shown in Figure 2–7, this information can be combined with some general information to compare and identify jobs using the *Dictionary of Occupational Titles* (DOT). Once the closest job in the DOT has been

Figure 2–7   Levels of worker functions

Data	People	Things
0 Synthesizing	0 Mentoring	0 Setting up
1 Coordinating	1 Negotiating	1 Precision working
2 Analyzing	2 Instructing	2 Operating-controlling
3 Compiling	3 Supervising	3 Driving-operating
4 Computing	4 Diverting	4 Manipulating
5 Copying	5 Persuading	5 Tending
6 Comparing	6 Speaking-signaling	6 Feeding-offbearing
	7 Serving	7 Handling
	8 Taking instructions-helping	

Note: The hyphenated factors: speaking-signaling, taking instructions-helping, operating-controlling, driving-operating, and feeding-offbearing are single functions.

Included in the concept of setting up, operating-controlling, tending, and feeding-offbearing is the situation in which the worker is actually part of the setup of the machine, either as the holder and guider of the material or holder and guider of the tool.

When a worker becomes part of the machine functioning, either by reason of holding and guiding the material or holding and guiding the tool, the worker function should be interpreted as machine related. In these cases the worker is either setting up, operating-controlling, tending, or feeding-offbearing.

When a worker is involved primarily with nonmachine activities, but also has a minor relationship to a machine, the approximate nonmachine, things worker function, should be assigned even though it may be lower in the hierarchy than the machines function.

Source: U.S. Department of Labor, *Handbook for Analyzing Jobs* (Washington, D.C.: U.S. Government Printing Office, 1972), p. 73.

located, the accompanying job description can then be modified as necessary to fit the specific job being analyzed. At the very least, the DOT job description provides a very good starting point. Functional job analysis has the advantages of being relatively easy to learn and of using a standardized format.

Dictionary of Occupational Titles (DOT) Compiled by the federal government, the DOT classifies and describes approximately 20,000 jobs. A nine-digit code is used to classify a job. The first digit indicates the occupational category, of which there are nine primary categories: Professional, Technical, and Managerial occupations is an example of one primary category. The second digit indicates a division within the primary occupational category. For example, occupations in education is a division within the primary category of professional, technical, and managerial occupations. The third digit indicates the group within the division into which the job is classified. For example, occupations in secondary school education is a group within the education division.

The fourth, fifth, and sixth digits reflect the difficulty of the job with regard to data, people, and things, respectively, using the numerical scheme shown in Figure 2–7.

The last three digits differentiate, in alphabetical order, those jobs that have the same first six digits. Thus, a number of occupations may have the same first six digits, but no two can have the same nine digits. If the first six digits apply to only one occupational title, then the last three digits are always 010. Figure 2–8 summarizes the nine-digit code used to classify jobs. Figure 2–9 shows how an elementary school teacher is classified by the DOT.

Questionnaires

Normally, job analysis questionnaires are three to five pages long and contain both objective and open-ended questions. Figure 2–10 shows the heading and some sample questions from such a questionnaire. For existing jobs, the incumbent completes the questionnaire, has it checked by his or her immediate manager, and returns it to the job analyst. If the job being analyzed is new, the questionnaire normally is sent to the manager who will supervise the employee in the new job. If the job being analyzed is vacant but is duplicated in another part of the organization, the questionnaire is completed by the incumbent in the duplicate job.

The questionnaire method has the advantage of obtaining information from a large number of employees in a relatively short period of time. Hence, questionnaires are used when a large input is needed and time and cost are limiting factors. A major disadvantage is the possibility of either the respondent or the job analyst misinterpreting the information. Also, questionnaires can be time-consuming and expensive to develop.

Figure 2–8   Nine-digit code used by the DOT

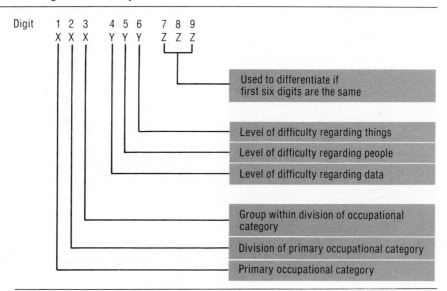

Figure 2–9　　　　　　　　　Elementary school teacher as classified by the DOT

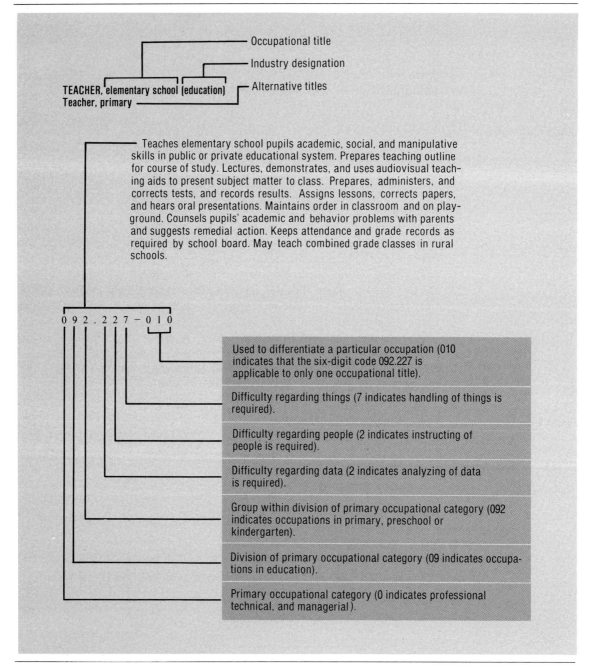

Occupational title

Industry designation

TEACHER, elementary school (education)
Teacher, primary

Alternative titles

Teaches elementary school pupils academic, social, and manipulative skills in public or private educational system. Prepares teaching outline for course of study. Lectures, demonstrates, and uses audiovisual teaching aids to present subject matter to class. Prepares, administers, and corrects tests, and records results. Assigns lessons, corrects papers, and hears oral presentations. Maintains order in classroom and on playground. Counsels pupils' academic and behavior problems with parents and suggests remedial action. Keeps attendance and grade records as required by school board. May teach combined grade classes in rural schools.

0 9 2 . 2 2 7 – 0 1 0

Used to differentiate a particular occupation (010 indicates that the six-digit code 092.227 is applicable to only one occupational title).

Difficulty regarding things (7 indicates handling of things is required).

Difficulty regarding people (2 indicates instructing of people is required).

Difficulty regarding data (2 indicates analyzing of data is required).

Group within division of primary occupational category (092 indicates occupations in primary, preschool or kindergarten).

Division of primary occupational category (09 indicates occupations in education).

Primary occupational category (0 indicates professional technical, and managerial).

Source: U.S. Dept. of Labor, *Dictionary of Occupational Titles*. U.S. Department of Labor, Employment and Training Administration, *Dictionary of Occupational Titles*, Fourth Edition, (Washington, D.C.: U.S. Government Printing Office, 1977).

Figure 2–10   Partial job analysis questionnaire

JOB ANALYSIS INFORMATION FORMAT

Your Job Title_____ Code_____ Date_____
Class Title_____ Department_____
Your Name_____ Facility_____
Superior's Title_____ Prepared by_____

Superior's Name_____ Hours Worked_____ $\frac{AM}{PM}$ ___ to $\frac{AM}{PM}$ ___

1. What is the general purpose of your job?

2. What was your last job? If it was in another organization, please name it.

3. To what job would you normally expect to be promoted?

4. If you regularly supervise others, list them by name and job title.

5. If you supervise others, please check those activities that are part of your supervisory duties:

☐ Hiring   ☐ Coaching   ☐ Promoting
☐ Orienting   ☐ Counseling   ☐ Compensating
☐ Training   ☐ Budgeting   ☐ Disciplining
☐ Scheduling   ☐ Directing   ☐ Terminating
☐ Developing   ☐ Measuring Performance   ☐ Other_____

6. How would you describe the successful completion and results of your work?

7. *Job Duties*—Please briefly describe WHAT you do and, if possible, HOW you do it. Indicate those duties you consider to be most important and/or most difficult

   (a) *Daily Duties*

   (b) *Periodic Duties* (Please indicate whether weekly, monthly, quarterly, etc.)

   (c) *Duties Performed at Irregular Intervals*

8. *Education*—Please check the blank that indicates the educational *requirements* for the job, not your *own* educational background.

   ☐ No formal education required.   ☐ 4-yr. college degree.
   ☐ Less than high school diploma.   ☐ Education beyond undergraduate
   ☐ High school diploma or equivalent.   degree and/or professional license.
   ☐ 2-yr. college certificate or equiva-
      lent

   List advanced degrees or specific professional license or certiciate required.

   Please indicate the education you had when you were placed on this job.

Source: Richard I Henderson, *Compensation Management* (Reston, Va.: Reston Publishing, 1976), pp. 98–99. Reprinted with permission of Reston Publishing Co., a Prentice-Hall Co., 11480 Sunset Hills Road, Reston, VA 22090.

A variation of the questionnaire method which has become popular is to have the incumbent write an actual description of the job, subject to the approval of his or her immediate supervisor. A primary advantage of this approach is that the incumbent is often the most knowledgeable about the job. Another benefit is that this method serves as a means of identifying any differences in perceptions about the job held by the incumbent and his or her manager.[12]

Position Analysis Questionnaire (PAQ)[13] The Position Analysis Questionnaire involves a highly specialized instrument for analyzing any job in terms of employee activities. Six major categories of employee activities are utilized, as described in Figure 2–11.

The PAQ uses a total of 194 descriptors, called job elements, to describe in detail the six activity categories. Each descriptor is judged as to the degree that it applies to the job being analyzed.

The primary advantage of PAQ is that it can be used to analyze almost any type of job. Also, it is relatively easy to use. The major disadvantage of the PAQ is the sheer length of the questionnaire.

Figure 2–11   Employee activities in the PAQ

Information input—where and how does the employee get the information he/she uses in performing his/her job?
Examples:
  Use of written materials.
  Near-visual differentiation.

Mental processes—what reasoning, decision-making, planning, and information-processing activities are involved in performing the job?
Examples:
  Level of reasoning in problem solving.
  Coding/decoding.

Physical activities—what physical activities does the employee perform and what tools or devices does he/she use?
Examples:
  Use of keyboard devices.
  Assembling/disassembling.

Relationships with other people—what relationships with other people are required in performing the job?
Examples:
  Instructing.
  Contacts with public, customers.

Job context—in what physical or social contexts is the work performed?
Examples:
  High temperature.
  Interpersonal conflict situations.

Other job characteristics—what activities, conditions, or characteristics other than those described above are relevant to the job?
Examples:
  Specified work pace.
  Amount of job structure.

Figure 2–12   Management position description factors

1. Product, marketing, and financial strategy planning.
2. Coordination of other organizational units and personnel.
3. Internal business control.
4. Products and services responsibility.
5. Public and customer relations.
6. Advanced consulting.
7. Autonomy of actions.
8. Approval of financial commitments.
9. Staff service.
10. Supervision.
11. Complexity and stress.
12. Advanced financial responsibility.
13. Broad personnel responsibility.

Source: W. W. Tornov and P. R. Pinto, "The Development of a Managerial Job Taxonomy: A System for Describing, Classifying, and Evaluating Executive Positions," *Journal of Applied Psychology* 61 (1976), p. 414.

Management Position Decription Questionnaire (MPDQ) The Management Position Description Questionnaire is a highly structured questionnaire designed specifically for analyzing managerial jobs. The MPDQ contains 208 items relating to managerial responsibilities, restrictions, demands, and other miscellaneous position characteristics.[14] These 208 items are grouped under the 13 categories shown in Figure 2–12. As with the PAQ, the MPDQ requires the analyst to check whether each item is appropriate to the job being analyzed.

POTENTIAL PROBLEMS WITH JOB ANALYSIS

In analyzing jobs, certain potential problems can arise. Some of these are the result of natural human behavior, while others result from the nature of the job analysis process.

Employee reactions

It is natural for employees to fear anything new or anything they don't completely understand. Before analyzing any job, the purpose and reasons for the analysis should be thoroughly explained to the jobholder. Unless a clear explanation is given, employees naturally will wonder why their jobs are being so closely scrutinized. They may think that they are doing something wrong or that management is looking for a way to make their jobs more difficult. On the other hand, employees may fear that the analysis will result in a more narrowly defined, and hence boring, job. Similarly, any changes in the job resulting from the job analysis should be clearly explained to the jobholder.

Job analysis
deficiencies

There is always the possibility that a job analysis will result in an incomplete or even inaccurate picture of the job. For several reasons, this can happen even when the most conscientious efforts are employed in the analysis. No two people see the same situation in exactly the same way. Thus, the human element required to analyze a job introduces a distinct possibility of error. Another reason for error is that many jobs change over time. These changes may occur because of alterations in the skill and experience of the jobholder, in the job methods, or in equipment. Therefore, it is important to review job descriptions periodically and ensure that they are up-to-date and accurately reflect the content of the respective jobs.

SUMMARY

A job is a group of positions which are identical with respect to their major or significant tasks and sufficiently alike to justify their being covered by a single analysis. A group of similar jobs forms an occupation. Job design defines the specific work tasks of an individual or group of individuals.

The basic idea behind job specialization is to produce more work with the same effort through increased efficiency. The major problem with job specialization is that it can result in boredom and even degradation of the employee.

Job scope refers to the number and variety of different tasks performed by the jobholder. Job depth refers to the freedom of jobholders to plan and organize their own work, to work at their own pace, and to move around and communicate as desired.

Job rotation is the practice of periodically rotating job assignments. Job enlargement involves giving a jobholder more tasks of a similar nature to perform. Job enrichment involves upgrading the job by increasing both scope and depth.

Several techniques have been developed to assist in determining the methods to be used for performing a job. These include motion study, process charts, time study, and work sampling. Several practical guidelines for designing jobs were offered.

Job analysis is the process of determining and reporting pertinent information relating to the nature of a specific job. In performing a job analysis, the job and its requirements are studied as opposed to the characteristics of the person currently holding the job. A job description and a job specification both result from job analysis. A job description explains what the job is and what the duties, responsibilities, and general working conditions are. A job specification describes the qualifications that the incumbent must possess.

A job analysis can be useful in the following areas: (1) job redesign, (2) recruitment, (3) selection and placement, (4) orientation, (5) training, (6) vocational counseling, (7) employee safety, (8) performance appraisal, and (9) compensation. Job analysis methods include observation, interviews, functional job analysis, and questionnaires. Functional job analysis uses the *Dictionary of Occupational Titles* (DOT) as an aid in classifying jobs. The Position Analysis Questionnaire (PAQ) is a highly specialized questionnaire for analyzing jobs in terms of employee activities. The Management Position Description Questionnaire (MPDQ) is a highly structured questionnaire designed specifically for analyzing managerial jobs. Problems can arise in the job analysis process because of human behavior or because of the nature of the analysis process.

REVIEW QUESTIONS

1. Describe vertical and horizontal divisions of labor.
2. What are job design and the three phases of the job-design process?
3. What is the difference between: job rotation, job enlargement, and job enrichment?
4. Name four different techniques that can be used to design the methods used in performing a job.
5. What is the sociotechnical approach to job design?
6. What are job descriptions and job specifications and how do they relate to the job analysis process?
7. What are the uses of job analysis?
8. Name four of the most frequently used methods for analyzing jobs.
9. What are some potential problems associated with job analysis?

DISCUSSION QUESTIONS

1. Discuss the pros and cons of job specialization. In what type of organization would job specialization be most efficient? Most inefficient?
2. Some people believe that any type of motion study (or time study) is undesirable because it almost always results in "oversimplifying" the job. Give your views regarding this issue.
3. After completing school, you will probably be entering the work force. What are the implications of job analysis and job design for you?
4. What method of job analysis do you think would be most applicable for jobs in a large grocery store?

REFERENCES AND ADDITIONAL READINGS

1. H. Koontz and C. O'Donnell, *Management: A Systems and Contingency Analysis of Managerial Functions,* 6th ed. (New York: McGraw-Hill, 1976), p. 275.
2. L. E. Davis, "Job Design and Productivity: A New Approach," *Personnel,* March 1957, p. 420.
3. R. A. Johnson, W. T. Newell, and R. C. Vergin, *Production and Operations Management: A Systems Concept* (Boston: Houghton Mifflin, 1974), p. 204.

4. Much of the next section is adopted for D. C. Geitgey, "Methods Engineering," in *Industrial Engineering Handbook*, 3d ed. (New York: McGraw-Hill, 1971), ed. H. B. Maynard, pp. 2–8.

5. E. E. Ghiselli and C. W. Brown, *Personnel and Industrial Psychology*, 2d ed. (New York: McGraw-Hill, 1955), p. 76.

6. Johnson, Newell, and Vergin, *Production and Operations Management*, p. 206.

7. P. B. Vaill, "Industrial Engineering and Socio-Technical Systems," *Journal of Industrial Engineering*, September 1967, p. 535.

8. War Manpower Commission, Division of Occupational Analysis, *Training and Reference Manual for Job Analysis*, (Washington, D.C.: U.S. Government Printing Office), June 1944, p. 7.

9. U.S. Department of Labor, *Handbook for Analyzing Jobs*, (Washington, D.C.: U.S. Government Printing Office, 1972).

10. Adapted from J. Markowitz "Four Methods of Job Analysis," *Training and Development Journal*, September 1981, p. 112.

11. D. Yoder and H. G. Heneman, Jr., eds., *ASPA Handbook of Personnel and Industrial Relations*, vol. 1 (Washington, D.C.: Bureau of National Affairs, 1974), pp. 4–58.

12. N. R. F. Maier, R. Hollman, J. J. Hoover, and W. H. Reed, *Superior-Subordinate Communication in Management* (New York: American Management Association, 1961).

13. The Position Analysis Questionnaire (PAQ) is copyrighted by the Purdue Research Foundation. The PAQ and related materials are available through the University Book Store, 360 West State Street, West Lafayette, Indiana 47906. Further information regarding the PAQ is available through PAQ Services, Inc., P. O. Box 3337, Logan, Utah, 84321. Computer processing of PAQ data is available through the PAQ Data Processing Division at that address.

14. W. W. Tornov and P. R. Pinto, "The Development of a Managerial Job Taxonomy: A System for Describing, Classifying, and Evaluating Executive Positions," *Journal of Applied Psychology* 61, no. 4 (1976), p. 413.

Case 2–1 **THE TAX ASSESSOR'S OFFICE**

A workday begins each morning at 8 A.M. in the tax assessor's office. The staff is composed of the director, two secretaries, two clerk-typists, and three file clerks. Although most of the work done in this office is clerical and the employee can pick it up where it was left off the previous day, the day normally begins with what appears to be a social hour. Clerical employees are at their desks, but instead of working, they are talking about activities of the previous night or the latest events of interest. The director does not come in until around 8:30 or 8:35 a.m.

When the director does arrive, he finds that most staff members are enjoying a party atmosphere. The conversations finally break up on his arrival, but not until after he has seen what goes on. The employees are obviously not in a big hurry to get down to work and appear unconcerned that he has witnessed their activities. The director has not discussed his feelings about this situation with anyone in the office. Even during the evaluation procedure, he has not voiced displeasure about what is taking place.

Each person in the office has a general job description that was written several years ago. However, the nature of most positions has changed considerably since then because of the implementation of a computer system. No attempt has been made to put these changes in writing. The director formerly held staff meetings to discuss problems that arose within the office; however, no meetings have been held in several months.

1. *What actions would you recommend to the director?*
2. *Why do you think that job descriptions are not updated in many organizations?*

Case 2–2

TURNOVER PROBLEMS

Ms. Shivers is the manager of a computer division in the federal government. Among her various responsibilities is the central data entry office, with 10 GS–4 data entry clerks and 1 GS–5 supervisor.

The starting salary range for a GS–4 data entry clerk with limited skills is comparable to the starting salary in private industry. However, after about six months of on-the-job experience, most data entry clerks can get a substantial pay increase by taking a job in private industry. It has become common knowledge in industry that Ms. Shivers has a very good training program for data entry clerks and that her division represents a good source of personnel. As a result of this reputation, Ms. Shivers has experienced a very heavy turnover over the last several months. In fact, the problem has recently become severe enough to create a tremendous work backlog in Ms. Shivers' division. Specifically, she has had such a large percentage of trainees that the division's overall productivity has declined.

Within the data entry section there are three notable exceptions who have worked for Ms. Shivers for several years. These three have recently been responsible for most of the work that has been turned out in the division. The GS–5 supervisor has been running the section for five years. Just recently, she informed Ms. Shivers that she has been offered a job with another company with a small pay increase and no supervisory responsibilities.

Ms. Shivers has always felt that data entry clerks should be upgraded to the GS–5 level and the supervisor's job to a GS–6. In fact, on several occasions Ms. Shivers has mentioned this idea to her boss, John Clayton. Not only does she believe that these jobs should be upgraded, but also that this action would go a long way toward solving her turnover problems. Unfortunately, Clayton has never shown much interest in Ms. Shivers' idea.

1. *What do you suggest that Ms. Shivers do to further promote the idea of upgrading the data entry clerk and supervisory positions?*
2. *Can you think of anything that Ms. Shivers might do from a job design standpoint to help with the turnover problem?*

Chapter 3

Human resource planning

Objectives

1. To develop an understanding of the relationship between organizational planning and human resource planning.
2. To discuss a general approach to human resource planning.
3. To introduce several tools that can be used in human resource planning.
4. To present several potential pitfalls in human resource planning.

Outline

How HRP relates to organizational planning
Steps in the HRP process
  Determining organizational objectives
  Determining the skills and expertise required
  Determining additional (net) human resource requirements
    Skills inventory
    Management inventory
    Anticipating changes in personnel
  Developing action plans
Specific role of the human resource department
Synthesizing the HRP process
Tools to aid in human resource planning
  Commitment Manpower planning (CMP)
  Ratio analysis
  Computer-based models
Time frame of HRP
Common pitfalls in HRP
  The identity crisis
  Sponsorship of top management
  Size of the initial effort

Coordination with other management and human resource functions
Integration with organization plans
Quantitative versus qualitative approaches
Involvement of operating managers
The technique trap

Glossary of terms

Aggregate human resource requirements Skills and expertise of employees required to meet organizational and departmental objectives.

Cascade approach Objective-setting process designed to involve all levels of management in the organizational planning process.

Commitment manpower planning (CMP) New and systematic approach designed to get managers and their subordinates thinking about and involved in human resource planning.

Human resource planning (HRP) Process by which an organization ensures that it has the right number of qualified people in the right jobs at the right time.

Management inventory Expanded form of a skills inventory for management personnel; in addition to basic types of information, it usually includes a brief assessment of past performance and potential for advancement.

Organizational objectives Statements of expected results that are designed to give an organization and its members direction and purpose.

Organizational replacement chart Chart that shows both incumbents and potential replacements for given positions within an organization.

Organizational vitality index (OVI) Index which results from ratio analysis; the index reflects the organization's human resource vitality as measured by the presence of promotable personnel and existing backups.

Ratio analysis Tool used in human resource planning to measure the organization's human resource vitality as indicated by the presence of promotable personnel and existing backups.

Skills inventory Consolidated list of biographical and other information on all employees in an organization.

In planning objectives related to profitability and growth, corporate management deals particularly with ideas and problems in terms of the future. Personnel managers must likewise deal more and more in concepts predicated on what lies ahead.

Albert F. Watters *

Human resource planning (HRP), also referred to as manpower planning or personnel planning, has been defined as the process of "getting the right number of qualified people into the right job at the right time."[1] Put another way, HRP is "the system of matching the supply of people—internally (existing employees) and externally (those to be hired or searched for)—with the openings the organization expects to have over a given time frame."[2] Basically all organizations engage in human resource planning, either formally or informally. Furthermore, some organizations do a good job while others do a poor job.

The long-term success of any organization ultimately depends on having the right people in the right jobs at the right time. Organization objectives and strategies to achieve these objectives have meaning only when people with the appropriate talent, skill, and desire are available to carry out the strategies.[3] Poor human resource planning can also cause substantial problems in the short term. For example, consider the following:

Despite an aggressive search, a vital middle-management position in a high-technology organization has gone unfilled for six months. Productivity in the section has plummeted.

In another company, employees hired just nine months ago have been placed on indefinite layoff because of an unforeseen lag in the workload in a specific production area.

In still another company, thanks to the spectacular efforts of a talented marketing manager, revenues have soared. However, that valued employee has just resigned because he wasn't able to identify career opportunities within the firm.[4]†

The necessity for HRP is due to the significant lead time that normally exists between the recognition of the need to fill a job and the securing of a qualified person to fill that need. In other words, it is usually not possible to go out and find an appropriate person over-

---

*A. F. Watters, "Personnel Management: Future Problems and Opportunities," *Personnel* 38, no. 1 (1961), p. 56.

†Excerpted, by permission of the publisher, from "Human Resource Planning: A Four-Phased Approach" by Craig B. Mackey, p. 17, *Management Review*, May 1981 © 1981 by AMACOM, a division of American Management Associations, New York. All rights reserved.

night. Effective HRP can also help reduce turnover by keeping employees appraised of their career opportunities within the company.

HOW HRP RELATES TO ORGANIZATIONAL PLANNING

HRP involves applying the basic planning process to the human resource needs of an organization. Any human resource plan, if it is to be effective, must be derived from the long-range plans of the organization. Unfortunately, HRP is often isolated from organization planning. A common error is for human resource planners to focus on the short-term replacement needs and not tie in with the long-range plans of the organization. Focusing on short-term replacement needs is a natural consequence of not integrating human resource planning with organizational planning. A nonintegrated approach almost always leads to surprises which force personnel planners to focus on short-term crises.

STEPS IN THE HRP PROCESS

HRP consists of four basic steps:[5]

1. Determining the impact of the organization's objectives on specific organizational units.
2. Defining the skills and expertise and the total number of employees (aggregate human needs) required to achieve the organization and departmental objectives.
3. Determining the additional (net) human resource requirements in light of the organization's current human resources.
4. Developing action plans to meet the anticipated human resource needs.

HRP is not strictly a human resource department function. All managers, and especially operating managers, should view human resource planning as one of their most important and accountable job responsibilities.[6] Unfortunately this is often not the case. Far too many managers view HRP as something to do only after everything else has been done. Furthermore, managers often think that HRP should be handled solely by the human resource department. The role of this department is to assist operating managers in developing their individual plans and integrating these different plans into an overall plan. The individual managers must, however, provide the basic data on which the plan is built. A joint effort is required by the individual managers and the human resource department in each of the four steps of HRP. In general, the human resource department provides the structure, the impetus, and assistance. However, individual managers must be actively involved. Figure 3–1 summarizes the steps in HRP.

Figure 3–1   Steps in the human resource planning process

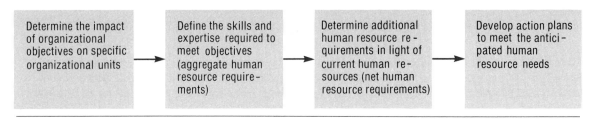

| Determine the impact of organizational objectives on specific organizational units | Define the skills and expertise required to meet objectives (aggregate human resource requirements) | Determine additional human resource requirements in light of current human resources (net human resource requirements) | Develop action plans to meet the anticipated human resource needs |

Determining
organizational
objectives

As mentioned earlier, human resource plans must be based on organizational plans. In actual practice, this means that the objectives of the human resource plan must be derived from organizational objectives. Specific human resource requirements in terms of numbers and characteristics of employees should be derived from the objectives of the entire organization.

Organizational objectives are designed to give an organization and its members direction and purpose, and should be stated in terms of expected results. The objective setting process begins at the top of the organization with a statement of central purpose. Organizational purpose defines an organization's current and future business. Long-range objectives and strategies are formulated based on the organization's statement of purpose. These can then be used to establish short-range performance objectives. Short-range performance objectives generally have a time schedule and are expressed quantitatively. Divisional and departmental objectives are then derived from the organization's short-range performance objectives. Establishing organizational, divisional, and departmental objectives in this manner has been called the "cascade approach" to objective setting. Figure 3–2 illustrates this approach.

The cascade approach is not a form of "top-down" planning whereby objectives are passed down to lower levels of the organization. The idea is to involve all levels of management in the planning process. Such an approach leads to an upward and downward flow of information during planning. This also ensures that the objectives are communicated and coordinated through all levels of the organization.

The cascade approach when properly used involves both operating managers and the human resource department in the overall planning process. During the early stages, the human resource department can influence objective setting by providing information about the organization's human resources. For example, if the human resource department has identified particular strengths and weaknesses in the organization's personnel, this information could significantly influence the overall direction of the organization.

Figure 3–2   Cascade approach to setting objectives

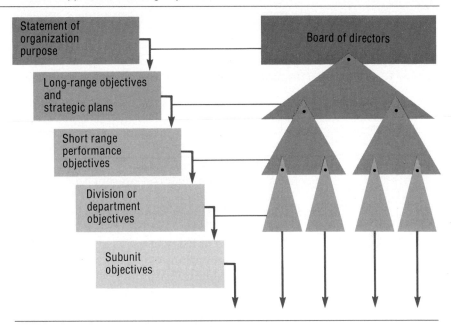

Source: Redrawn from *Managing by Objectives* by Anthony P. Raia. Copyright © 1974 by Scott, Foresman and Company. Reprinted by permission.

Determining the skills and expertise required

After organizational, divisional, and departmental objectives have been established, operating managers should determine the skills and expertise required to meet their respective objectives. The key here is not to look at the skills and abilities of present employees but rather to determine the skills and abilities required to meet the objectives. For example, suppose an objective of the production department is to increase total production of a certain item by 10 percent. Once this objective has been established, the production manager must determine precisely how this translates into human resources. A good starting point here is to review current job descriptions. Once this has been accomplished, managers are in a better position to determine the skills and expertise necessary to meet their objectives. The final step in this phase is to translate the needed skills and abilities into types and numbers of employees.

Determining additional (net) human resource requirements

Once a manager has determined the types and numbers of employees required, these estimates must be analyzed in light of the current and anticipated human resources of the organization. The first step in this process involves a thorough analysis of presently employed personnel as well as forecast changes in this status.

Skills inventory The purpose of a skills inventory, sometimes called a personnel register, is to consolidate information about the organization's human resources. It includes basic information on all employees. In its simplest form, a skills inventory includes a list of the names, certain characteristics, and skills of employees. Thomas H. Patten has outlined seven broad categories of information that should be included in a skills inventory.

1. Personal data—age, sex, marital status, etc.
2. Skills—education, job experience, training, etc.
3. Special qualifications—membership in professional groups, special achievements, etc.
4. Salary and job history—present and past salary, dates of raises, various jobs held, etc.
5. Company data—benefit plan data, retirement information, seniority, etc.
6. Capacity of individual—test scores on psychological and other tests, health information, etc.
7. Special preferences of individual—geographic location, type of job, etc.[7]

The popularity of skills inventories has increased rapidly since the proliferation of computers. Although most of the desired information traditionally was available from individual personnel files, compiling it was time-consuming before computers.

The primary advantage of a skills inventory is that it provides a means of quickly and accurately evaluating the skills that are available within the organization. In addition to helping determine net human resource requirements, this information is often necessary for making other decisions, such as whether to bid on a new contract or introduce a new product. A skills inventory also aids in planning future employee training and management development programs and in recruiting and selecting new employees. Figure 3–3 illustrates a skills inventory form.

Management inventory Because the type of information required about management personnel sometimes differs from that required about nonmanagerial employees, some organizations maintain a separate management inventory. In addition to biographical data, a management inventory often contains brief assessments of the manager's past performance and his or her strengths, weaknesses, and potential for advancement.[8]

Anticipating changes in personnel In addition to appraising present human resources through a skills inventory, managers must also take into account future changes. Certain changes in personnel can be es-

Figure 3–3   A form for a skills inventory

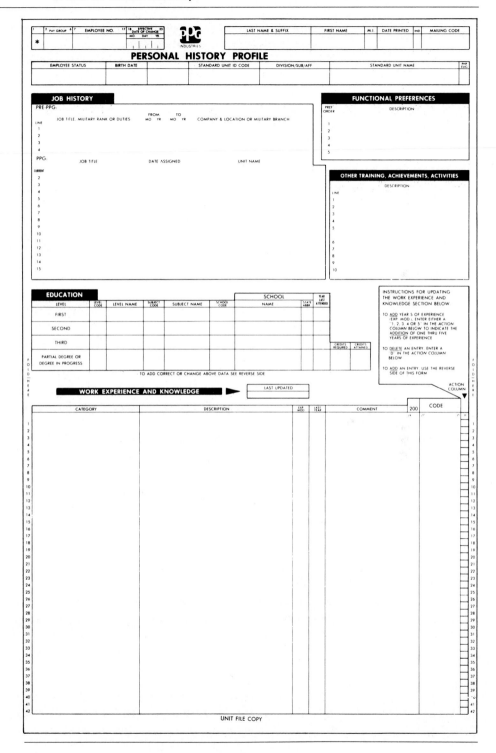

Source: Used with permission of PPG Industries, Pittsburgh, Pa.

timated accurately and easily, while other changes are not so easily forecast. However, information is almost always available to help make these forecasts. Changes such as retirements can be forecast reasonably accurately from information in the skills inventory. Others, such as transfers and promotions, can be estimated by taking into account such factors as the ages of individuals in specific jobs and the requirements of the organization. Individuals with potential for promotion can and should be identified. Other factors such as deaths, resignations, and discharges are much more difficult to predict. However, past experience and historical records can often provide useful information in these areas. Planned training and development experiences should also be considered when evaluating anticipated changes. By combining the forecast for the skills required with the information from the skills inventory and from anticipated changes, managers can make a reasonable prediction of their net human resource requirements for a specified time period.

Developing action plans

Once a manager has determined his or her net human resource requirements, action plans must be developed for achieving the desired results. If the net requirements indicate a need for additions, plans must be made to recruit, select, orient, and train new personnel. If a reduction in personnel is necessary, plans must be made to realize the necessary adjustments through attrition, layoffs, or discharges. Action plans should utilize the skills of present employees to the fullest extent possible.

Figure 3–4   Organizational and human resource planning

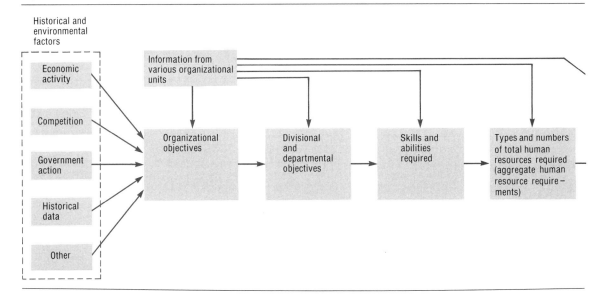

SPECIFIC ROLE OF THE HUMAN RESOURCE DEPARTMENT

As mentioned earlier, each of the steps in HRP requires a joint effort of the human resources department and the individual managers in the organization. The human resource department's primary roles are to coordinate, monitor, and synthesize the process. The human resource department usually provides the structure and establishes the timetable to be followed by operating managers. This helps ensure a unified effort. As individual managers determine their human resource needs this information should be channeled through the human resource department to be coordinated and synthesized. By funneling all the information through a central source, maximum efficiency in the process can be attained. For example, interdepartmental transfers and promotions can be used where feasible. Obviously, the information necessary to effect these types of actions would not always be available to individual managers, but would be available within the human resource department.

SYNTHESIZING THE HRP PROCESS

Figure 3–4 graphically depicts the relationship between organizational planning and human resource planning. As can be seen, organizational objectives are influenced by many historical and environmental factors. Once these objectives have been established, they are translated into department objectives. Individual managers then determine the human resources necessary to meet their respective objectives. The human resource department assimilates these different requirements into an aggregate human resource requirement forecast. Similarly, the additional (net) human resource requirements are deter-

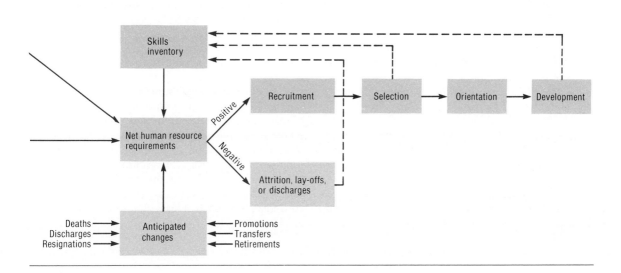

Management succession: A hard game to play

Management succession at most U.S. companies is a mess, and for a number of reasons. Some chief executives run their companies autocratically and are reluctant to give serious thought to who should succeed them. Others name a number of potential successors and let them compete against each other for the job, damaging corporate morale in the process. Most fundamentally, many CEOs simply do not invest the time and effort required to spot the most talented people in the company and groom them for higher jobs. They may give lip service to succession planning and draw up impressive replacement tables, but when an opening occurs, they ignore the table and the whole process goes out the window.

Noted expert Frank Gaines, Jr., who headed up succession planning at Exxon Corporation for many years and is now an independent consultant, puts it this way: "Too often, the CEO in a large corporation makes the mistake of thinking he is infallible. He is sure he can find the best people in the organization whenever he needs them to fill key jobs. But he can't. He must have a working system that will objectively identify the manager with the greatest potential."

Over the years, though, a few companies have consistently stood out from the crowd in their ability to plan management succession. Among them: General Electric, Mobil, General Motors, Citicorp, du Pont, International Business Machines, Eastman Kodak, Procter & Gamble, and Gaines's alma mater, Exxon.

These are all large companies that employ thousands of executives on whom they can compile detailed track records. And they have enough jobs at every level to allow capable people to rotate from one function to another, or one geographical area to another, to get the well-rounded experience they need to move up the corporate ladder. Thus, they use search firms sparingly, if at all, because they can fill the great bulk of their management needs by dipping into their own talent pools.

A way of life

Perhaps the company most totally committed to succession planning as a way of corporate life is Exxon. From the moment a young engineer, chemist or MBA joins the company, his or her performance is not only evaluated but continually compared with that of other employees doing similar work. Such comparative ranking, from the top to the bottom of the pyramid, is probably the most distinctive element of Exxon's master plan for finding and tracking executives of outstanding promise.

Every one of Exxon's scores of operating units has its own compensation and executive development committee, which keeps individual files on all employees in the unit. Each employee's job performance is evaluated on a scale of 1.0 (outstanding) to 4.0 (inadequate); so is his or her promotability, including a timetable for promotion. The unit also is required to maintain a list of replacements for every job, ranked in order of prefrence.

To make succession planning as objective as possible, Exxon has built cross-checks into the system. For example, each individual is evaluated by several superiors, rather than just one. Top management has found that a group of senior managers asked to rank people with whom they have had relatively close contact will almost invariably be in agreement, and consensus ranking obviously minimizes the bias of any one person. Comments one Exxon alumnus: "From the individual's viewpoint, the consensus approach at least guarantees that the person will always be treated fairly. The only trouble is that no individual is indispensable under the system, and some people may find that unsettling."

Perhaps most critical to the success of the Exxon system is the constant involvement of top management in the process. On most Monday afternoons throughout the year, Exxon Chairman Clifton Garvin, President Howard C. Kauffman, and the company's six senior vice presidents meet to review the progress of management training, development, and succession plans throughout the company. And once a year, the eight executives—who are the company's operating managers and also members of the board of directors—sit down for an entire day to go over the replacement schedules for filling all key management positions. As at the lower levels, they rank candidates for management jobs or the board of directors by a consensus judgment of their potential.

In filling Exxon's top job, the ultimate decision is, of course, made by the board, which includes a majority of 11 outside directors, who may or may not accept the recommendation of the out-going chairman. But over the years, observes T. H. Tiedemann, Jr., Gaines's successor as manager of compensation, organization, and executive development, those board members will have been exposed many times

to all the people at the level from which a new CEO is most likely to be chosen.

As a matter of corporate policy, Exxon consistently fills management positions from inside. "We go outside only in unusual circumstances—for instance, when we need some highly specialized expertise," Tiedemann says. "And we don't have to use a computer to find the best candidate for any given job in a hurry, because our system brings all the potential candidates to light."

At some companies, the list of management candidates is considered so important that it is kept secret from all but top management. As a key part of its management development program, for example, United Technologies Corporation maintains a special room in which it keeps detailed files on more than 100 of its best people. So secret are their names that only three people are allowed to enter the room—Chairman Harry Gray and two senior personnel executives. Citicorp also has a secret room, off limits to everyone but top management, in which are displayed the photographs of scores of middle managers who are considered to have a good chance of rising through the ranks.

Source: Reprinted with the special permission of *Dun's Business Month* (formerly *Dun's Review*), April 1981, pp. 54–55. © 1981, Dun & Bradstreet Publications Corporation.

mined based on the information submitted by the different organizational units in light of available resources and anticipated changes. If the net requirements are positive, the organization implements recruitment, selection, training, and development. If the requirements are negative, proper adjustments must be made through attrition, layoffs, or discharges. As these changes take place, they should be recorded in the skills inventory. Human resource planning is an ongoing process that must be continuously evaluated as conditions change.

TOOLS TO AID IN HUMAN RESOURCE PLANNING

Many tools are available to assist in the human resource planning process. The skills inventory, which was discussed in Chapter 2, is one of the most frequently used human resource planning tools. A second useful tool is an organization replacement chart. While there are many variations, a basic organization replacement chart shows both incumbents and potential replacements for given positions. Figure 3–5 is an example of a simple replacement chart.

Figure 3–5   Simple organization replacement chart

Organization replacement chart

	Director, Manufacturing	
Position	Director, Manufacturing	
Incumbent	J. L. Allen	
Backup	M. T. Barker	
Position	Manager, Manufacturing Engineering	
Potential/Promotability	HP	PN

	Manager, Plant Engineering		Manager, Manufacturing Engineering		Manager, Purchasing		Manager, Manufacturing	
Position	Manager, Plant Engineering		Manager, Manufacturing Engineering		Manager, Purchasing		Manager, Manufacturing	
Incumbent	J. M. Tyler		M. T. Barker		T. A. Barnes		D. B. Scott	
Potential Promotability		P(3)	HP	PN		NP	HP	P(1)
Backup	NBU		T. J. Bolles		NBU		K. D. Peters	
Position			Supervisor, Manufacturing Engineering				Superintendent, Manufacturing	
Potential Promotability				P(1)			HP	P(2)

Legend definitions

HP (high potential) = An above-average or outstanding performer with the potential to advance at least two levels above current position within five years.

PN (promotable now) = An individual who is promotable now to an identified position one level above current position.

P (years) = An individual who is promotable in "x" years to an identified position one level above current position.

NP (not promotable) = An individual who is not promotable above current position (e.g., individual desires to remain in current position, has retirement pending, has been promoted to maximum capabilities, etc.).

NBU (no backup) = No individual identified as a backup for this position.

Source: D. L. Chicci, "Four Steps to an Organization/Human Resource Plan," *Personnel Journal*, June 1979, p. 392.

Numerous sources that can be used to help forecast the availability of various human resource groups are periodically published by the U.S. government and others. Figure 3–6 lists some of these along with the frequency with which they are published.

Commitment Manpower Planning (CMP) Commitment manpower planning (CMP) is a new approach designed to get managers and their subordinates thinking about and involved in human resource planning.[9] In addition to encouraging managers and subordinates to think about human resource planning, the strength of CMP is that it provides a systematic approach to human resource planning.[10] CMP generates three reports which supply the following information: (1) the supply of employees and the promotability and placement status of each; (2) the organization's demand, arising from new positions and turnover and projected vacancies for each job title; and (3) the balance or status of supply versus demand, including the name, job, and location of all those suitable for promotions.

Ratio analysis Ratio analysis is another recently developed tool which can aid in human resource planning. Two basic premises underlie ratio analysis as it applies to human resource planning.[11] The first is that an organization is "vital" in terms of its human resources to the extent that it has people with high potential who are promotable, either now or in the near future, and backups identified to replace them. The second premise is that an organization is "stagnant" to the extent that employees are not promotable and no backups have been identified to replace the incumbents. The end product of ratio analysis is an overall

Figure 3–6   Source books and periodicals containing information useful for human resource planning

Daniels, Lorna M. *Business Information Sources.* Ch. 19. Berkeley: University of California Press, 1976.

Handbook of Labor Statistics. Washington, D.C.: U.S. Department of Labor, published annually.

Major Programs, Bureau of Labor Statistics, Report No. 552. Washington, D.C.: U.S. Department of Labor, 1980.

Monthly Labor Review. Washington, D.C.: U.S. Department of Labor, published monthly.

Occupational Outlook Handbook. Washington, D.C.: U.S. Department of Labor, published annually.

Occupational Projections and Training Data. Washington, D.C.: U.S. Department of Labor, published biannually.

Predicasts Forecasts. Cleveland, Ohio: Predicasts Forecasts, cumulative edition published annually.

Survey of Current Business. Washington, D.C.: U.S. Department of Labor, published monthly.

organizational vitality index (OVI), which can be used as a broad measure of an organization's human resource vitality. The index is calculated based on the number of promotable personnel and the number of existing backups in the organization.[12]

Computer-based models A vast number of computer-based human resource planning models have become available. These models usually provide a simplified view of the levels and flows of personnel through an organization.[13] The great majority of these models are designed to simplify the forecasting components of HRP by permitting the manipulation of available data using mathematical techniques. Computer-based human resource modeling is just in its infancy and is a field that should grow substantially in the future.

TIME FRAME OF HRP

Because HRP is so closely tied to the organizational planning process, the time frames covered by human resource plans should correspond with those covered by the organizational plans. Organizational plans are frequently classified as short range (0–2 years), intermediate range 2–5 years), or long range (beyond 5 years). Ideally, an organization prepares a plan for each of these horizons. Figure 3–7 presents a summary of the major factors affecting long-, intermediate-, and short-range human resource planning.

COMMON PITFALLS IN HRP

Unfortunately, HRP is not always successful. While a myriad of things can go wrong, the eight stumbling blocks described below are some of the most frequently encountered.[14]

Figure 3–7   Three ranges of human resource planning

Forecast	Short range (0–2 years)	Intermediate range (2–5 years)	Long range (beyond 5 years)
Demand	Authorized employment including growth, changes and turnover.	Operating needs from budgets and plans.	In some organizations the same as "intermediate"; in others, an increased awareness of changes in environment and technology—essentially judgmental.
Supply	Employee census less expected losses plus expected promotions from subordinate groups.	Human resource vacancies expected from individual promotability data derived from development plans.	Management expectations of changing characteristics of employees and future available human resources.
Net Needs	Numbers and kinds of employees needed.	Numbers, kinds, dates, and levels of needs.	Management expectations of future conditions affecting immediate decisions.

Source: Adopted from: J. Walker, "Forecasting Manpower Needs," in *Manpower Planning and Programming*, ed. E. H. Burack and J. W. Walker (Boston: Allyn & Bacon, 1972), p. 94.

The identity crisis Many managers and human resource specialists don't fully understand the HRP process. This is especially true for human resource personnel whose primary responsibility is HRP. Unless these specialists develop a strong sense of purpose, they are likely to flounder.

Sponsorship of top management For HRP to be successful in the long run, it must have the full support of at least one influential senior executive. Such high-ranking support can ensure the necessary resources, visibility, and cooperation necessary for the success of an HRP program.

Size of the initial effort Many HRP programs fail because of an over-complicated initial effort. Successful HRP programs start slowly and gradually expand as the program is successful. Developing an accurate skills inventory and a replacement chart are two good places to start.

Coordination with other management and human resource functions Human resource planning must be coordinated with the other management and human resource functions. Unfortunately, there is a tendency for HRP specialists to become absorbed in their own world and not interact with others.

Integration with organization plans As emphasized earlier in this chapter, human resource plans must be derived from organizational plans. The key here is to develop good communication channels between the organization planners and the human resource planners.

Quantitative versus qualitative approaches Some people view HRP as a numbers game designed to track the flow of people in, out, up, down, and across the different organizational units. These people take a strictly quantitative approach to HRP. Others take a strictly qualitative approach and focus on individual employee concerns such as individual promotability and career development. As is so often the case, a balanced approach usually yields the best results.

Involvement of operating managers HRP is not strictly a human resource department function. Successful HRP requires a coordinated effort on the part of operating managers and the human resources department.

The technique trap As HRP has become more and more popular, new and sophisticated techniques have been developed to assist in HRP. (Several of these were discussed earlier in this chapter.) Many of these are useful. However, sometimes there is a tendency to adopt one or more of these methods not for what they can do, but rather because "everyone is using them." HRP personnel should avoid becoming enamored of a technique merely because it is the "in thing."

SUMMARY

Human resource planning (HRP), also referred to as manpower planning or personnel planning, can be defined as the process of getting the right number of qualified people into the right jobs at the right time. Put another way, HRP is the system of matching the supply of people with the openings the organization expects to have over a given time frame.

A common error of many managers is to focus on the organization's short-term replacement needs. Any human resource plan, if it is to be effective, must be derived from the long-range plans and strategies of the organization.

HRP consists of four basic steps: (1) determining the impact of the organization's objectives on specific organizational units; (2) defining the skills and expertise and the total number of employees necessary to achieve the organization and departmental objectives; (3) determining the additional (net) requirements; and (4) developing action plans to meet the anticipated human resource needs. Successful HRP requires a joint effort by the human resource department and the operating managers of the organization. The human resource department's primary roles are to coordinate, monitor, and synthesize the process.

Several tools which can aid in HRP were discussed. These included the skills inventory, the organization replacement chart, specific reference sources, commitment manpower planning (CMP), ratio analysis, and computer-based planning models. Because HRP is so closely tied to the organizational planning process, the time frames covered should correspond with those covered by organizational plans.

Eight common pitfalls with HRP were discussed. These included: (1) the identity crisis, (2) sponsorship of top management, (3) size of the initial effort, (4) coordination with other managerial and human resource functions, (5) integration with organizational plans, (6) quantitative versus qualitative approaches, (7) involvement of operating managers, and (8) the technique trap.

REVIEW QUESTIONS

1. What is human resource planning (HRP)?
2. How does human resource planning relate to organizational planning?
3. What are the four basic steps in the human resource planning process?
4. What is the cascade approach to setting objectives?

5. Identify several tools that might be used as aids in the human resource planning process.

6. What is the role of human resource department in the human resource planning process?

7. What are eight common pitfalls in human resource planning?

DISCUSSION QUESTIONS

1. Comment on the following statement: "Human resource planning is something to do when you have nothing else to do."

2. Do you think that most human resource planning is undertaken on the basis of organizational objectives or on an "as-necessary" basis?

3. How is it possible to accomplish good organizational and, hence, good human resource planning, in light of the many changing environmental factors over which the organization has no control?

REFERENCES AND ADDITIONAL READINGS

1. C. F. Russ, Jr., "Manpower Planning Systems: Part I," *Personnel Journal,* January 1982, p. 41.

2. Ibid.

3. N. Scarborough and T. W. Zimmerer, "Human Resources Forecasting: Why and Where to Begin," *Personnel Administrator,* May 1982, p. 55.

4. C. B. Mackey, "Human Resource Planning: A Four-Phased Approach," *Management Review,* May 1981, p. 17.

5. Adapted from D. L. Chicci, "Four Steps to an Organization/Human Resource Plan," *Personnel Journal,* June 1979, pp. 290–92.

6. Ibid., p. 390.

7. T. H. Patten, *Manpower Planning and the Development of Human Resources* (New York: John Wiley & Sons, 1971), p. 243.

8. For an example of the use of a sophisticated skills inventory, see W. E. Bright, "How One Company Manages Its Human Resources," *Harvard Business Review,* January–February 1976, pp. 81–93.

9. Chicci, "Four Steps to an Organization," p. 393.

10. For a more in-depth discussion of CMP see C. F. Russ, Jr., "Manpower Planning Systems: Part II," *Personnel Journal,* February 1982, pp. 119–23.

11. Chicci, "Four Steps to an Organization," p. 392.

12. For a more in-depth discussion of ratio analysis see Chicci, "Four Steps to an Organization," pp. 392–94.

13. J. W. Walker, "Models in Manpower Planning," in *Manpower Planning and Programming,* ed. E. H. Burach and J. W. Walker (Boston: Allyn & Bacon, 1972), p. 131.

14. Adapted from Mackey, "Human Resource Planning," pp. 17–20.

| Case 3–1 | **HUMAN RESOURCE PLANNING—WHAT IS THAT?** |

You are a personnel consultant. You have been called by the newly appointed president of a large paper manufacturing firm.

President: I have been in this job for about one month now and all I seem to do is interview people and listen to personnel problems.

You: Why have you been interviewing people? Don't you have a human resource department?

President: Yes, we do. However, the human resource department doesn't hire top management people. As soon as I took over, I found out that two of my vice presidents were retiring and we had no one to replace them.

You: Have you hired anyone?

President: Yes, I have, and that's part of the problem. I hired a guy from the outside. As soon as the announcement was made, one of my department heads came in and resigned. He said he had wanted that job as vice president for eight years. He was angry because we had hired someone from the outside. How was I supposed to know he wanted the job?

You: What have you done about the other vice president job?

President: Nothing, because I'm afraid someone else will quit because they weren't considered for the job. But that's not half my problem. I just found out that among our youngest professional employees—engineers and accountants—there has been an 80 percent turnover rate during the past three years. These are the guys we promote around here. As you know, that's how I started out in this company. I was a mechanical engineer.

You: Has anyone asked them why they are leaving?

President: Yes, and they all give basically the same answer. They say they don't feel that they have a future here. Maybe I should call them all together and explain how I progressed in this company.

You: Have you ever considered implementing a human resource planning system?

President: Human resource planning? What's that?

1. *How would you answer the president's question?*
2. *What would be required to establish a human resource planning system in this company?*

| Case 3–2 | **A NEW BOSS** |

The grants management program of the Environmental Protection Agency (EPA) water division was formed four years ago. The program's main functions are to review grant applications, engineering design reports, and plans and specifications, change orders, and perform operation and maintenance inspections of wastewater treatment facilities. Paul Wagner, chief of the section, supervised four engineers, one technician, and one secretary. Three of the engineers were relatively new to the agency. The senior engineer, Waymon Burrell, had approximately three years' experience in the grants management program.

Because only Waymon Burrell had experience in grants management, Paul Wagner assigned him the areas with the most complicated projects within the state. The other three engineers were given regions with less complex projects; they were assigned to work closely with Waymon and to learn all they could about the program.

At the beginning of the year, Paul Wagner decided that the new engineers had enough experience to undertake more difficult tasks; therefore, the division's territory could be allotted on a geographical basis. The territory was divided according to river basins, with each engineer assigned two or three areas.

This division according to geography worked fine as the section proceeded to meet all its objectives. However, three months ago, Paul Wagner was offered a job with a consulting engineering company and decided to leave the EPA. He gave two months' notice to top management.

Time passed, but top management did not even advertise for a new section chief. People in the section speculated as to who might be chosen to fill the vacancy; most of them hoped that Waymon Burrell would be, since he knew most about the workings of the section.

On the Monday of Paul's last week, top executives met with him and the section members to announce that they had decided to appoint a temporary section chief until a new one could be hired.

The division chief announced that the temporary section chief would be Sam Kutzman, who was a senior engineer within another division of EPA. This came as quite a surprise to Waymon and the others in the grants management program.

Sam Kutzman had no experience in the program. His background was in technical assistance. His previous job had required that he do research in certain treatment processes so that he could provide more technical performance information to other divisions within EPA.

1. *Do you think Sam Kutzman was a good choice for temporary section chief?*
2. *How has human resource planning worked in this situation?*

Chapter 4

Equal employment opportunity

Objectives

1. To develop an understanding of equal employment opportunity legislation.
2. To describe how to develop an affirmative action plan.
3. To discuss current issues in equal employment opportunity.
4. To outline some of the record-keeping requirements of equal employment opportunity.

Outline

Title VII, Civil Rights Act
What is equal employment opportunity?
Enforcement agencies
Interpretation and application of Title VII
Affirmative action plans (AAP)
Landmark court cases
 Griggs v. Duke Power Company
 Albemarle Paper v. Moody
 Washington v. Davis
 University of California Regents v. Bakke
 United Steelworkers v. Weber
Uniform guidelines on employee selection procedures
 Adverse impact
 Eliminating adverse impact
Additional equal employment opportunity legislation
 Equal Pay Act
 Education Amendments Act
 Age Discrimination in Employment Act
 Veterans Readjustment Act
 Rehabilitation Act

Current issues in equal employment opportunity
 Sexual harassment
 Equal pay for work of comparable value
Record-keeping and equal employment opportunity

Glossary of terms

Adverse impact Condition that occurs when the selection rate for minorities or women in hiring, promotions, transfers, demotions or in any selection decision is less than 80 percent of the selection rate for the majority group.

Affirmative action plan Document outlining specific goals and timetables for remedying past discriminatory actions.

Bona fide occupational qualification (BFOQ) A selection decision based on sex or age because of business necessity.

Concentration More minorities and women in a job category or department than would reasonably be expected given their proportion in the labor market.

Employment parity Condition that exists when the proportion of minorities and women employed by an organization equals the proportion in the organization's relevant labor market.

Equal employment opportunity Refers to the right of all persons to work and to advance on the basis of merit, ability, and potential.

Equal Employment Opportunity Commission (EEOC) Agency of the federal government that was created under the Civil Rights Act of 1964 to administer Title VII of the act and to ensure equal employment opportunity.

Occupational parity Condition that exists when the proportion of minorities and women in various occupations in an organization is equal to their proportion in the organization's relevant labor market.

Office of Federal Contract Compliance Programs (OFCCP) An office within the U.S. Department of Labor that is responsible for ensuring equal employment opportunity by federal contractors and subcontractors.

Reverse discrimination Condition under which there is alleged preferential treatment of one group (minority or women) over another group rather than equal opportunity.

Sexual harassment Unwelcome sexual advances, requests for sexual favors, and other verbal or physical conduct of a sexual nature which influence employment decisions or interfere with an affected person's work performance.

Systemic discrimination Condition that exists when there are large differences in either occupational or employment parity.

Underutilization Condition that exists when fewer minorities or women are in a particular job category than would be reasonably expected given their proportion in the relevant labor market.

Many people who suffer effects of past and present discrimination are already qualified for better jobs, but continuing barriers throughout employment systems deny them equal opportunity.*

Two of the most important influences on human resource management are government legislation and court interpretations of this legislation. Numerous laws exist that influence the recruitment and selection of personnel, compensation, working conditions and hours, discharges, and labor relations. Because this legal framework is so comprehensive, it is impossible to analyze it in one chapter. Therefore, specific legislation and court decisions are described throughout this book. The purpose of this chapter is to develop an understanding of equal employment opportunity legislation and court interpretations of this legislation.

TITLE VII, CIVIL RIGHTS ACT

The keystone of federal equal employment opportunity legislation is Title VII of the Civil Rights Act of 1964. Two important provisions of the act are as follows:

Section 703(A):
It shall be an unlawful employment practice for an employer (1) to fail or refuse to hire or to discharge any individual, or otherwise to discriminate against any individual with respect to his compensation, terms, conditions, or privileges of employment, because of such individual's race, color, religion, sex, or national origin, or (2) to limit, segregate, or classify his employees in any way which would deprive or tend to deprive any individual of employment opportunities or otherwise adversely affect his status as an employee, because of such an individual's race, color, religion, sex or national origin.

Section 704(B):
It shall be an unlawful employment practice for an employer, labor organization, or employment agency to print or publish or cause to be printed or published any notice or advertisement relating to employment by such an employment agency indicating any preference, limitations, specification, or discrimination, based on race, color, religion, sex, or national origin. . . .

Title VII, as amended by the Equal Employment Opportunity Act of 1972, covers the following:

1. All private employers of 15 or more people.
2. All educational institutions, public and private.[1]
3. State and local governments.[1]

_____

Affirmative Action and Equal Employment, volume 1 (U.S. Equal Employment Opportunity Commission: Washington, D.C., 1974), p. 1.

4. Public and private employment agencies.
5. Labor unions with 15 or more members.
6. Joint labor-management committees for apprenticeship and training.

The Civil Rights Act, as amended, was passed by Congress to establish guidelines for ensuring equal employment opportunities for all people. As is true with most laws, ambiguities in the language of the law leave much room for interpretation by the federal agencies that enforce it. Furthermore, court decisions regarding the interpretation of the law often raise additional questions concerning interpretation. For these reasons and others, equal employment opportunity is one of the most challenging and complex aspects of human resource management.

WHAT IS EQUAL EMPLOYMENT OPPORTUNITY?

Equal employment opportunity refers to the right of all persons to work and to advance on the basis of merit, ability, and potential. One of the major focuses of equal employment opportunity efforts today is identifying and eliminating discriminatory employment practices. Such practices are any artificial, arbitrary, and unnecessary barriers to employment when the barriers operate to discriminate on the basis of race, sex, or other impermissible classification. The barriers identified by the Supreme Court include practices and policies of recruitment, selection, testing, systems of transfer, promotion, seniority, lines of progression, and other similar basic terms and conditions of employment.[2]

Title VII provides that when a court finds employment discrimination it may "order such affirmative action as may be necessary" to eliminate it. When the effects of employment practices, regardless of their intent, discriminate against a group protected by law, the courts have consistently ordered specific affirmative actions to eliminate present and future discrimination and to provide equitable remedies for the consequences of past discrimination.

ENFORCEMENT AGENCIES

Two federal agencies have major responsibility for enforcing equal opportunity legislation. The Equal Employment Opportunity Commission (EEOC) was created by the Civil Rights Act of 1964 to administer Title VII of the act and ensure equal employment opportunity for all people. The EEOC is composed of five members, not more than three of whom can be members of the same political party. Members of the commission are appointed by the president and with the advice and consent of the Senate for a term of five years. The EEOC investigates complaints of discrimination and develops guidelines to enforce Title

AT&T signs accord to review hiring of women, minorities

Washington—American Telephone & Telegraph Co. and the Labor Department agreed on new methods for keeping track of AT&T's progress in hiring and promoting women and minorities.

Under the accord, the department's Office of Federal Contract Compliance Program approved AT&T's affirmative-action program on a nationwide basis. A department official explained that investigators will use uniform standards to make sure AT&T carries out the program at various locations. The contract-compliance agency enforces a 1965 executive order barring job-bias by federal contractors.

"You won't have a problem of a GS-12 (investigator) in Peoria, (Ill.) saying the program ought to read this way and a GS-12 in New York saying it would read this way," said Ellen Shong, the program's director. "It allows us to focus energies on performance of the system rather than on the organization of the (affirmative-action) plan."

At the same time, AT&T agreed to provide the department with much more detail annually about the status of its affirmative-action efforts than ordinarily required by federal rules.

The result of the nationally approved program and additional data will be fewer compliance reviews, Miss Shong said. "What AT&T gets is: We're not willy nilly doing compliance reviews, which is costly to them, too."

The accord isn't related to any pending litigation or investigation. It affects all existing and future AT&T subsidiaries except Western Electric Co., which already has its own affirmative-action plan approved by the department.

A department spokesman said about a dozen other big concerns with federal contracts already have won approval of their national affirmative-action programs. But Miss Shong said "no other contractor agreed to provide the detailed information AT&T did. Contractors routinely must tell the departments about the proportion of various types of jobs held by women and minorities. AT&T will highlight changes in those numbers and explain why they're going up or down, Miss Shong said.

VII regulations. The 1972 amendment to Title VII gave the EEOC authority to take civil action against an organization that is using discriminatory employment practices. As a result, legal actions by the EEOC against organizations have increased substantially.

In some situations where the courts have upheld the EEOC's findings of discriminatory employment practices, significant monetary awards have been granted to the plantiffs. Some examples include:

A female chemistry professor formerly at the University of Minnesota was awarded $100,000 in compensatory damages in settlement of a sex discrimination suit brought against the university.[3]

Ford Motor Company was ordered to pay $23 million to make up for past discrimination against women and minorities.[4]

AT&T agreed to pay some $15 million in compensation for alleged discrimination against women and minorities.[5]

The Office of Federal Contract Compliance Programs (OFCCP) within the U.S. Department of Labor is responsible for ensuring equal employment opportunity among federal contractors and subcontractors, which include most major businesses in the United States. A special clause in their contracts makes equal employment opportunity and affirmative action an integral part of their agreements. Minorities, women, members of religious and ethnic groups, handicapped persons, Vietnam era veterans, and disabled veterans of all wars are protected by the equal opportunity and affirmative action requirements in federal government contracts.

Ensuring that the equal opportunity and affirmative action requirements are fulfilled is known as contract compliance. When a compliance review turns up problems which cannot be easily resolved, the OFCCP attempts to reach a conciliation agreement with the organization. Such an agreement might include back pay, seniority credit, promotions, new training programs, special recruitment efforts, or other measures.

Contractors or subcontractors who violate their equal employment and affirmative action requirements may lose their government contracts, may have payments withheld by the government, or may be declared ineligible for any federal contract work. In some cases, the Department of Justice, on behalf of the Department of Labor, may file suit in federal court against an employer for violation of the contract requirements. If a complaint involves discrimination against only one person, OFCCP can refer the case to the EEOC for processing.

INTERPRETATION AND APPLICATION OF TITLE VII

Title VII of the Civil Rights Act has probably been more fully interpreted by the courts than any of the other equal opportunity laws. Courts have decided that whether the employer intended to discriminate is not an important factor in discrimination.[6] Employment practices which deny opportunities to persons protected by Title VII are illegal, no matter what the organization's intent. For instance, an employer who requires a college degree for a certain job may be required to show that the college degree is both job related and an accurate predictor of future success in the job.

There are very few exceptions to Title VII. The exceptions that do exist have been interpreted very narrowly by the courts. Justifying any practice or policy which has a disparate effect on groups protected by the law requires the employer to demonstrate a compelling business necessity and to show that no alternative nondiscriminatory practice can achieve the required purposes.[7] Business necessity has been narrowly interpreted to mean that the employer must show overriding evidence that a discriminatory practice is essential to the safe and efficient operation of the business and/or show extreme adverse financial impact.[8]

State laws which in the past may have contributed to discriminatory practices have also been ruled by the courts to be superseded by Title VII. Title VII allows for sex discrimination only when sex is a bona fide occupational qualification (BFOQ). BFOQ refers to selection based on sex or age by reason of business necessity. BFOQ has been very narrowly interpreted by the courts to occupations such as actors, models, rest room attendants, wet nurses, or security guards in a maximum security prison. Title VII does not provide for race or color as a BFOQ. Age may be considered a BFOQ when there is concrete evidence that this is a job-related factor and a business necessity. For example, age may be a BFOQ when public safety is involved, such as with airline pilots or interstate bus drivers.

Another exception to Title VII is discrimination based on a bona fide seniority system. The Supreme Court has ruled that such systems are protected under Title VII, even though they may perpetuate the effects of pre-act discrimination.[9] The Court in this decision concluded that in the passage of Title VII, Congress did not intend to destroy or water down the vested seniority rights of employees simply because their employers had engaged in discrimination prior to the passage of the act.

Contractual agreements between a union and employer are not legal or binding if they violate equal employment opportunity laws. Clauses which limit certain jobs to one group or pay one group more for equal work are not binding. Contract negotiations must be reopened as soon as this type of discrimination is discovered by either management or the union.

Two methods can be used by EEOC to determine whether discrimination against groups protected by the law has occurred: (1) employment parity and (2) occupational parity. When employment parity exists, the proportion of minorities and women employed by an organization equals the proportion in the organization's relevant labor market. Occupational parity exists when the proportion of minorities and women employed in various occupations in an organization is equal to their proportion in the organization's relevant labor market. Large differences in either occupational or employment parity are called systemic discrimination. EEOC also can examine the underutilization or concentration of minorities and/or females in certain jobs. Underutilization refers to the practice of having fewer minorities or females in a particular job category than would reasonably be expected by their presence in the relevant labor market. Concentration means having more minorities and women in a job category or department than would reasonably be expected by their presence in the relevant labor market. When statistics reveal significant underutilization, concentration, or systemic discrimination, the employer is likely to be required to engage in affirmative action.

AFFIRMATIVE ACTION PLANS (AAP)

An affirmative action plan is a written document outlining specific goals and timetables for remedying past discriminatory actions. All federal contractors and subcontractors with contracts over $50,000 and 50 or more employees are required to develop and implement written affirmative action programs which are monitored by the OFCCP. While Title VII and EEOC do not require any specific type of affirmative action program, court rulings have often required affirmative action when discrimination is found. For example, the American Telephone & Telegraph Company (AT&T) in a consent decree with the EEOC and Department of Labor agreed to the following affirmative actions:

1. Hiring and promotion targets to increase significantly the utilization of women and minorities in every job classification. Progress in accomplishing these targets was to be reviewed regularly by EEOC and OFCCP.
2. Goals for employing men in previously all-female jobs.
3. Allowing women and minorities in noncraft jobs to compete for craft jobs based on their qualifications and seniority.
4. Assessing all female college graduates hired since 1965 to determine their interest and potential for higher-level jobs and implementing a specific development program to prepare these women for promotions.[10]

A number of basic steps are involved in the development of an effective affirmative action plan. The EEOC has suggested the following eight steps:

1. The chief executive officer of an organization should issue a written statement describing his or her personal commitment to the plan, legal obligations, and the importance of equal employment opportunity as an organizational goal.
2. A top official of the organization should be given the authority and responsibility for directing and implementing the program. In addition, all managers and supervisors within the organization should clearly understand their own responsibilities for carrying out equal employment opportunity.
3. The organization's policy and commitment to the policy should be publicized both internally and externally.
4. Present employment should be surveyed to identify areas of con-

centration and underutilization and to determine the extent of underutilization.

5. Goals and timetables for achieving the goals should be developed to improve utilization of minorities, males, and females in each area where underutilization has been identified.

6. The entire employment system should be reviewed to identify and eliminate barriers to equal employment. Areas for review include: recruitment, selection, promotion systems, training programs, wage and salary structure, benefits and conditions of employment, lay-offs, discharges, disciplinary action, and union contract provisions affecting these areas.

7. An internal audit and reporting system should be established to monitor and evaluate progress in all aspects of the program.

8. Company and community programs that are supportive of equal opportunity should be developed. Programs might include training of supervisors on their legal responsibilities and the organization's commitment to equal employment and job and career counseling programs.[11]

Organizations without affirmative action plans will find that it makes good business sense to identify and revise employment practices which have discriminatory effects before the federal government requires such action. Increased legal action and the consistent record of court-required affirmative action emphasize the advantage of writing and instituting an affirmative action plan.

LANDMARK COURT CASES

Several Supreme Court decisions have provided guidance in the interpretation and application of equal employment opportunity laws. Some of the more important decisions are described in the following sections.

Griggs v. Duke Power Company

The Griggs case concerned the promotion and transfer policies of the Duke Power Company, which provides electricity to customers in both North and South Carolina. Duke required certain categories of employees to have a high school diploma and to obtain a score at least equal to the national median for high school graduates on the Wonderlic Intelligence Test and the Bennett Mechanical Comprehension Test. In a class action suit, black employees argued that these practices were contrary to Title VII, since a much higher percentage of blacks failed these tests and a higher percentage of blacks did not have high school diplomas. The suit also contended that neither of these requirements was necessary for successful performance of the jobs in question.[12]

The Supreme Court in 1971 ruled unanimously for the black employees. The decision stated that if an employment practice cannot be shown to be related to job performance, the practice is prohibited. Furthermore, the courts placed the burden on the employer to prove that employment practices are related to job performance. The Griggs decision established the standard that employment practices which deny opportunities to persons protected by Title VII are illegal regardless of the organization's intent. Thus, the effect and not the intent of an employment practice determines whether it is discriminatory.

Albemarle Paper v.
Moody[13]

The Albemarle decision in June 1975 was also concerned with the use of tests in employment practices. In its decision, the Supreme Court held a plaintiff can establish that discrimination exists by showing the tests in question select applicants for hire or promotion in a racial pattern significantly different from the pool of applicants. The Court ruled that once the plaintiff has established this, the employer must then prove that the tests being used are job related. The Albemarle decision, as a practical matter, meant that the burden is on the employer to show that its tests are in compliance with *EEOC Guidelines on Testing*.[14]

Washington v.
Davis[15]

The Washington decision made by the Supreme Court in 1976 was concerned with an 80-question test of general verbal ability used by the District of Columbia Metropolitan Police Department to screen applicants for the police training academy. The problem with the test was that a much higher percentage of women and blacks were failing the test. The Metropolitan Police Department had statistical evidence to show a relationship between the test scores and academy performance. However, the plaintiffs contended that this evidence was of no use since the police department had not demonstrated a relationship between academy performance and job performance.

The Supreme Court ruled in favor of the Metropolitan Police Department. The decision stated that the test was directly related to the requirements of the training program and that a positive relationship between the test and training course performance was sufficient to justify the use of the test, regardless of its possible relationship to actual performance as a police officer. This decision may have signaled a shift in emphasis from the Griggs and Albemarle decisions. In this case, the Court seemed to say that showing a relationship between test scores and performance on the job is not the only consideration in determining whether a test can be used for selection purposes.

University of
California Regents v.
Bakke [16]

The Medical School of the University of California at Davis opened in 1968 with an entering class of 50 students. No black, Hispanic, or native American students were in this class. Over the next two years, the faculty developed a special admissions program to increase the participation of minority students. In 1971, the size of the entering class was doubled, and 16 of the 100 positions were to be filled by "disadvantaged" applicants chosen by a special admissions committee. In actual practice, disadvantaged meant minority applicant.

Allan Bakke, a white male, was denied admission to the medical school in 1973 and 1974. Contending that minority students with lower grade averages and test scores were admitted under the special program, Bakke brought suit. He argued that he had been discriminated against because of his race when he was prevented from competing for the 16 reserved positions and alleged that the medical school's special two-track admissions system violated the Civil Rights Act of 1964. Thus, the Bakke case raised the issue of reverse discrimination, i.e., alleged preferential treatment of one group (minority or female) over another group rather than equal opportunity.

On June 28, 1978, the Supreme Court ruled in a 5 to 4 decision that Allan Bakke should be admitted to the Medical School of the University of California at Davis and found the school's two-track admissions system to be illegal. However, by another 5 to 4 vote, the Court held that at least some forms of race-conscious admissions procedures are constitutional. Justice Powell in his opinion stated as follows: "race or ethnic background may be deemed a 'plus' in a particular applicant's file, yet it does not insulate the individual from comparison with all other candidates for the available seats."[17] As could be expected, the somewhat nebulous decision in the Bakke case provided an environment for further court tests of the legal status of reverse discrimination.

United Steelworkers
v. Weber [18]

In 1974, the Kaiser Aluminum and Chemical Corporation and the United Steelworkers of America signed a collective bargaining agreement that contained an affirmative action plan designed to reduce racial imbalances in Kaiser's then almost exclusively white work force. The plan set hiring goals and established on-the-job training programs to teach craft skills to unskilled workers. Under the plan, 50 percent of the openings in the training programs were reserved for blacks.

At Kaiser's Gramercy, Louisiana plant, Brian F. Weber, a white male, filed a class action suit against the company because black employees were accepted into the company's in-plant craft training program before white employees with more seniority. In its 1979 decision on this case, the Supreme Court ruled that the voluntarily agreed-upon plan between Kaiser and the Steelworkers was permissible. The Court stated that the Title VII prohibition against racial discrimination did not condemn all private, voluntary, race-conscious affirmative action programs. The decision also hinted at the Court's criteria for a permissible affirmative action plan: (1) the plan must be designed to break down old patterns of segregation; (2) must not involve the discharge of innocent third parties; (3) must not have any bars to the advancement of white employees, and (4) must be a temporary measure to eliminate discrimination.[19]

Some guidance on the status of reverse discrimination has been given in both the Bakke and Weber cases. However, the issue is far from being settled, and more court cases are likely in the future.

UNIFORM GUIDELINES ON EMPLOYEE SELECTION PROCEDURES[20]

In 1978, the EEOC, the Civil Service Commission, the Department of Justice, and the Department of Labor adopted and issued a document titled *Uniform Guidelines on Employee Selection Procedures.* These guidelines were intended to establish the federal government's position concerning discrimination in employment practices. Virtually all areas of human resource management (recruitment, selection, training, promotions, demotions, transfers, and performance appraisal systems) are affected by these guidelines.

Adverse impact

The fundamental principle underlying the guidelines is that employment policies and practices which have an adverse impact on the employment opportunities of any racial, sexual, or ethnic group are illegal under Title VII unless justified by business necessity. Normally, justification on the basis of business necessity means that the employer must demonstrate a relationship between the selection procedure and performance on the job.

The guidelines specify the "four-fifths" or "80 percent" rule as a practical means of determining adverse impact. Adverse impact occurs when the selection rate for minorities or women is less than 80 percent of the selection rate for the majority group (white males). Figure 4–1

Figure 4–1   Determination of adverse impact

Selection rate for white males:

$$\text{Number of applicants} = 25$$
$$\text{Number hired} = 15$$
$$\text{Selection rate} = {}^{15}/_{25} = 60\%$$

Selection rate for women:

$$\text{Number of applicants} = 20$$
$$\text{Number hired} = 5$$
$$\text{Selection rate} = {}^{5}/_{20} = 25\%$$

Adverse impact rate:
$4/5$ (or 80%) of selection rate for white males = $4/5$ (60%) = 48%
A selection rate for women below 48% indicates adverse impact

Thus, in this example, since the selection rate for women is 25%, adverse impact exists.

illustrates the calculations used in determining adverse impact. This example shows adverse impact in hiring. However, adverse impact can also occur in promotions, transfers, demotions, or in any selection decision.

Eliminating adverse impact

The uniform guidelines provide two basic options for eliminating adverse impact. First, the employer can modify or eliminate the selection procedure which produces the adverse impact. If the employer does not do that, then he or she must, in most circumstances, justify the procedure on the basis of business necessity. This generally means that the employer must show a clear relation between the selection procedure and performance on the job. Showing this relationship is called validation. Methods of validation are discussed in depth in Chapter 6.

ADDITIONAL EQUAL EMPLOYMENT OPPORTUNITY LEGISLATION

Discrimination in employment has been prohibited by court rulings under the Civil Rights Act of 1866 and 1870 and the equal protection clauses of the 14th Amendment. Discrimination because of race, religion, and national origin have also been found to violate rights guaranteed by the National Labor Relations Act, which is described in depth in Chapter 16. Many state and local government laws also prohibit employment discrimination. The following paragraphs provide a brief description of some of the more current and important laws dealing with equal employment opportunity.

Equal Pay Act

The Equal Pay Act was passed in 1963 and was later amended by Title IX of the Education Amendments Act of 1972. The law requires all employers covered by the Fair Labor Standards Act (and others included in the 1972 amendment) to provide equal pay to men and women who perform work which is similar in skill, effort, and responsibility. Title VII of the Civil Rights Act also requires equal pay regardless of race, national origin, or sex. This includes base pay as well as opportunities for overtime, raises, bonuses, commissions, and other benefits. The employer is also responsible for ensuring that fringe benefits are available to employees without regard to sex. Offering and paying higher wages to women and minorities to attract these groups is also illegal. Wage disparities between sexes are permitted when such payment is based on a seniority system, a merit system, a system which measures earnings by quantity or quality of production, or a differential based on any other factor other than sex.

Education
Amendments Act

Title IX of the Education Amendments Act of 1972 extended coverage of the Equal Pay Act of 1963. Title IX prohibits sex discrimination against employees or students in any educational institution receiving financial aid from the federal government.

Age Discrimination
in Employment Act

The Age Discrimination in Employment Act was enacted in 1967 and amended in 1978. The act prohibits discrimination against people between the ages of 40 and 70 in any area of employment. This law applies to employers of 25 or more persons. This law does not apply where age is a bona fide occupational qualification, such as with airline pilots or interstate bus drivers.

Veterans
Readjustment Act

The Vietnam Era Veterans Readjustment Act of 1974 requires federal government contractors and subcontractors to take affirmative action to hire and promote Vietnam and disabled veterans. Contractors and subcontractors with contracts of $10,000 or more must list all suitable job openings with state employment services. Contractors and subcontractors with contracts of $50,000 or more and 50 or more employees are required to have written affirmative action plans for Vietnam and disabled veterans.

Rehabilitation Act

The Rehabilitation Act of 1973, which was amended in 1977, prohibits employers from denying jobs to individuals merely because of a handicap. This law applies to government contractors and subcontractors with contracts of $50,000 or more and 50 or more employees. The act requires contractors and subcontractors to make reasonable and necessary accommodations enabling qualified handicapped people to work as effectively as other employees. This law defines a handicapped person as one who has a physical or mental impairment which significantly limits one or more major life activities.

**CURRENT ISSUES
IN EQUAL
EMPLOYMENT
OPPORTUNITY**

Over the past several years, new issues have regularly surfaced concerning equal employment opportunity. As these issues have arisen, new guidelines have been proposed by the federal government to clarify its position on the issue, and, of course, court decisions have provided further clarification.

Sexual harassment[21]

One of the more current issues in equal opportunity is sexual harassment. On March 11, 1980, the EEOC published guidelines on sexual harassment in the workplace. The EEOC has taken the position that the Civil Rights Act prohibits such harassment, just as it prohibits harassment based on race, religion, or national origin.

Under the EEOC guidelines, employers are considered responsible for the acts of managers or agents, regardless of whether the acts were authorized or forbidden by the employer and regardless of whether the employer knew or should have known of the acts. An employer is considered responsible for the actions of nonmanagerial employees only when the employer knows or should have known of their misconduct. The employer has the opportunity to rebut this liability by showing that immediate and appropriate corrective action was taken to remedy the situation.

The guidelines established three basic criteria to determine whether an act, including unwelcome sexual advances, requests for sexual favors, and other verbal or physical conduct of a sexual nature, constitutes unlawful harassment:

1. If submission to the conduct is either an explicit or implicit term or condition of employment.
2. If submission to or rejection of the conduct is used as a basis for an employment decision affecting the person rejecting or submitting to the conduct.
3. If the conduct has the purpose or effect of unreasonably interfering with an affected person's work performance or creating an intimidating, hostile, or offensive work environment.

The guidelines also emphasize the importance of employers taking positive action to prevent sexual harassment in the workplace. They suggest that employers take the following steps: affirmatively raise the subject; express strong disapproval; develop appropriate sanctions; inform employees of their right to raise sexual harassment claims; and develop methods to sensitize all employees to the issue.

Equal pay for work of comparable value

A controversial and unresolved issue in equal employment opportunity is the so-called "comparable value" or "worth" theory. This theory holds that entire classes of jobs are traditionally undervalued and underpaid because they are held by women, and that this inequality amounts to sex discrimination in violation of Title VII of the Civil Rights Act. Proponents of this theory argue that the Equal Pay Act offers little protection to women workers because most jobs continue to be illegally segregated by sex and because the act only applies to those job classifications in which men and women are employed.[22] Proponents further argue that the most serious form of wage discrimination occurs when women arrive at the workplace with equivalent education, training, and ability to that of men and are assigned jobs held mainly by females and which are normally lower paid than predominantly male jobs. For example, proponents of this theory contend that clerical employees should be paid the same as plant employees.[23]

Presently, the few court cases that have been concerned with the issue of comparable value have given little indication as to what the ultimate outcome will be. In the case of *County of Washington* v. *Gunther*,[24] the Supreme Court considered a claim of sex-based wage discrimination between prison matrons and prison guards. Prison matrons were being paid approximately 70 percent of what the guards were being paid. In a 5 to 4 decision, the Court ruled that sex-based wage discrimination violates Title VII of the Civil Rights Act and that the plaintiffs could file suit under the law, even if the jobs were not equal. However, the Court's decision specifically stated that it was not ruling on the comparable worth issue. Thus, it is likely that this issue will be the focal point of many more cases.

RECORD-KEEPING AND EQUAL EMPLOYMENT OPPORTUNITY

All organizations that have 15 or more employees are required by law to keep records and to make reports to the EEOC and OFCCP as deemed necessary by these two agencies. The most basic report required is Standard Form 100. Every employer with 15 or more employees must make and keep records and statistics necessary for completion of Standard Form 100. However, only those employing 100 or more persons (excluding state and local governments); those with fewer than 100 employees, but that are subsidiaries of organizations with more than 100 employees; and all federal government contractors and subcontractors must file Standard Form 100. Figure 4–2 illustrates Standard Form 100.

In fact, all employment records made and kept by an employer are subject to review when requested by the EEOC and OFCCP. This includes application forms and records on recruitment, hiring, job placements, selection for training, rates of pay, promotions, discharges, layoffs, and transfers.

SUMMARY

The keystone of federal equal employment opportunity legislation is Title VII of the Civil Rights Act of 1964. Equal employment opportunity refers to the right of all persons to work and advance on the basis of merit, ability, and potential.

The Equal Employment Opportunity Commission (EEOC) and the Office of Federal Contract Compliance Programs (OFCCP) are the two federal agencies with primary responsibility for enforcing equal employment opportunity legislation.

Two criteria are used by EEOC to determine whether discrimination has occurred. Employment parity i.e., the proportion of minorities and women employed by an organization equals the proportion in the or-

Figure 4–2   Standard Form 100

Standard Form 100
(Rev. 12/78)
O.M.B. No. 3046-0007
100-210

EQUAL EMPLOYMENT OPPORTUNITY
EMPLOYER INFORMATION REPORT EEO-1

Joint Reporting
Committee

- Equal Employment Opportunity Commission
- Office of Federal Contract Compliance Programs

Section A - TYPE OF REPORT
Refer to instructions for number and types of reports to be filed.

1. Indicate by marking in the appropriate box the type of reporting unit for which this copy of the form is submitted (MARK ONLY ONE BOX).

(1) ☐ Single-establishment Employer Report

Multi-establishment Employer:
(2) ☐ Consolidated Report
(3) ☐ Headquarters Unit Report
(4) ☐ Individual Establishment Report (submit one for each establishment with 25 or more employees)
(5) ☐ Special Report

2. Total number of reports being filed by this Company (Answer on Consolidated Report only) _____

Section B - COMPANY IDENTIFICATION *(To be answered by all employers)*

OFFICE USE ONLY

1. Parent Company

a. Name of parent company (owns or controls establishment in item 2) omit if same as label

Name of receiving office		Address (Number and street)	
City or town	County	State	ZIP code

b. Employer Identification No.

a.

b.

2. Establishment for which this report is filed. (Omit if same as label)

a. Name of establishment

Address (Number and street)	City or town	County	State	ZIP code

b. Employer Identification No.   (If same as label, skip.)

c.

d.

3. Parent company affiliation   (Multi-establishment Employers Answer on Consolidated Report only)

a. Name of parent-affiliated company   b. Employer Identification No.

Address (Number and street)	City or town	County	State	ZIP code

Section C - EMPLOYERS WHO ARE REQUIRED TO FILE *(To be answered by all employers)*

☐ Yes ☐ No   1. Does the entire company have at least 100 employees in the payroll period for which you are reporting?

☐ Yes ☐ No   2. Is your company affiliated through common ownership and/or centralized management with other entities in an enterprise with a total employment of 100 or more?

☐ Yes ☐ No   3. Does the company or any of its establishments (a) have 50 or more employees AND (b) is not exempt as provided by 41 CFR 60-1.5, AND either (1) is a prime government contractor or first-tier subcontractor, and has a contract, subcontract, or purchase order amounting to $50,000 or more, or (2) serves as a depository of Government funds in any amount or is a financial institution which is an issuing and paying agent for U.S. Savings Bonds and Savings Notes?

NOTE: If the answer is yes to ANY of these questions, complete the entire form, otherwise skip to Section G.

Figure 4–2 (*concluded*)

Section D - EMPLOYMENT DATA

Employment at this establishment—Report all permanent, temporary, or part-time employees including apprentices and on-the-job trainees unless specifically excluded as set forth in the instructions. Enter the appropriate figures on all lines and in all columns. Blank spaces will be considered as zeros.

JOB CATEGORIES	OVERALL TOTALS (SUM OF COL B THRU K) A	MALE					FEMALE				
		WHITE (NOT OF HISPANIC ORIGIN) B	BLACK (NOT OF HISPANIC ORIGIN) C	HISPANIC D	ASIAN OR PACIFIC ISLANDER E	AMERICAN INDIAN OR ALASKAN NATIVE F	WHITE (NOT OF HISPANIC ORIGIN) G	BLACK (NOT OF HISPANIC ORIGIN) H	HISPANIC I	ASIAN OR PACIFIC ISLANDER J	AMERICAN INDIAN OR ALASKAN NATIVE K
Officials and Managers											
Professionals											
Technicians											
Sales Workers											
Office and Clerical											
Craft Workers (Skilled)											
Operatives (Semi-Skilled)											
Laborers (Unskilled)											
Service Workers											
TOTAL											
Total employment reported in previous EEO-1 report											

(The trainees below should also be included in the figures for the appropriate occupational categories above)

Formal On-the job trainees	White collar										
	Production										

1. NOTE: On consolidated report, skip questions 2-5 and Section E
2. How was information as to race or ethnic group in Section D obtained?
   1 ☐ Visual Survey   3 ☐ Other—Specify ....
   2 ☐ Employment Record   ....
3. Dates of payroll period used -

4. Pay period of last report submitted for this establishment
   _____
5. Does this establishment employ apprentices?
   This year? 1 ☐ Yes   2 ☐ No
   Last year? 1 ☐ Yes   2 ☐ No

Section E - ESTABLISHMENT INFORMATION

1. Is the location of the establishment the same as that reported last year?
   1 ☐ Yes   2 ☐ No   3. ☐ Did not report last year.   4. ☐ Reported on combined basis.

2. Is the major business activity at this establishment the same as that reported last year?
   1 ☐ Yes   2 ☐ No   3. ☐ No report last year   4. ☐ Reported on combined basis.

OFFICE USE ONLY

3. What is the major activity of this establishment? (Be specific, i.e., manufacturing steel castings, retail grocer, wholesale plumbing supplies, title insurance, etc. Include the specific type of product or type of service provided, as well as the principal business or industrial activity.

e.

Section F - REMARKS

Use this item to give any identification data appearing on last report which differs from that given above, explain major changes in composition or reporting units and other pertinent information.

Section G - CERTIFICATION (See Instructions G)

Check one
1 ☐ All reports are accurate and were prepared in accordance with the instructions (check on consolidated only)
2 ☐ This report is accurate and was prepared in accordance with the instructions.

Name of Certifying Official	Title	Signature	Date

Name of person to contact regarding this report (Type or print)	Address (Number and street)		

Title	City and State	ZIP code	Telephone Area Code	Number	Extension

All reports and information obtained from individual reports will be kept confidential as required by Section 709 (e) of Title VII
WILLFULLY FALSE STATEMENTS ON THIS REPORT ARE PUNISHABLE BY LAW, U.S. CODE, TITLE 18, SECTION 1001

ganization's relevant labor market; and occupational parity i.e., the proportion of minorities and women employed in various occupations in the organization is equal to their proportion in the organization's relevant labor market.

An affirmative action plan is a written document outlining specific goals and timetables for remedying past discriminatory actions. The following landmark court decisions further interpret equal employment opportunity: *Griggs* v. *Duke Power Company, Albemarle Paper* v. *Moody, Washington* v. *Davis,* the *University of California Regents* v. *Bakke,* and the *United Steelworkers* v. *Weber.*

The *Uniform Guidelines on Employee Selection Procedures* established the federal government's position on prohibiting discrimination in employment practices. Adverse impact occurs when the selection rate for any protected group is less than 80 percent of the selection rate for the majority group.

Additional equal employment opportunity legislation described in this chapter includes: the Equal Pay Act, Education Amendments Act, Age Discrimination in Employment Act, Veterans Readjustment Act, and Rehabilitation Act. Sexual harassment and equal pay for work of comparable value are two current issues relating to equal employment opportunity.

REVIEW QUESTIONS

1. What is equal employment opportunity?
2. Outline the coverage of Title VII of the Civil Rights Act of 1964.
3. What two federal government agencies have the primary responsibility for enforcing equal employment opportunity legislation?
4. What is a bona fide occupational qualification (BFOQ)?
5. What is an affirmative action plan?
6. Describe the impact of the following Supreme Court decisions:
   a. Griggs v. *Duke Power Company*
   b. Albemarle Paper v. *Moody*
   c. Washington v. *Davis*
   d. University of California Regents v. *Bakke*
   e. United Steelworkers v. *Weber*
7. What is adverse impact?
8. Explain the significance of the following legislation:
   a. Equal Pay Act.
   b. Education Amendments Act.
   c. Age Discrimination in Employment Act.
   d. Veterans Readjustment Act.
   e. Rehabilitation Act.
9. What is sexual harassment?
10. Explain the "equal pay for work of comparable value" controversy.

DISCUSSION QUESTIONS

1. Do you feel that telling an off-color joke or using profanity in front of women would be considered sexual harassment? Discuss.

2. How do you feel about the "equal pay for work of comparable value" controversy?

3. What area of human resource management is most affected by equal employment opportunity legislation? Discuss.

4. Do you feel that most organizations meet the requirements of equal employment opportunity? Why or why not?

REFERENCES AND ADDITIONAL READINGS

1. New coverage added by the 1972 amendment.

2. EEOC Commission Decision No. 72-0427.

3. "Women Chemist Wins Discrimination Case" *Chemical and Engineering News*, 30 June 1980, p. 23.

4. "Read the Fine Print" *Forbes*, 16 February 1981, p. 38.

5. "Equality of Result, Not Equality of Opportunity," *Across the Board*, March 1978, pp. 56–58.

6. *Griggs* v. *Duke Power Company*, 401 U.S. 424 (1971).

7. Ibid.

8. *Gregory* v. *Litton*, 316 F. Supp. 401 (C.D. California 1970).

9. *International Brotherhood of Teamsters* v. *United States*, 431 U.S. 324 (1977).

10. *Affirmative Action and Equal Employment*, vol. 1 (Washington, D.C.: U.S. Equal Employment Opportunity Commission, 1974), pp. 10–11.

11. Ibid., pp. 16–64.

12. *Griggs* v. *Duke Power Company*.

13. *Albemarle Paper* v. *Moody*, 10 FEP 1181 (1975).

14. Holt, "A View from Albemarle" *Personnel Psychology*, Spring 1977, p. 71. Also see "EEOC Guidelines on Employment Testing," *Federal Register* 1 August 1970, p. 12333.

15. *Washington* v. *Davis* 96 Sup. Ct. 2040 (1976).

16. *University of California Regents* v. *Bakke*, 483 U.S. 265 (1978).

17. *Toward an Understanding of Bakke* (Washington, D.C.: United States Commission on Civil Rights, 1974), p. 57.

18. *United Steelworkers* v. *Weber*, 99 S. CT 2721 (1979).

19. N. D. McFeeley, "Weber versus Affirmative Action?" *Personnel*, January–February 1980, p. 50.

20. "Uniform Guidelines on Employee Selection Procedures," *Federal Register*, 25 August 1978, pp. 38290–315.

21. "EEOC Issues Guidelines Banning Sexual Harassment in the Workplace," *Daily Labor Report*, 11 March 1980, p. A-7.

22. W. Newman "Pay Equity Emerges as a Top Labor Issue in the 1980s," Monthly Labor Review, April 1982, p. 49.

23. Eleanor Holmes Norton, Chair of the U.S. Equal Employment Opportunity Commission, as quoted in *Washington Report*, 19 May 1980, p. 7.
24. *County of Washington* v. *Gunther*, 101 Sup. Ct. 2242 (1981).

Case 4–1 | **ACCEPT THINGS AS THEY ARE**

Jane Harris came to work at the S&J Department Store two years ago. In Jane's initial assignment in the finance department, she proved to be a good and hard worker. It soon became obvious to both Jane and her department head, Rich Jackson, that she could handle a much more responsible job than the one she presently held. Jane discussed this matter with Rich. It was obvious to him that if a better position could not be found for Jane, S&J would lose a good employee. As there were no higher openings in the finance department, Rich recommended her for a job in the accounting department, which she received.

Jane joined the accounting department as payroll administrator and quickly mastered her position. She became knowledgeable in all aspects of the job and maintained a good rapport with her two employees. A short time later, Jane was promoted to assistant manager of the accounting department. In this job, Jane continued her outstanding performance.

Two months ago, Bob Thomas suddenly appeared as a new employee in the accounting department. Ralph Simpson, vice president of administration for S&J, explained to Jane and Steve Smith, head of the accounting department, that Bob was a trainee. After Bob had learned all areas of the department, he would be used to take some of the load off both Jane and Steve and also undertake special projects for the department. Several days after Bob's arrival, Jane learned that Bob was the son of a politician who was a close friend of the president of S&J. Bob had worked in his father's successful election campaign until shortly before he joined S&J.

Last week, Steve asked Jane to help him prepare the accounting department's budget for next year. While working on the budget, Jane got a big surprise. She found that Bob had been hired at a salary of $2,000 per month. At the time of Bob's hiring, Jane, as assistant manager of the accounting department, was making only $1,700 per month.

After considering her situation for several days, Jane went to see Ralph Simpson, the division head, about the problem. She told Ralph that she had learned of the difference in salary while assisting Steve with the budget and stated that it was not right to pay a trainee more than a manager. She reminded Ralph of what he had said several times, that Jane's position should pay $22,000 per year considering her responsibility, but that S&J just could not afford to pay her that much. Jane told Ralph that things could not remain as they presently were, and she wanted to give S&J a chance to correct the situation. Ralph told Jane he would get back to her in several days.

About a week later, Ralph gave Jane a reply. He stated that while the situation was wrong and unfair he did not feel that S&J could do anything about it. He told her that sometimes one has to accept things as they are, even if they are wrong. He further stated that he hoped this would not cause S&J to lose a good employee.

1. *What options does Jane have?*
2. *What influence, if any, would the federal government have in this case?*

Case 4–2   **AFFIRMATIVE ACTION**

Allen Russell was attending a management development program offered by his company, Southwestern Gas Company. Allen considered this an honor because only a small number of managers are selected for the program each year. The program consists of two sessions each lasting for one week. The first week consists mostly of classroom training with very little class participation.

At the end of the first week, the personnel director of Southwestern, Larry Rankin, announced that each of the participants would be required to make a 30-minute presentation to the group during the second week of the program. He stated that the subject should be of interest to managers at Southwestern and that each person would be graded on the presentation. Larry asked that each of the participants inform him of their topic within two days.

Allen knew it was important that he do a good job in this presentation if he wanted to move up at Southwestern. After thinking it over, Allen decided to talk about Southwestern's affirmative action program and the manager's role in the program. When Allen called Larry to give him his topic, Larry was delighted. He told Allen, "You know the affirmative action program is very important, and I don't believe most managers understand their role in it. I'll really be looking forward to hearing your presentation."

1. *Do you think most managers understand their role in affirmative action programs?*
2. *If you were Allen, what points would you cover in the presentation?*

**TROUBLE
BETWEEN
PERSONNEL AND
OPERATIONS**

The Central Bank of Detroit is one of 12 district banks of a large central banking institution in the United States. The parent institution has 12 district banks supported by 25 branches and a number of other satellite facilities. Central Bank has six branch offices in Michigan and Wisconsin. There are approximately 2,400 salaried employees in the Bank, with 750 of these in the main office in Detroit. The branch office staffs vary in size from the smallest office, with approximately 200 employees, to the largest branch, which has about 450 employees. The composition and makeup of the offices are approximately uniform, with a slightly higher concentration of professional and managerial level staff in Detroit. With this exception, the staff is similarly organized at each office. The general composition of Central Bank's staff is as follows: 15 per cent managers and supervisors, 10 per cent professional (such as systems analysts, programmers, nurses, human resource specialists, and so forth), and the remaining 65 per cent are secretaries, typists, stenographers, and clerks. In addition to the staff, there are 65 officers in the Central Bank. Forty-four officers are in the Detroit office, while the remaining officers are equally distributed at each of the five branch offices.

The total district payroll amounts to about $28 million per year for regular personnel. The fringe benefits package is generous by industry standards. It is estimated that these benefits amount to approximately 36 percent of total payroll costs. Fringe benefits include a subsidized cafeteria operation, full health insurance, free checking accounts, low-interest loans, free term insurance, and parking.

Central Bank can best be described as a "banker's bank." In this role, Central Bank makes available a flow of credit and money for the purpose of facilitating orderly economic growth, stabilizing the dollar, and balancing our international payments. Specifically for commercial banks, it services reserve accounts, furnishes currency for circulation, facilitates the collection and clearance of checks, and acts as a fiscal agent of the U.S. government. Although it is subject to strict government regulation, Central Bank may be classified as a "quasigovernmental" institution in that it is not a branch of government per se and it does not come under civil service regulations.

The management style at Central Bank is conservative and paternalistic. At the same time, a number of bank programs and policies are moderately progressive. This is especially true in the compensation area and with regard to the general emphasis placed on efficiency of operations. The bank's management believes in taking care of its people, encourages loyalty and longevity, and rewards on the basis of merit by placing heavy emphasis on programs to retain key performers. The general environment in the bank is good and most employees feel that Central Bank is "a great place to work."

The Human Resource Department at Central Bank consists of two divisions: (1) Human Resource Development and Staffing, and (2) Compensation/Benefits and Personnel Services. Human Resource Development and Staffing has 10 people in three functional units: 4 people in Training, 2 people in Employee Relations/Publications, and 4 people in Employment. Jayne Fox is the Employment Supervisor. The Compensation/Benefits and Personnel Services Department has 34 employees, 22 of whom are in the cafeteria operation.

The Check Processing Department, with 120 employees, is the largest department in Central Bank. It is the principal operations department and processes over 2 million checks a day. Kemp Smith is one of several operations managers in this department.

Bill Heck, Vice President of Human Resources, approached Jayne Fox in early 1983 and asked her to assist him with a problem. His discussion with Jayne went as follows.

"Jayne, the Human Resource Committee met this morning to discuss a problem the Systems Department is having with one of their employees, Chuck Ford. It seems that Chuck is a programmer who is just not making it. As you may recall, about two years ago Chuck was one of the first people we placed through our new job posting program. He moved from Senior Settlement Clerk, Grade 7, in Check Collection to Programmer Trainee, Grade 8, in the Systems Department. He made satisfactory progress in the 'trainee' job and one year and three months later he was promoted to Programmer, Grade 9. That was about nine months ago. But the Systems Department claims he has been slow in coming up to an acceptable level of performance in the new position. Usually six months is the customary probationary period for an employee in a new position, but in order to 'give him a chance' to succeed they gave him an extra three months to come up to standard. However, they have now concluded that he is not going to make it as a programmer and to carry him any longer would hurt the operation."

Jayne asked Mr. Heck what alternatives were available. He went on:

"The Systems Department considered extending his probationary period, but they feel this would only delay the inevitable. It appears that he 'peaked out' early and that even if he were able to bring himself up to the acceptable level of performance, the stark reality is that they could never expect him to progress beyond that point."

Jayne then asked Mr. Heck what he wanted her to do. He informed her that since Chuck Ford had a total of five-and-a-half years' service with the bank, he would like her to pursue the possibility of transferring Chuck back to his old job in the Check Processing Department. Bill informed Jayne that he would like her to act quickly because the

Systems Department was under a lot of pressure and needed to fill Chuck's job with a more competent person as soon as possible. Jayne responded by saying that she understood the situation and she would give the matter her immediate attention.

That same afternoon Jayne met with Kemp Smith, an operations manager in the Check Processing Department. After informing Kemp of the details of the case, Jayne asked him to consider the possibility of taking Chuck back in his old job. Kemp's response to this was, "You know, Jayne, I'm getting a little tired of dealing with situations like this. It seems to me that all departments in the bank view Check Processing as the 'dumping ground' for employees they don't want. I don't understand why we get everybody's rejects. You know we have to get those checks out every day and we have enough problems already without taking on additional ones."

Jayne replied, "I can appreciate how you feel, and correct me if I'm wrong, but prior to his moving to systems as a programmer I understood that Chuck was one of your best employees. In fact, I had the impression that your department was very high on him and actually hated to see him go."

In response to this Kemp offered a few comments. "Yes, for the most part Chuck was a good employee prior to leaving for systems. But remember that was over two years ago. A lot has happened since that time . . . and I seem to remember that Chuck had a bit of an attendance problem. Let me review the situation and then let's get together." Jayne responded that this sounded okay to her.

After getting back to her office, Jayne reflected on what was said during the conversation. In reality, she could not help but feel a little miffed over Kemp's reaction to her request; it troubled her that he was so negative. Also, she was a bit surprised at his apparent low opinion of Chuck's performance and especially at his mention of Chuck's supposedly poor attendance record. Because this was in conflict with what Heck had told her, she decided to investigate the facts. Her findings turned up some very interesting information.

First, Chuck had made rapid progress from a trainee position at the Grade 5 level to Senior Settlement Clerk at the Grade 7 level in the three and a half years he had worked in Check Processing. His performance reviews had progressed from "good" in the early stages to "very good" in the later stages prior to his transfer and promotion to the Systems Department. A review of his performance reviews revealed no apparent weaknesses in his performance history, or at least none were noted on his reviews. There were no notations of any attendance problems. Jayne then decided to review additional information concerning Chuck's attendance record. The record revealed that during 1980 Chuck had been out a total of 11 days, six of which were consecutive days associated with one illness. This total exceeded the bank average of five to six days per year, but was still in the acceptable range of 5 to 12 days. For the other two and a half years, Chuck's attendance record was better than the average. Jayne also examined his attendance records for the two years since he had left Check Processing. His record in systems was also better than the average for both years. Jayne concluded from these findings that Chuck had no attendance problem, unless he had a problem with tardiness or time away from work for personal reasons. If this was the case, there was no evidence in the official records.

With these facts in mind and Chuck Ford's personnel record in front of her, she called Kemp Smith first thing the next morning. She asked Kemp if he had given Chuck Ford's placement more consideration since they had talked the previous evening. Kemp indicated that he still had serious reservations about bringing Chuck back and that he would need more time to "think it over." Kemp also indicated that he wanted to discuss it with his boss before a final decision was made. Although Jayne was getting more steamed by the minute, she controlled herself and asked Kemp when he felt he would be in a position to give her an answer. He indicated that he would give her a final decision in a day or so. Jayne ended by reminding him again that the Human Resources Committee needed a prompt answer because the situation in systems was becoming critical. Kemp acknowledged that he understood their problem.

Later that same day, Jayne bumped into Jerry Conigan, who was also an operations manager in Check Processing. Briefly, Jayne advised Jerry of the situation with Chuck Ford. Jerry's reaction was one of genuine surprise. "I don't understand what's up with Kemp. Chuck Ford was a fine employee . . . in my opinion Check Processing would be fortunate to have him back. I was never aware of any attendance problem he had. I don't know what Kemp is up to . . . whether he's bitter because Chuck left for a different job, sour grapes, wants to 'blackball' him, or what, but there is no reason in my opinion why we couldn't slot him back in his old job." Jayne thanked him for his opinion and returned to her office.

Late that same afternoon, Jayne called Kemp to discuss the clearance of two new employees that Kemp was hiring in his area. Johnnie Jones was 18 years old, had two months' experience working for a local bank, and had applied for an entry-level position with Kemp. Jayne had noted that his reference checks appeared satisfactory but could not be classified as outstanding. Jayne informed Kemp that Johnnie had been cleared for hiring. Jayne then referred to the reference checks on Terri Hall, who was applying for a position as a typist in Check Processing. Ms. Hall was 22 years old, had three years of experience, and had been rated very highly on her interviews. Her typing test scores were average, and she got high marks on appearance, personality, and verbal communication skills. Jayne expressed some concern to Kemp concerning her references. Two prior employers had given her "below average" ratings in attendance and maturity. One employer said that they would not consider her for rehire. Jayne made these facts known to Kemp and wanted to know if he wanted to withdraw the tentative offer of employment on the basis of these findings. Kemp said, "No, I think we ought to give Ms. Hall a chance. She's young and I think she will grow into the job."

Jayne paused for a moment. "You know, Kemp, I can't help but reflect back on our conversations on Chuck Ford. Chuck has a proven track record at the bank with five and a half years of service. Although these two individuals are in different capacities, it seems that he should be given equal if not greater opportunity to be returned to his old position. After all, Chuck is a proven commodity."

Kemp replied, "I guess you are right but I still have reservations about the guy. I never did like him leaving Check Processing and I had a hunch he wouldn't make it as a programmer. Something still hangs in my mind concerning his attendance. He had a problem of some sort, but I just can't recall exactly what it was. I'll be back in touch with you in a day or so."

SECTION TWO

Obtaining and developing employees

Recruiting employees

Objectives

1. To show the relationships among job analysis, personnel planning, recruitment, and selection.
2. To describe the advantages and disadvantages of filling job vacancies from internal and external sources.
3. To discuss the most frequently used methods of recruitment.
4. To describe the impact of equal employment opportunity on the recruitment process.

Outline

Recruitment—A two-way street
Sources of qualified personnel
   Internal sources
   External sources
Methods of recruitment
   Job posting
   Advertising
   Campus recruiting
   Employment agencies
   Employee referrals and walk-
      ins/write-ins
   Effectiveness of recruitment methods
Who does the recruiting?
Organizational inducements
The recruitment interview
Equal employment opportunity and
    recruitment

Glossary of terms

Campus recruiting The recruitment activities of employers on college and university campuses.

Job advertising The placement of help-wanted advertisements in daily newspapers and in trade and professional publications, and on radio and television.

Job bidding Requirement that employees bid for a job based on seniority, experience, or other specific qualifications.

Job matching Fitting the needs of the potential job applicant with the requirements of the job.

Job posting Method of making employees aware of job vacancies by posting a notice in central locations throughout an organization and giving a specified period to apply for the job.

Organizational inducements Positive features and benefits offered by an organization to attract job applicants.

Recruitment Process of seeking and attracting a pool of people from which qualified candidates for job vacancies can be chosen.

Realistic job previews Provide complete job information, both positive and negative, to the job applicant.

Assembling resources is one of the major divisions of administrative work, along with planning, organizing, directing, and controlling. People to man the positions in the organization, funds to purchase the necessary materials and equipment and to provide working capital, physical facilities with which to work, all must be brought together for the use of the enterprise if it is to function.

*William H. Newman**

Recruitment involves seeking and attracting a pool of people from which qualified candidates for job vacancies can be chosen. The magnitude of an organization's recruiting effort and the methods to be used in that recruiting effort are determined from the personnel planning process and the requirements of the specific jobs that are to be filled. As will be recalled from Chapter 3, if the forecast human resource requirements exceed the net human resource requirements, the organization must actively recruit new employees.

On the other hand, recruitment should be concerned with seeking and attracting only qualified job candidates. Regardless of whether the job to be filled has been in existence or is newly created, its requirements must be defined as precisely as possible for recruiting to be effective. Successful recruiting is difficult if the jobs to be filled are vaguely defined. As discussed in Chapter 2, job analysis provides information about the nature and requirements of specific jobs.

Figure 5–1 illustrates the relationships between human resource planning, job analysis, recruitment, and the selection process. Job analysis gives the nature and requirements of specific jobs. Human resource planning determines the specific number of jobs that is to be filled. Recruitment is concerned with providing a pool of people who are qualified to fill these vacancies. Questions that are addressed in the recruitment process include: What are the sources of qualified personnel? How are these qualified personnel to be recruited? Who is to be involved in the recruiting process? And what inducements does the organization have to attract qualified personnel? The selection process, which is discussed in detail in the next chapter, is concerned with choosing the individual or group of individuals who is most likely to succeed on a job from the pool of qualified candidates.

RECRUITMENT—A TWO-WAY STREET

Corporate recruiting practices have traditionally involved attempts to sell the organization and the job to the prospective employee by making both look good. Normally, this is done to obtain a favorable selection ratio, that is, a large number of applicants in relation to the number of job openings. Then, of course, the company can select the

---

*W. H. Newman, *Administrative Action* (Englewood Cliffs, N.J.: Prentice-Hall, 1951), p. 317.

Figure 5–1   Relationships between job analysis, personnel planning, recruitment, and selection

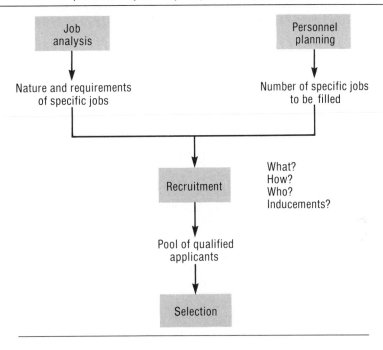

"cream of the crop." Unfortunately, these attempts sometimes set the initial job expectations of the new employees too high and can produce dissatisfaction and high turnover among employees recruited in this manner.

Research suggests that recruitment can be made more effective through the use of realistic job previews (RJP).[1] Realistic job previews provide complete job information, both positive and negative, to the job applicant. Figure 5–2 illustrates the typical consequences of traditional and realistic job preview procedures. Studies conducted at Southern New England Telephone Company, the Prudential Insurance Company, the U.S. Military Academy, and Texas Instruments have shown that several benefits can be gained from the use of the RJP approach. Major findings from these studies indicated that:

Newly hired employees who received realistic job previews have better job survival than those hired using traditional recruiting methods.

Employees hired after RJPs indicate higher job satisfaction.

Figure 5–2   Typical consequences of job preview procedures

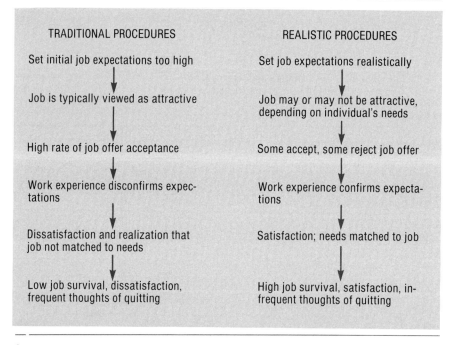

An RJP can "set" the job expectations of new employees at realistic levels.

RJPs do not reduce the flow of highly capable applicants.[2]

Another approach used to avoid inaccurate job expectations is job matching. Job matching involves fitting the needs of the potential job applicant with the requirements of the job. Citibank has implemented an automated job-matching system for its nonprofessional employees.[3] Basically, two types of records are kept for Citibank's job matching system: the candidate profile and the job profile. Both have identical task vocabularies. A sample of the task vocabulary is shown in Figure 5–3. The system works as follows:

1. The manager with a job opening defines the job using the task vocabulary.
2. Job applicants use the same task vocabulary to identify tasks they have performed and tasks they would prefer on future job assignments.
3. A computer program calculates the match scores and provides a printout listing of potential job candidates.[4]

Figure 5–3   Sample job matching task vocabulary

Job task description
Posts financial records
Does credit examining/analyzes financial records
Prepares financials/budgets
Negotiates financial agreements (contracts, loan applications, etc.)
Conducts auditing procedures
Makes investment agreements for clients
Evaluates financial needs of clients
Maintains periodic records (time sheets, attendance records, etc.)
Prepares and processes standard bank forms
Maintains adequate supply quantities
Makes appointments and reservations
Addresses, distributes, screens mail
Conducts investigations
Researches information, uses reference materials
Writes memoranda/letters
Writes reports
Organizes data for presentations
Conducts planned presentations
Conducts telephone inquiries
General telephone reception
Proofreads copy/forms
Scans letters, forms, etc, for specific information
Edits rough or typed copy
Takes dictation
Meets and directs people
Handles requests for information
Performs financial transactions with customers
Sells Citicorp services

Source: P. Sheibar, "A Simple Selection System Called 'Jobmatch'," *Personel Journal*, January 1979, p. 27. Used with permission.

Both realistic job previews and job matching are attempts to make recruitment a two-way street. Effective recruitment not only must meet the needs of the organization but also must meet the needs of job applicants.

SOURCES OF QUALIFIED PERSONNEL

An organization may fill a particular job with someone already employed by the organization or someone from outside. Each of these sources has advantages and disadvantages.

Internal sources

If an organization has been effective in recruiting and selecting employees in the past, one of the best sources of talent is its own employees. Organizations such as Delta Airlines and IBM have always followed a policy of promotion from within. This has several advantages. First, an organization should have a good idea of the strengths and weaknesses of its employees. If an organization maintains a skills inventory, this can be used as a starting point for recruiting from within. In addition, performance evaluations of employees are available. Present and prior managers of the employee being considered can be interviewed to obtain their evaluations of the employee's potential for promotion. In general, more accurate data are normally available concerning employees within the organization; thus, the chance of making a wrong decision should be reduced.

Not only does the organization know more about its current employees, but also, the employees know more about the organization and how it operates. Therefore, the likelihood of the employee having inaccurate expectations and/or becoming dissatisfied with the organization is reduced when recruiting is done from within.

Another advantage is that recruitment from within can have a significant, positive effect on employee motivation and morale when it creates promotion opportunities or prevents layoffs. When employees know that they will be considered for openings, they have an incentive for good performance. On the other hand, if outsiders usually are given the first opportunity to fill job openings, the effect can be the opposite.

A final advantage relates to the fact that most organizations have a sizable investment in their work force. Full use of the abilities of an organization's employees improves the organization's return on its investment.

However, there are disadvantages to recruiting from within. One that has been widely publicized is the so-called Peter Principle,[5] i.e., that successful people are promoted until they finally reach a level at which they are unable to perform adequately. Another danger associated with promotion from within is that infighting for promotions can become overly intense and have a negative effect on the morale and performance of people who are not promoted.

A final danger involves the inbreeding of ideas. When recruiting is only from internal sources, precautions must be taken to ensure that new ideas and innovations are not stifled by such attitudes as "We've never done it before" or "We do all right without it."

There are two major issues involved if an organization promotes from within. First, the organization needs a strong employee and management development program to ensure that its people can handle larger responsibilities. The second issue concerns the desirability of using seniority as the basis for promotions. Unions generally prefer promotions based on seniority for jobs within the bargaining unit. On the other hand, many organizations seem to prefer promotions based on prior performance and potential to do the new job.

External sources　　　Organizations have at their disposal a wide range of external sources for recruiting personnel. External recruiting is often needed in organizations that are growing rapidly or that have a large demand for technical, skilled, or managerial employees.

One inherent advantage of recruiting from outside is that the pool of talent is much larger than when recruiting is restricted to internal sources. Another advantage is that employees hired from outside can bring new insights and perspectives to the organization. In addition, it is often cheaper and easier to hire technical, skilled, or managerial people from the outside rather than training and developing them internally. This is especially true when the organization has an immediate demand for this type of talent.

One disadvantage to external recruitment is that attracting, contacting, and evaluating the potential employees is more difficult. A second potential disadvantage is that employees hired from the outside need a longer adjustment or orientation period. This can cause problems because even jobs that do not appear unique to the organization require familiarity with the people, procedures, policies, and special characteristics of the organization in which they are performed.[6] A final problem is that recruiting from outside may cause morale problems among those people within the organization who feel qualified to do the job. Figure 5–4 summarizes the advantages and disadvantages of internal and external sources of qualified personnel.

Figure 5–4　　　Advantages and disadvantages of internal and external sources of qualified personnel

Internal Sources	
Advantages	*Disadvantages*
Company has a better knowledge of strengths and weaknesses of job candidate.	People can be promoted to the point where they cannot successfully perform the job.
Job candidate has a better knowledge of company.	Infighting for promotions can negatively affect morale.
Morale and motivation of employees is enhanced.	Inbreeding can stifle new ideas and innovation.
The return on investment that an organization has in its present work force is increased.	

External Sources	
Advantages	*Disadvantages*
The pool of talent is much larger.	Attracting, contacting, and evaluating potential employees is more difficult.
New insights and perspectives can be brought to the organization.	Adjustment or orientation time is longer.
Frequently, it is cheaper and easier to hire technical, skilled, or managerial employees from outside.	Moral problems can develop among those employees within the organization who feel qualified to do the job.

**METHODS OF
RECRUITMENT**

Many different methods are available for recruiting personnel. These can generally be classified as either formal or informal. Although such a classification scheme is necessarily imprecise, it is based on the fact that some methods make more use of established channels of job availability information than do others. For example, job posting, advertising, campus recruiting, and the use of employment agencies are generally classified as formal methods of recruitment. Persons referred by employees and write-in/walk-in applicants are informally recruited. An organization selects its recruiting methods on the basis of the general circumstances it faces, such as the number and type of vacancies, the general state of the economy, the labor environment, and government requirements. The exact reasons why specific methods are chosen by a particular organization are difficult to identify. Past experience and convenience are two variables that significantly influence the choice of a recruitment method. Contrary to widespread belief, some research has indicated that informal methods of recruitment often yield results as good as those from formal methods.[7]

Job posting

Job posting is a method of making employees aware of job vacancies. Notices of available jobs are posted in central locations throughout the organization and employees are given a specified length of time to apply. Other methods used in publicizing jobs include memos to supervisors and listings in employee publications.[8] Normally, the job notice specifies the job title, rate of pay, and qualifications necessary. The usual procedure is for all applications to be sent to the human resource department for an initial review. The next step is an interview by the prospective manager. Then a decision is made based on qualifications, performance, length of service, and other pertinent criteria.

If a job-posting program is to be successful, specific policies should be developed concerning the implementation of the program. Some suggestions include:

Both promotions and transfers should be posted.

Openings should be posted for a specified time period before external recruitment begins.

Eligibility rules for the job-posting system need to be developed and communicated. For example, one eligibility rule might be that no one can apply for a posted position unless the employee has been in his or her present position for six months.

Specific standards for selection should be included in the notice.

Job bidders should be required to list their qualifications and reasons for requesting a transfer or promotion.

Unsuccessful bidders should be notified by the personnel department and advised as to why they were not accepted.[9]

Naturally, the actual specifications for a job-posting program must be tailored to the particular organization's needs.

Job bidding, which is closely associated with job posting, requires employees to bid for a job based on seniority, experience, or other specific qualifications. In unionized organizations, job-posting and bidding procedures are usually spelled out in the collective bargaining agreement. Most unions insist on seniority being one of the primary determining factors.

Advertising

One of the more widely used methods of recruitment is the help-wanted advertisement. Help-wanted ads are commonly placed in daily newspapers and in trade and professional publications. Other, less frequently used media for advertising include radio, television, and billboards. In a study of 188 peronnel executives, the Bureau of National Affairs found that newspaper advertising was used by more than 8 out of 10 companies for recruiting professional/technical, plant, and managerial personnel.[10] The same study found that three fourths of the companies use newspaper advertising for recruiting sales employees, and slightly more than two thirds use this method to recruit office employees.

Research on the effectiveness of advertising has been limited. One study found that newspaper advertisements were poorer sources for recruiting than were professional journal/convention advertisements.[11] The same study found that employees recruited through newspaper ads missed almost twice as many days as did those recruited with any other source.[12]

Furthermore, in the past, human resource managers were encouraged to ensure that their ads accurately described the job opening and the requirements or qualifications needed to secure the position. However, one study found that the difference in reader response to a given recruitment advertisement which contained a specific description of the candidate qualifications and one containing a nonspecific description of the candidate qualifications was not significant.[13] This same study found that corporate image was a more important factor in reader response. In other words, people responded more frequently to advertisements from companies with a positive corporate image than to those from companies with a lower company image.[14]

In light of these studies and others, the widespread use of advertising is probably more a matter of convenience than proven effectiveness. If advertising is to be used as a primary source of recruitment by an organization, planning and evaluation of the advertising program should be a primary concern of the human resource department.

Some concerns are recruiting by computer

When Southwestern Bell Telephone Company proposed a computerized yellow pages for Austin, Texas, two years ago, newspaper publishers went to court to stop it. They didn't want to lose any of their classified-ad business.

The phone company soon backed off, but the idea didn't die.

Now several entrepreneurs have started to offer computerized listings of jobs or job candidates. Some people argue that there aren't enough people with access to computers to make the services profitable, and newspaper trade groups say they aren't worried. But the entrepreneurs believe their offerings can find a market.

One approach is to aim the service at groups that use computers regularly. Connexions, of Cambridge, Massachusetts, charges high-technology companies $600 for an eight-paragraph help-wanted ad. Job hunters—mostly engineers and scientists—are charged $15 to look at the ads for two hours. In business two months, Connexions claims three dozen employers, advertising more than 100 jobs, and says several hundred job hunters have signed on.

Some managers like service

If a job hunter sees a job he wants, Connexions helps him apply immediately from his own terminal. It asks questions about education, job history, and objectives so that the applicant can compose a resume that is sent electronically to both the potential employer and to Connexions. Connexions also retypes the resume on quality stationery and mails it to the company.

Some personnel managers believe computerized services are already an attractive, economical alternative to newspaper advertising and recruiting firms. The $600 that keeps a help-wanted ad on Connexions for two months would buy only one four-inch-square ad in the Sunday *Boston Globe*.

One of Connexions' advertisers is Digital Equipment Corporation, a computer maker based in Maynard, Massachusetts. William Baker, Digital's U.S. human resources manager, believes computerized recruiting "will evolve to be a major factor in the next two or three years." He says "almost everyone in the computer industry has five terminals in a 20-foot radius." Digital itself plans to post company job openings electronically by next year. That will eliminate the delays that result from spreading the word by mail to numerous plants.

Mitre Corporation, an engineering laboratory in Bedford, Massachusetts, expects to have 340 technical job openings this year. Rather than go to an outside firm, it put its job listings on its computer and ran ads in area newspapers inviting engineers to dial in electronically and see what was available. "This field is unique in that the people we want have this kind of machine," says Robert J. Smith, Director of Personnel.

About 2,800 people checked the listings. Some 200 were interested enough to leave their names so Mitre could contact them. (Another 600 left obscenities and other "computer graffiti.") Smith says that for Mitre, which spends an average of $5,500 to hire each new technical employee, the cost of setting up the system was relatively low.

Still, there are some doubters. Steven Weissman, a researcher at International Resource Development, Inc. of Norwalk, Connecticut, believes electronic help-wanted ads "may be premature." His research shows that most people buy personal computers for a particular job and are slow to use them for other purposes.

Listing potential employees

Ira Gordon, a researcher for the Newspaper Advertising Bureau, says that "so far people aren't actually accessing the information as much as the entrepreneurs behind it would like them to." He also predicts that "the newspaper will continue to be a primary source of job information on the local, regional, and national level."

Meanwhile, other entrepreneurs are setting up services that list potential employees. Job/Net Inc., in Bedford, Massachusetts, sells a data base of high-tech resumes to companies. An employer pays either $20,000 a year or up to $2,000 for each new hire for the right to examine resumes by various criteria. To encourage engineers to add their resumes, Job/Net lets them use their personal computers to look at help-wanted listings from client companies free. The Job/Net computer is programmed so that personnel directors can't learn which of their employees are job hunting.

Personnel officers using a Job/Net terminal "can find people in 15 minutes that it would take eight hours to find going through paper resumes," says Janice Kempf, a vice president and cofounder. M/A-Com, Inc., a microwave and telecommunications company in Burlington, Massachusetts, recently hired a $30,000 quality-control engineer through Job/Net. "If we had paid an agency fee, it would have been $6,500 to $7,000," says Richard L. Bove, the staffing and development manager. He adds that the service lets him see more resumes of qualified people and lets him choose people who don't require expensive relocation.

Recruiting Consortium, Inc. of Littleton, Massachusetts, keeps a computerized data base of technical people who want to work for small, new companies. Corporate subscribers can study resumes and then ask the firm to screen potential candidates. Members are charged $375 a month, and they must pay 5 percent of the first-year salary for new hires.

Some companies make job seekers pay to put their resumes in the computer. Plenum Publishing Corporation's Career Placement Registry, Inc. in Alexandria, Virginia, says it has 11,000 resumes on file after a year of operation. "Employers can punch in the qualifications they want and have the resume come on line," says Robert A. Goldberg, Marketing Manager. Job hunters pay $15 to $40, depending on salary expectations.

Career Systems, Inc., in West Palm Beach, Florida, charges $49.50 each to list resumes. It has already received 7,000, 40 percent of them from people who are unemployed. Within two years, its president, William Berry, a former International Business Machines Corporation personnel official, hopes to have a service for job seekers that will track job availability and salary ranges based on job, geographic region, and experience.

Source: William M. Bulkeley, in *The Wall Street Journal*, 8 February 1983, p. 35.

Campus recruiting

Recruiting on college and university campuses is a common practice of both private and public organizations. These activities are usually coordinated by the university or college placement center. Generally, organizations send one or more recruiters to the campus for initial interviews. The most promising recruits are then invited to visit the office or plant before a final employment decision is made.

There is evidence that campus recruiters are often undertrained in terms of knowledge of their company and use of effective interviewing skills.[15] This is sometimes due to the fact that relatively new employees with little organizational experience are chosen for campus recruiting.[16] If campus recruiting is used, steps should be taken by the human resource department to ensure that recruiters are knowledgeable concerning the jobs that are to be filled and the organization, and understand and use effective interviewing skills. Recruitment interviewing is discussed later in this chapter. Figure 5–5 lists some common mistakes made by organizations in campus recruiting. Correcting these mistakes should be of primary concern to the human resource department.

Another method of tapping the products of colleges, universities, technical/vocational, and high schools is through cooperative work programs. In these programs, students may work part-time and go to school part-time, or they may go to school and work at different times of year. These programs attract people because they offer an opportunity for both a formal education and work experience. As an added incentive to finish their formal education and stay with the organization, employees are often promoted when their formal education is completed.

Employment agencies

Both public and private employment agencies can be helpful in recruiting new employees. There are state employment agencies in most cities of the United States with populations of at least 10,000. Although these agencies are administered by their respective states, they must comply with the policies and guidelines of the Employment and Training Administration of the U.S. Department of Labor to receive federal funds. The Social Security Act requires all eligible individuals to register with the state employment agency before they can receive unemployment compensation. Thus, state employment agencies generally have an up-to-date list of unemployed persons.

Figure 5–5	Common mistakes made in campus recruiting

Failure to utilize a full-time professional recruiter. Often recruitment is used as a training experience for new employees; this results in rapid turnover in the recruitment office.

The recruiter is not professionally trained in interviewing. Professionally trained as used here means a minimum training period of three days of principles and practices using live interviews that are audio- or videotaped and critiqued.

The recruiter does not have the authority to make decisions with regard to hiring. Often this is reserved for the boss, who does not know how to conduct an evaluative interview.

The actual plant visit is mishandled. Recruits are left waiting for scheduled appointments; constant interruptions occur during the visit; accompanying spouses are not properly attended to.

The recruiter does not get involved in the development of the new employee. Because the recruiter often has the best rapport with the new employee, he or she should become involved.

Source: R. W. Walters, "Want to Be a Pro?" *Journal of College Placement*, Summer 1976, pp. 42–43.

The nature and level of services provided by the state employment agencies varies from state to state and even from city to city. One study of 28 state employment agencies found the following types of information and services being provided:

Labor market information.

Recruiting services.

Testing, including test validation.

Design and implementation of on-the-job training programs.

Information on record-keeping and interview techniques.

Seminars.[17]

Private employment agencies, sometimes called search firms or "headhunters", are found more frequently in larger cities. These agencies usually charge a flat fee for their services or a percentage of the salary earned by the hired employee during the first year. Some organizations pay the fee for the new employee, while others require the new employee to pay the fee. Many private employment agencies concentrate on white-collar and executive recruiting because of the higher fees involved. The fees charged by these agencies are regulated by law in many states. In general, private agencies offer more specialized recruitment services than do state employment agencies.

Employee referrals and walk-ins/write-ins

Many organizations involve their employees in the recruiting process. These recruiting systems may be informal and operate by word-of-mouth or they may be structured with definite guidelines to be followed. Incentives and bonuses are sometimes given to employees referring persons who are subsequently hired. One drawback to the use of employee referrals is that cliques may develop within the organization because employees have a tendency to refer only close friends and relatives.

Walk-ins/write-ins are also a source of qualified recruits. Corporate image has a significant impact on the number and quality of people applying to an organization in this manner. Compensation policies, working conditions, relationships with labor, and participation in community activities are some of the many factors that can positively or negatively influence an organization's image.

Effectiveness of recruitment methods

One study found a relationship between the method of recruitment and turnover rates.[18] This study was conducted with employees hired through seven different sources: (1) newspaper ads, (2) the major employment agency used by the organization, (3) other employment agencies, (4) employee referrals, (5) referrals by high schools, (6) walk-ins, and (7) rehiring employees who had previously been with the organization. Turnover rates for the first three sources were significantly higher than those associated with the last four.

Another study examined the relationship between employee performance, absenteeism, work attitudes, and methods of recruitment.[19] This study showed that individuals recruited through a college placement office and, to a lesser extent, those recruited through newspaper advertisements were lower in performance (i.e., quality and dependability) than individuals who made contact with the company on their own initiative or through a professional journal/convention advertisement. Furthermore, employees recruited through newspaper ads missed almost twice as many days as did those recruited through any of the other sources. Finally, college recruits showed significantly lower levels of job involvement and satisfaction with their managers than did employees recruited in other ways. This study concluded that campus recruiting and newspaper advertising were poorer sources of employees than were journal/convention advertisements and self-initiated contacts.

The effectiveness of the particular method or methods used by an organization in its recruitment program is influenced by a number of variables. Some of the more important ones are compensation policies, career opportunities, and organizational reputation.

WHO DOES THE RECRUITING?

In most large and middle-sized organizations the human resource department is responsible for recruiting. These organizations normally have an employment office within the human resource department. The employment office has recruiters, interviewers, and clerical personnel who handle the recruitment activities both at the organizations's offices and elsewhere.

The role of those in the employment office is crucial. Walk-ins/write-ins, respondents to advertising, and present employees responding to job postings develop an impression of the organization through their contacts with the employment office. If the applicant is treated indifferently or rudely, a lasting negative impression can be developed. On the other hand, if the applicant is greeted, provided with pertinent information about job openings, and treated with dignity and respect, then a lasting positive impression is likely to result. Having employees trained in effective communication and interpersonal skills is essential in the employment office.

When recruiting away from the organization's offices, the role of the recruiter is equally critical. Job applicants' impressions about the organization are significantly influenced by the knowledge and expertise of the recruiter.

In small organizations, the recruitment function, in addition to many other responsibilities, is normally handled by one person—frequently the office manager. It is also not unusual for line managers in small organizations to recruit and interview job applicants.

ORGANIZATIONAL INDUCEMENTS

The objective of recruitment is to attract a number of qualified personnel for each particular job opening. Organizational inducements are all the positive features and benefits offered by an organization that serve to attract job applicants to the organization. Three of the more important organizational inducements are organizational compensation systems, career opportunities, and organizational reputation.

The components of organizational compensation systems are described at length in Chapters 10, 11, and 12. Starting salaries, frequency of pay raises, incentives, and the nature of the organization's fringe benefits can all serve as inducements to potential employees. For example, in 1982, Delta Airlines gave pay increases to its employees when other companies in the industry were either giving no pay increases or laying off people. This decision not only served to motivate Delta's employees, but also helped attract potential employees.

Organizations that have a reputation for providing employees with career opportunities are also more likely to attract a larger pool of qualified candidates through their recruiting activities. Employee and management development opportunities enable present employees to grow personally and professionally and also attract good people to the organization. Assisting present employees in career planning develops feelings that the company cares and also acts as an inducement to potential employees.

Finally, the organization's overall reputation or image serves as an inducement to potential employees. Factors that affect an organization's reputation include its general treatment of employees, the nature and quality of its products and services, and its participation in worthwhile social endeavors. Unfortunately, some organizations accept a poor image as "part of our industry and business." Regardless of the type of business or industry, organizations should strive for a good image.

THE RECRUITMENT INTERVIEW

The recruitment interview can be viewed as either part of the recruitment process or part of the selection process. For example, in campus recruiting, the recruiter's impression of the job applicant plays a role in determining whether the applicant is invited for a visit to the company or, in some cases, whether the job applicant is offered a job.

In this case, the recruitment interview serves as part of the recruitment process and as the first step in the selection process.

The content and quality of the recruitment interview influence an applicant's decision to join an organization. Indifferent interviewers can turn applicants away from the organization. However, in spite of the importance of recruitment interviews, many interviewers have little or no training. Additionally, many interviewers acknowledge that they are looking for certain personality characteristics that may or may not relate to successful performance of the job.[20]

The entire subject of recruitment interviewing is made even more complex by equal employment opportunity legislation and related court decisions relating to this legislation. For example, if an interviewer asks for certain information such as race, sex, age, marital status, and number of children during the interview, the company risks the chance of an employment discrimination suit. Prior to employment, interviewers should not ask for information that is potentially prejudicial unless the company is prepared to prove (in court, if necessary) that the requested information is job related.[21] Interviewing is discussed further in Chapter 6.

EQUAL EMPLOYMENT OPPORTUNITY AND RECRUITMENT

Recruitment activities have been significantly influenced by the equal employment opportunity legislation discussed in Chapter 4. All recruitment procedures for each job category should be analyzed and reviewed to identify and eliminate discriminatory barriers. For example, the EEOC encourages organizations to avoid recruitment primarily by employee referral and walk-ins because these practices tend to perpetuate the present composition of an organization's work force. If minorities and females are not well represented at all levels of the organization, reliance on such recruitment procedures has been ruled by the courts to be a discriminatory practice.

EEOC also suggests that the content of help-wanted ads should not indicate any race, sex, or age preference for the job unless age or sex is a bona fide occupational qualification (BFOQ). Organizations are also encouraged to advertise in media directed toward minorities and women. Advertising should indicate that the organization is an equal opportunity employer and does not discriminate.

Campus recruiting visits should be scheduled at colleges and universities with large minority and female enrollment. EEOC also recommends that employers develop and maintain contact with minority, female, and community organizations as sources of recruits.

Employers are encouraged to contact nontraditional recruitment sources, such as women's colleges and organizations that place physically and mentally handicapped persons. It is certain that hiring of both females and minority groups will continue to receive attention, and increased emphasis is likely to be placed on hiring from ethnic and religious groups.

Recruiters will also more than likely have to pay more attention to the spouse, male or female, of the person being recruited. It may become necessary to assist in finding jobs for spouses of recruits. In hiring women, especially for managerial and professional jobs, it may be necessary to consider hiring the husband, as well.

SUMMARY

Recruitment involves seeking and atracting a pool of people from which qualified candidates for job vacancies can be chosen. Questions that are addressed in the recruitment process include: What are the sources of qualified personnel? How are these qualified personnel to be recruited? Who is to be involved in the recruitment process? And what inducement does the organization have to attract qualified personnel?

Approaches to making recruitment a two-way street are realistic job previews (RJP) and job matching. RJPs give the potential employee a realistic set of job expectations. Job matching involves fitting the needs of the potential job applicant with the requirements of the job.

Organizations may fill a particular job with someone already employed by the organization or with someone from outside. The advantages and disadvantages of each of these sources were described in this chapter.

Formal methods of recruitment, discussed in this chapter, include job posting, advertising, campus recruiting, and the use of employment agencies. Informal methods include employee referrals and write-in/walk-in applicants.

Organizational inducements are all the positive features and benefits offered by an organization that serve to attract job applicants. Compensation systems, career opportunities, and organizational reputation were discussed.

The influence of equal employment opportunity legislation on recruitment was also dealt with. Specific recommendations for meeting EEOC recruitment requirements were presented.

REVIEW QUESTIONS

1. What is recruitment?
2. Describe the relationships between job analysis, personnel planning, recruitment, and selection.
3. Define realistic job previews (RJP) and job matching.
4. Give several advantages of recruiting from internal sources; external sources.
5. Name and describe at least five methods of recruiting.
6. What are organizational inducements?
7. Outline some specific EEOC recommendations for job advertising.

DISCUSSION QUESTIONS

1. Discuss the following statement: "If an individual owns a business he or she should be able to recruit and hire whomever he or she pleases."

2. Employees often have negative views on the policy of hiring outsiders rather than promoting from within. Naturally, employees feel that they should always be given preference for promotion before outsiders are hired. Do you think this is in the best interest of the organization?

3. As a potential recruit who will probably be looking for a job upon completion of school, what general approach and method or methods of recruiting do you think would be most effective in attracting you?

REFERENCES AND ADDITIONAL READINGS

1. J. P. Wanous, "Tell it Like it is at Realistic Job Previews," *Personnel,* July–August 1975, p. 51. Also see J. P. Wanous, "Realistic Job Previews: Can a Procedure to Reduce Turnover Also Influence the Relationship Between Abilities and Performance?" *Personnel Psychology,* Summer 1978, pp. 249–58.

2. Wanous, "Tell It Like It Is," p. 51.

3. P. Sheibar, "A Simple Selection System Called 'Jobmatch'," *Personnel Journal,* January 1979, pp. 26–29.

4. Ibid.

5. L. J. Peter and R. Hall, *The Peter Principle* (New York: Bantam Books, 1979).

6. L. R. Sayles and G. Strauss, *Managing Human Resources* (Englewood Cliffs, N.J.: Prentice-Hall, 1977), p. 147.

7. G. L. Reid, "Job Search and the Effectiveness of Job-Finding Methods," *Industrial and Labor Relations Review,* July 1972, pp. 479–95.

8. *Employee Promotion and Transfer Policies,* Bureau of National Affairs, *PPF Survey no. 120,* (Washington, D.C., 1978), pp. 2–3.

9. D. R. Dahl and P. R. Pinto, "Job Posting: An Industry Survey," *Personnel Journal,* January 1977, pp. 41–42. Reprinted with the permission of *Personnel Journal,* Costa Mesa, Calif.; all rights reserved.

10. *Recruiting Policies and Practices,* Bureau of National Affairs, PPF Survey no. 126 (Washington, D.C., 1979), p. 1.

11. J. A. Breaugh, "Relationships Between Recruiting Sources and Employee Performance, Absenteeism, and Work Attitudes," *Academy of Management Journal,* March 1981, p. 145.

12. Ibid., p. 145.

13. J. A. Belt and J. G. P. Paolillo, "The Influence of Corporate Image and Specificity of Candidate Qualifications on Response to Recruitment Advertisement," *Journal of Management,* Spring 1982, p. 110.

14. Ibid.

15. L. R. Drack, R. H. Kaplan, and R. A. Stone, "Organizational Performance as a Function of Recruitment Criteria and Effectiveness," *Personnel Journal,* October 1973, pp. 885–92.

16. H. F. O'Neill, "Isn't it Time to Change Our Hiring Policies?" *Personnel Journal,* August 1973, pp. 732–34.

17. W. S. Hubbartt, "The State Employment Service: An Aid to Affirmative Action Implementation," *Personnel Journal,* June 1977, pp. 289–91.

18. M. J. Gannon, "Sources of Referral and Employee Turnover," *Journal of Applied Psychology,* June 1971, pp. 226–28.

19. Breaugh, "Relationships Between Recruiting Sources," p. 145.

20. J. Bucalo, "The Balanced Approach to Successful Screening Interviews," *Personnel Journal,* August 1978, p. 420.

21. C. M. Koen, Jr., "The Pre-Employment Inquiry Guide," *Personnel Journal,* October 1980, p. 825. Reprinted with the permission of *Personnel Journal,* Costa Mesa, Calif.; all rights reserved.

Case 5–1

INSIDE OR OUTSIDE RECRUITING

Powermat, Inc. has encountered difficulty over the last few years in filling its middle-management positions. The company, which manufactures and sells complex machinery, is organized into six semiautonomous manufacturing departments. Top management believes that it is necessary for the managers of these departments to know the product lines and the manufacturing process, because many managerial decisions must be made at that level. Therefore, the company originally recruited strictly from within. However, they soon found that employees elevated to the middle-management level often lacked the skills necessary to discharge their new duties.

A decision then was made to recruit from outside, particularly from colleges with good industrial management programs. Through the services of a professional recruiter, the company was provided with a pool of well qualified industrial management graduates. Several were hired and placed in lower management positions as preparation for the middle-management jobs. Within two years, all these people had left the company.

Management reverted to its former policy of promoting from within and experienced basically the same results as before. Faced with the imminent retirement of employees in several key middle management positions, the company decided to call in a consultant who could suggest solutions.

1. *Is recruiting the problem in this company?*
2. *If you were the consultant, what would you recommend?*

Case 5–2

MALPRACTICE SUIT AGAINST A HOSPITAL

By 1980, "hospital jumping" had been steadily increasing. The term is used by hospital personnel people to describe the movement of incompetent and potentially negligent employees from hospital to hospital. One factor that had contributed to this increase was the reluctance of hospitals to release information to other hospitals that were checking references.

In mid-1981, Ridgeview Hospital was sued for negligence in its screening of employees. The case involved the alleged incorrect administration to an infant of a medication that nearly caused the child's death. The party bringing suit, contended that the nurse who administered the drug was negligent, as was the hospital because it had failed to make a thorough investigation of the nurse's work history and background. It was learned that the nurse had been hired by Ridgeview before it had received a letter of reference from her previous employer verifying her employment history. In support of the plantiff's case, uncontested information was presented about a similar incident of negligence in patient care by the nurse in her previous employment.

Ridgeview Hospital's personnel director, John Reeves, took the position that reference checks were a waste of time because area hospital personnel directors would not provide information about former employees which they thought might be defamatory. He further stated that these same personnel directors would request information in checking reference sources that they themselves would not give.

Reeves' lawyers concluded that the hospital would have to choose between two potentially damaging alternatives in adopting a personnel screening policy. It could continue not to verify references, thereby risking malpractice suits such as the one discussed. Alternatively, it could implement a policy of giving out all information on past employees and risk defamation suits. The lawyers recommended the second alternative because they thought that the potential cost would be significantly less if the hospital were convicted of libel or slander than if it were judged guilty of negligence.

1. *What would you recommend to the hospital?*
2. *What questions could be asked in a recruitment interview to help eliminate the problem?*

Chapter 6

Selecting employees

Objectives

1. To describe in detail the validation process for selection procedures.
2. To explain the equal employment opportunity requirements for validating selection procedures.
3. To outline and discuss in detail the steps in the selection process.
4. To present several methods used in employment testing.

Outline

Validation of selection procedures
  Empirical validity
    Predictive validity
    Concurrent validity
  Content and construct validity
Reliability
Uniform Guidelines on Employee
    Selection Procedures
The selection process
  The application form
    EEOC requirements
    Processing the application form
    Accuracy of application form
        information
    Applicant flow record
  Preliminary interview
Applicant testing
  Aptitude tests
  Psychomotor tests
  Job knowledge and proficiency tests
  Interest tests
  Psychological tests
  Polygraph tests
  Graphology (handwriting analysis)
Diagnostic interview
  Types of interviews

Problems in conducting interviews
Conducting effective interviews
Reference checking
Physical examination
Making the final selection decision

Aptitude test Measures a person's capacity or latent ability to learn and perform a job.

Applicant flow record Form completed voluntarily by a job applicant and used by an employer to obtain information and data which might be viewed as being discriminatory if it is included on an application form.

Concurrent validity Validity that is established by identifying a criterion predictor, such as a test, administering the test to an organization's current employees, and correlating the test scores with the current employees' performance on the job.

Construct validity The extent to which a criterion predictor, such as a test, measures a theoretical construct, such as verbal ability or perceptual speed.

Content validity The extent to which a criterion predictor, such as a test, contains a sample of the knowledge, skills, and behavior necessary for successful performance of the job.

Criterion of job success Specifies how successful performance of the job is to be measured.

Criterion predictors Factors such as education, previous work experience, and scores on company-administered tests that are used to predict successful performance of the job.

Graphology (handwriting analysis) Using a trained analyst to examine a person's handwriting to assess the person's personality, performance, emotional hang-ups, and honesty.

Interest tests Tests designed to determine how a person's interests compare with the interests of successful people in a specific job.

Job knowledge tests Tests used to measure the job related knowledge of an applicant.

Polygraph Commonly known as a "lie detector." A machine which records fluctuations in a person's blood pressure, respiration, and perspiration on a moving roll of graph paper in response to questions asked of the person.

Predictive validity Validity that is established by identifying a criterion predictor, such as a test, administering the test to all job applicants, hiring people without regard to their test scores, and, at a later date, correlating the test scores with the performance of these people on the job.

Proficiency tests Tests which measure how well a job applicant can do a sample of the work that is to be performed.

Psychological tests Tests which attempt to measure personality characteristics.

Psychomotor tests Tests which measure a person's strength, dexterity, and coordination.

Reliability Refers to the reproducibility of results of a criterion predictor.

Selection Process of choosing from those available the individuals who are most likely to perform successfully in a job.

Validity How well a given criterion actually predicts successful performance on the job.

Weighted application form Assigns different weights or values to different questions on an application form.

Select for farm hands those who are fitted for heavy labor and have some aptitude for agriculture, which can be ascertained by trying them on several tasks and by inquiring as to what they did for their former master. The foreman should have some education, a good disposition and economical habits, and it is better that he should be older than the hands, for they will be listened to with more respect than if they were boys. The foreman should be very experienced in agricultural work so that workers may appreciate that it is greater knowledge and skill which entitles the foreman to command. The foreman should never be authorized to enforce his discipline with the whips if he can accomplish his result with words. It is wise to choose a foreman who is married because marriage will make him more steady and attach him to the place. The foreman will work more cheerfully if rewards are offered him.

Varro [*]

The purpose of the selection process is to choose from those available the individuals most likely to perform successfully in a job. The development of job analyses, human resource planning, and recruitment are necessary prerequisites to the selection process. A breakdown in any of these processes can make even the best selection system ineffective.

VALIDATION OF SELECTION PROCEDURES

The objective of the selection decision is to choose the individual who can most successfully perform the job from the pool of qualified candidates. This decision requires the decision maker to know what distinguishes successful performance from unsuccessful performance in the available job and to forecast a person's future performance in that job.

Job analysis is essential in the development of a successful selection system. As discussed in Chapter 2, both job descriptions and job specifications are developed through job analysis. A job description facilitates determining how successful performance of the job is to be measured. This measure is called the criterion of job success. Possible criteria include performance appraisals, production data, such as quantity of work produced, and personnel data, such as rates of absenteeism and tardiness.

A job specification facilitates identifying the factors that can be used to predict successful performance of the job. These factors are called criterion predictors. Possible predictors include education, previous work experience, scores on company-administered tests, data from application blanks, previous performance appraisals or evaluations, and results of preliminary interviews.

Validity refers to how well a criterion of job success actually predicts successful performance on the job. For example, a job applicant for a typist position who types 120 words per minute should be able to

---

[*]Varro, "Selection of Farm Hands," in *Roman Farm Management* (New York: Macmillan 1913), p. 277.

Figure 6–1   Relationship between job analysis and validity

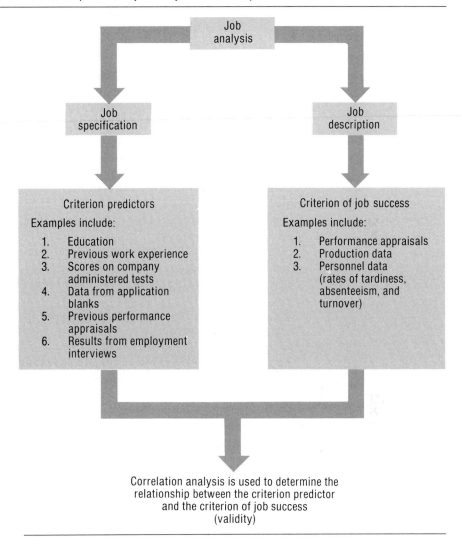

Correlation analysis is used to determine the
relationship between the criterion predictor
and the criterion of job success
(validity)

perform well in the job if typing speed is a valid predictor of successful performance. Any criterion that is used in a selection decision must
be valid. Figure 6–1 shows the relationship between job analysis and
validity.

Validity is an extremely important concept in human re-
source/personnel management. Validity in selection decisions can be
demonstrated using empirical, content, and construct methods. Each
of these is discussed in detail in the following sections.

Empirical validity

Empirical (also known as criterion-related) validity is established by collecting data and using correlation analysis (a statistical method used to measure the relationship between dependent and independent variables) to determine the relationship between the criterion predictor and the criterion of job success. The independent variable is the criterion predictor, and the dependent variable is the criterion of job success. The degree of validity for a particular criterion predictor is indicated by the magnitude of the coefficient of correlation (r), which can range from $+1$ to -1. Both $+1$ and -1 represent perfect correlation or validity. Zero represents total lack of correlation or validity. A positive sign ($+$) on the coefficient of correlation means that the independent and dependent variables are moving in the same direction, whereas a negative ($-$) sign means that the variables are moving in opposite directions.

Rarely does a criterion predictor have perfect, positive validity ($+1$). More commonly, validity is less than perfect. A minimum $r = +0.60$ is necessary to indicate any correlation at all between a criterion predictor and the criterion of job success. Generally, a minimum $r = +0.80$ is required to indicate a high degree of correlation or validity for a criterion predictor.

Two primary methods for establishing empirical validity are predictive validity and concurrent validity.

Predictive validity Predictive validity involves identifying a criterion predictor such as a test, administering the test to the entire pool of job applicants, and then hiring people to fill the available jobs without regard to their test scores. At a later date, the test scores are correlated with the criterion of job success to see whether those people with high test scores performed substantially better than those with low test scores.

For example, suppose a company wanted to determine the validity of a test for predicting future performance of production workers. In this example, test scores would be the criterion predictor. Further suppose that the company maintains records on the quantity of output of individual workers and that that quantity of output is to be used as the criterion of job success. In a predictive validation study, the test would be administered to the entire pool of job applicants, but people would be hired without regard to their test scores. The new employees would be given the same basic orientation and training. Some time later (e.g., one year) the test scores would be correlated to quantity of output. If a high correlation exists (e.g., $r = +0.80$ or higher), then the test is shown to be valid and can be used for selection of future employees. Figure 6–2 summarizes the steps in performing a predictive validation study.

Predictive validation is infrequently used because it is costly and

Figure 6–2   Predictive validation process

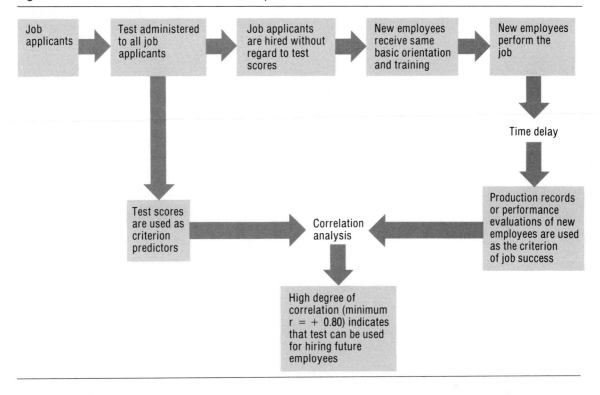

slow.[1] To use this method, a large number of new employees must be hired at the same time without regard to their test scores. Potentially, an organization may hire both good and bad employees. Furthermore, for criteria to be predictive, all new employees must have equivalent orientation and training.

Concurrent validity Concurrent validity involves identifying a criterion predictor, such as a test, administering the test to present employees, and correlating the test scores with the present employees' performance on the job. If a high correlation exists (e.g., $r = +0.80$ or higher), then the test can be used for selection of future employees. Figure 6–3 summarizes the concurrent validation process.

One disadvantage to concurrent validation is that in situations in which either racial or sexual discrimination has been practiced in the past, minorities and women will not be adequately represented. Another potential drawback is that among present employees with a particular job, the poorer performers are more likely to have been discharged or quit, and frequently the best performers have been

Figure 6–3   Concurrent validation process

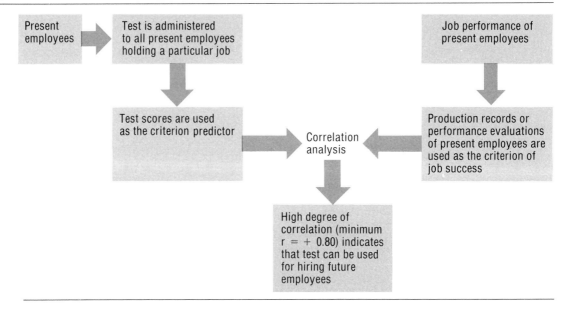

promoted. Obviously, a correlation coefficient obtained under these conditions can be misleading.

Empirical validation procedures (either predictive or concurrent) are preferred by the Equal Employment Opportunity Commission (EEOC) in validation studies. However, because of the cost and difficulties associated with empirical validation, nonempirical methods are frequently used. Nonempirical validation is also accepted by the EEOC.

Content and construct validity

Two nonempirical methods of validation are content and construct validity. Content validity requires a systematic analysis of the test that is to be used in hiring new employees and the job that is to be performed to determine whether the content of the test contains a sample of the knowledge, skills, and behavior necessary for successful performance of the job. Thus, a typing test is content valid for hiring secretaries, although it does not cover all of the skills required to be a good secretary. Content validity is especially useful in those situations where the number of employees is not large enough to justify the use of empirical validation methods. To use content validity, an employer must determine the exact requirements of a specific job and develop a test around an actual sample of the work that is to be performed.

Construct validity refers to the extent to which a test measures a theoretical construct. In psychology, a construct is mental process—a synthesis or ordering of terms, elements, or factors. Examples of job-related constructs include verbal ability, space visualization, and perceptual speed. For example, if a job requires blueprint reading, a test of space visualization might be construct valid for use in employment decisions.

Both of the nonempirical methods of validation are dependent on judgment. However, in many validation situations, they may be the only available options.

RELIABILITY

Another important consideration of a selection system is reliability. Reliability refers to the reproducibility of results with a criterion predictor. For example, a test is reliable to the extent that the same person working under the same conditions produces approximately the same test results at different time periods. A test is not reliable if a person fails it on one day but in taking it again a week later makes an A.

Three methods can be used to demonstrate the reliability of a criterion predictor. Suppose a given test is used. One method of showing the reliability of the test is *test-retest*. This involves testing a group and later, usually in about two weeks, giving the group the same test. The degree of similarity between the sets of scores determines the test's reliability. Obviously, the results can be influenced by whether the individual studied during the time between tests. A second method of showing reliability, *parallel forms*, involves giving two separate but similar forms of the test at the same time. The degree to which the sets of scores coincide determines reliability. The third method, *split halves*, involves dividing the test into halves to determine whether performance is similar on both sections. Again, the degree of similarity determines reliability.

A test or other criterion predictor can be reliable without being valid. However, it cannot be valid if it is not reliable. Consequently, the reliability of a criterion predictor plays an important role in determining its validity.

UNIFORM GUIDELINES ON EMPLOYEE SELECTION PROCEDURES[2]

The "Uniform Guidelines on Employee Selection Procedures" contain technical standards and documentation requirements for the validation of selection. The guidelines are broadly defined to include not only hiring, but also making promotion decisions, selection for training programs, and virtually every selection decision made by an organization.

Selection procedures which have no adverse impact on minority groups do not have to be validated. However, if one way of using a procedure results in greater adverse impact than another, the procedure must be validated for that use. Generally, it is good practice for an organization to validate all of its selection procedures.

Empirical, content, and construct validity studies are permitted under the guidelines. In conducting a validity study, employers are also encouraged to consider available alternatives for achieving business purposes with less adverse impact.

All validation studies must be thoroughly documented, and the guidelines specify in detail the types of records that must be kept in any study. Since job analysis is an essential part of a validation study, specific guidelines are also provided for conducting job analyses.

As was discussed in Chapter 4, the guidelines define the four-fifths or 80 percent rule for determining adverse impact. Furthermore, the relationship between the guidelines and voluntary affirmative action programs is defined. Compliance with the guidelines does not relieve an employer of its affirmative action obligations. In fact, the guidelines encourage employers to implement voluntary affirmative action programs.

THE SELECTION PROCESS

A series of steps is normally followed in processing an applicant for a job. Figure 6–4 illustrates the steps in a typical selection process. The size of the organization, the types of jobs to be filled, the number of people to be hired, and outside pressures from EEOC or unions all influence the exact nature of an organization's selection process. Most organizations use a multiple cutoff technique in selection. With this technique, an applicant must be judged satisfactory through a series of screening devices, such as application blanks, interviews, and tests. The applicant is eliminated from consideration for the job if any of these is unsatisfactory. It is also important to remember that all of these screening devices must be valid.

The application form

Completing an application form is normally the first step in most selection procedures. It provides basic employment information for use in later steps of the selection process and can be used to screen out unqualified applicants. For example, if the job opening requires the ability to type 60 words per minute and the applicant indicates that he or she cannot type, then there is no need to process the application further.

EEOC requirements EEOC and the courts have found that many application and interview inquiries disproportionately reject minorities and females and frequently are not job related. Many questions have

Figure 6–4   Steps in the selection process

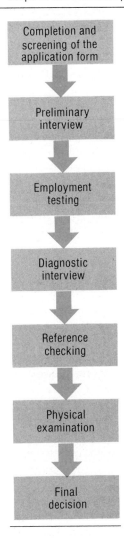

therefore been explicitly prohibited. Some of the major questions which should be eliminated from preemployment inquiries (both application forms and interviews) or carefully reviewed to ensure their use is job related and nondiscriminatory include:

Race, color, national origin, and religion—Inquiries about race, color, religion, or national origin are not illegal per se, but asking or recording this information in employment records is carefully examined if discrimination charges are filed against an employer.

Arrest and conviction records—An individual's arrest record has been ruled by the courts to be unlawful basis for refusal to employ unless a business necessity for such a policy can be established.[3]

Credit rating—An applicant's poor credit rating has also been ruled by the courts to be an unlawful basis for refusal to employ unless a business necessity for such a policy can be established.[4] Inquiries about charge accounts and home or car ownership may be unlawful unless required because of business necessity.

Appendix A at the end of this text provides a comprehensive listing of permissible questions and questions to be avoided on application forms and in preemployment interviews. One study of 151 of the largest employers in the United States revealed that all but two employers had at least one inappropriate question on their application forms. Fifty-seven of the employers had 10 or more inappropriate questions, indicating that many employers need to examine and redesign their application forms.[5]

Processing the application form Normally, the information on the application form is reviewed by a member of the human resource department to determine the applicant's qualifications in relation to the requirements of currently available jobs. Another screening procedure is the use of weighted application forms. These assign different weights to different questions. Weights are developed by determining which item responses were given more frequently by applicants who proved to be higher performers but less frequently by applicants who proved to be poorer performers. Weighted application forms are subject to the validity requirements discussed earlier in this chapter. Studies have shown the weighted application form to be useful in the selection of salespeople, clerical workers, production workers, secretaries, and supervisors.[6]

Accuracy of application form information The accuracy of information given on application forms is open to debate. Avaiable research has indicated some degree of distortion.[7] This research suggests that placing full reliance on information provided on the application form may not be prudent unless some means of verification is employed. Some of the information on the application form can be verified through reference checking, which is described later in this chapter.

Many employers, in an attempt to ensure that accurate information is given, require the applicant to sign a statement similar to the following:

> I hereby certify that the answers given by me to the foregoing questions and statements made are true and correct, without reservations of any kind whatsoever and that no attempt has been made by me to con-

ceal pertinent information. Falsification of any information on this application can lead to immediate discharge at the time of disclosure.

Whether this statement actually increaes the accuracy of information provided is not known. However, employers view falsification of an application form as a serious offense which, if uncovered, frequently leads to discharge.

Applicant flow record At the time the applicant is completing the application form, he or she is frequently asked to complete an applicant flow record. This record is completed voluntarily by the applicant. Figure 6–5 shows a sample combination application form and applicant flow record. Employers use this form to obtain information and data

Figure 6–5   Application form and applicant flow record

132

Figure 6–5 (*concluded*)

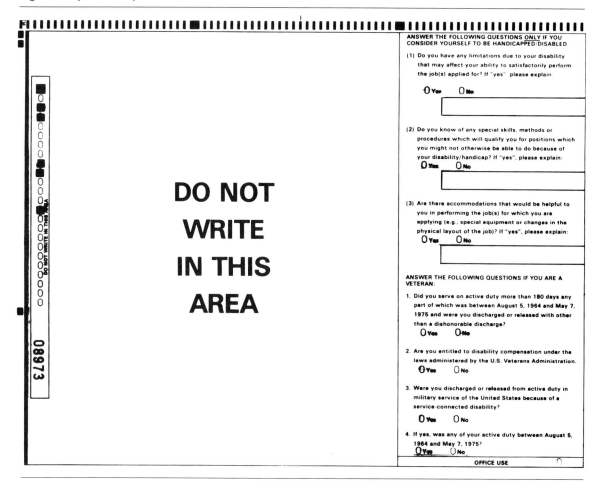

which might be viewed as discriminatory. Data and information from the applicant flow form can then be used to provide statistical reports to EEOC concerning the employer's recruitment and selection activities involving women and minorities.

Preliminary interview

The preliminary interview is used to determine whether the applicant's skills, abilities, and job preferences match any of the available jobs in the organization, to explain to the applicant the available jobs and their requirements, and to answer any questions the applicant has about the available jobs or the employer. A preliminary interview can be conducted either before or after the applicant has completed the application form. It is generally a brief, exploratory interview that is normally conducted by a specialist from the human resource department. Unqualified or uninterested applicants are screened out in this interview. Interview questions must be job related and are subject to questions of validity. Appendix A at the end of this text provides a summary of permissible inquiries and inquiries to be avoided during the preliminary interview.

Applicant testing

Applicant testing is one of the most controversial aspects of employee selection procedures. If a test is to be used in the selection process, EEOC requires the employer to establish validity and reliability using the procedures outlined in the "Uniform Guidelines on Employee Selection." Prior to the issuance of these guidelines, the legal requirements for the use of tests were uncertain. This uncertainty caused many employers to reduce the use of tests in their selection procedures during the 1970s. However, the issuance of the uniform guidelines may lead to an increased use of tests in the future.

Many types of tests are available to organizations for use in the selection process.[8] For the purposes of this text the following five categories of tests are examined: aptitude, psychomotor ability, job knowledge and proficiency, interests, and psychological. In addition, the use of polygraphs and graphology is examined.

Aptitude tests Aptitude tests measure a person's capacity or potential ability to learn and perform a job. Some of the more frequently used tests measure verbal ability, numerical ability, perceptual speed, spatial ability, and reasoning ability. Verbal aptitude tests measure a person's ability to use words in thinking, planning, and communicating. Numerical tests measure ability to add, subtract, multiply, and divide. Perception speed tests measure a person's ability to recognize similarities and differences, and spatial tests measure ability to visualize objects in space and determine their relationships. Reasoning tests measure ability to analyze oral or written facts and make correct judgments concerning these facts on the basis of logical implications.

One of the oldest and, prior to the passage of equal employment opportunity legislation, most frequently used aptitude tests was the general intelligence test. The EEOC views this type of test with disfavor because it has frequently been found to adversely affect minorities. Furthermore, such tests often contain questions that are not related to successful performance of the job. It is for these reasons that employers have largely abandoned the use of intelligence tests in employee selection.

Psychomotor tests Psychomotor tests are used to measure a person's strength, dexterity, and coordination. Finger dexterity, manual dexterity, wrist-finger speed, and speed of arm movement are some of the psychomotor abilities that can be tested. Abilities such as these might be tested for hiring people to fill assembly line jobs.

Job knowledge and proficiency tests Job knowledge tests are used to measure the job related knowledge possessed by the applicant. These tests can be either written or oral. The applicant must answer questions that differentiate experienced and skilled workers from less experienced and less skilled workers. Proficiency tests measure how well the applicant can do a sample of the work that is to be performed. A typing test given to applicants for a secretarial job is an example of a proficiency test.

Interest tests Interest tests are designed to determine how a person's interests compare with the interests of successful people in a specific job. These tests indicate the occupations or areas of work in which the person is most interested. The basic assumption in the use of interest tests is that people are more likely to be successful in jobs they like. The primary problem with using interest tests for selection purposes is that responses to the questions are not always sincere.

Psychological tests Psychological tests attempt to measure personality characteristics. These tests are generally characterized by low validity and reliability and presently have limited use for selection purposes. Two of the better-known psychological tests are the Rorschach "inkblot" test and the Thematic Apperception Test (TAT). In the Rorschach test, the applicant is shown a series of cards which contain inkblots of varying sizes and shapes. The applicant is asked to tell what the inkblot looks like to him or her. With the TAT the applicant is shown pictures of real life situations for interpretation. With both of these methods the individual is encouraged to report anything that immediately comes to mind. Interpretation of these responses requires subjective judgment and the services of a qualified psychologist. Furthermore, responses to psychological tests can also be easily fabricated. It is for these reasons that psychological tests presently have limited application in selection decisions.

Polygraph tests The polygraph, popularly known as the "lie detector," is a device that records physical changes in the body as the test subject answers a series of questions. The polygraph records fluctuations in blood pressure, respiration, and perspiration on a moving roll of graph paper. The polygraph operator makes a judgment as to whether the subject's response was truthful or deceptive by studying the physiological measurements recorded on the paper.

The use of a polygraph rests on a series of cause-and-effect assumptions: stress causes certain physiological changes in the body; fear and guilt cause stress; lying causes fear and guilt. The theory behind the use of a polygraph test assumes a direct relationship between the subject's responses to the questions and the physiological responses recorded on the polygraph. However, it is important to note that the polygraph machine itself does not detect lies. It only detects physiological changes. The operator must interpret the data recorded by the machine, and thus it is the operator, not the machine, that is the real lie detector.

A study of the use of polygraph tests found that 20 percent of the 400 major U.S. corporations use polygraphs.[9] The businesses that tend to use polygraph tests are normally those in which employees have direct access to cash or to goods that are easy and potentially profitable to steal.[10] These include: jewelers, department stores, banks, chemical plants, and restaurants.

Despite its use by organizations, serious questions have been raised about the validity of polygraph tests. Difficulties involve situations in which a person lies without guilt (a pathological liar) or lies believing the response to be true. Furthermore, it is difficult to prove that the physiological responses recorded by the polygraph occur only because a lie has been told. In addition, some critics argue that the use of the polygraph violates fundamental principles of the Constitution: the right of privacy, the privilege against self-incrimination, and the presumption of innocence. Regardless of these criticisms, employers are likely to continue the use of polygraph tests for selection purposes unless legislation is passed to restrict its usage.

Graphology (handwriting analysis) Graphology involves using a trained analyst to examine the lines, loops, hooks, strokes, curves, and flourishes in a person's handwriting to assess the person's personality, performance, emotional hang-ups, and honesty. As with the polygraph, the use of graphology is dependent on the training and expertise of the person (called a graphologist) doing the analysis.

Graphology has had limited acceptance by organizations in the United States. Questions of validity and just plain skepticism have limited its use. In Europe, it is frequently used in selection decisions. For example, in West Germany, some 2,000 graphologists are kept busy doing analyses for corporate clients. Lloyd's of London has long used graphology in the bonding of people who handle large sums of money.[11]

Diagnostic interview

The diagnostic interview is used by virtually all organizations as an important step in the selection process. Its purpose is to supplement information gained in other steps in the selection process to determine the suitability of an applicant for a specific opening in the organiza-

Neo-Diogenes uses tests, not lantern

There's only one degree of honesty, but there are many degrees of dishonesty," says Carl Klump, who has built his business, The Stanton Corporation, on being able to tell companies where prospective employes fall on that scale.

After eight and one-half years in the army, the last three in military intelligence, Klump studied criminology at the University of California at Berkeley. He became so fascinated with the polygraph, and the written tests that were used with it, that he decided to make it his carrer.

After graduation, Klump joined a firm to learn to be a polygraph examiner. One day in a test situation, three subjects, when asked to sit down, moved the chair away from its location near the table with the polygraph machine before sitting. All three were shown to have lied on the test. Klump made a note of this and in later tests found that of 45 people who moved the chair away from the machine, 43 were not telling the truth. He also noticed that people who disregarded a tester's instructions, such as "sit quietly or look straight to the front," were usually found to be deceptive and guilty of some previous criminal offense.

As a result of his studies, Klump came up with a series of written questions that he developed into The Stanton Survey. "The written test can do just as good a job as the polygraph at weeding out poor employment risks," says Klump, "but people like machines, and I still get a lot of calls for polygraph tests."

Of his research, Klump says, "I wish I could tell you I studied the questions carefully and found just the right ones, but it was a case of stumbling on them.

"I didn't think it would be too easy to market a test called the Klump Test so I decided to use my middle name—Stanton—for my corporation," he says.

The company's first client was Interstate Service Corporation, now a division of Globe Security, and still a client. That first year Klump grossed $3,400 and barely squeaked by. Since then, business has picked up, helped by increases in crime and greater caution on the part of employers. Stanton's gross now is about $450,000 annually.

The Stanton Corporation, headquartered in Chicago, has offices in Canada, South Africa, Australia, and the Philippines and sells several different written tests to business firms. Among them are tests to measure attitudes toward honesty among job applicants and current employees. A new test, still in the works, will measure productivity.

"It didn't take me long in this business to learn that people steal because of greed, not need," Klump says.

He also found that people stereotype themselves in the phrases they use to explain how they would behave, and why, in certain situations. "They usually use almost the same words, no matter what language they are using," he says.

From his wealth of experience, Klump, 49, has some advice for employers looking over applications: "Be very cautious about hiring people who leave dirty fingerprints on the form, and those who have passed through the educational system but make gross spelling errors."

Source: *Nation's Business*, vol. 69, June 1981, p. 91. Chamber of Commerce of the United States, 1615 H Street, N.W., Washington, D.C. 20062.

tion. It is important to remember that all questions asked during an interview must be job related. Equal employment opportunity legislation has placed limitations on the types of questions that can be asked during an interview. As mentioned earlier, Appendix A at the end of this text summarizes inquiries that can and cannot be made.

Types of interviews Several different types of interviews are used by organizations. The structured interview is conducted using a predetermined outline. Through the use of this outline, the interviewer maintains control of the interview so that all pertinent information on the applicant is covered systematically. Advantages to the use of structured interviews are that it provides the same type of information on all interviewees and allows systematic coverage of all questions deemed necessary by the organization. Furthermore, research studies have recommended the use of a structured interview to increase reliability and accuracy. [12]

Unstructured interviews are conducted using no predetermined checklist of questions. Opened-ended questions such as "Tell me about your previous job" are used. Interviews of this type pose numerous problems such as a lack of systematic coverage of information, and are very susceptible to the personal biases of the interviewer. This type of interview, however, does provide a more relaxed atmosphere.

Three other types of interviewing techniques have been used to a limited extent by organizations. The stress interview is designed to place the interviewee under pressure. In the stress interview, the interviewer assumes a hostile and antagonistic attitude toward the interviewee. The purpose of this type of interview is to detect the highly emotional person. In board or panel interviews, two or more interviewers conduct a single interview with the applicant. Group interviews, in which several job applicants are questioned together in a group discussion, are also sometimes used. Panel interviews and group interviews can involve either a structured or unstructured format.

Problems in conducting interviews Although interviews have widespread use in selection procedures, a host of problems exist. The first and certainly one of the most significant problems is that interviews are subject to the same legal requirements of validity and reliability as other steps in the selection process. Furthermore, research has indicated that the validity and reliability of most interviews is very questionable. [13]

One of the primary reasons for the lack of validity and reliability in interviews seems to be that it is easy for the interviewer to become either favorably or unfavorably impressed with the job applicant for the wrong reasons. Several common pitfalls may be encountered in interviewing a job applicant. Interviewers, like all people, have personal biases. These biases play a role in the interviewing process. For example, a qualified male applicant should not be rejected merely because the interviewer dislikes long hair on males.

Closely related is the problem of the halo effect which occurs when the interviewer allows a single prominent characteristic to dominate judgment of all other traits. For instance, it is often easy to overlook other characteristics when a person has a pleasant personality. However, merely having a pleasant personality does not necessarily ensure that the person will be a good employee.

Overgeneralizing is another common problem. An interviewee may not behave exactly the same way on the job as during the interview. The interviewer must remember that the interviewee is under pressure during the interview and that some people just naturally become very nervous during an interview.

Conducting effective interviews The problems associated with interviews can be partially overcome through careful planning. The following suggestions are offered to increase the effectiveness of the interviewing process.[14]

Careful attention must be given to the selection and training of interviewers. Interviewers should be outgoing and emotionally well-adjusted persons. Interviewing skills can be learned, and the persons responsible for conducting interviews should be thoroughly trained in these skills.

The plan for the interview should include an outline specifying the information that is to be obtained and the questions that are to be asked. The plan should also include room arrangements. Privacy and some degree of comfort are important. If a private room is not available, the interview should be conducted in a place where other applicants are not within hearing distance.

The interviewer should also attempt to put the applicant at ease. He or she should not argue with the applicant or put the applicant on the spot. A brief conversation about a general topic of interest or offering the applicant a cup of coffee can help ease the tension. The applicant should be encouraged to talk. However, the interviewer must maintain control and remember that the primary goal of the interview is to gain information that will aid in the selection decision.

The facts obtained in the interview should be recorded immediately. Generally notes can and should be kept during the interview. Finally, the effectiveness of the interviewing process should be evaluated. One way to evaluate effectiveness is to compare the performance appraisal of individuals who are hired against assessments made during the interview. This cross-check can serve to evaluate the effectiveness of individual interviewers as well as the total interviewing program.

Reference checking

Reference checking can take place either before or after the diagnostic interview. Many organizations realize the importance of reference checking and provide space on the application form for listing references. Most prospective employers contact individuals from one or more of the three following categories: personal, school, or past employment references. For the most part, contacting individuals who are personal references has limited value because generally no applicant is going to list someone who will not give a positive recommendation. Contacting individuals who have taught the applicant in a school, college, or university is also of limited value for similar reasons. Previous employers are clearly the most used source and are in a position to supply the most objective information.

Reference checking is most frequently conducted by telephoning previous employers. However, many organizations will not answer questions about a previous employee unless the questions are put in writing. The amount and type of information that a previous employer is willing to divulge varies from organization to organization. The least that normally can be accomplished is to verify the information that has been given on the application form. Other information that might be obtained includes reasons for leaving and whether or not the organization would be willing to rehire the person and why.

Government legislation has significantly influenced the process of reference checking. The Privacy Act of 1974 prevents government agencies from making their employment records available to other organizations without the consent of the individual involved. The Fair Credit and Reporting Act (FCRA) of 1971 requires private organizations to give job applicants access to information obtained from a reporting service. It is also mandatory that an applicant be made aware that a check is being made on him or her. Because of these laws, most employment application forms now contain statements which must be signed by the applicant, authorizing the employer to check references and conduct investigations.

Physical examination

Many organizations require a physical examination before an employee is hired. This is given not only to determine whether he or she is physically capable of performing the job, but also to determine the applicant's eligibility for group life, health, and disability insurance. Because of the expense, physical examinations are normally given as one of the last steps in the selection process. The expense of physical examinations has also caused many organizations to have applicants complete a health questionnaire when they fill out their application form. If no serious medical problems are indicated on the medical questionnaire, the applicant is not normally required to have a physical examination.

The Rehabilitation Act of 1973 has caused many employers to reexamine the physical requirements for many jobs. This act prohibits discrimination against handicapped persons and requires government contractors to take affirmative action to employ qualified handicapped persons, i.e., persons who, with reasonable accommodations, can perform the essential functions of a job. This act does not prohibit employers from giving medical exams. However, it does encourage employers to make medical inquiries which are directly related to the applicant's ability to perform job-related functions and encourages employers to make reasonable accommodations in helping handicapped people to perform the job.

Making the final
selection decision

The final step in the selection process is choosing one individual for the job. The assumption made at this point is that there will be more than one qualified person. If this is true, a value judgment based on all of the information gathered in the previous steps must be made to select the most qualified individual. If the previous steps have been performed properly, chances of making a successful judgment are improved dramatically.

The responsibility for making the final selection decision is assigned to different levels of management in different organizations. In many organizations, the personnel department handles the completion of application forms, conducts preliminary interviews, testing, and reference checking, and arranges for physical exams. The diagnostic interview and final selection decision are usually left to the manager of the department with the job opening. Such a system relieves the manager of the time-consuming responsibility of screening out unqualified and uninterested applicants. In other organizations, the human resource department handles all of the steps up to the final selection decision. Under this system, the human resource department gives the manager with a job opening a list of three to five qualified applicants. The manager then chooses the individual that he or she feels will be the best employee based on all the information provided by the human resource department. Many organizations leave the final choice to the manager with the job opening, subject to the approval of higher levels of management. In some organizations, the human resource department handles all of the steps in the selection process, including the final selection decision. In small organizations, the owner often makes the final choice.

An alternate approach is to involve peers in the final selection decision. Peer involvement has been used primarily with the selection of upper-level managers and professional employees. Peer involvement naturally facilitates the acceptance of the new employee by the work group.

In the selection of managers and supervisors, assessment centers are also sometimes used. An assessment center utilizes a formal procedure involving interviews, tests, and individual and group exercises aimed at evaluating an individual's potential as a manager/supervisor and determining his or her developmental needs. Assessment centers are described at length in Chapter 8.

SUMMARY

The purpose of the selection process is to choose individuals who are most likely to perform successfully in a job from those available to do the job. A criterion of job success specifies how performance on the job is to be measured. Criterion predictors identify the factors that can be used to forecast successful performance in the job. Validity refers to how well a criterion of job success actually predicts successful performance in the job, and may involve predictive validity, concurrent validity, content validity, and construct validity. Reliability refers to the reproducibility of results on a criterion predictor. A criterion predictor cannot be valid if it is not reliable. The "Uniform Guidelines on Employee Selection Procedures" contain technical standards and documentation requirements for the validation of selection procedures.

A series of steps is normally followed in the selection process. These include: completion and screening of the application form, preliminary interview, employment testing, diagnostic interview, reference checking, physical examination, and making the final selection decision.

An application form provides basic information for use in later steps of the selection process and can be used to screen out unqualified applicants. The preliminary interview is used to determine whether the applicant's skills, abilities, and job preferences match any of the available jobs in the organization, to explain the available jobs and their requirements, and to answer any questions the applicant has about the available jobs or the employer. Tests may also be used to screen applicants. Five types of such tests were examined in this chapter: aptitude, psychomotor ability, job knowledge and proficiency, interests, and psychological tests.

The diagnostic interview is conducted to supplement information gained in other steps in the selection process to determine the suitability of an applicant for a specific opening in the organization. In reference checking, most prospective employers contact individuals from one or more of the three following categories: personal, school, or past employment references. Based on information gathered in these steps, a certain degree of judgement is usually required in making the final selection decision.

REVIEW QUESTIONS

1. Define the following terms:
    a. Criterion of job success.
    b. Criterion predictor.
    c. Validity.
    d. Reliability.
2. Describe the following methods of validation:
    a. Predictive.
    b. Concurrent.
    c. Content.
    d. Construct.
3. Outline the steps in the selection process.
4. Describe some preemployment inquiries that should be eliminated or carefully reviewed to ensure their job relatedness.
5. What is a weighted application form?
6. How is an applicant flow record used?
7. Outline and briefly describe five categories of tests.
8. What is a polygraph test?
9. What is graphology?
10. What is reference checking?
11. Briefly describe some of the methods used by organizations in making the final selection decision.

DISCUSSION QUESTIONS

1. "Tests often do not reflect an individual's true ability." What are your views on this statement?
2. "Organizations should be able to hire employees without government interference." Do you agree or disagree? What do you think would happen if organizations could do this?
3. "Reference checking is a waste of time." Do you agree or disagree? Why?
4. How do you feel about the establishment of minimum entrance scores on national tests for acceptance to a college or university?

REFERENCES AND ADDITIONAL READINGS

1. D. Yoder and H. G. Heneman, *ASPA Handbook of Personnel and Industrial Relations* (Washington, D.C.: Bureau of National Affairs, 1979), p. 4-125.
2. "Uniform Guidelines on Employee Selection Procedures," *Federal Register,* 25 August 1978, pp. 38290–315.
3. *Gregory* v. *Litton,* 316 F. Supp. 401 (C.D. California 1970).
4. Commission Decision No. 72-0427, *CCH Employment Practice Guide* 6312 (August 31, 1971).

5. E. C. Miller, "An EEO Examination of Employment Applications," *Personnel Administration,* March 1980, pp. 63–69.

6. Yoder and Heneman, *ASPA Handbook,* p. 4-131.

7. I. L. Goldstein, "The Application Blank: How Honest are the Responses," *Journal of Applied Psychology* 55 (1971), pp. 491–92.

8. O. K. Buros, *Mental Measurements Yearbook* (Highland Park, N.J.: Gryphon Press, 1981).

9. J. A. Belt and P. B. Holden, "Polygraph Usage among Major U.S. Corporations," *Personnel Journal* February 1978, p. 82.

10. T. Hayden "Employers Who Use Lie Detector Tests," *Business and Society Review,* Spring 1982, p. 19.

11. R. Levy "Handwriting and Hiring," *Dun's Review,* March 1979, p. 78.

12. E. D. Pursell, M. A. Campion, and S. R. Gaylord, "Structured Interviewing: Avoiding Selection Problems," *Personnel Journal,* November 1980, p. 908.

13. Yoder and Heneman, *ASPA Handbook,* pp. 4-146–4-148.

14. Ibid., pp. 4-152–4-154.

Case 6–1

PROMOTIONS AT OMG

The Old Money Group is a mutual fund management company based in Seattle. It operates four separate funds, each with a different goal: one each for income growth and income interest production, one for a combination or balance of growth and production, and one for dealing in short-term securities (a money market fund). OMG, which was formed in early 1964 as a financial management firm, started its growth fund in 1967. The balanced fund and the income fund were added in 1969, while the money market fund was not added until 1977. By the end of 1982, OMG had almost $47 million under its management. Over this time period, the company had slightly outperformed the Standard & Poor's 500 average, and done slightly better than the stock market as a whole.

In 1962, Congress passed the Keogh Act, which permits self-employed individuals to set up retirement plans. All contributions to and earnings from the plans are tax exempt until the money is withdrawn by the individual on retirement.

In 1967, OMG recognized the great potential of using Keogh plans to help market shares in its mutual funds. It launched an aggressive marketing program aimed at persuading those with Keogh plans to buy into the fund; this was very successful.

As a result of this success, OMG found it necessary at the end of 1967 to establish a separate department to handle only Keogh plans.

This new department was placed in the corporate account division under division vice president Ralph Simpson. The Keogh department grew rapidly, and by the end of 1982 was managing approximately 3,000 separate Keogh plans. The department was responsible for all correspondence, personal contact, and problem solving involved with these accounts.

John Baker, who had graduated from college the previous fall with a degree in history, joined OMG in February. In his interview, John had impressed the human resource department as having potential managerial ability. The human resource department wanted to place him in an area where he could move into such a position, but at that time, there were none available.

A job that could be used as a stepping stone to more responsible positions came open in the Keogh department. In February, John became assistant to the administrator of the department. He was told that if he handled this position well, he would be considered for a job as plan administrator when an opening occurred. This was communicated to John both by the human resource department and by the head of the Keogh department, Jane Haris.

Over the next six months, it became apparent that John was not working out well. He seemed to show little interest in his work and did only what he had to do to get by; at times, his work was unsatisfactory. He appeared to be unhappy and not suited to the job. John let it be known that he had been looking for another position.

Jane Harris left OMG in June. Her assistant, Roy Johnson, took her place as head of the Keogh department. In August, Roy gave John his six-month review. Knowing that John was looking for another job, Roy decided to take the easy way out. Instead of giving John a bad review and facing the possibility of having to fire him, he gave John a satisfactory performance review. He hoped that John would find another job so that the problem would go away.

In early October, one of the plan administrators said that she would be leaving OMG in late December. Roy was faced with the task of selecting someone to fill her position. Of those who had expressed an interest in the job, Fran Jenkins appeared the best suited for it. Fran was secretary to the head of the corporate division. She had become familiar with the plan administrators' work because she had helped them during their peak periods for the past three years. The only problem was Fran's lack of a college degree which was stipulated as a requirement in the job description. Although she was currently taking night courses, she had completed only two and one-half years of college. After Roy discussed the problem with the head of personnel, this requirement was waived. Roy then announced that Fran would assume the position of plan administrator in December.

Two weeks later, John Baker informed the head of the human resource department that he had talked to his lawyer. He felt that he had been discriminated against and believed he should have gotten the position of plan administrator.

1. *Do you think that John has a legitimate point?*
2. *What went wrong in this selection process?*

Case 6–2

THE POLE CLIMBERS

Ringing Bell Telephone Company has implemented an affirmative action plan in compliance with the Equal Employment Opportunity Commission. Under the current plan, women must be placed in jobs traditionally held by men to eliminate discrimination based on sex. Therefore, the human resource department has emphasized recruiting and hiring women for such positions. Women who apply for craft positions are encouraged to try for outdoor craft jobs, such as those described as installer-repairer and line worker.

All employees hired as outside technicians must first pass basic installation school, which includes a week of training for pole climbing. During this week, employees are taught to climb 30-foot telephone poles. At the end of the week, they must demonstrate the strength and skills necessary to climb the pole and perform exercises while on it, such as lifting heavy tools and using a pulley to lift a bucket. Only those who pass this first week of training are allowed to advance to the segment dealing with installation.

Records have been maintained on the rates of success or failure for employees who attend the training school. For men, the failure rate has remained fairly constant at 30 percent. However, it has averaged 70 percent for women.

The human resource department has become concerned because hiring and training the employees who must resign at the end of one week is a tremendous expense. In addition, the goal of placing women in outdoor craft positions is not being reached.

As a first step in solving the problem, the human resource department has started interviewing the women who have failed the first week of training. Each employee is asked her reasons for seeking the position and encouraged to discuss probable causes for failure. Interviews over the last two months disclosed that employees were motivated to accept the job because of their wishes to work outdoors, to work without close supervision, to obtain challenging work, to meet the public, to have variety in their jobs, and to obtain a type of job unusual for women. Reasons for failure were physical inability to climb the pole, fear of height while on it, an accident during training such as a fall from the pole, and change of mind about the job after learning that strenuous work was involved.

In many instances, the women who mentioned physical reasons also stated that they were not physically ready to undertake the training; many had no idea it would be so difficult. Even though they still wanted the job, they could not pass the physical strength test at the end of one week.

Some stated that they felt "influenced" by their interviewer from the human resource department to take the job; others said they had accepted it because it was the only job available with the company at the time.

1. *What factors would you keep in mind in designing an effective selection process for the position of outdoor craft technician?*
2. *What would you recommend to help Ringing Bell reduce the failure rate of women trainees?*

Chapter 7

Orientation and employee training

Objectives

1. To discuss the employee orientation process.
2. To explain how to train a new employee in his or her new job.
3. To describe the process of training employees in updating and acquiring new skills, concepts, or attitudes.
4. To present principles of learning applicable to all phases of training.

Outline

Glossary of terms

Apprenticeship training Method of training personnel in skilled trades; the trainee works under the guidance of a skilled and licensed worker.

Company-level orientation Phase of orientation including information of relevance and interest about the company normally presented to all new employees by the personnel department.

Cross training *See* job rotation.

Departmental and job orientation Phase of orientation including topics unique to the new employee's specific department and job which are normally presented by the new employee's manager.

Job rotation Requires an individual to learn several different jobs in a work unit or department and perform each for a specified time period; also called cross training.

On-the-job training Method of training normally given by a senior employee or supervisor that involves showing the employee how to perform the job and allowing him or her to do it under the trainer's supervision.

Orientation Introduction of new employees to the organization, work unit, and job.

Orientation kit Package of written information which is given to a new employee to supplement the verbal orientation program.

Training Learning process that involves the acquisition of skills, concepts, rules, or attitudes to increase employee performance.

Vestibule training Method of training in which a special place separate from the normal working area is established for training with procedures and equipment similar to those used in the actual job.

After we have studied the workman, so that we know his possibilities, we then proceed, as one friend to another, to try to develop every workman in our employ, so as to bring out his best faculties and to train him to do a higher, more interesting and more profitable class of work than he has done in the past.

*Frederick W. Taylor**

After employees have been hired, they must be introduced to the organization and to their jobs. In addition, they must also be trained to perform their jobs. Furthermore, present employees must periodically have their skills updated and must learn new skills. The orientation and training of new employees and the training of longer-term employees are major responsibilities of the human resource department.

The need for orientation and employee training is directly related to the human resource planning process which was discussed in Chapter 3. Figure 7–1 shows the relationship between orientation, employee training, and other phases of human resource management. The objectives and strategies of the organization, the skills of the organization's present work force as indicated by its skills inventory, and anticipated changes in its work force determine the quantity and quality of personnel required by an organization. If new personnel are required, they must be recruited and go through the selection process. The personnel that are hired must then be oriented and trained in their new jobs. Later, these personnel will periodically require training to update their present skills or training in new skills. Even in situations where an organization hires no new personnel, training is still required to update the skills of present employees and /or to train them in new skills.

ORIENTATION

Orientation is the introduction of new employees to the organization, work unit, and job. Employees receive orientation from their fellow workers and from the company. The orientation received from fellow workers is usually unplanned and unofficial, and often provides the new employee with misleading and inaccurate information.[1] This is one of the reasons the official orientation provided by the company is important. An effective orientation program has an immediate and lasting impact on the new employee and can make the difference between a new employee's success or failure.

Job applicants get some orientation to the company even before they are hired. The organization has a reputation as to the type of company that it is and the types of products or services it provides. Generally, during the selection process, the new employee learns other general

---

*F. W. Taylor, "On Scientific Management," *Addresses and Discussions at the Conference on Scientific Management* Hanover, N.H., Dartmouth College, 1912), p. 33.

Figure 7–1   Relationship between orientation, training, and other phases of human resource management

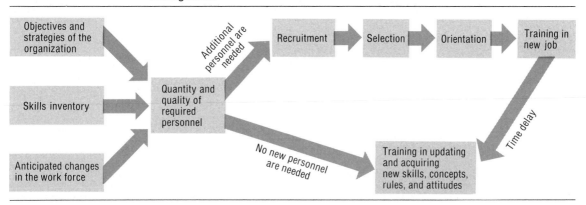

aspects of the organization and what his or her duties, working conditions, and pay will be.

After the employee is hired, the organization's formal orientation program begins. Regardless of the type of company or industry, orientation should usually be conducted at two distinct levels:

1. General company orientation—presents topics of relevance and interest to all employees.
2. Departmental and job orientation—describes topics that are unique to the new employee's specific department and job.

Shared responsibility

Since there are two distinct levels of orientation, the responsibility for orientation is normally shared between the human resource department and the new employee's immediate manager. The human resource department is responsible for initiating and coordinating both levels of orientation, training line managers in procedures for conducting department and job orientation, conducting general company orientation, and following up the initial orientation with the new employee. The new employee's manager is usually responsible for conducting department and job orientation. Some organizations have instituted a "buddy system" in which the job orientation is conducted by one of the new employees' fellow workers. If a buddy system is to work successfully, the person chosen for this role must be carefully selected and properly trained for his or her orientation responsibilities.

Company orientation

The topics presented in the company orientation should be based on both the needs of the company and the needs of the employee.

Generally, the company is interested in making a profit, providing good service to customers and clients, satisfying employee needs and well-being, and being socially responsible. New employees, on the other hand, generally are more interested in pay, benefits, and specific terms and conditions of employment. A good balance between the company's and the new employee's needs is essential if the orientation program is to have positive results. Figure 7–2 provides a listing of suggested topics that might be covered in an organization's orientation program.

Figure 7–2   Possible topics for a company orientation program

1. Overview of the company
- ☐ Welcoming speech
- ☐ Founding, growth, trends, goals, priorities and problems
- ☐ Traditions, customs, norms, and standards
- ☐ Current specific functions of the organization
- ☐ Products/services and customers served
- ☐ Steps in getting product/service to customers
- ☐ Scope of diversity of activities
- ☐ Organization, structure and relationship of company and its branches
- ☐ Facts on key managerial staff
- ☐ Community relations, expectations and activities

2. Key policies and procedures review

3. Compensation
- ☐ Pay rates and ranges
- ☐ Overtime
- ☐ Holiday pay
- ☐ Shift differential
- ☐ How pay is received
- ☐ Deductions: required and optional, with specific amounts
- ☐ Option to buy damaged products and costs thereof
- ☐ Discounts
- ☐ Advances on pay
- ☐ Loans from credit union
- ☐ Reimbursement for job expenses
- ☐ Tax shelter options

4. Fringe benefits
- ☐ Insurance:
- ☐ Medical-dental
- ☐ Life
- ☐ Disability
- ☐ Workers' compensation
- ☐ Holidays and vacations (e.g., patriotic, religious, birthday)
- ☐ Leave: personal illness, family illness, bereavement, maternity, military, jury duty, emergency, extended absence
- ☐ Retirement plans and options
- ☐ On-the-job training opportunities
- ☐ Counseling services
- ☐ Cafeteria
- ☐ Recreation and social activities
- ☐ Other company services to employees

5. Safety and accident prevention
- ☐ Completion of emergency data card (if not done as part of employment process)
- ☐ Health and first aid clinics
- ☐ Exercise and recreation centers
- ☐ Safety precautions
- ☐ Reporting of hazards
- ☐ Fire prevention and control
- ☐ Accident procedures and reporting
- ☐ OSHA requirements (review of key sections)
- ☐ Physical exam requirements
- ☐ Use of alcohol and drugs on the job

6. Employee and union relations
- ☐ Terms and conditions of employment review
- ☐ Assignment, reassignment, and promotion
- ☐ Probationary period and expected on-the-job conduct
- ☐ Reporting of sickness and lateness to work
- ☐ Employee rights and responsibilities
- ☐ Manager and supervisor rights
- ☐ Relations with supervisors and shop stewards
- ☐ Employee organizations and options
- ☐ Union contract provisions and/or company policy

Figure 7–2 (concluded)

□ Supervision and evaluation of performance
□ Discipline and reprimands
□ Grievance procedures
□ Termination of employment (resignation, layoff, discharge, retirement)
□ Content and examination of personnel record
□ Communications: channels of communication—upward and downward—suggestion system, posting materials on bulletin board, sharing new ideas
□ Sanitation and cleanliness
□ Wearing of safety equipment, badges, and uniforms
□ Bringing things on and removing things from company grounds
□ On-site political activity
□ Gambling
□ Handling of rumors

7. Physical facilities
□ Tour of facilities
□ Food services and cafeteria
□ Restricted areas for eating
□ Employee entrances
□ Restricted areas (e.g., from cars)
□ Parking
□ First aid
□ Rest rooms
□ Supplies and equipment

8. Economic factors
□ Costs of damage by select items with required sales to balance
□ Costs of theft with required sales to compensate
□ Profit margins
□ Labor costs
□ Cost of equipment
□ Costs of absenteeism, lateness, and accidents

Source: W. D. St. John, "The Complete Employee Orientation Program," *Personnel Journal*, May 1980, p. 376–77. Reprinted with the permission of *Personnel Journal*, Costa Mesa, California; all rights reserved.

Departmental and job orientation

The content of departmental and job orientation depends on the specific needs of the department and the skills and experience of the new employee. Experienced employees are likely to need less job orientation. However, even experienced personnel usually need some basic orientation. Both experienced and inexperienced workers should receive a thorough orientation concerning departmental matters. Figure 7–3 provides a checklist for the development of departmental and job orientation programs.

Orientation kit

It is desirable for each new employee to receive a kit or packet of information to supplement the verbal orientation program. This kit is normally prepared by the human resource department and can provide a wide variety of materials. Care should be taken in the design of this kit to ensure not only that essential information is provided, but also that too much information is not given. Some materials that might be included in an orientation kit include:

A company organization chart.

A map of the company's facilities.

Copy of policy and procedures handbook.

Figure 7–3 Possible topics for departmental and job orientation programs

---

1. **Department functions**
   - ☐ Goals and current priorities
   - ☐ Organization and structure
   - ☐ Operational activities
   - ☐ Relationship of functions to other departments
   - ☐ Relationships of jobs within the department

2. **Job duties and responsibilities**
   - ☐ Detailed explanation of job based on current job description and expected results
   - ☐ Explanation of why the job is important, how the specific job relates to others in the department and company
   - ☐ Discussion of common problems and how to avoid and overcome them
   - ☐ Performance standards and basis of performance evaluation
   - ☐ Number of daily work hours and times
   - ☐ Overtime needs and requirements
   - ☐ Extra duty assignments (e.g., changing duties to cover for an absent worker)
   - ☐ Required records and reports
   - ☐ Checkout on equipment to be used
   - ☐ Explanation of where and how to get tools, have equipment maintained and repaired
   - ☐ Types of assistance available; when and how to ask for help
   - ☐ Relations with state and federal inspectors

3. **Policies, procedures, rules, and regulations**
   - ☐ Rules unique to the job and/or department
   - ☐ Handling emergencies
   - ☐ Safety precautions and accident prevention
   - ☐ Reporting of hazards and accidents
   - ☐ Cleanliness standards and sanitation (e.g., cleanup)
   - ☐ Security, theft problems and costs
   - ☐ Relations with outside people (e.g., drivers)
   - ☐ Eating, smoking, and chewing gum, etc., in department area
   - ☐ Removal of things from department
   - ☐ Damage control (e.g., smoking restrictions)
   - ☐ Time clock and time sheets
   - ☐ Breaks/rest periods
   - ☐ Lunch duration and time
   - ☐ Making and receiving personal telephone calls
   - ☐ Requisitioning supplies and equipment
   - ☐ Monitoring and evaluating of employee performance
   - ☐ Job bidding and requesting reassignment
   - ☐ Going to cars during work hours

4. **Tour of department**
   - ☐ Rest rooms and showers
   - ☐ Fire-alarm box and fire extinguisher stations
   - ☐ Time clocks
   - ☐ Lockers
   - ☐ Approved entrances and exits
   - ☐ Water fountains and eye-wash systems
   - ☐ Supervisors' quarters
   - ☐ Supply room and maintenance department
   - ☐ Sanitation and security offices
   - ☐ Smoking areas
   - ☐ Locations of services to employees related to department
   - ☐ First aid kit

5. **Introduction to department employees**

List of holidays and fringe benefits.

Copies of performance appraisal forms, dates, and procedures.

Copies of other required forms (e.g., expense reimbursement form).

Emergency and accident prevention procedures.

Sample copy of company newsletter or magazine.

Telephone numbers and locations of key company personnel (e.g., security personnel).

Copies of insurance plans.[2]

Many organizations require employees to sign a form indicating that they have received and read the orientation kit. This is commonly required in unionized organizations to protect the company if a grievance arises and the employee alleges that he or she was not aware of certain company policies and procedures. Whether signing a document actually encourages new employees to read the orientation kit is questionable.

Orientation length
and timing

It is virtually impossible for a new employee to absorb all of the information in the company orientation program in one long session. Brief sessions, not to exceed a maximum of two hours, spread over several days increase the likelihood that the new employee will understand and retain the information presented. Too many organizations conduct a perfunctory orientation program lasting for a half day or full day. Programs of this nature can result in a negative attitude on the part of new employees.

Unfortunately, many departmental and job orientation programs produce the same results. Frequently, upon arriving in a department, new employees are given a departmental procedures manual, told to read the material, and ask any questions that occur to them. Another frequently used departmental and job orientation method is to give new employees menial tasks to perform. Both of these methods are likely to produce poor results.

Departmental orientations should also be brief and spread over several days. Job orientations should be well planned and conducted using appropriate techniques.

Follow-up and
evaluation

Formal and systematic follow-up to the initial orientation is essential. The new employee should not be told to drop by if any problems occur. The manager should regularly check on how well the new employee is doing and answer any questions that may have arisen after the initial orientation. This follow-up should occur a minimum of twice during the new employee's first week of work and at least once a week during the next two or three weeks. The human resource department should have a scheduled follow-up after the employee has been on the job for a month.

The human resource department should also conduct an annual evaluation of the total orientation program. The purpose of this evaluation is to determine whether the current orientation program is meeting the company's and new employee's needs and to ascertain ways of improving the present program.

Feedback from new employees is one method of evaluating the effectiveness of an organization's orientation program. Feedback can be obtained using the following methods:

Unsigned questionnaires completed by all new employees.

In-depth interviews of randomly selected new employees.

Group discussion sessions with new employees who have settled comfortably into their jobs.[3]

Feedback of this type enables an organization to adapt its orientation program to the specific suggestions of actual participants in the program. Finally, organizations should realize that new employees are going to receive an orientation that has an impact on their performance either from their fellow workers of from the company. With this in mind, it is certainly in the best interests of the company to have a well-planned and executed orientation program.[4]

TRAINING EMPLOYEES

Training is a learning process that involves the acquisition of skills, concepts, rules, or attitudes to increase the performance of employees. Generally, the new employee's manager has primary responsibility for training him or her in how to perform the job. Sometimes this training is delegated to a senior employee in the department. Regardless of who has the responsibility, the quality of this initial training can have significant influence on the employee's attitude toward the job and productivity on the job.

Furthermore, economic, social, technological, and governmental changes significantly influence the objectives and strategies of all organizations. Changes in these areas can make the skills learned today obsolete in a short time. Also, planned organizational changes and expansions can make it necessary for employees to update their skills or acquire new ones.

Determining training needs

Training must be directed toward the accomplishment of some organizational objective such as more efficient production methods, improved quality of products/services, or reduced operating cost. This means that an organization should only commit its resources to those training activities that can best help in achieving its objectives. Determining specific training activities in a particular organization requires a systematic and accurate analysis of training needs.

A variety of methods can be used for determining an organization's training needs.[5] Company reports and records provide clues to trouble spots within the organization. Records on absenteeism, turnover, tardiness, and accident rates provide objective evidence of problems. Because this type of information already exists, it can be collected and examined with a minimum of effort and interruption to the work flow. Interviews conducted with individual employees, questionnaires, and group discussions can be used to identify training needs. Personal observations of work being performed can also give insight into performance problems that may be corrected through training.

Establishing training objectives

After training needs have been determined, objectives must be established for meeting these needs. Unfortunately, many organizational training programs have no objectives. "Training for training's sake" appears to be the maxim. With this philosophy, it is virtually impossible to evaluate the strengths and weaknesses of a training program.

In general, objectives specify the skills, concepts, rules, or attitudes that should result from training. They should be in writing and be measurable. Until an organization determines what results it expects from the training experience, it is in no position to determine the content or method of instruction.[6]

Evaluating training

When the results of a training program are evaluated, a number of benefits accrue. Less effective programs can be withdrawn to save time and effort. Weaknesses within established programs can be identified and remedied.

Evaluation of training can be broken down into four logical steps:

Step 1—Reaction. How well did the trainees like the program?

Step 2—Learning. What principles, facts, and concepts were learned in the training program?

Step 3—Behavior. Did the job behavior of the trainees change because of the program?

Step 4—Results. What were the results of the program in terms of factors such as reduced costs or reduction in turnover?[7]

Reaction evaluation is generally determined through questionnaires administered at the end of the training program. Trainee reactions can be checked both immediately following the training and several weeks later. The major flaw in using only reaction evaluation is that the enthusiasm of trainees cannot necessarily be taken as evidence of improved ability and performance.

Learning evaluation measures how well the trainee has learned the principles, facts, and concepts presented in the program. Behavior evaluation measures how the training has influenced the employees' behavior on the job. Evaluation of learning and behavior requires testing of the trainee's knowledge and behavior both before and after training. Furthermore, control groups which do not receive the training but match the training group as closely as possible in all other respects are required for conducting learning and behavior evaluation. Comparison of the pre- and post-test data on trainees identifies the changes in knowledge and behavior. Comparison of data from the control group and the trainee group helps to identify factors other than training that may have produced the change.

Results evaluation attempts to measure changes in variables such as turnover, absenteeism, accident rates, tardiness, and productivity. As with learning and behavior evaluation, pretests, post-tests, and control groups are required in performing an accurate results evaluation.

Even when great care is taken in designing evaluation procedures, it is difficult to determine the exact effect of training on learning, behavior, and results. Because of this, the evaluation of training is still limited and often superficial.[8]

METHODS OF TRAINING

Several methods can be used to satisfy an organization's training needs and accomplish its objectives. Some of the more commonly used methods include on-the-job training, job rotation, vestibule training, apprenticeship training, and classroom training. The following paragraphs describe these methods.

On-the-job training and job rotation

On-the-job training (OJT) is normally given by a senior employee or manager. The employee is shown how to perform the job and allowed to do it under the trainer's supervision.

One form of on-the-job training is job rotation, sometimes called cross training. In job rotation, an individual learns several different jobs within a work unit or department and performs each for a specified time period. One of the main advantages of job rotation is that it makes flexibility possible in the department. For example, when one member of a work unit is absent, another can perform his or her job.

The advantages of on-the-job training are that no special facilities are required and the new employee does productive work during the learning process. Its major disadvantage is that the pressures of the workplace can cause instruction of the employee to be haphazard or neglected.

In training an employee on the job, several steps can be taken to ensure that the training is effective. The following paragraphs summarize five steps that should be followed in any type of on-the-job training.

Prepare the employee for learning the job The desire to learn a new job is almost always present in an employee. Showing an interest in the person, explaining the importance of the job, and explaining why it must be done correctly enhance the employee's desire to learn. Determining the employee's previous work experience in similar jobs enables the trainer to use that experience in explaining the present job or to eliminate explanations that are unnecessary.

Break down the work into components and identify the key points This breakdown consists of determining the segments which make up the total job. In each segment, something is accomplished to advance the work toward completion. This breakdown can be viewed as a detailed road map which helps guide the employee through the entire work cycle in a rational, easy to understand manner, without injury to the person or damage to the equipment.

A key point is any directive or information that helps the employee perform a work component correctly, easily, and safely. Key points are the "tricks of the trade" and are given to the employee to help reduce learning time. Observing and mastering the key points help the employee to acquire needed skill and perform the work more effectively.

Demonstrate the proper way to perform the job Simply telling an employee how to perform the job is usually not sufficient. An employee must not only be told but also must be shown how to do the job. Each component of the job must be demonstrated. While each is being demonstrated, the key points for that component should be explained. Employees should be encouraged to ask questions about each component.

Allow the employee to perform the job An employee should perform the job under the guidance of the trainer. Generally, an employee should be required to explain what he or she is going to do at each component of the job. If the explanation is correct, the employee is then allowed to perform the component. If the explanation is incorrect, the mistake should be corrected before the employee is allowed to actually perform the component. Praise and encouragement are essential in this phase.

Gradually put the employee on his or her own When the trainer is reasonably sure that an employee can do the job on his or her own, the employee should be encouraged to work at his or her own pace while developing skills in performing the job and should be left alone. The trainer should return periodically to answer any questions and see that all is going well. An employee should not be turned loose and forgotten. An employee will have questions and will make better progress if the trainer is around to help with problems and answer questions.

Figure 7–4 outlines the job instruction training (JIT) system, which is an old, and yet still effective, method for ensuring that on-the-job training is properly conducted.

Vestibule training

In vestibule training, procedures and equipment similar to those used for the actual job are set up in a special working area, called a vestibule. The trainee is then taught how to perform the job by a skilled person and is able to learn the job at his or her own rate without the pressures of production schedules.

Banks training workers to market a new wave of financial services

Chicago—Banks are finding they have a big problem with all the new financial instruments and services they're spewing forth: The people in the lobby who are supposed to explain them to customers are mostly holdovers from simpler times, when the most complex task was opening a checking account.

To cope with the rapid change, a growing number of banks are using training and incentive programs to try to transform their employees from passive application-takers into aggressive, knowledgeable salesmen. At North Shore National Bank here, for instance, customer-service people are being drilled on the nuances of such things as money-market accounts, individual-retirement accounts and certificates of deposit. The counselors are coached on how to sell more than one service to each customer because the bank has learned that the more ties it has to a customer, the more likely it is to keep him.

North Shore also is hoping to upgrade the status of customer service by calling the employees financial counselors, and it is trying to improve their appearance by banning soda-drinking and cigarette-smoking on the job.

The effort puts North Shore ahead of many banks. "Every bank is talking about upgrading customer-service people and salesmanship, but not enough are doing it," says George Morvis, president of Financial Shares Corp., a Chicago training concern that is working with North Shore's employees.

In each of the past two years, 20% more banks and thrifts have started using the salesmanship courses offered by Xerox Learning Systems, the training-services division of Xerox Corp. But that's up from a very low base, especially compared with banks' competitors.

Rivals' higher salaries

In suddenly trying to improve customer services, banks are competing with financial-service companies that have long been sales-oriented and that pay much higher salaries to employees who deal with the public.

At Merrill Lynch & Co., retail-account officers spend much of the final quarter of the 17 weeks of training working on salesmanship. The brokerage firm's training director, Jerome J. Donovan, says banks are trying to move in that direction, but he notes: "I don't think they fully understand the enormity of their task. They're going to have to go through a long time frame before they take people from saying, 'I'm a transaction-taker' to 'I'm a doer.'"

Indeed, Vicki Unangst, a Financial Shares trainer, spends a lot of time on the bare basics with customer-service bankers: getting them to stand up and shake hands, give out business cards, and carry on conversations rather than just do heads-down paperwork.

"They're so ingrained with just filling out the forms that it's hard to get them to interview and probe for customer needs," she says. "One of the industry's problems is that its products are designed for up-scale people but they aren't being sold by up-scale people. They have a hard time relating to somebody who should be getting sold $300,000 of CDs."

Improving wardrobes

Ann White, a Lincolnshire, Ill., training consultant, spends a third of her sessions with bankers on "professional image," with an emphasis on improving wardrobes, (Men: Shine those shoes, unless they are white, in which case jettison them. Women: Wear sensible blazers, eschew sexy sundresses.) "People's money is too important to them to entrust it to somebody who doesn't look the part," she says.

Some banks are anxious to get better people to fill the part, too. "It used to be that as long as a girl smiled and could carry on a conversation we kept her at customer-service forever," says Donald Menefee, president of little University Bank, Green Bay, Wis. "Now we need someone sitting there who knows 18 products and can spot a sales opportunity. There's no life tenure."

His customer-service people—retitled "bank product counselors"—now are screened for the job by personality testing. Salesmanship is honed by critiquing videotapes of their conversations with customers. Periodic product-knowledge tests are required, and there's a $20 reward for good scores.

Northwestern Financial Corp., a $2.3 billion Greensboro, N.C., bank-holding company, is forming an elite cadre of "deposit counselors" in its 195 branches. Plucked from the ranks of customer-service representatives, they get more training for handling more sophisticated customer needs.

Even a bank as small as $46 million Randolph (Vt.) National Bank has added a full-time training director in the past year, while another small one, Central Bank & Trust Co. of Provo, Utah, is one of a growing number paying customers to rate the quality of service.

Many banks have doubled or tripled their training budgets in the past year, redirecting resources away from advertising, according to Jack W. Whittle, a Chicago bank-marketing consultant. But banks still lag badly in the technology to support salesmanship, he adds. At most brokerage firms, account officers have instant access to data on each customer. Many banks, though, don't have that data pulled together, and they haven't equipped officers with video-display terminals.

That's a big reason many "personal-banker" programs prove ineffectual, according to James T. Brewer, retail banking head of Wachovia Bank & Trust Co., a big Winston-Salem, N.C., regional bank. Personal bankers are supposed to open accounts and thereafter serve as the bank's liaison with the new customer. But, says Mr. Brewer, "If you're having relationship banking, you need to know what the relationship is. You need computer capability, and that takes a lot of time and money." Wachovia is getting terminals for its personal bankers.

Norwest Corp., Minneapolis, is another big regional outfit that is trying to change. Under the code name "Operation Asset Growth," it is promoting aggressive selling of consumer loans. Bankers are expected to increase their loan portfolios by 20% a year by, among other things, making at least five solicitation phone calls a day and by scanning applications for one service for other possible customer needs.

Checking auto titles

Innovation is encouraged. Loan-makers at a Norwest bank in Sioux Falls, S.D., recently invaded the local Register of Deeds office to check auto titles registered 18 months ago. Then they called 30 car owners who had financed elsewhere, telling them rates were down and they should refinance with Norwest. The result: 15 loans. Outstanding performers in the campaign got an "Operation Asset Growth" T-shirt and adoring mention in the employee newspaper.

Source: John Helyar, *The Wall Street Journal*, 20 July 1983, pp. 29, 36. Reprinted by permission of *The Wall Street Journal*, © Dow Jones & Co., Inc., (1983). All rights reserved.

The primary advantage of this method is that the trainer can emphasize theory and use of proper techniques rather than output, while the student can learn by actually doing the job. However, this method is expensive and the employee still must adjust afterward to the actual production environment. Vestibule training has been used for training

Figure 7–4   Steps in the JIT system

Determining the training objectives and preparing the training area.
1. Decide what the trainee must be taught so he or she can do the job efficiently, safely, economically, and intelligently.
2. Provide the right tools, equipment, supplies, and material.
3. Have the workplace properly arranged, just as the employee will be expected to keep it.

Presenting the instruction.
Step 1. Preparation of the trainee.
    1. Put the trainee at ease.
    2. Find out what the trainee already knows about the job.
    3. Get him or her interested in and desirous of learning the job.
Step 2. Presentation of the operations and knowledge.
    1. Tell, show, illustrate, and question to put over the new knowledge and operations.
    2. Instruct slowly, clearly, completely, and patiently, one point at a time.
    3. Check, question, and repeat.
    4. Make sure the trainee understands.
Step 3. Performance tryout.
    1. Test the trainee by having him or her perform the job.
    2. Ask questions beginning with why, how, when, or where.
    3. Observe performance, correct errors, and repeat instructions, if necessary.
    4. Continue until the trainee is competent in the job.
Step 4. Follow-up
    1. Put the trainee on his or her own.
    2. Check frequently to be sure the trainee follows instructions.
    3. Taper off extra supervision and close follow-up until the trainee is qualified to work with normal supervision.

Source: Adapted from *The Training Within Industry Report* (War Manpower Commission: Bureau of Training, 1945), p. 195

typists, word processor operators, bank tellers, clerks, and others in similar jobs.

Apprenticeship training

Apprenticeship training dates back to biblical times and is frequently used to train personnel in skilled trades such as carpenters, bricklayers, electricians, mechanics, and tailors. The apprenticeship period generally lasts from two to five years. During this time, the trainee works under the guidance of a skilled licensed worker, but receives lower wages than the licensed worker.

Classroom training

Classroom training is conducted off the job and is probably the most familiar method. Classroom training is an effective means of imparting information quickly to large groups with limited or no knowledge of the subject being presented. It is useful for teaching factual material, concepts, principles, and theories. Portions of orientation programs, some aspects of apprenticeship training, and safety programs are usually presented utilizing some form of classroom instruction. Generally, however, classroom instruction is more frequently used for technical, professional, and managerial employees. Several specific techniques used in classroom training are discussed in Chapter 8.

PRINCIPLES OF LEARNING

Previous sections of this chapter have discussed not only how training needs are determined but also how they can be met. The use of sound learning principles during the development and implementation of these programs helps to ensure that the programs will succeed.

Motivation to achieve personal goals

People will strive to achieve objectives they have set for themselves. The most frequently identified objectives of employees are job security, financially and intellectually rewarding work, recognition, status, responsibility, and achievement. If a training program helps employees achieve some of these objectives, the learning process is greatly facilitated. For example, an unskilled worker who is given the opportunity to learn a skilled trade may be highly motivated because he or she can see that more money and job security probably will result.

Knowledge of results

Knowledge of results (feedback) influences the learning process. When the individual is informed of his or her progress as measured against some standard, this helps in setting goals for what remains to be learned. The continuous process of analyzing progress and establishing new objectives greatly enhances learning. However, precautions should be taken to ensure that goals are not so difficult to achieve that the person becomes discouraged. Oral explanations and demonstrations by the trainee and written examinations are frequently used tools for providing feedback to both the trainee and the trainer. In addition, the progress of an individual or a group can be plotted on a chart to form what is commonly called a learning curve. The primary purpose of a learning curve is to provide feedback on the trainee's progress. It can also be used to help in deciding when to increase or decrease training or when to change methods. Figure 7–5 illustrates two different learning curves. In the curve labeled decreasing returns, the trainee initially learns rapidly but later his or her learning rate slows. In the plateau curve, the trainee initially shows rapid improvement, this improvement levels off, and then shows rapid improvement again. Although the decreasing returns curve is most frequently encountered, many other shapes of learning curves are possible.

Figure 7–5 Learning curves

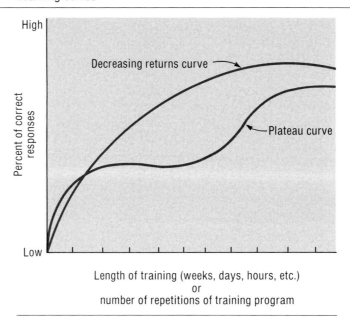

Length of training (weeks, days, hours, etc.)
or
number of repetitions of training program

Reinforcement

The principle involved in this technique is that reinforced behavior is likely to be repeated and behavior that is not reinforced is not likely to be repeated. Praise and recognition are two typical positive reinforcers. If a trainee is praised for good performance, he or she is likely to continue to strive to do better work.

Punishment, which is negative reinforcement, can be either the withholding of a reward or the use of an unpleasant act in an attempt to stop some type of behavior. For example, criticizing an employee for an act is a form of punishment. Punishment should be used carefully because it can produce harmful effects. By attracting unwelcome attention, punishment can cause some people to become so self-conscious that they continue their poor performance.

Flow of the training program

Each segment of training should be organized so that the individual can see not only its purpose but also how it fits in with other parts of the program. In addition, later segments should build on those presented earlier. Gaps and inconsistencies in material are not conducive to effective learning.

Practice and repetition

The old adage "practice makes perfect" is applicable in learning. Having trainees perform a particular operation or discuss their ideas helps them concentrate on the subject. Repeating a task several times develops facility in performing it. Effective learning is almost always enhanced by practice.

Spacing of sessions

Organizations frequently want to get an individual out of training and into a productive job as quickly as possible. However, it must be decided whether the training should be given on consecutive days or at longer intervals. Generally, it has been found that spacing out training over a period of time facilitates the learning process. But the interval most conducive to learning depends on the type of training.

Whole or part training

It must be decided whether to give complete training for a job at once or to train separately for each different job component. The decision should be based on the content of the specific job, the material being taught, and the needs of the those being trained. One method that is often successful is first to give trainees a brief overview of the job as a whole and then divide it into portions for in-depth instruction.

SUMMARY

Orientation is the introduction of new employees to the organization, work unit, and job. A general company orientation presents topics of relevance and interest to all employees. Specific department and job orientation describe topics that are unique to the new employee's department and job. The responsibility for orientation is normally shared by the human resource department and the new employee's immediate manager. An orientation kit provides written material to supplement the verbal orientation program. Formal and systematic follow-up to the initial orientation is essential.

Training is a learning process that involves the acquisition of skills, concepts, rules, or attitudes to increase the performance of employees. On-the-job training (OJT) is normally given by a senior employee or the new employee's manager; with this method the new employee is shown how to perform the job and allowed to do it under the trainer's supervision. Job rotation requires the employee to learn several different jobs within a work unit or department and perform each for a specified time period. Steps that can be taken to train a new employee in a job include: preparing the new employee for learning the job, breaking down the work into components and identifying the key points, demonstrating the proper way of performing the job, allowing the employee to perform the job, and gradually putting the new employee on his or her own.

Training employees in updating or acquiring new skills requires determining training needs and establishing objectives to meet those needs. After the needs and objectives have been determined, several methods of training that can be used include on-the-job training, job rotation, vestibule training, apprenticeship training, and classroom training. Evaluation of training can be conducted using reaction evaluation, learning evaluation, behavior evaluation, and results evaluation.

Sound learning principles that should be used in all training programs include: motivation to achieve personal objectives, knowledge of results, reinforcement, flow of the training program, practice and repetition, spacing of sessions, and whole or part training.

REVIEW QUESTIONS

1. What is orientation? General company orientation? Departmental and job orientation?
2. Outline several possible topics for a general company orientation.
3. What is an orientation kit?
4. What is training?
5. Define:
   a. On-the-job training.
   b. Job rotation.
6. Outline five steps that should be followed in training a new employee in how to perform a job.
7. Define:
   a. Apprenticeship training.
   b. Vestibule training.
8. What are four logical steps for evaluating training?
9. Outline several learning principles that should be used in all training programs.

DISCUSSION QUESTIONS

1. Why are most training programs not evaluated?
2. Which principles of learning are applied in college classrooms? Which ones are most appropriate for use in college classrooms?
3. Why are training programs one of the first areas to be eliminated when an organization's budget must be cut?
4. If you were asked to develop a training program for taxicab drivers, how would you do it? How would you evaluate the program?

REFERENCES AND ADDITIONAL READINGS

1. See, for instance, M. R. Louis, "Surprise and Sense Making: What Newcomers Experience in Entering Unfamiliar Organizational Settings," *Administrative Science Quarterly*, June 1980, pp. 226–51.

2. W. D. St. John, "The Complete Employee Orientation Program," *Personnel Journal*, May 1980, p. 375. Reprinted with the permission of *Personnel Journal*, Costa Mesa, California; all rights reserved.

3. Ibid., p. 378.

4. For additional suggestions on evaluating orientation programs see M. Lubliner, "Employee Orientation," *Personnel Journal*, April 1978, pp. 207–8.

5. S. V. Steadham, "Learning to Select a Needs Assessment Strategy," *Training and Development Journal*, January 1980, pp. 56–61.

6. For more information, see R. F. Mager, *Preparing Instructional Objectives* (Belmont, Calif.: Fearon Publishers, 1972).

7. D. L. Kirkpatrick, *Evaluation of Training*, in R. L. Craig and L. R. Bittel, *Training and Development Handbook* (New York: McGraw-Hill, Inc., 1967), p. 88.

8. D. Yoder and H. G. Heneman, *Handbook of Personnel and Industrial Relations* (Washington, D.C.: Bureau of National Affairs, 1979), p. 5-56.

Case 7–1

STARTING A NEW JOB

Jack Smythe, branch manager for a large computer manufacturer, had been told by Bob Sprague, his marketing manager, that Otis Brown had just given two weeks notice. When Jack had interviewed Otis, he had been convinced of his tremendous potential in sales. Otis was bright and personable, an MIT honor graduate in electrical engineering who had the qualifications that the company looked for in computer sales. Now he was leaving after only two months with the company. Jack called Otis into his office for an exit interview.

Jack: Come in, Otis, I really want to talk to you. I hope I can change your mind about leaving.

Otis: I don't think so.

Jack: Well, tell me why you want to go. Has some other company offered you more money?

Otis: No—in fact. I don't have another job. I'm just starting to look.

Jack: You've given us notice without having another job?

Otis: Well, I just don't think this is the place for me!

Jack: What do you mean?

Otis: Let me see if I can explain. On my first day at work, I was told that my formal classroom training in computers would not begin for a month. I was given a sales manual and told to read and study it for the rest of the day.

The next day I was told that the technical library, where all the manuals on computers are kept, was in a mess and needed to be organized. That was to be my responsibility for the next three weeks.

The day before I was to begin computer school, my boss told me that the course had been delayed for another month. He said not to worry, however, because he was going to have James Crane, the branch's leading salesperson, give me some on-the-job training. I was told to accompany James on his calls. I'm supposed to start the school in two weeks, but I've just made up my mind that this place is not for me.

Jack: Hold on a minute, Otis. That's the way it is for everyone in the first couple of months of employment in our industry. Any place you go will be the same. In fact, you had it better than I did. You should have seen what I did in my first couple of months.

1. *What do you think about the philosophy of this company pertaining to a new employee's first few weeks on the job?*
2. *What suggestions do you have for Jack to help his company avoid similar problems of employee turnover in the future?*

Case 7–2

IMPLEMENTING ON-THE-JOB TRAINING

The first-year training program for professional staff members of a large national accounting firm consists of classroom seminars and on-the-job training. The objectives of the training are to ensure that new staff members learn fundamental auditing concepts and procedures, and develop technical, analytical, and communication skills that, with further experience and training, will help them achieve their maximum potential with the organization.

Classroom training is used to introduce concepts and theories applicable to the work environment. It consists of three two-day and two three-day seminars presented at varying intervals during the staff member's first year. Although new staff members do receive this special training, actual work experience is the principal method for them to develop many skills necessary to become good auditors.

Most of the firm's audits are performed by teams supervised by the senior member. This individual is responsible for conducting the review and producing the required reports. Teams normally are assembled primarily on the basis of member availability. For this reason, a senior auditor may be assigned one or more first-year employees for a team that must undertake a complex assignment. Because senior auditors are measured on productivity, their attention usually is focused on the work being produced. Therefore, they assign routine tasks to new staff employees with little or no thought to furthering the career development of these employees. Most senior auditors assume that the next supervisor or the individuals themselves will take care of their training and development needs.

Recently, the firm has lost some capable first-year people. The reason most gave for leaving was that they were not learning or advancing in their profession.

1. *What, if anything, do you think the company should do to keep its young employees?*
2. *Do you think that on-the-job training will work in a situation such as the one described?*

Chapter 8

Management and organization development

Objectives

1. To define and outline the management development process.
2. To describe several methods used in management development.
3. To discuss the use of assessment centers in management development.
4. To define and describe some of the methods used in organization development.

Outline

The management development
    process
Organizational objectives
Management inventory and
    succession plan
Changes in the management team
Needs assessment
    Organizational needs
    Needs of individual managers
Establishing management
    development objectives
Methods used in management
    development
    Understudy assignments
    Coaching
Experience
Job rotation
Special projects and committee
    assignments
Classroom training
University and professional
    association seminars
Evaluation of management
    development activities
Assessment centers
Organization development
    Sensitivity training
    Grid training
    Behavior modeling

Glossary of Terms

Assessment center An approach to training and/or selection aimed at evaluating an individual's potential as a manager by exposing the individual to simulated problems that he or she would face in a real-life managerial situation.

Business game Method of classroom training which simulates an organization and its environment and requires a team of players to make operating decisions based on the situation.

Case study Method of classroom training in which the student analyzes real or hypothetical situations and suggests not only what to do but also how to do it.

Coaching Method of management development conducted on the job that involves experienced managers advising and guiding trainees in solving managerial problems.

Grid training Method of training used in organization development and designed to make managers more conscious of being part of a team.

In-basket technique Method of classroom training in which the trainee is required to simulate the handling of a specific manager's mail and telephone calls and to react accordingly.

Incident method A form of case study in which students are initially given the general outline of a situation and are given additional information by the instructor only as they request it.

Management development Process that is concerned with developing the experience, attitudes, and skills necessary to become, or remain, an effective manager.

Management inventory A specialized type of skills inventory which provides certain types of information concerning an organization's current management team.

Management succession plan A chart or schedule that shows potential successors for each management position within an organization.

Organization development An organizationwide, planned effort, managed from the top, with a goal of increasing organizational performance through planned interventions and training experiences.

Programmed instruction Method of classroom training in which material is presented in text form or on computer video displays; students are required to answer correctly questions about the subject presented before progressing to more advanced material.

Sensitivity training Method of training normally used in organization development and designed to make the participants more aware of themselves and their impact on others.

Understudy assignments Method of on-the-job training in which one individual, designated as the heir to a job, learns the job from the present job holder.

> There was a time when it was widely believed that management development was an automatic process requiring little attention. It was felt that the normal operation of the industrial organization would permit the cream to rise to the top, where it would become visible and could be skimmed off as needed. . . . Particularly since World War II we have seen an unprecedented growth in management development programs and activities throughout the whole western world. It is rare to find a large or even medium-sized company today which does not have a formal program and a staff to administer it.
>
> *Douglas McGregor**

The previous chapter was concerned with the orientation and training of new employees and the training of longer-term employees. In addition, an organization must be concerned with developing the abilities of its management team, including supervisors, middle-level managers, and executives. The development and implementation of programs to improve management effectiveness is a major responsibility of the human resource department.

THE MANAGEMENT DEVELOPMENT PROCESS

Management development is concerned with developing the experience, attitudes, and skills necessary to become, or remain, an effective manager. If management development is to be successful, it must have the full support of the organization's top executives. Management development should be designed, conducted, and evaluated on the basis of the objectives of the organization, the needs of the individual managers that are to be developed, and anticipated changes in the organization's management team. Figure 8–1 summarizes the total management development process, while the following sections of this chapter discuss each of the elements in depth.

Organizational objectives

An organization's objectives play a significant role in determining its requirements for managers. For instance, if an organization is undergoing a rapid expansion program, new managers will be needed at all levels. If, on the other hand, the organization is experiencing limited growth, few new managers may be needed, but possibly the skills of the present management team should be upgraded.

Management inventory and succession plan

A management inventory, which is a specialized type of skills inventory, provides certain types of information on an organization's current management team. Management inventories often include information such as present position, length of service, retirement date, education, and past performance evaluations. Figure 8–2 illustrates a simplified management inventory.

---

*D. McGregor, *The Human Side of Enterprise.* (New York: McGraw-Hill, 1960), p. 190.

Figure 8–1 Management development process

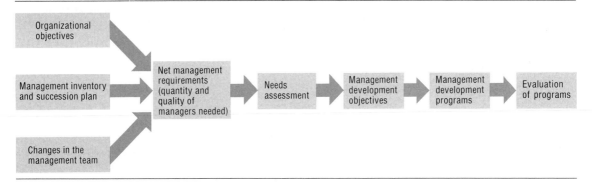

A management inventory can be used to fill vacancies that occur unexpectedly, for example, as a result of resignations or deaths. Another use is in planning the development needs of individual managers and in using these to pinpoint development activities for the total organization. A management inventory can also be used to develop a management succession plan, sometimes called a replacement chart or schedule. A management succession plan records potential successors for each manager within an organization. Usually presented in chart form, similar to an organization chart, this plan may be simply a list of positions and potential replacements. Other information such as length of service, retirement data, past performance evaluations, and salary might also be shown on the replacement chart.

Figure 8–2 Simplified management inventory

Name	Present position	Length of service	Retirement year	Replacement positions	Previous training received
James W. Burch	Industrial Relations Manager, Greenville plant	5 years	1997	Corporate industrial relations staff Industrial Relations Manager, Atlanta plant	B.B.A. University of South Carolina, Middle Management Program, Harvard
George S. Chesser	Engineering trainee	9 months	2017	Plant Engineering Manager, Corporate Engineering staff	Bachelor of Electrical Engineering, Purdue
Thomas R. Lackey, Jr.	Supervisor, Receiving Department, night shift	15 years	1992	Department Manager, Shipping and Receiving	High school diploma Supervisory skills training
Edward C. Sabo	Eastern Regional Marketing Manager	2 years	1982	Vice President, Marketing	B.B.A., UCLA M.B.A., USC Executive Development Program, Stanford

Figure 8–3 illustrates a possible replacement chart for a company's administrative division.

Management inventories and succession plans are generally kept confidential and can be computerized. They are also maintained by the human resource department for the use of top executives of the organization.

Changes in the management team

Certain changes in the management team can be estimated fairly accurately and easily, while other changes are not so easily determined. Changes such as retirements can be predicted from information in the management inventory. Other changes, such as transfers and promotions, can be estimated from such factors as the planned retirement of individuals in specific jobs and the objectives of the organization. Deaths, resignations, and discharges are, of course, difficult to forecast. However, when these changes do occur, the management inventory and succession plan can be used to fill these vacancies.

Analyzing the organization's objectives, studying the management inventory and succession plan, and evaluating changes in the management team can give the human resource department a good picture of both the quantity and quality of managers that will be needed by the organization in the future. Only after this analysis has been completed can the management development needs of individual managers and the total organization be determined.

Needs assessment

Numerous methods have been proposed for use in assessing management development needs. The management development needs of any organization are composed of the aggregate or overall needs of the organization and the development needs of individual managers within the organization.

Organizational needs In addition to the analysis described above, the most common source for determining organizational management development needs is an analysis of problem areas within the organization.[1] For example, increases in the number of grievances or accident rates within a particular area of the organization often signal the need for management development. High turnover rates and high rates of absenteeism or tardiness might also indicate management development needs.

Projections of management requirements based on the organization's objectives and changes in its management team are also used to determine an organization's management development needs. Organizational objectives and strategies are used to describe the nature and scope of future position requirements, which, when compared with

Figure 8–3

Replacement plan for administrative division of a typical company

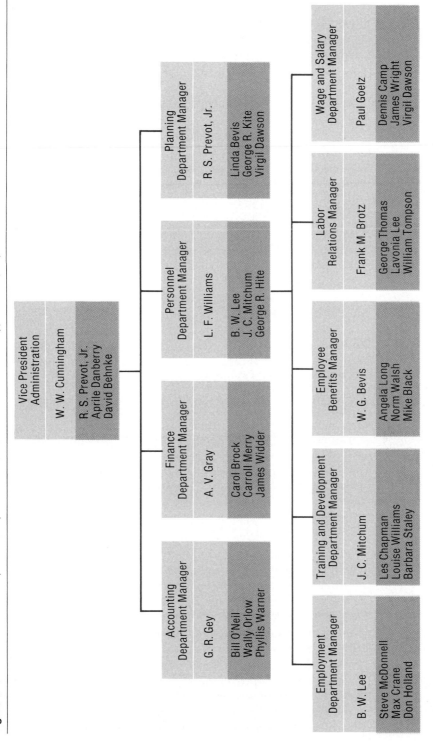

Key: Potential replacements

the current inventory of management, highlight gaps that define over-all management development needs.[2] Projected personnel changes such as promotions, also are used in determining an organization's management development needs.

Needs of individual managers The performance of the individual is the primary indicator used in determining indiviual development needs.[3] Performance evaluations of each manager can be examined to determine areas that need strengthening. The existence of problem situations within a manager's work unit can also signal individual development needs. Planned promotions or reassignments also frequently indicate the need for development.

Establishing management development objectives

After the management development needs of an organization have been determined, objectives for the overall management development program and for individual programs must be established to meet these needs. Both types of objectives should be expressed in writing and should be measurable.

One classification system for the preparation of overall management development objectives involves establishing routine, problem-solving, and innovative objectives.[4] Routine or regularly occurring objectives might include those related to supervisory training for new managers. Specifically, these objectives might incorporate targets relating to the number of trainees, hours of training, cost per trainee, and time required for trainees to reach a standard level of knowledge.

The second category of objectives is concerned with problem areas within the organization that are to be addressed through management development. These objectives would result from a needs assessment of management reports on such factors as absenteeism, turnover, safety, and number of grievances. In addition, managers could be interviewed or polled through questionnaries.

Innovative objectives are concerned with the achievement of higher levels of performance through the development of new kinds of behavior. These objectives are also concerned with new techniques to improve the quality of management, to reduce the cost of management development, or to ensure that development activities are more effective. The difference between problem-solving and innovative management development objectives is illustrated by the following example. Suppose that an organization notices a sudden increase in employee grievances. To correct this, a new supervisory development program is designed to improve the human relations skills of supervisors. If, through this program, the number of grievances returns to normal or is reduced even further, the situation has been remedied. The problem-solving objective has been met. Suppose that in another company, new supervisors have received most of their training in the form of classroom lectures and that this method appears to be meeting the organization's needs. However, the human resource department, believing that this training can be improved, institutes a program of combined home study and programmed learning. If this system allows the new supervisors to build their skills faster or at a lower cost, an innovative objective has been achieved.

After the overall management development objectives have been established, individual program objectives must be identified. Objectives for individual programs specify the skills, concepts, or attitudes that should result. After these objectives are developed, course content and method of instruction can be specified. Figure 8–4 shows the relationship between needs assessment, objectives, identification of overall management development objectives and identification of objectives for each individual management development program.

Methods used in management development

After the previous steps have been completed, management development programs must be implemented. This section examines some of the more frequently used methods of management development. At this point, it would also be worthwhile to recall the list of conditions for effective learning discussed in the previous chapter. These conditions also apply to management development programs.

Figure 8–4   Relationship between needs assessment, identifying overall management development objectives, and identifying objectives for each individual management development program

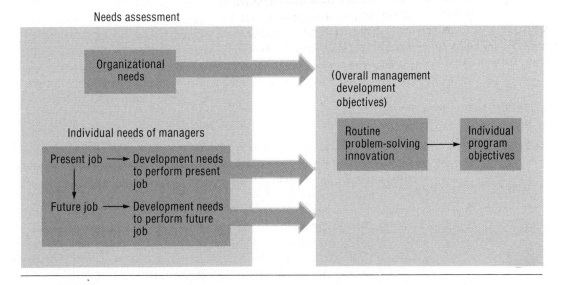

Figure 8–5   Selected methods used in management development

Type of method

On the job
   Understudy assignments
   Coaching
   Experience
   Job rotation
   Special projects and committee assignments
Off the job
   Classroom training
      Lectures
      Case studies
      Role playing
      In-basket techniques
      Programmed instruction
      Business games
   University and professional association seminars

As with employee training, management development can be achieved both on the job and off the job. Some of the most popular methods of management development are summarized in Figure 8–5 and are discussed below.

Understudy assignments Understudy assignments generally are used to develop an individual's capabilities to fill a specific job. An individual who will eventually be given a particular job works for the incumbent. The title of the heir to the job is usually assistant manager, administrative assistant, or assistant to a particular manager.

The advantage of understudy assignments is that the heir realizes the purpose of the training and can learn in a practical and realistic situation without being directly responsible for operating results. On the negative side, however, the understudy learns the bad as well as the good practices of the incumbent. In addition, understudy assignments that are maintained over a long period can become expensive. If an understudy assignment system is used, it should generally be supplemented with one or more of the other management development methods.

Coaching Coaching by experienced managers emphasizes the responsibility of all managers for developing subordinates. Experienced managers advise and guide trainees in solving managerial problems. The idea behind coaching should be to allow the trainee to develop his or her own approaches to management with the counsel of a more experienced person.

One advantage to coaching is that the trainee gets practical experience and sees the results of his or her decisions. However, there is a danger that the coach may neglect the training responsibilities or pass on inappropriate management practices. The coach's expertise and experience are of critical importance with this method.

Experience Development through experience is used in many organizations. Under this method, individuals are promoted into management jobs and allowed to learn on their own, from their daily experiences. The primary advantage in this method is that the individual, in attempting to perform a specific job, may recognize the need for management development and look for a means of satisfying it. However, employees who are allowed to learn management only through experience can create serious problems by making mistakes. Also, it is frustrating to attempt to manage without the necessary background and knowledge. Serious difficulties can be avoided if the experience method is supplemented with other management development techniques.

Job rotation Job rotation is designed to give an individual broad experience through exposure to many different areas of the organization. In understudy assignments, coaching, and experience, the trainee generally receives training and development for one particular job. In job rotation, the trainee goes from one job to another within the organization, generally remaining in each from six months to a year. This technique is used frequently by large organizations for training recent college graduates.

One advantage of job rotation is that the trainees can see how management principles can be applied in a cross section of environments. Also, the training is practical and allows the trainee to become familiar with the entire operation of the company. One serious disadvantage of this method is that the trainee is frequently given menial assignments in each job. Another disadvantage is the tendency to leave the trainee in each of the jobs longer than necessary. Both of these disadvantages can produce a negative attitude.

Special projects and committee assignments Special projects require the subordinate to learn about a particular subject. For example, a trainee may be told to develop a training program on safety. This would require that he or she learn about the organization's present safety policies and problems, and the safety training procedures used by other companies. The individual must also learn to work with and relate to other employees. However, it is of critical importance that the special assignments provide a developing and learning experience for the student and not just "busywork."

Committee assignments, which are similar to special projects, can be used if the organization has regularly constituted or ad hoc committees. In this approach, an individual works with the committee on its regularly assigned duties and responsibilities. Thus, the person exercises skills in working with others and learns through the activities of the committee.

Classroom training In this, the most familiar type of training, several methods can be used. Classroom training is used not only in management development programs, but also widely in the orientation and training activities discussed in the previous chapter. Therefore, some of the material in this section is also applicable to those activities. In addition, several of the approaches used in organization development, which is discussed later in this chapter, involve classroom training.

Lectures With lecturing, the instructor has control over the situation and can present the material exactly as he or she desires. Although the lecture is useful for presenting facts, its value in changing attitudes and in teaching skills is somewhat limited.

Case studies In this technique, which was popularized by the Harvard Business School, real and hypothetical situations are presented for the student to analyze. Ideally, the case should force the trainee to think through problems, propose solutions, choose among them, and analyze the consequences of the decision. One primary advantage of the case method is that it brings a note of realism to the instruction. However, case studies often are simpler than the real situations faced by managers. Another drawback is that, when cases are discussed, there is often a lack of emotional involvement on the part of the participants, and thus attitude and behavioral changes are less likely to occur. Also, the success of the case study method depends heavily on the skills of the instructor.[5]

One variation of case study is the incident method. The student is initially only given the general outline of a situation. The instructor then provides additional information as the trainee requests it. Theoretically, the incident method makes the student probe the situation and seek additional information, much as he or she would be required to do in real life.

Role playing In this method, participants are assigned different roles and are required to act out these roles in a realistic situation. The idea is for the participants to learn from playing out the assigned roles. The success of this method depends on the ability of participants to assume the roles realistically. Videotaping allows for review and evaluation of the exercise to improve its effectiveness.

In-basket techniques This teaching technique simulates a realistic situation by requiring the trainee to answer one manager's mail and telephone calls. Important duties are interspersed with routine matters. For instance, one call may come from an important customer who is angry, while a letter from a local civic club may request a donation. The trainee analyzes the situation and suggests alternative actions. He or she is evaluated on the basis of the number and quality of decisions and on the priorities assigned each situation. The in-basket technique has been used not only for management development but also in assessment centers, which are discussed later in this chapter.

Programmed instruction Programmed instruction requires the trainee to read material on a particular subject and then to answer questions about the subject. If the trainee's answers are correct, he or she moves on to more advanced or new material. If the trainee's answers are incorrect, he or she is required to reread the material and answer additional questions. The material in programmed instruction is presented either in text form or on computer video displays. Regardless of the type of presentation, programmed instruction provides active practice, a gradual increase in difficulty over a series of steps, immediate feedback, and an individualized rate of learning. Programmed instruction normally is used to teach factual information. The increased availability and lower cost of small computers may increase the use of programmed instruction, not only in management development but also in employee training and orientation.

Business games Business games generally provide a setting of a company and its environment and require a team of players to make decisions involving operating the company. Business games also normally require the use of computer facilities. Generally, in a business game, several different teams will act as companies within a type of industry. This method forces individuals not only to work with other group members but also to function in an atmosphere of competition within the industry. Advantages of business games are that they simulate reality, decisions are made in a competitive environment, feedback is provided concerning decisions, and decisions are made using less-than-complete data. The main disadvantage is that many participants simply attempt to determine the key to winning. When this occurs, the game is not used to its fullest potential as a learning device.[6]

University and professional association seminars Many colleges and universities offer both credit and noncredit courses, intended to help meet the management development needs of various organizations. These offerings range from courses in principles of supervision to advanced executive management programs. Professional associations, such as the American Management Association, also offer a wide variety of management development programs. Many of the previously discussed classroom techniques are used in these programs.

EVALUATION OF MANAGEMENT DEVELOPMENT ACTIVITIES

In the previous chapter, four areas were described for evaluating employee training. These were reaction evaluation, learning evaluation, behavior evaluation, and results evaluation. All four of these areas are equally applicable to the evaluation of management development activities. Unfortunately, too many such activities are evaluated solely

Monopoly with paperwork:
Sony's latest tack? Playing games

*Executive contest shuns
electronics, but offers
glimpse into Japan Inc.*

Japan's Sony Corporation is carting still another product to the United States. But this one isn't like its usual lineup of electronic wares. It's a game—not an advanced electronic gadget, but a made-in-Japan management training simulation that abandons computers for pencils, paper, chips, and cards. Players fight for market share as each runs a "company" as "president."

After test-marketing the game in San Francisco, Seattle, and Hawaii this month, Sony will gage its appeal in Los Angeles and Vancouver, B. C., in July and expects to launch a full-scale marketing effort late this year.

Sony's business game resembles a complex version of Monopoly—with paperwork. But the pace "comes closer to duplicate bridge," says one of the American executives who've already tried the game in Tokyo. It is played over three days, in a seminar-type session.

American executives who test their skills may gain a benefit even Sony may not have anticipated when it developed its English-language version with the aid of Career Development International (CDI), its Tokyo-based management recruiting and training subsidiary; familiar economic forces and management tools are set in motion in an environment that's subtly unfamiliar to current-day American management.

Inside look

The result, some say, gives U. S. players an insight into what shapes Japanese corporate strategies and management outlooks by the shortest possible route: *taiken gakushu, or learning by experience.* "The fundamental value of running close to what would be bankruptcy

by Western standards is built into the game," observes one American player.

The game's primary objective, explains Tetsuo Mirua, CDI's president, is to pull a player out of his normal business specialty and force him to see business as a whole. In the game he must handle his "company's" planning, investment, research and development, purchasing, hiring, production, and sales through five fiscal years. Between fast-paced rounds of play (one per fiscal year), each player plots his actions and calculates performance figures using management accounting practices, which are explained in minilectures scheduled during the three-day session.

As the game proceeds, wall charts track year-to-year changes in each player's market share, shareholder equity, and other performance factors.

"After playing," assures CDI's overseas manager, Masao Ogura, "anyone can easily prepare a balance sheet or earnings statement. And he has a feel for which figures and ratios must be changed to improve his [real] company's performance."

Surprises

Americans playing the game may find themselves running their "companies" in untypical fashion after a round or two. Once hired, the staff can't be fired, for example. Production workers and salespeople can readily be rotated. Borrowing to the hilt isn't frowned upon. Market share "is all."

"When I started the game," says Steven Myers, representative director of Amway (Japan) Ltd. of Tokyo, "I had American reactions like: 'It's wrong to borrow this much. I should pay as I go. Where's my return on investment? Why should I invest so much in R&D so soon?'"

Those who come out on top in the Sony–CDI game often have a long streak of lousy return on investment. And, as in real-life Japan, banks keep putting up capital as long as players hang on to their market share and push R&D. "That ethic seeps right into you—you'd never get that in an American game," adds Myers.

Sony's gamesmanship began several years ago with a critique of the company's own management-training program by Kazuo Iwama, now Sony's president. He judged it was weak in practical accounting for managers and lacked balance among operating performance, organization, motivation, and strategic planning. Sony's Personnel Division was challenged to come up with a mode of training more stimulating than reading and lectures.

Its answer: a game. A task force was assembled from CDI and several Sony divisions to design it. The player, it was soon decided, should experience the whole management cycle—not be a specialist on a team. And he should work out the results of his decisions, not relegate the figuring to a computer.

Two models

Designing the Sony–CDI game took 30 months. Both an industrial version (emphasizing manufacturing) and a commercial version (stressing wholesaling and retailing) are offered, each in both basic and advanced forms.

Launched in Japan in 1976, they're now part of the regular in-house training programs of 1,000 Japanese companies. This month, Japan Steel Corporation will run 300 newly hired university graduates through the basic industrial game at five steel-making centers.

The game is also being played in South Korea. A French-language version is in the works, and a management-control delegation from Beijing recently sat down to a one-day version of the game in Tokyo—played in Mandarin Chinese.

The U. S. marketing effort likely will be handled by new American offices of CDI, and the cost of playing the game is expected to be between $500 and $600. However, the game itself will be backed by Sony and identified as such.

Source: Michael McAbee, in *Industry Week* 1 June 1981, pp. 83, 87. Penton Publishing, Pittway Corporation, Perton Plaza, 1111 Chester Ave., Cleveland, Ohio 44114.

on the basis of participant reactions to the training. Objective evaluation of management development is still limited and often superficial.[7]

In summary, it is unrealistic to assume that the very difficult job of managing complex organizations can be accomplished by untrained managers. Unfortunately, there are very few managers who have an intuitive and workable approach to the management process. One realistic method of acquiring managerial skills is through effectively planned, conducted, and evaluated management development programs.

ASSESSMENT CENTERS

An assessment center utilizes a formal procedure aimed at evaluating an individual's potential as a manager and his or her developmental needs. Assessment centers are used both in the selection and development of managers. Basically, these centers simulate the problems that a person might face in a real-life managerial situation. Presently, more than 2,000 companies use assessment centers, and, because of their validity, their use has continued to grow.[8] In the typical assessment center, 10 to 15 participants of approximately equal organizational rank are brought together for three to five days to work on individual and group exercises similar to ones they would be handling in a typical managerial job. Business games, situational problems, interviews, and cases are normally used to simulate managerial situations. These exercises involve the participants in decision making, leadership, written and oral communication, planning, organizing, and motivation. Assessors observe the participants and evaluate their performance, and then provide feedback to the participants concerning performance and developmental needs.

Generally, assessors are selected from management ranks several levels above those of the participants. Also, professional psychologists from outisde the organization frequently serve as assessors. For a program to be successful, the assessors must be rigorously trained in the assessment process, the mechanics of the exercises that are to be observed, and the techniques of observing and providing feedback.

ORGANIZATION DEVELOPMENT

Organization development (OD) seeks to improve the performance of groups, departments, and the overall organization. Specifically, OD is an organizationwide, planned effort, managed from the top, with a goal of increasing organizational performance through planned interventions and training experiences. In particular, OD looks in depth at the human side of organizations. OD seeks to change attitudes, values, organizational structures, and managerial practices in an effort to improve organizational performance. The ultimate goal of OD is to structure the organizational environment so that managers and employees can use their developed skills and abilities to the fullest.

An OD effort has as its initial phase a recognition by management that organizational performance can and should be improved. Following this initial recognition, most OD efforts include the following phases:

1. Diagnosis.
2. Strategy planning.
3. Education.
4. Evaluation.

Diagnosis involves gathering information from organization members through the use of questionnaires or attitude surveys. Strategy planning is concerned with developing a plan for organization improvement based on these data. Strategy planning identifies problem areas in the organization and outlines steps to be taken to resolve the problems. Education consists of sharing the information obtained in the diagnosis with people who are affected by it, and helping them to realize the need for changed behavior. The education phase often involves the use of outside consultants working with individual employees or employee groups. This phase can also involve the use of the management development programs that were discussed earlier. Other techniques that might be used in the education phase are examined in the following sections of this chapter. The evaluation phase is very similar to the diagnostic phase. Following diagnosis, strategy planning, and education, additional data are gathered through attitude surveys or questionnaires to determine the effects of the OD effort on the total organization. This information can then, of course, lead to additional planning and educational efforts.

Sensitivity training

Sensitivity training is frequently used in OD programs and is designed to make the participants more aware of themselves and their impact on others. Unfortunately, some people tend to equate sensitivity training and OD. It is important to note, however, that sensitivity training is only one technique that can be used in organizational development. In fact, one OD program was described as follows: "This effort has reached a point where sensitivity training, per se, represents only 10 to 15 percent of the effort in our program. The rest of the effort . . . is in on-the-job situations, working real problems with the people who are really involved in them."[9]

Sensitivity training involves a group, normally called a training group or T group, which has no agenda or particular focus. Normally the group consists of from between 10 to 15 people who may or may not know each other. Since the group has no planned structure, the behavior of individual group members in attempting to deal with the lack of structure becomes the agenda. While engaging in dialogue with the group, each member is encouraged to learn about himself or herself and others in the nonstructured environment. The objectives of sensitivity training are to:

1. Increase self-insight and self-awareness of the participant's behavior and its meaning in a social context.
2. Increase sensitivity to the behavior of others.
3. Increase awareness and understanding of the types of processes that facilitate or inhibit group functioning and the interactions between different groups.
4. Heighten diagnostic skills in social, interpersonal, and intergroup situations.
5. Increase the participant's ability to intervene successfully in inter- or intragroup situations so as to increase member satisfaction, effectiveness, or output.
6. Increase the participant's ability to analyze continually his or her

own interpersonal behavior for the purpose of helping himself or herself and others achieve more effective and satisfying interpersonal relationships.[10]

Although sensitivity training sessions have no agenda, there is a desired pattern of events. The group usually meets with no directive leadership patterns, no authority positions, no formal agenda, and no power and status positions. Therefore, a vacuum exists. Nonevaluative feedback received by each individual on his or her behavior from other group members is the method of learning. From this feedback and from limited guidance given to the group by the trainer, feelings of openness and mutual trust emerge while the members of the group serve as resources for one another. Collaborative behavior develops. Finally, the group explores the relevance of the experience as it relates to the management of their organizations.

There are many misconceptions and misunderstandings about sensitivity training. To correct some of these the following list defines what sensitivity training is *not:*

1. A set of hidden, manipulative processes used to brainwash individuals into thinking, believing, and feeling the way someone might want them to without realizing what is happening to them.
2. An educational process guided by a leader who is covertly in control and hides this fact from the participants by some means.
3. Designed to suppress conflict and get everyone to like one another.
4. An attempt to teach people to be callous and disrespectful of society, and to dislike those who live a less open life.
5. Psychoanalysis nor intensive group therapy.
6. Necessarily dangerous.
7. A guarantee that a participant who attends a session will change behavior.[11]

For sensitivity training to be effective, some guidelines need to be followed. These are summarized below:

1. The trainer(s) should be closely evaluated.
2. Trainees should be carefully screened.
3. Trainees should know in advance the nature of the training.
4. The training should be administered to each individual participant outside the normal work group.

Sensitivity training has been criticized and defended as to its relative value for organizations. In general, the research on sensitivity training indicates that individuals who have attended training sessions tend to show increased sensitivity, more open communication, and increased flexibility.[12] However, the same research studies indicate that it is difficult to predict exactly what the outcome of a sensitivity training session will be for any one individual.[13] Thus, the research indicates that the outcomes from sensitivity training are beneficial in general, but are individually unpredictable.

Grid training   Grid training is an extension of the Managerial Grid®. Basically, the Managerial Grid, depicted in Figure 8–6, is a two-dimensional framework characterizing a manager according to his or her concern for people and his or her concern for production. A questionnaire is used to locate a particular individual's style of management on the grid.

The methods used in grid training can be divided into six phases.

Figure 8–6   The managerial grid®

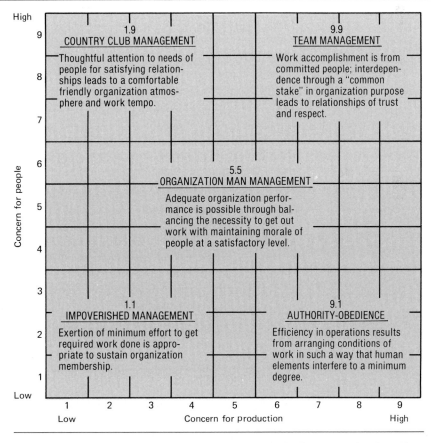

Source: R. R. Blake and J. S. Mouton, *The New Managerial Grid®* (Houston: Gulf Publishing, 1978), p. 11. Copyright © 1978 by Gulf Publishing Company. Reproduced by permission.

1. Laboratory-seminar training—this phase is designed to introduce the participant to the Managerial Grid concepts and material. Each manager determines where he or she falls on the Managerial Grid.
2. Team development—this phase involves establishing the ground rules and relationships necessary for 9,9 management.
3. Intergroup development—this phase involves establishing the ground rules and relationships necessary for 9,9 management for group-to-group working relationships.
4. Organizational goal setting—management by objectives is used to establish individual and organizational goals.
5. Goal attainment—goals established in Phase 4 are pursued.
6. Stabilization—changes brought about in the other phases are evaluated, and an overall evaluation of the program is made.[14]

As with sensitivity training, grid training has had mixed success in organizations. Little research has been conducted on grid training, and more is needed before determinations of its effectiveness can be made.[15]

Behavior modeling

A relatively recent approach that can be used in traditional management development programs and in OD is called behavior modeling or interaction management.[16] Basically, behavior modeling involves identifying interaction problems faced by managers, such as gaining acceptance, overcoming resistance to change, motivating employees, and reducing tardiness. The sequence of learning activities in behavior modeling then involves:

1. A filmed model or demonstration of the skills necessary to solve the problem being studied.
2. Practice in solving the problem through role playing for each trainee.
3. Reinforcement of the correct behaviors in solving the problem during the practice situation.
4. Planning by each trainee of how to transfer the skills back to his or her specific job situation.[17]

While behavior modeling is a new technique, results have been encouraging. In one study, behavior modeling resulted in better performance than found with no training or more traditional management development methods.[18]

SUMMARY

Management development is concerned with developing the experience, attitudes, and skills necessary to become, or remain, an effective manager. Management development should be designed, conducted, and evaluated on the basis of the objectives of the organization, the needs of the individual managers who are to be developed, and anticipated changes in the organization's management team.

A management inventory provides certain types of information about an organization's current management team. A management succession plan records prospective successors for management positions within an organization.

Objectives should be established for the overall management development program and for individual programs. One classification system for the preparation of overall management development objectives involves establishing routine, problem-solving, and innovative objectives.

Management development can be achieved through both on-the-job and off-the-job methods. Some on-the-job methods include understudy assignments, coaching, experience, job rotation, special projects, and committee assignments. Off-the-job methods include classroom training and university and professional association seminars. Methods used in classroom training include lectures, case studies, role playing, in-basket techniques, programmed instruction, and business games.

An assessment center utilizes a formal procedure aimed at evaluating an individual's potential as a manager and his or her developmental needs. Assessment centers are used in both the selection and development of managers.

Organization development (OD) is an organizationwide, planned effort, managed from the top, with a goal of increasing organizational performance through planned interventions and training experiences. Sensitivity training, grid training, and behavior modeling are three techniques used on OD.

REVIEW QUESTIONS

1. What is management development?
2. What is a management inventory? A succession plan?
3. Name three classifications for overall management development objectives and give examples of each.
4. Describe the following on-the-job methods of management development:
   a. Understudy assignments.
   b. Coaching.
   c. Experience.
   d. Job rotation.
   e. Special projects.
   f. Committee assignments.
5. Describe the following methods of classroom training:
   a. Lectures.
   b. Case studies.
   c. Role playing.
   d. In-basket technique.

    e. Programmed instruction.

    f. Business games.

6. What is an assessment center?

7. What is organization development (OD)?

8. Outline the phases of organization development.

9. What is sensitivity training?

10. Outline the six phases involved in grid training.

DISCUSSION QUESTIONS

1. Outline a system for evaluating a management development program for supervisors.

2. "It is impossible to evaluate the effectiveness of a supervisory development program." Discuss.

3. "Management games are fun, but you don't really learn anything from them." Discuss.

4. Organization development generally takes several years to produce any positive results. Describe some of the positive results that might accrue from such a program.

REFERENCES AND ADDITIONAL READINGS

1. L. A. Digman, "Determining Management Development Needs," *Human Resource Management*, Winter 1980, p. 13.

2. B. Hawrylyshyn, "Management Education—A Conceptual Framework," in ed. *Management Development and Training Handbook,* B. Taylor and G. L. Lippitt (London: McGraw-Hill, 1975), pp. 169–181.

3. Digman, "Determining Management Development Needs," pp. 14–15.

4. G. Odiorne, *Personnel Administration by Objectives* (Homewood, Ill.: Richard D. Irwin, 1971), pp. 338–51.

5. For an in-depth discussion on the case method, see C. Argyris, "Some Limitations of the Case Method: Experiences in a Management Development Program," *Academy of Management Review,* April 1980, pp. 291–98.

6. For a further discussion of business games, see B. Hunter and M. Price, "Business Games: Underused Learning Tools?" *Industry Week,* 18 August 1980, pp. 52–56.

7. For a discussion of evaluation procedures, see L. A. Digman "How Companies Evaluate Management Development Programs," *Human Resource Management,* Summer 1980, pp. 9–13.

8. L. A. Digman, "How Well-Managed Organizations Develop Their Executives," *Organizational Dynamics*, Autumn 1978, pp. 65–66. See also the entire February 1980 issue of *The Personnel Administrator,* which is devoted to an analysis of assessment centers.

9. S. A. Davis, "Organic Problem Solving Method of Organization Change," *Journal of Applied Behavioral Science* vol. 3, no. 1 (1967), p. 5.

10. J. P. Campbell and M. D. Dunnette, "Effectiveness of T-Group Experiences in Managerial Training and Development," *Psychological Bulletin,* August 1968, pp. 73–104.

11. C. Argyris, "T-Groups for Organizational Effectiveness," *Harvard Business Review,* March–April 1964, pp. 68–70.

12. M. Beer, "The Technology of Organization Development," in *Handbook of Industrial and Organizational Psychology,* ed. M. D. Dunnette (Skokie, Ill.: Rand McNally, 1976), p. 941.

13. Ibid.

14. R. R. Blake, J. S. Mouton, L. B. Barnes, and L. E. Greenes, "Breakthrough in Organization Development," *Harvard Business Review,* November–December 1964, pp. 137–38.

15. Beer, "Technology of Organization Development," p. 943.

16. W. Byham and J. Robinson, "Interaction Modeling: A New Concept in Supervisory Training," *Training and Development Journal,* February 1976, pp. 25–33.

17. J. Hinrichs, "Personnel Training," in *Handbook of Industrial and Organizational Psychology,* ed. M. D. Dunnette (Skokie, Ill.: Rand McNally, 1976), p. 832.

18. J. Moses and R. Richie, "Supervisory Relationship Training: A Behavioral Evaluation of a Behavior Modeling Program," *Personnel Psychology* 29 (1976), pp. 337–43.

Case 8–1   **THE 30-YEAR EMPLOYED**

John Brown, who is 52 years old, has been at the State Bank for 30 years. For the past 20 years, he has worked in the bank investment department. During his first 15 years in the department, it was managed by Bill Adams. The department consisted of Bill, John, and two women. Bill made all decisions, while the others performed manual record-keeping functions. When Bill retired five years ago, John held the position of assistant cashier.

Tom Smith took over the bank investment department after Bill Adams retired. Tom, 56, has worked for the State Bank for the past 28 years. Shortly after taking control of the department, Tom recognized that it needed to be modernized and staffed with people capable of giving better service to the bank's customers. As a result, he increased the department work force to 10 perple and installed two different computer systems. Of the 10 employees, only John and Tom are older than 33.

When Tom Smith took over the department, John was able to be helpful since he knew all about how the department had been run in the past. Tom considered John to be a capable worker; after about a year, he promoted John to assistant vice president.

After he had headed the department for about a year and a half, Tom purchased a computer package to handle the bond portfolio and its accounting. When the new system was implemented, John said that he did not like computers and would have nothing to do with them. At this time, his attitude created no real problem, since there were still many manual records to be kept. John continued to handle most of the daily record-keeping.

Over the next two years, further changes came about. As the other employees in the department became more experienced, they branched into new areas of investment work. The old ways of doing things were replaced by new, more sophisticated methods. John resisted these changes; he refused to accept or learn new methods and ideas. He slipped more and more into doing only simple but time-consuming drudgery.

Presently, a new computer system is being acquired for the investment section, and another department is being put under Tom's control. John has written Tom a letter stating that he wants no part of the new computer system but would like to be a manager of the new department. In his letter, John said he was tired of being given routine tasks while the young people got all the exciting jobs. John contended that since he had been with the bank longer than anyone else, he should be given first shot at the newly created job.

1. *Who has failed, John or the company?*
2. *Does the company owe something to a 30-year employee? If so, what?*
3. *What type of development program would you recommend for John?*

Case 8–2   **CONSOLIDATING THREE ORGANIZATIONS**

Sitting at his desk, Ray McGreevy considered the situation he faced. His small but prosperous real estate firm had tripled in size because of two simultaneous acquisitions. He now needed to develop a management team that could coordinate the three previously independent companies into one efficient firm. He knew that this would be no easy task because the two companies he had acquired had each been operated as independent entities.

In the seven years since Ray had started his real estate brokerage business, he had compiled an enviable record of growth and profits. His staff originally had consisted of himself and a secretary; it had grown to more than 25 employees. His organization included himself as president, two vice presidents, 16 sales representatives, four secretaries, and two clerical workers. These employees were distributed equally between the two branches that were each supervised by a vice president. The sales representatives reported to the vice president in their particular branch. The two branches covered a large geographic area that was divided into two regions.

About a year ago, Ray had decided to add a branch in a new area. After doing considerable research, he had decided that it might be more feasible to acquire one of the smaller firms already operating in the area. A bank officer whom he had contacted approved his plans and promised to help in locating a company to buy and in financing the acquisition.

Several months had gone by, and Ray had discussed possible mergers with two firms; however, satisfactory terms could not be reached. He was becoming slightly discouraged when the banker called him to set up a meeting with the owner of another real estate firm. This firm had been in business for approximately 30 years, and the owner had only recently decided to retire. The company, which was almost equal in size to Ray's, did not sell in his firm's geographic area. Therefore, it appeared to be a natural choice, and he was quite excited about prospects for acquiring it. The owner had agreed to accept payment over several years. Although the price was higher than Ray had originally intended to pay, the deal was too good to refuse.

Then, when the deal seemed ready to be closed, the owners of one of the other firms that he had been interested in buying called and said they wished to renegotiate. Ray was able to make a favorable arrangement with them. After he had discussed his situation with the banker, he finally decided to purchase both firms. Although this plan far exceeded his original intentions, he knew that opportunities such as these did not happen every day.

Now Ray pondered his next step. He had been so busy in the negotiations that he had not had time to develop a plan for managing his enlarged company. As an entrepreneur, he knew that he needed to develop a professional team to manage the new business properly. He now had three more branches and about 45 additional employees.

There were so many questions to be answered. Would it be better to operate the three as independent divisions? Should he retain the individual identities of the two new firms, or should he rename them after his original one? He needed answers to these and all his other questions.

1. *Does organizational development hold the key to Ray's questions?*
2. *As a personnel consultant, what recommendations would you make him?*

TRANS-STATES AIRLINES

Ken Morton groaned to himself as he examined the contents of the rather lengthy legal document that lay before him. "What next?" he wondered, as the full impact of what the document contained traveled through his senses.

Ken held the formerly sought-after position of Vice President, Personnel, of Trans-States Airlines, one of the nation's largest and most profitable air carriers. The term "formerly sought-after position" is used because of the rash of problems that had faced Ken in the last few months. None, however, held as much potential for catastrophe as the document he now held in his hand. He picked up the telephone and rapidly punched out the number of the company legal department.

"Bill Simpson, please," said Ken. Bill Simpson, as Trans-States' general counsel and chief lawyer, had a reputation as a shrewd courtroom adversary. However, he was known to be somewhat cavalier as far as the corporate entity was concerned.

In a moment Bill came on the line. "What can I do for you?" he said.

"For starters, you can get over here and explain what this lovely piece of legalese is, and tell me how we ended up in this mess," responded Ken. "For an encore, you can tell me how we're going to get out of it."

"I can help you with the former but not with the latter," said Bill. "I'll see you in 15 minutes."

Precisely 15 minutes later, a knock sounded on Ken's office door. "Good morning!" bellowed Bill.

"For you, maybe," replied Ken. "What is all this about, anyway?" he said, brandishing the document.

"Well, basically, it's a consent decree which we signed with the Justice Department and the EEOC boys," said Bill. "I suppose we should have kept you guys informed, but at the time the thing came up we felt that it would stay in legal channels. We also felt that we could easily defeat it, and we didn't want to get you all steamed up."

"I'm steamed up now," retorted Ken. "I don't see how we're going to live with this thing."

"Let me finish," said Bill. "We don't want this thing anymore than you do. Besides, we're not convinced that the whole concept of minority quotas isn't unconstitutional anyway. We plan to go back into court and fight it as a result of the outcome of the *Bakke* case. For the time being, however, we have to abide by the agreement and begin implementation of it."

"That's great!" said Ken. "However, you overlook one small point. According to the way I read things, we have 90 days to comply with the order. You're talking about a two- or three-year time frame with your appeals and court battles. By the time that comes to pass, this will be a moot case. And just what does all this stuff mean, anyway?''

"Well, essentially, this is how it stands," said Bill. "We have to hire half the number of women and minority people of the total number of women and minorities who apply for positions as pilots for the next 500 pilots we hire, up to a maximum of 50 percent of the total, or 250.''

"What does all that mean?" asked Ken. "No wonder I can't understand it. You can't even explain it.''

"Let me try an example," said Bill. "Suppose you plan to hire 100 pilots. If 40 women and 40 minorities applied, we'd have to hire 20 women and 20 minorities out of the total of 100. We couldn't be forced to hire more than 25 of each. It's that simple!''

"Do black women count against both quotas?" asked Ken.

"Unfortunately, no," replied Bill. "A black or minority woman would go against one quota or the other, but not both.''

"Where do you propose that we find that many qualified women and minority pilots?" asked Ken.

"That's your problem," said Bill. "I really don't foresee any difficulty, though. I read somewhere the other day that there are something like 1.7 million licensed pilots in the United States. Just put an ad in *The New York Times* and *The Wall Street Journal* and you'll have 'em crawling out of the woodwork.''

"It's not that simple," said Ken. "We normally hire pilots with about 2,500 flying hours, who have an Airline Transport Pilot certificate. They must also have a college degree and be somewhere between 23 and 32 years of age. Of the 1.7 million pilots you mentioned, only about 100,000 have active ATP certificates. Probably even fewer fall into our age and experience brackets. Throw in the degree requirement, and the fact that 4,000 of that total are already on our payroll, and you don't have too large a base to begin with. Delta, Eastern, United, TWA, and American probably account for at least as many as we have, and of what's left, how many are black or female? Besides that, about the only place you can get the kind of experience we're talking about is in the military, and they just didn't train that many black pilots—and all the women pilots they've trained have been trained within the last five years. They still have time to go on their obligations and won't be available for at least another year at the earliest. I sure wish you'd have consulted me before signing this thing!''

"Look, it could have been worse," said Bill. "United got hit with the same deal, except that their's extends over the next 1,200 pilots not 500. Also, you'd better be careful with that maximum age thing, or they'll be after us on that, too!''

"This is really wild! We'll be in a recruiting race with the other carriers that will make the NBA and NFL look tame by comparison. I can see it now: 'Trans States offers $1 million bonus to a 23-year-old woman with a private license and 50 hours for signing up for the pilot training program.' Do you realize how much this could cost us? Literally millions!'' Ken said.

Bill remained silent.

"I can tell you one thing," Ken continued. "It's going to cost us plenty, both in training and recruiting. Maybe I was being a bit facetious about the bonus babies, but I can see an immediate need to set up an entry-level training program for new hires. Because the pilots we've been getting from the military are highly qualified, we haven't had to have an entry-level training program since 1964. Our training time has been minimal, and our washout rate has been extremely low. We'll have to double or triple the training time required, and I'm sure the washout rate will skyrocket. That means money lost in partially training someone who will never spend one productive day with the company. It's like throwing money down the drain!"

"Well, at least you've got a little time to get on it," said Bill.

"I wish I could afford that luxary," replied Ken. "Marketing called me yesterday and said that they planned to add several new flights at the end of next month. That means that we have about 60 days to begin turning out the finished product. I just don't see how we'll do it."

"Why the short fuse?" asked Bill. "I know that we've added plenty of flying time in the past with no problem."

"Well, that's the way it may have appeared to your group over in legal," said Ken. "I can tell you, though, that there has always been a big scramble, even with a pool of fully qualified pilots to pick from. For example, if we begin running an entry-level course, we'll have to triple the amount of simulator time that each student receives. The two simulators we've got are already overbooked and the lead time to get a new simulator is about 18 months. Besides that, you'd have to yank more pilots off the line and train them as instructors, right when we can least afford it! The ground school times will increase, and we'll have to get some more ground school instructors for that program."

"What are your alternatives?" asked Bill.

"Unfortunately, there are only two; neither of them is very practical at this point in time," said Ken. "One alternative would be to rent time on a simulator from another airline. We've done that in the past, but right now everyone is expanding and I doubt that anyone has any slack time available. The other alternative, which is what I think we'll have to go to, is to negotiate some type of overtime flying agreement with the pilot's union. Knowing those greedy pilots, they'll probably insist on triple time or something equally outrageous. There's also a time factor involved. Negotiations with the pilots usually drag, and I'm sure they'll play this one to the bitter end, since they know they have the upper hand. Jim McBain, their negotiating chairman, is no dummy. He'll try to squeeze everything he can out of us."

"How about just ignoring the problem and not hiring anyone?" asked Bill. "Sometimes if you ignore a problem, it'll just go away. We do that all the time in the legal profession."

"If we did that, Delta and Eastern would clobber us," said Ken. "We'd be losing passengers to them and every study I've ever seen shows that once you lose a passenger, you almost never get him back. No, we can't ignore the challenge—expensive as it will be, we've got to add time."

"Well, things can't be as bad as all that," said Bill patronizingly. "We've already got some black pilots and some women pilots, and they've done okay on the shorter training course, haven't they?"

"Yes, we do have some black pilots." replied Ken, "about 20 out of 4,000—and those guys were all exmilitary and fully qualified. You just can't find enough of them! That was a problem long before this consent decree hit us. As for the women—they're even more of a problem. There is no supply of exmilitary women pilots, and there won't be for another year or two. We've hired some women, sure, just to stay ahead of the EEOC—or so we thought. By the way, that reminds me—what are we going to do about all the reverse discrimination suits that are bound to crop up? It seems to me that the problem is just going to get worse, and we're caught in the middle regardless of what we do."

"I wish you hadn't mentioned that," said Bill. "It's one of the reasons I suggested ignoring the problem if we could. The answer is, we'll probably be inundated with suits. I really can't blame them. If I were a white male with 3,500 hours of heavy jet time and had a master's degree, I'd be mad at being passed over in favor of a woman with a private license and 50 hours in a Cessna 150. No doubt about it—we'll get the pants sued off us."

"Bill, thanks for your help, such as it was," said Ken. "I guess I'd better start getting things organized to see if we can solve this problem. First, I'd better get Bob Siderholm to begin work on a recruiting program. Then I've got to get hold of Niles Gray over in Flight Training so they can start gearing up for an entry-level program. Patsy, please get me Captain McBain on the phone, and tell him I'd like to see him at once about some overtime flying. . . ."

SECTION THREE

Compensating employees

Motivation, satisfaction, and rewards

Objectives

1. To develop an understanding of the motivation process.
2. To present current theories of motivation and to clarify the relationships among them.
3. To explore how motivation, satisfaction, performance, and rewards are related.
4. To show how the human resource department can influence the motivation and satisfaction of employees.

Outline

Glossary of terms

Equity theory Theory of motivation based on the idea that if a person perceives an imbalance between his or her job inputs and the resulting outcomes, then the person will take the necessary actions to produce a balance between inputs and outcomes.

Extrinsic rewards Rewards that are directly controlled and distributed by the organization.

Intrinsic rewards Rewards that are internal to an individual and normally derived from involvement with the job.

Job enlargement Making a job structurally larger by giving an employee more of the same types of operations or tasks to perform.

Job enrichment Upgrading a job by adding more meaningful work, more recognition, more responsibility, and more opportunities for advancement.

Job satisfaction An individual's general attitude, which may be either positive or negative, about the job; usually a function of the difference between what a person wants from a job and what he or she obtains from it.

Morale Feeling of being accepted by and belonging to a group of employees through adherence to common goals and confidence in the desirability of these goals.

Motivation The incentive to work toward an objective; a causative sequence involving a need that provides the drive to achieve an objective.

Motivation-maintenance theory Motivation theory based on the idea that all work-related factors can be grouped into one of two categories: maintenance factors which will not provide motivation but can prevent it and motivators which can encourage motivation.

Need hierarchy Five different levels of individual needs (physiological, safety, social, esteem or ego, and self-actualization) that exist within individuals; identified by Abraham H. Maslow.

Reinforcement theory A motivation theory based on the idea that reinforced behavior will be repeated and behavior that is not reinforced is less likely to be repeated.

THE MODERN LITTLE RED HEN

Once upon a time, there was a little red hen who scratched about the barnyard until she uncovered some grains of wheat. She called her neighbors and said, "If we plant this wheat, we shall have bread to eat. Who will help me plant it?"

"Not I," said the cow.

"Not I," said the duck.

"Not I, " said the pig.

"Not I," said the goose.

"Then I will," said the little red hen. And she did. The wheat grew tall and ripened into golden grain. "Who will help me reap my wheat?" asked the little red hen.

"Not I," said the duck

"Out of my classification," said the pig.

"I'd lose my seniority," said the cow.

"I'd lose my unemployment compensation," said the goose.

"Then I will," said the little red hen, and she did.

At last it came time to bake the bread. "Who will help me bake the bread?" asked the little red hen.

"That would be overtime for me," said the cow

"I'd lose my welfare benefits," said the duck.

"I'm a dropout and never learned how," said the pig.

"If I'm to be the only helper, that's discrimination," said the goose.

"Then I will," said the little red hen.

She baked five loaves and held them up for her neighbors to see.

They all wanted some and, in fact, demanded a share. But the little red hen said, "No, I can eat the five loaves myself."

"Excess profits!" cried the cow.

"Capitalist leech!" screamed the duck.

"I demand equal rights!" yelled the goose.

And the pig just grunted. And they painted "unfair" picket signs and marched round and round the little red hen, shouting obscenities.

When the government agent came, he said to the little red hen, "You must not be greedy."

"But I earned the bread," said the little red hen.

"Exactly," said the agent. "That is the wonderful free enterprise system. Anyone in the barnyard can earn as much as he wants. But under our modern government regulations, the productive workers must divide their product with the idle."

And they lived happily ever after, including the little red hen, who smiled and clucked," "I am grateful. I am grateful."

But her neighbors wondered why she never again baked any more bread.

From an advertisement for the Pennwalt Corporation, Philadelphia, Pa.

"Our employees are just not motivated." "Half the personnel problems we have come about because workers aren't interested in producing more." "How can I encourage my employees to work harder?" Statements and questions such as these are often expressed by managers at all levels of organizations.

The problem of motivation did not develop recently. Research conducted by William James in the late 1800s indicated the importance of

Figure 9–1   Potential influence of motivation on performance

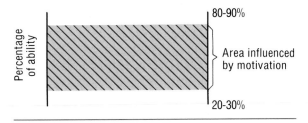

Source: P. Hersey and K. H. Blanchard, *Management of Organizational Behavior: Utilizing Human Resources*, 4th ed. (Englewood Cliffs, N.J.: Prentice-Hall, © 1982), p. 4. Reprinted by permission.

motivation.[1]* James found that workers paid on an hourly basis could keep their jobs by using approximately 20 to 30 percent of their ability. He also found that highly motivated employees work at approximately 80 to 90 percent of their ability. Figure 9–1 illustrates the potential influence of motivation on performance. Highly motivated employees tend to be more productive and have lower rates of absenteeism, turnover, and lateness.

THE MEANING OF MOTIVATION

Numerous definitions are given for the word motivation, usually involving such concepts as aim, desire, end, impulse, intention, objective, and purpose. Motivation comes from the Latin word movēre, which means "to move." Two formal definitions of motivation are:

> all those inner striving conditions described as wishes, desires, drives, etc. . . . It is an inner state that activates or moves[2]

> the combination of forces which initially direct and sustain behavior toward a goal[3]

The process of motivation can best be illustrated by the following causative sequence:

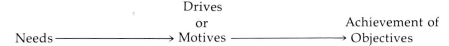

In the motivation process, needs produce motives that lead to the accomplishment of objectives. Needs are caused by either physical or psychological deficiences. For instance, a physical need will develop if an individual goes without sleep for 48 hours. When a person has no

---

*P. Hersey and K. H. Blanchard, *Management of Organization Behavior: Utilizing Human Resources*, 4th ed. (Englewood Cliffs, N.J.: Prentice-Hall, © 1982), p. 4. Reprinted by permission.

friends or companions, a psychological need exists. Needs of people will be explored more deeply in a later section of this chapter.

A motive is a stimulus leading to an action that satisfies a need; in other words, motives produce action. Lack of sleep (the need) activates the physical condition of fatigue (the motive) that produces sleep (the action, or, in this example, inaction.)

In the motivation process, achievement of the objective satisfies the need and reduces the motive. When an objective is reached, balance is restored. However, other needs arise that can be satisfied through the same sequence of events.

REWARDS AND MOTIVATION

The types of rewards that an organization offers its employees play a crucial role in determining their level of motivation. In addition, rewards have an impact on the quality and quantity of personnel that an organization is able to recruit, hire, and retain. Organizational rewards include both intrinsic and extrinsic rewards that are received as a result of employment by the organization. Intrinsic rewards are internal to an individual and are normally derived from involvement with the job. Job satisfaction and feelings of accomplishment are examples. Most extrinsic rewards are directly controlled and distributed by the organization and are more tangible than intrinsic rewards. Pay and benefits are examples of extrinsic rewards. Figure 9–2 provides examples of both types.

Although intrinsic and extrinsic rewards are different, they are also closely related. An extrinsic reward can result in intrinsic rewards. For example, if an employee receives a raise, the individual may also experience feelings of accomplishment (intrinsic rewards) by interpreting the pay raise as a sign of a job well done. It should also be realized that many formal rewards are unrelated to what the employee produces. These rewards are usually dispersed as a result of employment with the organization. While these rewards can significantly affect an organization's ability to attract personnel, they have little effect on motivating employees. Rewards in this category are called benefits and include paid vacations, insurance plans, and paid holidays.

Figure 9–2 Extrinsic versus intrinsic rewards

Extrinsic rewards	Intrinsic rewards
Fringe benefits	Achievement
Incentive payments	Feeling of accomplishment
Pay	Informal recognition
Promotion	Job satisfaction
Social relationships	Personal growth
	Status

Almost all theories of motivation are concerned with rewards offered by the organization. Some theories focus on intrinsic rewards while others focus on extrinsic rewards. Several motivation theories are described below to provide a broader understanding of what motivates people and a basis for understanding the importance of the role of human resource management in designing compensation systems.

TRADITIONAL THEORY

The traditional theory of motivation evolved from the work of Frederick W. Taylor and others in the scientific management movement, which was active at the beginning of this century. Taylor's ideas were based on his belief that existing reward systems had not been designed to compensate a person for high production. Taylor thought that when a highly productive person discovered that he or she was being compensated basically the same as someone producing less, his or her productivity would decrease. Taylor's solution to this problem of inequality of compensation was simple. He designed a system whereby a worker was compensated according to the amount he or she produced. Realizing that a reasonable standard of performance needed to be devised, Taylor broke jobs down into components and measured the time necessary to accomplish each. In this way, he was able to establish standards of performance "scientifically."

Taylor's plan was unique in that he advocated one rate of pay for units produced up to the standard. A significantly higher rate was paid not only for the number of units more than the standard, but also for all the units produced during the day. Thus, under Taylor's system, workers could in many cases significantly increase their pay by producing more than the standard.

The traditional motivation theory is based on the assumption that money is the primary motivator. On the basis of this assumption, financial rewards are related directly to performance in the belief that, if the reward is great enough, workers will produce more.

NEED HIERARCHY THEORY

In the need hierarchy theory, it is assumed that workers are motivated to satisfy a number of needs and that money can satisfy, directly or indirectly, only some of these. The need hierarchy theory is based largely on the work of Abraham Moslow.[4]

Need levels

Maslow thought that several different types of needs exist within individuals and that these relate to each other in the form of a hierarchy. Maslow's hierarchy consists of the five levels of needs shown in Figure 9–3. The physiological needs are shown as being strongest;

Figure 9–3   Maslow's need hierarchy

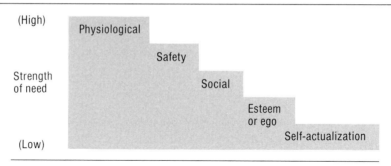

they tend to dominate all others until they are substantially satisfied. Once the physiological needs have been met, safety needs become dominant. This process continues with different needs emerging as the preceding level is satisified. Figure 9–4 shows a situation in which safety has become the dominant need.

Physiological needs are basically bodily needs that must be satisfied to sustain life; food, sleep, water, exercise, clothing, and shelter. Safety needs are concerned with protection against imminent or threatened danger, or deprivation. Since all employees, to some degree, depend on the organization, safety needs can be critically important. Favoritism, discrimination, and arbitrary administration of organizational policies are all actions that arouse uncertainty among employees and therefore affect safety needs.

It is important to note that, in our society, the physiological and the safety needs, the so-called lower-order needs, are more easily and therefore more generally satisfied than the others. In fact, Maslow estimated the percentage of satisfaction of the five needs as follows: physiological, 85 percent; safety, 70 percent; social, 50 percent; esteem, 40 percent; and self-actualization, 10 percent. Extrinsic rewards, such as wages and fringe benefits, provided by today's organizations are normally used to satisfy physiological and safety needs.

Figure 9–4   Dominant safety needs

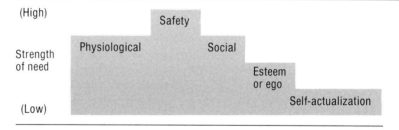

The third level of the hierarchy is the social needs. This level and the next two are called higher-order needs. Generally placed in the third level are needs for love, affection, belonging—all of which are concerned with establishing one's position in relationship to others. This level does not necessarily include sex, which, of course, would be categorized with the basic physiological drives. Rather, this concept of social need is exemplified by the development of meaningful personal relationships and acceptance in groups. Developing a sense of belonging to a corporate entity and identifying with work groups are means of satisfying these needs in organizations.

The esteem needs compose the fourth level; they involve the drive to value oneself and to inspire the esteem of others. Maslow contended that all people want a stable, firmly based, high evaluation of themselves—that is, self-respect and self-esteem—and the respect of others. These needs are met by forming various relationships based on adequacy, independence, and the giving and receiving of indications of regard and acceptance.

The next level in Maslow's need hierarchy, self-actualization or self-fulfillment, is attained through use of the person's abilities and interests to the fullest in functioning in his or her environment. In striving to reach their highest potential, people seek the rewards that are the result of that attainment. The rewards may not be only economic and social, but may also be psychological. As Maslow puts it, "What a man can be, he must be."[5] The need for self-actualization or self-fulfillment is never completely satisfied; one can always reach one step higher. Figure 9–5 lists several examples from each need level in the hierarchy.

Figure 9–5	Examples of needs

Physiological needs	Social needs
Food and water	Acceptance
Sleep	Feeling of belonging
Health	Membership in group
Bodily needs	Love and affection
Exercise and rest	Group participation
Sex	
	Esteem (or ego) needs
Safety needs	Recognition and prestige
Security and safety	Confidence and leadership
Protection	Competence and success
Comfort and peace	Strength and intelligence
No threats or danger	
Orderly and neat	Self-actualization needs
surroundings	Fulfillment of potential
Assurance of long-term	Doing things for the challenge
economic well-being	of accomplishment
	Intellectual curiosity
	Creativity and aesthetic
	appreciation
	Acceptance of reality

The most important contention of need hierarchy theory is that a satisfied need is not a motivator. Consider the basic physiological need for oxygen—only when an individual is deprived of oxygen can it motivate his or her behavior. Many of today's ogranizations apply the logic of the need hierarchy to build motivation in their employees. For instance, wage and salary systems and fringe benefit programs generally are meant to satisfy the lower-order needs—physiological and safety. On the other hand, interesting work and opportunities for advancement will appeal to higher-order needs. Designing jobs and compensation systems that enable a person to satisfy his or her needs within the organization is an important function of human resource management.

MOTIVATION-MAINTENANCE THEORY

Frederick Herzberg has developed a theory of work motivation that has been widely accepted in management circles. His hypothesis is referred to by several names: motivation-maintenance, dual factor, or the motivation-hygiene theory.

The formulation of this theory involved extensive interviews with approximately 200 engineers and accountants from 11 industries in the Pittsburg area.[6] In conducting the interviews, Herzberg and his colleagues, Bernard Mausner and Barbara Snyderman, used what is called the critical incident method. They requested employees to recall work situations in which they had experienced periods of high and low motivation. Specific questions were asked about the situation and the effect of the experience over a period of time.

Through analysis of the interviewees' statements, it was found that different factors were associated with good and bad feelings. These conditions were classified into two major categories. Factors most frequently mentioned in association with a favorably viewed incident concerned the work itself; these were achievement, recognition, responsibility, advancement, and the characteristics of the job. But when subjects felt negatively about a work incident, they were more likely to mention factors associated with the work environment. Examples of these included status; relations with supervisors, peers, and subordinates; technical aspects of supervision; company policy and administration; job security; working conditions; salary; and aspects of personal life that were affected by the work situation. Herzberg refers to the latter category as hygiene or maintenance factors. The researchers believed that these factors are preventive in nature. In other words, they will not motivate, but can prevent motivation from occurring. Thus, proper attention to hygiene factors is a necessary but not sufficient condition for motivation.

The first set of factors are called motivators. Herzberg contends that these conditions, when present in addition to the hygiene factors, en-

Figure 9–6   Hygiene and motivator factors

Hygiene factors (environmental)	Motivator factors (job related)
Policies and administration	Achievement
Supervision	Recognition
Working conditions	Challenging work
Interpersonal relations	Increased responsibility
Personal life	Advancement
Money, status, security	Personal growth

able true motivation. Herzberg maintains that motivation comes from within the individual, not from the manager. At best, maintenance of hygiene factors will keep an individual from being highly dissatisfied but will not cause him or her to be motivated. Both hygiene and motivator factors must be present for true motivation. These factors are summarized in Figure 9–6.

As a solution to motivation problems, Herzberg developed an approach called job enrichment. Unlike job enlargement, which merely involves giving a worker more of the same tasks to perform, or job rotation, the practice of periodically rotating assignments, job enrichment involves upgrading the job by adding motivator factors. Designing positions that provide meaningful work, achievement, recognition, responsibility, advancement, and growth is the key to job enrichment.

As can be seen from Figure 9–7 Herzberg's motivation-maintenance theory is closely related to the need hierarchy theory of motivation; thus, it is subject to many of the same criticisms.

In terms of application, many researchers have attempted to apply the motivation-maintenance theory in controlled studies; these have produced mixed results. The majority have shown that when the subjects were similar to Herzberg's initial subjects, accountants and engineers, the results were supportive of the theory.[7] In studies of supervisors, blue-collar workers, and low-level white-collar workers in routine jobs, the results have been nonconfirming.[8]

PREFERENCE-EXPECTANCY THEORY

An additional theory of motivation was developed by Victor H. Vroom.[9] Called the preference-expectancy theory, it can be analyzed with the aid of the following diagram:

$$\text{Effort} \xrightarrow[\text{Expectancy}]{\text{E-P}} \text{Performance} \xrightarrow[\text{Expectancy}]{\text{P-O}} \text{Outcomes}$$

Theoretically, a probability or likelihood is either consciously or unconsciously developed by an employee about the expectancy that in-

Figure 9–7 A comparison of Maslow's need hierarchy theory and Herzberg's motivation-maintenance theory

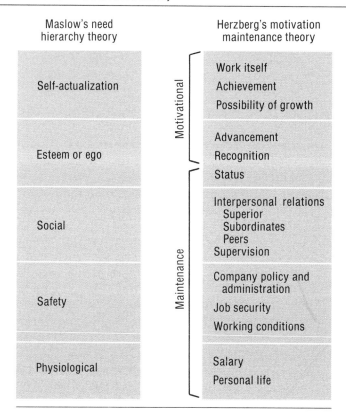

creased effort will lead to increased performance (E-P Expectancy). For example, there is some probability that more sales calls (effort) by a salesperson will add to total sales (performance). In addition, each individual expects that increased performance will produce certain outcomes (P-O Expectancy). For instance, a noncommissioned salesperson may think that there is a high probability (high expectancy) of receiving a pay raise if sales increase. On the other hand, the person might think that greater sales would not result in a pay raise (low expectancy). The expectancy of increased effort leading to increased performance (E-P) multiplied by the expectancy of increased performance leading to a particular outcome (P-O) yields a measure of the individual's total expectation about increased effort.

The preference component is the value that an individual places on a particular outcome. This could range from a +1.0 to a −1.0. Thus, if a person desires a promotion, he or she would assign a high positive value or preference to this outcome; on the other hand, the same person, if not interested in a promotion, would give a low or even a negative value to the outcome.

Under the preference-expectancy theory, an individual's level of motivation is determined by multiplying his or her total expectations by his or her preference (a number close to +1.0 indicates extremely high motivation).

$$\text{Motivation} = (\text{E-P Expectancy}) \times (\text{P-O Expectancy}) \times \text{Preference}$$
$$(0 \text{ to } +1) \qquad (0 \text{ to } +1) \qquad (+1 \text{ to } -1)$$

Thus, if an individual has a high expectation that increased effort will lead to a desirable outcome, his or her level of motivation will be high. If either the expectation of obtaining the outcome or the value of the outcome is low, the level of motivation will be low. Vroom's theory is based on the belief that individual expectations and preferences do exist, even though they may be unconscious.

The following example is intended to illustrate the preference-expectancy theory. Assume that John Que, an employee, regularly comes to work late. His effort (or, in this case, his lack of effort) is producing a performance record of tardiness. His E-P expectancy is high. In other words, the probability of his behavior producing a record of tardiness is 1.0. Past experience has shown that management does not enforce a policy that employees must be on time for work. Therefore, the likelihood of his record of performance (tardiness) producing an outcome (disciplinary action) is relatively low and his P-O expectancy is likely to be close to zero. Finally, even if John places a high value or preference on the avoidance of disciplinary action, he still will not be motivated to get to work on time because of his low P-O expectancy.

REINFORCEMENT THEORY

The work of B. F. Skinner forms the primary basis for the reinforcement theory. The general idea behind this theory is that reinforced behavior will be repeated and behavior that is not reinforced is less likely to be repeated. For instance, if an employee is given an increase in wages when performance is high, the employee is likely to continue to strive for high performance. Reinforcement theory assumes that the consequences of an individual's behavior determine his or her level of motivation. Thus, an individual's motives are considered to be relatively minor in this approach.

Reinforcers are not necessarily rewards and do not necessarily have to be positive. For instance, in the example of tardiness given in the discussion of the preference-expectancy theory, the desire of the employee to avoid disciplinary action would be an avoidance reinforcer. Similarly, cutting a salesperson's salary when his or her sales decrease

Ohio firm relies on incentive-pay system to motivate workers and maintain profits

Lots of companies these days are huffing and puffing to find some good way to motivate workers. Lincoln Electric Co. found the way it wanted in 1907 and says it has liked the results ever since.

The company relies on incentives. It pays most of its 2,500 employees on a piecework basis. In 1933, it added an annual bonus system. Based on performance, bonuses may exceed regular pay, and they apply far more extensively than in most companies. A secretary's mistakes, for example, can cut her bonus.

Some employees complain of pressure. But they stay around. Turnover is only 0.3% a month. The Cleveland company has no unions, and it avoids strikes. It says employees have *averaged* as much as $45,000 a year in good times. Sales and earnings have risen at a respectable pace.

"You really can ask, 'Is Lincoln Electric behind the times or ahead of the times?'" says Norman Berg, a Harvard Business School professor who has studied the company since 1975. But the nation would have fewer problems with foreign competition "if more companies in the U.S. operated like Lincoln," he says. And perhaps they will. Mr. Berg has used Lincoln as a case study in a course he taught iin Japan.

Pushing a message

John C. Lincoln founded the company in 1895 to make an electric motor he had developed. His brother, James, joined the concern in 1907 and began emphasizing employee motivation. Ever since, the company has pushed its message that the business must prosper if employees are to benefit.

By letting employees buy stock at book value, the company has encouraged workers to own a stake in its prosperity. (Employees must sell the stock at book value when they leave.) About 70% of the employees own stock, and together they hold nearly 50% of the shares outstanding. Members of the Lincoln family, who aren't directly involved in company operations, own most of the remaining stock in the maker of motors and welding equipment.

But the heart of Lincoln's approach is the incentive-pay system, which the company calls "the low cost of high wages." Given the weakness in the company's industrial market, employees now work only 30 hours a week. But even with the reduced work-week, they would average between $30,000 and $35,000 a year, including bonus, says Richard S. Sabo, an official.

In 1981, employees earned an average of about $45,000 including the bonus, Mr. Sabo adds. These pay figures include earnings of all employees. But the production workers alone earn well above the norm. At the average manufacturing wage of $8.69 an hour last year, an employee working full-time every week would earn just over $18,000 a year.

Cost defects

Each employee is responsible for the quality of his own work. He inspects his own parts and must correct any imperfect work on his own time. The company keeps records on who worked on each piece of equipment. Defects that slip by the worker and are discovered by customers or by Lincoln's quality-control people lower the worker's merit rating, bonus and pay.

Lincoln employees don't mind the high pay— or the company's guarantee of at least 30 hours of work each week for workers with at least two years of service. But they say there is a price.

"It's physically and mentally tough on you,"

says one former worker who quit after eight years. "You work so fast."

Lorenzo Hilles, a 42-year-old worker with 17 years of service, says, "There comes a time when you want to slow down." He says he'd like to move out of the piecework factory environment "if something comes available" elsewhere in the company. But as Lincoln hasn't any seniority system, he'll have to compete on a merit basis with the newest employees for one of the few jobs that doesn't involve piecework.

In order to guarantee steady work, Lincoln hire cautiously in boom times. This means employees may work 50 hours a week or more for prolonged periods. And they must accept any position in any department, even if it means a pay cut.

Merit point tension

Some employees say the system can generate unfriendly competition, too. A certain number of merit points are allotted to each department. An unusually high rating for one person usually means a lower rating for another. "There's a saying around here that you don't have a friend at Lincoln Electric," says a worker with nearly 20 years service.

But management defends the system. "We don't feel hard work is harmful," Mr. Sabo says. It certainly hasn't hurt the company itself. Though the recession slashed earnings last year by 42% and sales by 28% compared with a year earlier, volume and profits have risen over the years. The company passes out few financial details. But in the seven years through 1981, sales advanced to a record $526.9 million from $232.8 million. Earnings in the period rose to $39.7 million, also a record, from $17.5 million.

Among other things, Lincoln is now one of the leading makers of arc-welding equipment. Its success in this market has "encouraged the exit of several major companies from the industry and caused others to seek more-specialized market niches," says Harvard's Prof. Berg.

Customers praise the company's product quality, too. "I don't ever remember having one problem with quality from Lincoln," says Samuel Flager, purchasing agent for an Ashland Oil Corp. unit that buys $1.8 million of Lincoln welding equipment a year. "We'd expect some problems with this volume of business," he adds.

Source: Maryann Mrowca, in *The Wall Street Journal*, 12 August, 1983, p. 23. Reprinted by permission of *The Wall Street Journal*, © Dow Jones & Co., Inc., 1983. All rights reserved.

illustrates a negative reinforcer. The phrase negative reinforcer is used because for the individual to stop the action that is being taken (decrease in salary), his or her behavior (selling) must change.

The current emphasis in organizations is on positive reinforcement. The Emery Air Freight Corporation has reported exceptionally good results from a positive reinforcement program.[10] On the basis of Emery's success, several other corporations, such as United Airlines, IBM, IT&T, and Ford Motor Company, have implemented positive reinforcement approaches with results that, while still incomplete, are similarly good.[11]

The effects of negative reinforcement have not been determined scientifically. While punishment had been shown to weaken a specific behavior, the usual effect of negative reinforcement is some form of fear or withdrawal.[12] Thus, at least until further research has been conducted, any negative reinforcement in organizations should be used with extreme caution.

EQUITY THEORY

Equity theory is based on the belief that employees will take whatever actions are necessary to produce feelings of equity with respect to their jobs. All employees bring a certain set of inputs to their jobs in the form of education, previous work experience, etc., and all employees receive certain outcomes in the form of pay, benefits, job satisfaction, prestige, etc. Equity theory states that if a person perceives an imbalance between his or her job inputs and the resulting outcomes, then the person will take the actions necessary to produce a balance between perceived inputs and outcomes. For example, it is not unusual for an employee to feel that he or she is underpaid for what he or she does when compared to other employees. According to equity theory, such an employee's level of effort would be reduced to balance the inputs and outcomes. Other possible actions would be to quit or become more dissatisfied. Although it occurs much less frequently, it is possible for an employee to feel that the outcomes received outweigh the inputs. In this situation, equity theory postulates that the employee would work harder to balance the inputs and outcomes.

An important point regarding equity theory is that an individual's feelings of equity are based on his or her *perceptions* of inputs versus outcomes. Naturally, these perceptions are heavily influenced by what the individual sees as the inputs and outcomes of others. For instance, an employee might feel good about his or her pay until he or she finds out that others doing the same job are receiving substantially higher pay.

Much of the work on equity theory has centered around compensation. This aspect of equity theory is discussed at length in Chapter 11. Figure 9–8 summarizes the major components of equity theory.

Figure 9–8   Major components of equity theory

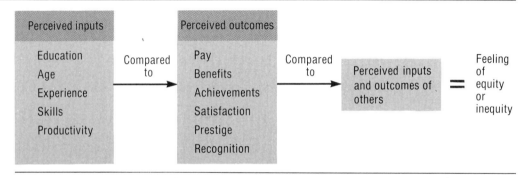

INTEGRATING THE THEORIES OF MOTIVATION

    All the previously discussed theories present motivation as goal-directed behavior. Although the theories may appear to be quite different, most of them are not in conflict but rather treat a different segment of the overall motivational process or look at the same segment from a different perspective Figure 9–9 presents a model that reflects the overall motivational process and indicates relationships among the major motivational theories.

    Vroom's preference-expectancy theory is reflected at the heart of the model by the three factors that are shown to influence effort; note the arrows leading to the effort box. Maslow's theory is represented by the value of the reward as a function of the nature and strength of the individual's current needs (upper left portion of the model). Herzberg's ideas are represented by the influence of the perceived nature and quantity of the rewards issued on the value of the reward (upper right portion). Herzberg's theory can be understood better if one thinks of rewards as being both intrinsic and extrinsic. Reinforcement theory is represented through the effort-performance-reward relationship (middle and lower portions of the model). The inputs of the equity theory are represented by the abilities and traits and the effort components. The outcomes are represented by the perceived nature and quantity of rewards.

Figure 9–9 The overall motivational process

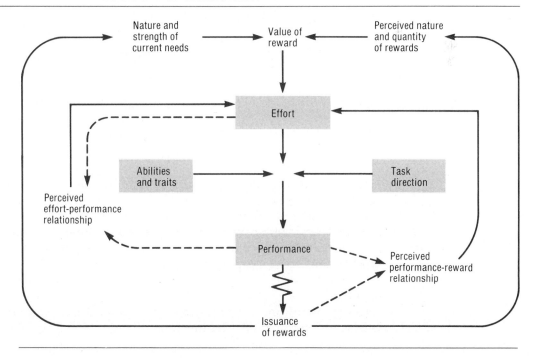

Thus, as indicated in Figure 9–9 no single motivation theory provides all the answers. Today's human resource manager plays an important role in the motivation process because he or she influences not only the extrinsic reward system (wage and salary determination) but also the intrinsic reward system (recognition systems and job design/satisfaction, etc.).

JOB SATISFACTION

Because human resource managers often serve as intermediaries between employees and management in conflicts, they are concerned with job satisfaction or general job attitudes of the employees. Phillip Applewhite has listed the five major components of job satisfaction as "(1) attitude toward work group, (2) general working conditions, (3) attitude toward company, (4) monetary benefits, and (5) attitude toward supervision.[13] Other components that should be added to these five are the indivual's state of mind about the work itself and about life in general. The individual's health, age, level of aspiration, social status, and political and social activities can all contribute to job satisfaction. A person's attitude toward his or her job may be positive or negative.

Job satisfaction is not synonymous with organizational morale, which is the possession of a feeling of being accepted by and belonging to a group of employees through adherence to common goals and confidence in the desirability of these goals. Morale is the by-product of a group, while job satisfaction is more an individual state of mind. However, the two concepts are interrelated in that job satisfaction can contribute to morale and morale can contribute to job satisfaction.[14]

The satisfaction-performance controversy

For many years, managers generally have believed that a satisfied worker is necessarily a good worker. In other words, if management could keep all the workers "happy," good performance would automatically follow. Charles Greene has suggested that many managers subscribe to this belief because it represents "the path of least resistance."[15] Greene's thesis is that, if a performance problem exists, increasing an employee's happiness is far more pleasant then discussing with the worker his or her failure to meet standards. Before the satisfaction-performance controversy is discussed further, it might be wise to point out that there are subtle but real differences between being satisfied and being happy. Although happiness eventually results from satisfaction, this feeling goes much deeper and is far less tenuous than happiness.

The following incident illustrates two propositions concerning the satisfaction-performance relationship:

As Ben walked by smiling on the way to his office, Ben's boss remarked to a friend. "Ben really enjoys his job and that's why he's the best damn worker I ever had. And that's reason enough for me to keep Ben happy." The friend replied, "No, you're wrong! Ben likes his job because he does it so well. If you want to make Ben happy, you ought to do whatever you can to help him further improve his performance."[16]

Ben's boss holds the traditional view that satisfaction causes performance. The second proposition, as expressed by his friend, is that satisfaction is the effect rather than the cause of performance. This proposition says that effort in a job leads to rewards, which result in a certain level of satisfaction. Thus, rewards constitute a necessary intervening variable in the relationship. In another proposition, both satisfaction and performance are considered to be functions of rewards. This proposition not only views satisfaction as being caused by rewards but also postulates that current effort in a job affects later effort if rewards are based on current performance. Research generally rejects the more popular view that satisfaction causes performance. The evidence does, however, provide moderate support for the view that job effort causes satisfaction. The evidence also strongly indicates that rewards constitute a more direct cause of satisfaction than does performance and that rewards based on current effort cause subsequent performance.[17] Research also indicates that a high level of job satisfaction does have a positive impact in reducing turnover, absenteeism, tardiness, accidents, grievances, and strikes.[18]

In addition, recruitment efforts by current employees generally are more successful if these employees are well satisfied. Satisfied employees are preferred simply because they affect the work environment positively. Thus, even though a well-satisfied employee is not necessarily an outstanding performer, there are numerous reasons for taking steps to encourage employee satisfaction.

Rewards and satisfaction

As mentioned earlier, a wide range of factors affect an individual's level of satisfaction. While organizational rewards can and do have an impact, job satisfaction is primarily determined by factors that are usually not directly controlled by the organization. The top portion of Figure 9–10 summarizes the major factors that influence an individual's level of satisfaction. The lower portion shows the behaviors generally associated with high and low levels of satisfaction. A high level of satisfaction leads to organizational commitment, while a low level, or dissatisfaction, results in behavior detrimental to the organization (turnover, absenteeism, tardiness, accidents). For example, employees who like their jobs, supervisors, and factors related to the job will probably be loyal and devoted. However, employees who strongly

Figure 9–10   Determinants of satisfaction and dissatisfaction

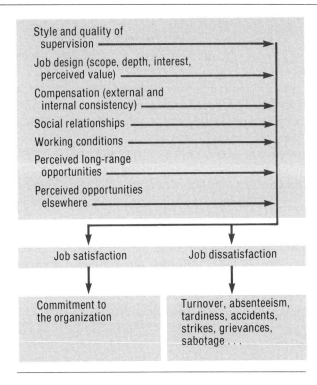

dislike their jobs or any related factors will probably act out their feelings by being late or absent, or by taking more covert actions to disrupt the organization.

It must be remembered that satisfaction and motivation are not synonymous. Motivation is a drive to perform, whereas satisfaction reflects the individual's attitude toward the situation. The factors that determine whether an individual is adequately satisfied with the job differ from those that determine whether he or she is motivated. The level of satisfaction is largely determined by the comforts offered by the environment and the situation. Motivation, on the other hand, is largely determined by the value of rewards and their dependence on performance. Motivation results in added effort that, in turn, leads to increased performance if the individual has the ability and if the effort is directed properly. The result of high satisfaction is increased commitment to the organization, which may or may not result in better performance. This increased commitment normally will lessen the number of personnel-related problems, such as strikes, excessive absenteeism, tardiness, and turnover.

SUMMARY   The motivation process centers on needs, which produce motives that lead to the accomplishment of objectives. Needs are caused by deficiencies or imbalances. Motives, or stimuli, produce an action taken to satisfy the need. In the motivation process, the achievement of the objective satisfies the need and reduces the motive. When the objective is reached, balance is restored; of course, other needs then arise. These new needs must then be satisfied by the motivation process.

The types of rewards that an organization offers its employees play a crucial role in determining the level of motivation. In addition, rewards have an impact on the quality and quantity of personnel that the organization is able to recruit, hire, and retain. Organizational rewards include both intrinsic and extrinsic rewards.

Six basic theories of motivation are the traditional, need hierarchy, motivation-maintenance preference-expectancy, reinforcement and equity theories. The traditional theory is based on the assumption that money is a primary motivator—employees will produce more for greater financial gain.

The need hierarchy theory is based on the assumption that employees are motivated to satisfy a variety of needs, only some of which can be satisfied by money. The needs of an individual are said to exist in a hierarchy as follows: physiological, safety, social, esteem, and self-actualization. Once a need has been sufficiently satisfied, it no longer serves as a motivator.

The motivation-maintenance theory involves two categories of factors that relate to motivation. The first category, called hygiene or maintenance factors, concerns the work environment and includes status, interpersonal relations, supervision, company policy and administration, job security, working conditions, salary, and personal life. These factors must receive proper attention in the job for motivation to occur. However, the hygiene factors do not motivate employees but rather keep them from being dissatisfied. The second category of factors, called motivators, relates to the work itself. They relate to recognition, advancement, achievement, growth potential, and responsibility. Only if both the hygiene and motivator factors are properly maintained will motivation occur.

The preference-expectancy theory implies that motivation depends on the preferences and expectations of an individual. This theory emphasizes the need for organizations to relate rewards directly to performance and to be sure that the rewards are desired by the recipients.

The reinforcement theory of motivation is based on the idea that reinforced behavior will be repeated and behavior that is not reinforced will not be repeated. The theory assumes that the consequences of an individual's behavior determine his or her level of motivation.

Equity theory is based on the belief that employees will take whatever actions are necessary to produce feelings of equity with respect to their jobs. Equity theory holds that if a person perceives an imbalance between his or her job inputs and job outcomes, then the person will take the actions necessary to produce a balance between job inputs and outcomes.

Although each of the basic motivation theories may appear to be different, most are not in conflict but rather deal with a different segment of the overall motivational process or the same segment from different perspectives.

Job satisfaction, which is an individual's attitude about the job, is influenced by many factors. The complex relationship between job satisfaction and performance has been debated for years. Current theory holds that performance should determine rewards. Rewards, in turn, affect an individual's level of satisfaction through their impact on current needs. Research has shown that the level of job satisfaction can directly affect many personnel problems, such as excessive absenteeism, turnover, tardiness, and even grievances and sabotage.

REVIEW QUESTIONS

1. Explain the motivation sequence.
2. What are intrinsic and extrinsic rewards? Give examples of each.
3. Describe the following theories of motivation:
   a. Traditional.
   b. Need hierarchy.
   c. Motivation-maintenance.
   d. Preference-expectancy.
   e. Reinforcement.
   f. Equity.
4. What is job satisfaction? What are its major components?
5. What is organizational morale?
6. Discuss the satisfaction-performance controversy.
7. From a personnel standpoint, what are the real benefits of having satisfied employees?

DISCUSSION QUESTIONS

1. "Most people can be motivated with money." Discuss your views on this statement.

2. Do you think that a loyal employee is necessarily a good employee?

3. As a personnel manager, would you prefer a highly motivated or a well-satisfied group of employees?

4. The XYZ Company has just decided to take all 200 of its employees to Las Vegas for a three-day weekend to show its appreciation for their high level of performance. What is your reaction to this idea?

5. Discuss the following statement: "A satisfied employee is one who is not being pushed hard enough."

REFERENCES AND ADDITIONAL READINGS

1. P. Hersey and K. H. Blanchard, *Management of Organizational Behavior*, 4th ed. Englewood Cliffs, N. J.: Prentice-Hall, 1982), p. 4.

2. B. Bereison and G. A. Steiner, *Human Behavior* (New York: Harcourt, Brace & World, 1964), p. 240

3. D. B. Lindsley, *Psychophysiology and Motivation, Nebraska Symposium on Motivation,* (Lincoln: University of Nebraska Press, 1957), p. 48.

4. A. H. Maslow, *Motivation and Personality* (New York: Harper & Row, 1954).

5. *Ibid.,* p. 91.

6. F. Herzberg, B. Mausner, and B. Snyderman, *The Motivation to Work* (New York: John Wiley & Sons, 1959), p. ix.

7. M. Mayers, "Who Are the Motivated Workers?" *Harvard Business Review,* January–February 1964, pp. 73–88. M. M. Swartz, E. Janusailts, and H. Stark, "Motivational Factors among Supervisors in the Utility Industry," *Personnel Psychology,* Spring 1963, pp. 45–53. F. Friedianger and E. Walton, "Positive and Negative Motivations Toward Work," *Administrative Science Quarterly,* September 1964, pp. 194–207. T. M. Lodahl, "Patterns of Job Attitudes in Two Assembly Technologies," *Administrative Science Quarterly*, March 1964, pp. 482–519.

8. M. D. Dunnette, "Factor Structures of Unusually Satisfying and Unusually Dissatisfying Job Situations for Six Occupational Groups" (Paper presented at Mid-Western Psychological Association Meeting, Chicago, 1965). R. B. Ewen, "Some Determinants of Job Satisfaction: A Study of the Generality of Herzberg's Theory," *Journal of Applied Psychology* 47 (1963), pp. 246–50. A. W. Kornhauser, *Mental Health of the Industrial Worker.* (New York: John Wiley & Sons, 1965). P. F. Wernicht, "Intrinsic and Extrinsic Factors in Job Satisfaction" (Ph.D Thesis, University of Minnesota, Minneapolis, 1964).

9. V. H. Vroom, *Work and Motivation* (New York: John Wiley & Sons, 1967).

10. E. J. Feeney, "At Emery Air Freight: Positive Reinforcement Boosts Performance," *Organizational Dynamics,* Fall 1973, pp. 41–50.

11. D. Hellriegel, and J. W. Slocum, Jr., and R. Woodman, *Organizational Behavior,* 3ed. (St. Paul, Minn.: West Publishing Company, 1983), p. 101.

12. J. P. Campbell and R. D. Pritchard, "Motivation Theory in Industrial Psychology," in *Handbook of Industrial and Organizational Psychology,* ed. M. D. Dunnette (Skokie, Ill.: Rand McNally, 1976), p. 71.

13. P. B. Applewhite, *Organizational Behavior* (Englewood Cliffs, N.J.: Prentice-Hall, 1965), p. 22. Reprinted by permission of Prentice-Hall, Inc., Englewood Cliffs, N.J.

14. M. L. Blum, *Industrial Psychology and Its Social Foundations.* (New York: Harper & Row, 1956), p. 126.

15. C. N. Greene, "The Satisfaction-Performance Controversy," *Business Horizons,* October 1972, p. 31. Copyright 1972 by the Foundation for the School of Business at Indiana University. Reprinted by permission.

16. Ibid., p. 31.

17. F. J. Roethlisberger, *Management and Morale* (Cambridge, Mass.: Harvard University Press, 1941), p. 40.

18. D. P. Schwab, and L. L. Cummings, "Theories of Performance and Satis-

faction: A Review," *Industrial Relations,* October 1970, pp. 408–29; also E. A. Locke, "The Nature and Causes of Job Satisfaction," in *The Handbook of Industrial and Organizational Psychology,* ed. M. D. Dunnette (Skokie, Ill.: Rand McNally, 1976), p. 343.

Case 9–1 | **ARE CAREER EXPECTATIONS REALLY CHANGING?**

One of the authors recently had a discussion with the personnel director of a large national insurance company. This person was female. Her comments follow:

> Recent news articles and publications have focused a great deal of attention on the changing profile of career women moving into mid-level and executive positions; the realities indicate that women are still concentrated in low-skilled, low-paying jobs. Recent Census Bureau data show that the average man earns about $5,000 more than the average woman and that this is a significantly worsened condition in comparison to 1955 figures. More than 80 percent of the regularly employed women earned less than $15,000, while only 38 percent of the men working regularly earn under $15,000. In business, the majority of women are still among the clerical-secretarial ranks, which are low-paying positions.
>
> As regional director, I have been faced with problems of high turnover and low productivity among clerical employees, almost all of whom are female. Departments with a high concentration of such employees have a significantly higher turnover rate and are not producing the quality or quantity of work that management desires.
>
> While low pay is obviously a factor contributing to these problems, it is not the only one. Frustration and lack of motivation affect turnover and productivity and, I believe, do not result solely from low pay. In fact, I believe that it is largely the career orientation of most working women that accounts for the majority of the problem. At a time when many women are achieving acceptance as career employees, our female employees still view themselves as temporarily in the work force. Because of this orientation, they have merely taken a job rather than planned toward a lifetime of paid work.
>
> Further, as part of the society as a whole, they are caught between the cultural stereotypes that encourage or demand duty to home and family and the urgings of some to become personally fulfilled through a career. Such conflicts do nothing to help resolve a woman's role as a lifetime worker.

Through such a job orientation and a lack of career planning, women in business have been educationally unprepared and have taken low-skilled, low-pay clerical and secretarial positions. If they were content doing such work and being compensated accordingly, problems would be minor. But, in part due to rising expectations in society as a whole as well as within themselves, these duties are not sufficiently satisfying. The result is often lack of motivation and its attendant ills.

1. *Do you agree with this human resource director?*
2. *What can the human resource department do to help in this situation?*
3. *What percentage of motivational problems do you think are created by employees themselves versus those created by the organization? Discuss.*

| Case 9–2 | **A SUDDEN CHANGE IN ATTITUDE** |

Bob Watson was a young sailor assigned to a navy attack squadron on an aircraft carrier. He had just been married when he was ordered to begin duty with his squadron. Basically, Bob was a bright young man; he had joined the navy after dropping out of high school. After enduring a boot camp experience that he thought was degrading, he had found himself at the bottom of the rank structure. Because of the timing of his placement in the squadron and its current staffing, no position was open in his job specialty of engine mechanic. Therefore, he was temporarily assigned to the leading chief to run errands and perform any menial tasks that were necessary for the squadron The leading chief, who had been in the navy for 28 years, was a strict disciplinarian.

Shortly after beginning this assignment, Bob began to rebel by showing indifference toward his role in meeting the squadron goals. He would disappear for hours, perform tasks poorly, and talk back to the chief. At the time of each incident, the chief would respond with disciplinary action. Bob was on report and in trouble with his superiors continually.

After a port visit, Bob missed the ship's sailing; this is a mortal sin in the navy. He had to be flown by helicopter back to the ship. At that point, the leading chief decided to bring Bob before the commanding officer in two weeks to discuss whether he should be given an undesirable discharge. Bob had told the leading chief that he simply wanted out of the navy and did not care how such a discharge would affect his future.

The personality clash between the leading chief and Bob had become so severe that he had Bob transferred to the line division for the two-week period. This division consisted mostly of young men who had the important job of assisting the pilots by launching and recovering the squadron aircraft. These men, called plane captains, were each assigned to a particular plane. Each was responsible for his plane whenever a pilot was not in it.

When the time came to meet with the commanding officer, Bob's new supervisor requested that he not be given a discharge. He said that Bob was a superior performer with a good attitude.

1. *How do you explain this change in Bob's attitude?*
2. *What motivation theories would apply in this case?*

Chapter 10

Base wage and salary systems

Objectives

1. To develop an understanding of the base wage or salary component of employee compensation.
2. To discuss and illustrate different methods of job evaluation.
3. To describe how to conduct wage surveys and construct wage curves.

Outline

The importance of fair pay
  Pay equity
Compensation policies
  Government and union influence on compensation policies
    The Fair Labor Standards Act (FLSA)
    The Davis-Bacon Act
    The Walsh-Healey Public Contracts Act
    The Federal Wage Garnishment Law
    Equal Pay Act
  Union contracts
Pay secrecy
Job evaluation
  Point method
    Selection of key jobs
    Selecting compensable factors
    Assigning weights to factors
    Assigning points to specific jobs
  Factor comparison method
  Job classification method
  Job ranking method
  Similarities and differences among job evaluation methods

Pricing the job
  Wage surveys
  Wage curves
  Pay grades/ranges
Base wage/salary structure

Base wage (salary) The hourly, weekly, or monthly pay that employees receive for their work.

Benefits Rewards that employees receive as a result of their employment and position with an organization.

Compensable factors Characteristics of jobs that are deemed important by the organization to the extent that it is willing to pay for them.

Compensation system Policies, procedures, and rules that the organization follows in determining employee compensation.

Degree Written statements used to further break down job subfactors.

Exempt employees Managerial, administrative, and professional employees who are exempt from coverage by the Fair Labor Standards Act (FLSA). These employees do not have to be paid overtime and are not subject to a minimum wage.

External equity What employees in an organization are being paid compared to employees in other organizations performing similar jobs.

Factor comparison method Job evaluation technique that uses a monetary scale for evaluating jobs on a factor-by-factor basis.

Garnishment A legal procedure by which an employer is empowered to withhold wages for payment of an employee's debt to a creditor.

Incentives Rewards that are offered in addition to the base wage or salary and are usually directly related to performance.

Internal equity What an employee is being paid for doing his or her job compared to what other employees in the same organization are being paid to do their jobs.

Job classification method Job evaluation method that determines the relative worth of a job by comparing it to a predetermined scale of classes or grades of jobs.

Job evaluation A systematic determination of the value of each job in relation to other jobs in the organization.

Job ranking method Job evaluation method that ranks jobs in order of their difficulty from simplest to most complex.

Nonexempt employees Employees who are covered by the Fair Labor Standards Act (FLSA). These employees must be paid overtime and are subject to a minimum wage.

Point method Job evaluation method in which a quantitative point scale is used to evaluate jobs on a factor-by-factor basis.

Subfactor A detailed breakdown of a single compensable factor of a job.

Wage curve Graphical depiction of the relationship between the relative worth of jobs and their wage rates.

Wage survey Survey of selected organizations within a geographical area or industry designed to provide a comparison of reliable information on policies, practices, and methods of payment.

Employees who do not have sufficient funds to support their reasonable family needs are distracted from their efforts. Accordingly, the organization should attempt to have salary measure the job itself and provide enough money for reasonable living costs. Incentive compensation is to measure variations in performance.

*Robert Townsend**

Compensation refers to the extrinsic rewards that employees receive in exchange for their work. Usually, compensation is composed of the base wage or salary, any incentives or bonuses, and any benefits. The base wage or salary is the hourly, weekly, or monthly pay that employees receive for their work. Incentives are rewards offered in addition to the base wage or salary and are usually directly related to performance. Benefits are rewards which employees receive as a result of their employment and position with an organization. Paid vacations, health insurance, and retirement plans are examples of benefits. Figure 10–1 presents some examples of the different types of compensation.

An organization's compensation system consists of the policies, procedures, and rules that it follows in determining employee compensation. This chapter is concerned primarily with the base wage or salary component of compensation. Chapters 11 and 12 deal, respectively, with incentive systems and employee benefits.

Figure 10–1	Components of employee compensation		
	Base wage or salary	*Incentives*	*Benefits*
	Hourly wage	Bonuses	Paid vacation
	Weekly, monthly, or annual salary	Commissions	Health insurance
		Profit sharing	Life insurance
	Overtime pay	Piece rate plans	Retirement pension

THE IMPORTANCE OF FAIR PAY

Employee motivation is closely related to the types of rewards offered and their method of disbursement. While there is considerable debate over the motivational aspect of pay, there is little doubt that inadequate pay can have a very negative impact on an organization. Figure 10–2 presents a simple model that summarizes the reactions of employees when they are dissatisfied with their pay. According to this model, pay dissatisfaction can influence an individual's feelings about his or her job in two ways: (1) it can increase the desire for more money, and (2) it can lower the attractiveness of the job. When an individual's desire for more money increases, he or she is likely to engage in actions that can increase his or her pay. These actions might

*R. Townsend, *Up the Organization* (New York: Alfred A. Knopf, 1970), p. 76.

Figure 10–2   Model of the consequences of pay dissatisfaction

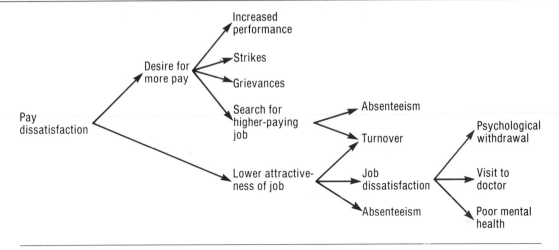

Source: E. E. Lawler III, *Pay and Organizational Effectiveness: A Psychological View* (New York: McGraw-Hill, 1971), p. 233.

include joining a union, looking for another job, performing better, or going on strike. With the exception of performing better, all of the consequences are generally classified as being undesirable by management. Better performance happens only in those cases where pay is perceived as being directly related to performance. On the other hand, when the job decreases in attractiveness, the individual is more likely to be absent, tardy, and become dissatisfied with the job itself. After studying compensation systems in Great Britain for more than 10 years, Elliot Jacques reported that "underpayment by more than 10 percent brings about enough dissatisfaction to make employees want to act to get their compensation boosted, and that underpayment by roughly 20 percent produces an explosive situation."[1] Thus, while its importance may vary somewhat from situation to situation, pay satisfaction can and usually does have a significant impact on both individual and organizational performance.

Pay equity

The question of fair pay involves two general factors: (1) what the employee is being paid for doing his or her job compared to what other employees in the same organization are being paid to do their jobs (*internal equity*); and (2) what employees in other organizations are being paid for performing similar jobs (*external equity*). It is not at all unusual for an individual to feel good about internal equity and bad about external equity or vice versa. For example, employees may feel very good about their pay in comparison to what their friends working in other organizations are making. However, a person may be very unhappy about his or her pay relative to several other people in the same organization.

If organizations are to avoid dissatisfaction with pay, employees must be convinced that both internal and external equity exist. A sound job evaluation system is usually the best method for ensuring internal equity. External equity is usually established through wage surveys. Job evaluation and wage surveys are discussed at length later in this chapter.

COMPENSATION POLICIES

Certain policies must be formulated before a successful compensation system can be developed and implemented.[2]* Naturally, these policies are strongly influenced by an organization's objectives and its environment. Policies must be determined concerning the following issues:

1. Minimum and maximum levels of pay (taking into consideration ability to pay, government regulations, union influences, and market pressures).
2. The general relationships among levels of pay (between senior management and operating management, operative employees and supervisors).
3. The division of the total compensation dollar (i.e., what portion goes into base pay, what portion into incentive programs, and what portion into benefits?)[3]

In addition to the above areas, decisions must be made concerning how much money will go into pay increases for the next year, who will recommend them, and generally, how raises will be determined. Another important decision concerns whether pay information will be kept secret or made public. The pros and cons of pay secrecy are discussed later in this chapter.

Compensation policies provide the guidelines necessary to develop and implement a wage and salary structure. Normally, the specifics of the structure are worked out by the human resource department. Figure 10–3 outlines specific policy issues that must be addressed by those developing and implementing the wage and salary structure.

Government and union influence on compensation policies

Many factors external to the organization also affect compensation policies and hence the wage and salary structure. Two of the most important are government legislation and union contracts.

---

*R. I. Henderson, *Compensation Management: Rewarding Performance*, 3d ed., 1979, pp. 264–65. Reprinted with permission of Reston Publishing Co., a Prentice-Hall Co., 11480 Sunset Hills Road, Reston, VA 22090.

Figure 10–3   Specific policy issues to be addressed when developing and implementing a wage
and salary structure

1. What is the lowest rate of pay that can be offered for a job that will entice the quality of employees the organization desires to have as its members?
2. What is the rate of pay that must be offered to incumbents to ensure that they remain with the organization?
3. Does the organization desire to recognize seniority and meritorious performance through the base pay schedule?
4. Is it wise or necessary to offer more than one rate of pay to employees performing either identical or similar work?
5. What is considered to be a sufficient difference in base rates of pay among jobs requiring varying levels of knowledge and skills, and responsibilities and duties?
6. Does the organization wish to recognize dangerous and distressing working conditions within the base pay schedule?
7. Should there be a difference in changes in base pay progression opportunities among jobs of varying worth?
8. Do employees have a significant opportunity to progress to higher-level jobs? If so, what should be the relationship between promotion to a higher job and changes in base pay?
9. Will policies and regulations permit incumbents to earn rates of pay higher than established maximums and lower than established minimums? What would be the reasons for allowing such deviations?
10. How will the pay structure accommodate across-the-board, cost-of-living, or other adjustments not related to employee tenure, performance, or responsiblity and duty changes?

Source: R. I. Henderson, *Compensation Management: Rewarding Performance*, 3d ed. 1979, pp. 264–65. Reprinted with permission of Reston Publishing Co., a Prentice-Hall Co., 11480 Sunset Hills Road, Reston, VA 22090.

The Fair Labor Standards Act (FLSA) The FLSA, commonly called the Wages and Hours Act, was passed in 1938 and has been amended several times. The primary requirements of the FLSA are that individuals employed in interstate commerce or in organizations producing goods for interstate commerce must be paid a certain minimum wage and must be paid time-and-a-half for hours worked over 40 in one week. Table 10–1 shows how the minimum wage has changed over the years. In addition, the FLSA places restrictions on the employment of individuals between the ages of 14 and 18. The most complex parts of the FLSA deal with possible exemptions. Amendments to the law have reduced the number of exemptions, but careful study of the FLSA is necessary to determine an organization's obligations.

In discussions of compensation systems, the terms exempt and non-exempt personnel are often used. Non-exempt employees are covered by the FLSA and must be paid overtime and are subject to a minimum wage. Managerial, administrative, and professional personnel are exempt from coverage by the FLSA.

The Davis-Bacon Act The Davis-Bacon Act was passed by Congress on March 3, 1931. The act requires that contractors and subcontractors

Table 10–1	History of minimum wage rates

Date	Rate per hour
October 24, 1938	$0.25
October 24, 1939	0.30
October 24, 1945	0.40
January 25, 1950	0.75
March 1, 1956	1.00
September 3, 1961	1.15
September 3, 1963	1.25
February 1, 1967	1.40
February 1, 1968	1.60
May 1, 1974	2.00
January 1, 1975	2.10
January 1, 1976	2.30
January 1, 1978	2.65
January 1, 1979	2.90
January 1, 1980	3.10
January 1, 1981	3.35

on federal construction contracts in excess of $2,000 pay the prevailing wage rates for the locality of the project. This prevailing wage rate, which is determined by the Secretary of Labor, has normally been the same as the prevailing union rate for the area.

The Walsh-Healey Public Contracts Act The Walsh-Healey Public Contracts Act was passed by Congress on June 30, 1936. This act requires that organizations manufacturing or furnishing materials, supplies, articles, or equipment to the federal government in excess of $10,000 pay at least the minimum wage for the industry, as determined by the Secretary of Labor.

The Federal Wage Garnishment Law Garnishment is a legal procedure by which an employer is empowered to withhold wages for payment of an employee's debt to a creditor. The Federal Wage Garnishment Law, which became effective on July 1, 1970, limits the amount of an employee's disposable earnings that can be garnished in any one week and protects the individual from discharge because of garnishment.[4] However, the law did not substantially alter state laws on this subject. For instance, if the state law prohibits or provides for more limited garnishment than the federal law, the state law is applied. Thus, a human resource manager must be familiar with his or her state laws relating to garnishment.

Equal Pay Act The Federal Equal Pay Act was signed into law on June 10, 1963, as an amendment to the Fair Labor Standards Act, eliminating pay differentials based solely on sex. The law makes it illegal to pay different wages to men and women on jobs that require equal

Open salary administration the polaroid way

Open salary administration means that information about pay is shared with and influenced by those people whose pay is being administered.

The Polaroid Corporation, like many other companies, has established a pay-level structure for its exempt salaried employees and, in keeping with its policy of openness, involves its employees in making salary-related decisions. According to Richard G. Terry, Manager of Salary Administration, "If employees know how they are being paid and why they are being paid that way, and if they know that they have a say in these matters, the need for earning more pay won't be foremost in their minds."

Polaroid's policy

Each salaried position at Polaroid is slotted into a particular pay level on the basis of its value to the company. When a new job is created, or when a job's requirements change, management conducts a detailed review of the position and then slots the job into its appropriate pay level.

Terry explains that an employee knows when his or her job is being reevaluated. As part of the process, both the incumbent and the managers who frequently interact with him or her are often asked to assist in the job analysis.

The job analyst's decision regarding a job's salary level is reviewed by a committee of compensation managers. It must receive final approval from a committee of division managers and corporate officers.

"The extensive attention each slotting determination receives provides a broad understanding of the process by·which job value is established," said Terry.

Salary adjustments

To make sure that its salaries are competitive, Polaroid conducts an annual survey of the salary levels of key jobs in its major divisions and at certain grade levels. These salaries are compared with those of similar jobs in a select group of high-technology industrial firms and the overall results are made available to Polaroid's work force.

"Using this and other surveys," Terry said, "Polaroid determines an adjustment to the salary range structure for each job and a salary increase budget to keep salaries competitive with the marketplace for the upcoming year. The adjustment to the salary range structure is announced in a letter from the president and posted companywide.

"Consulting a grid that relates the size of merit increases to performance level," he continued, "managers budget pay increases for employees. Before an employee's annual pay increase date (which usually occurs at the same time each year), the manager discusses the employee's performance level and salary increase with him or her—in the process informing the employee about the minimum, midpoint, and maximum of the pay range for the job, and his or her current position within the range. The employee is already familiar with the current structure because it is printed on pocket-size cards and distributed throughout the company."

Source: *Personnel*, May–June 1981, pp. 45–47. AMA-COM, a division of American Management Association, 135 West 50th St., New York, N.Y. 10020.

skill, effort, and responsibility and that are performed under similar conditions.

This law does not prohibit the payment of wage differentials based on:

1. A seniority system.
2. A merit system.
3. A system that measures earnings by quantity and quality of production.
4. A system based on any factor other than sex.

Union contracts

If an organization is unionized, the wage structure usually is largely determined through the collective bargaining process (Chapter 17). Because wages are a primary concern of unions, current union contracts must be considered in formulating compensation policies. Union contracts can even affect nonunionized organizations. For example, the wage rates and increases paid to union employees often influence the wages paid to employees in nonunioned organizations.

PAY SECRECY

Some organizations have a policy of keeping pay-related information secret. The justification for pay secrecy is usually to avoid any discontent that might result from employees knowing what everybody else is being paid. Further justification is that many employees, and especially high achievers, feel very strongly that their pay is nobody else's business.[5] On the other hand, pay secrecy makes it difficult for individuals to determine whether pay is related to performance. Also, pay secrecy does not eliminate pay comparisons but it may (1) cause employees to overestimate the pay of their peers, and (2) cause employees to underestimate the pay of supervisors.[6] Both situations can create unnecessary feelings of dissatisfaction. A good compromise on the issue of pay secrecy is to disclose the pay ranges for various job levels within the organization. This approach clearly communicates the general ranges of pay for different jobs but it does not disclose exactly what any particular individual is making.

JOB EVALUATION

Job evaluation is a systematic determination of the value of each job in relation to other jobs in the organization. This process is used for designing a pay structure, not for appraising the performance of individuals holding the jobs. The general idea of job evaluation is to enumerate the requirements of a job and the job's contribution to the organization, and then to classify it according to importance. For instance, a design engineer's job would involve more complex require-

Figure 10–4   Potential uses of job evaluations

To provide a more workable internal wage structure to simplify and make rational the relatively chaotic wage structure resulting from chance, custom, and such individual factors as favoritism or aggressive tendencies.

To provide an agreed-upon device for setting rates for new or changed jobs.

To provide a means whereby realistic comparisons may be made of the wage and salary rates of different organizations.

To provide a base for measuring individual performance.

To reduce grievances over wage and salary rates by reducing the scope of grievances and providing an agreed-upon means of solving disputes.

To provide incentives for employees to strive for higher-level jobs.

To provide facts for wage negotiations.

To provide facts on job relationships for use in selection, training, transfers, and promotions.

Source: D. W. Belcher, *Compensation Administration* (Englewood Cliffs, N.J.: Prentice-Hall, 1974), pp. 91–92. © 1974 by Prentice-Hall, Inc. Reprinted by permission.

ments and a potentially greater contribution to an organization than that of an assembler of the designed product. Although both jobs are important, a determination must be made concerning the relative worth of each. While the overriding purpose of job evaluation is to establish the relative worth of jobs, it can serve several other purposes. Fig 10–4 presents a list of potential uses of job evaluations.

The first step in a job evaluation program is to gather information on the jobs being evaluated. Normally information is obtained from current job descriptions. If current job descriptions do not exist, then it is usually necessary to analyze the jobs and create up-to-date descriptions.

The job evaluation process then identifies the factor or factors that are to be used in determining the worth of different jobs to the organization. Some factors frequently used are skill, responsibility, and working conditions.

The job evaluation process also involves developing and implementing a plan that uses the chosen factors for evaluating the relative worth of the different jobs to the organization. Such a plan should consistently place jobs requiring more of the factors at a higher level in the job hierarchy than jobs requiring fewer of the factors. Most job evaluation plans are variations or combinations of four basic methods: the point method, the factor comparison method, the job classification method, and the job ranking method.

Point method

Surveys have shown the point method has historically been the most widely used job evaluation plan in the United States.[7] It has the advantages of being relatively simple to use and reasonably objective.

When this method is used, a quantitative point scale is developed for the jobs being evaluated. One scale usually cannot be used to evaluate all types of jobs. For example, different scales are normally required for clerical and production jobs. Another scale is usually required to evaluate management and professional jobs. Usually, the human resource department decides which jobs are to be included in a specific evaluation scale.

Selection of key jobs After deciding which jobs are to be evaluated on each specific scale, key or benchmark jobs are selected from each type of job within the organization. Rather than evaluate each separate job, these representative jobs, usually numbering 15 to 20, are evaluated. Key jobs should be easy to recognize and well understood by the persons developing the evaluation scale. If there is any disagreement about the description of the job or what its pay should be, it should not be selected as a key job.

Selecting compensable factors Compensable factors are those factors or characteristics of jobs that are deemed important by the organization to the extent that it is willing to pay for them. The degree to which a specific job possesses these compensable factors determines its relative worth.

Early approaches to job evaluation proposed a set of "universal" factors. The belief was that a given set of factors, usually skill, responsibility, and working conditions, should apply to all jobs. This theory has gradually been replaced by one postulating that each organization must tailor its compensable factors to fit its own special requirements. Thus, complete adoption of any set of "universal" factors is not recommended.[8] For example, the compensable factors selected for evaluating production jobs might include skill, effort, and working conditions, whereas, the compensable factors selected for evaluating managerial or professional jobs might be knowledge, responsibility, and decision-making requirements. Compensable factors selected for unionized jobs must be acceptable to both management and the union.

In the point method, subfactors are used to describe compensable factors in more detail. For instance, the compensable factor of responsibility might include subfactors of responsibility for the work of others, for developing organizational policy, or for organizational assets. Degrees, or profile statements, as they are sometimes called, describe the specific requirements of each subfactor. Because each profile is unique, degree statements usually are in the form of written phrases. Figure 10–5 presents possible degrees and subfactors for the compensable factor of responsibility. Breaking compensable factors into subfactors and degrees allows for a more precise definition of the job and facilitates the evaluation process.

Figure 10–5   Possible subfactors and degrees for the compensable factor of responsibility

Subfactors	First degree	Second degree	Third degree	Fourth degree
Determining organizational policy.	May make suggestions to superior as to changes, most often minor, in organizational policy.	Often suggests changes in procedures applying mostly to affairs within departments.	May determine minor policies of organization with close control of supervisors; may interpret organizational policy to subordinates.	Determines organizational policy for large group of workers; incorrect execution would result in considerable loss.
Work of others; managerial ability required.	Responsible only for own work, including individual work or work of "flow" nature.	Small amount of supervision; performs mechanical operations and may control some work.	Supervises many workers or a department, organizing and coordinating with other supervisors.	Responsible for coordination of groups of departments.
Development and maintenance of goodwill with customers and public.	Very little contact with customers or public.	Only contact with customers and public is checked communications or occasional telephone calls.	Tact needed to avoid possible loss of goodwill through close contact with customers through letters or personal interviews.	Considerable contact with customers, other organizations, and public; tact and diplomacy needed.
Organization cash expenditures. Judgment needed in expenditures of organization funds.	Cash expenditures of not more than $100 monthly.	Cash expenditures of from $101 to 300 monthly.	Cash expenditures of $200 to 1,000 monthly.	Cash expenditures of from $1,001 to 5,000 monthly.

Source: adapted from J. L. Otis and R. H. Leukart, *Job Evaluation*, 2d ed. (Englewood Cliffs, N.J.: Prentice-Hall, 1959), pp. 110–11.

Assigning weights to factors Weights are assigned to each of the factors, subfactors, and degrees to reflect their relative importance. Naturally, the weight assigned varies from job to job. For example, skill might be the most important factor used in evaluating a machinist's job, while responsibility might be more critical to a supervisor's job.

While there are some systematic and helpful approaches for assigning weights, there is no one best method. Regardless of the technique used, both past experience and judgment play a major role in assigning weights. Generally, weights are assigned on the basis of a maximum number of points for any job; the maximum number allowed is often decided arbitrarily. Points are then assigned to the compensable factors, subfactors, and degrees on the basis of their relative importance. Table 10–2 presents a possible point breakdown that totals 1,200 points.

Assigning points to specific jobs After the point scale has been agreed upon, point values are derived for key jobs using the following steps:

Table 10-2   Example point values

Compensable factors	Subfactors	Degrees				
		1	2	3	4	5
Skill	Job knowledge	35	70	105	140	175
(325 points)	Experience	20	40	60	80	100
	Initiative	10	20	30	40	50
Effort	Physical	20	40	60	80	100
(300 points)	Mental	40	80	120	160	200
Responsibility	For company policy	20	40	60	80	100
(400 points)	For work of others	30	60	90	120	150
	For goodwill and public relations	20	40	60	80	100
	For company cash	10	20	30	40	50
Job Conditions	Working conditions	20	40	60	80	100
(175 points)	Hazards	15	30	45	60	75
					Total points	1,200

1. Examine the job descriptions.
2. Determine the degree statement that best describes each subfactor for each compensable factor.
3. Add the total number of points.

The point totals should bear the same general relationships as the actual pay scales do for the key jobs. For example, a rank ordering of the key jobs according to point totals should be approximately equivalent to a rank ordering of key jobs according to pay. This serves as a check on the appropriateness of the points that have been assigned to the degrees, subfactors, and factors. Nonkey jobs can then be evaluated in the same manner by determining the appropriate points for each factor from the scale and then totaling the points. Table 10–3 illustrates possible point totals for several banking jobs.

One drawback to the point method is the amount of time required to develop the point scale. However, once a scale has been properly formulated, it does not take long to evaluate the remaining jobs.

Table 10-3   Possible point totals for clerical jobs

Job	Points
Head teller	980
L & D (loan) teller	900
Teller	870
Secretary	750
Vault custodian	650
Proof-transit operator	600
Bookkeeper	540
Courier	500
Janitor	460

Factor comparison method

The factor comparison method of job evaluation was originated by Eugene Benge in 1926 to overcome the inadequacies that he perceived in the point method. The factor comparison method is similar to the point method, except that it involves a monetary scale instead of a point scale.

As with the point method, key jobs are selected. It is absolutely essential that the rates of pay of key jobs are viewed as reasonable and fair to all those making evaluations. Compensable factors then are identified just as with the point method. Unlike the point method, however, the factor comparison method does not break down the compensable factors into subfactors and degrees. Another difference between the two techniques involves the ranking of the compensable factors. In the factor comparison method, each factor is ranked according to its importance in each of the key jobs. This is done by assigning a rank to every key job on one factor at a time, rather than ranking one job at a time on all factors. For example, Table 10–4 gives a factor-by-factor ranking of key jobs within a bank. Many proponents of the factor comparison method suggest that these rankings be done once or twice at later dates without reference to the previous rankings to validate the rankings.

After each job has been ranked on a factor-by-factor basis, the next step is to allocate the wage or salary for each job according to the ranking of the factors. It is important to remember that one of the selection criteria of a key job is that its pay rate must be viewed as reasonable and fair to all the evaluators. Some proponents of the factor comparison method say that the pay should be allocated without reference to the factor rankings; others believe that the evaluators should refer to the factor rankings when apportioning the pay. Regardless of the approach that is used, the money allocation and the factor rankings must ultimately be consistent. If descrepancies occur that cannot

Table 10–4 Factor-by-factor ranking of key banking jobs

| Job | Compensable factor | | | | |
	Mental require-ments	Skill	Physical	Respon-sibility	Working condi-tions
Head teller	1	5	9	1	9
L & D (loan) teller	2	3	5	2	5
Teller	3	4	4	3	4
Secretary	4	6	8	5	7
Vault custodian	5	7	3	4	6
Proof-transit operator	6	1	7	7	2
Bookkeeper	7	2	6	6	8
Courier	8	9	1	8	3
Janitor	9	8	2	9	1

238

Table 10–5

	Compensable factor				
Job	Mental	Skill	Physical	Respon-sibility	Working condi-tions
Head teller	$120.00	$39.00	$15.00	$75.00	$12.00
L & D (loan) teller	95.00	46.00	33.00	60.00	19.00
Teller	90.00	45.00	39.00	51.00	21.00
Secretary	85.00	44.00	18.00	30.00	15.00
Vault custodian	58.00	21.00	60.00	36.00	16.00
Proof-transit operator	50.00	69.00	24.00	15.00	28.00
Bookkeeper	45.00	65.00	27.00	18.00	13.00
Courier	40.00	16.00	71.00	9.00	27.00
Janitor	30.00	18.00	66.00	6.00	31.00

be resolved, the position in question should be eliminated from the list of key jobs. Table 10–5 presents a sample pay allocation for the key jobs in Table 10–4.

As the final step in the factor comparison method, a monetary scale is prepared for each compensable factor. Each scale not only shows the order of ranking of the jobs, but also establishes the relative difference in pay for the jobs. Table 10–6 illustrates a monetary scale for the compensable factor of responsibility for banking jobs.

Other jobs are evaluated by studying their respective job descriptions and locating each job on the monetary scale for each compensable factor. The total worth of a given job is then determined by adding the dollar amounts assigned to each compensable factor.

Table 10–6   Monetary scale for responsibility requirements in banking jobs

Monetary	Key job	Monetary value	Key job
$ 6.00	Janitor		
9.00	Courier	$42.00	
12.00		45.00	
15.00	Proof-transit operator	48.00	
18.00	Bookkeeper	51.00	Teller
21.00		54.00	
24.00		57.00	
27.00		60.00	L&D (loan) teller
30.00	Secretary	63.00	
33.00		66.00	
36.00	Vault custodian	69.00	
39.00		72.00	
		75.00	Head teller

Job classification method

A third type of job evaluation plan is the job classification or job grading method. Certain classes or grades of jobs are defined on the basis of differences in duties, responsibilities, skills, working conditions, and other job-related factors. The relative worth of a particular job is then determined by comparing its description with the description of each of the classes and assigning the job to the appropriate class. This method has the advantage of simplicity, but it is also less precise because it evaluates the job as a whole. The number of required classes or grades depends upon the range of skills, responsibilities, duties, and other requirements that exist among the jobs being evaluated. Normally, 5 to 15 classes will suffice. Since 1949, the U.S. government has used the classification method to evaluate all civil service jobs.

Job ranking method

This is the simplest, oldest, and least used job evaluation technique. The evaluator ranks whole jobs from the simplest to the most difficult. Often, the evaluator prepares cards with basic information about the jobs and then arranges the cards in the order of importance of the positions. The job ranking method produces only an ordering of jobs and does not indicate the relative degree of difference between them. For example, a job with a ranking number of four is not necessarily twice as difficult as a job with a ranking of two.

Similarities and differences among job evaluation methods

The point and factor comparison methods are commonly referred to as quantitative plans because a number or dollar value ultimately is assigned to each job being evaluated. Numbers or dollars are assigned on the basis of the degree to which the job contains the predetermined compensable factors. The job classification and ranking methods, called nonquantitative techniques, compare whole jobs. The point system and the job classification system have a common feature in that they evaluate jobs against a predetermined scale or class, whereas the factor comparison and job ranking methods evaluate jobs only in comparison to the other positions in the organization. Figure 10–6 illustrates the similarities and differences in these four basic methods.

PRICING THE JOB

The factor comparison method of evaluation is the only technique that relates the worth of jobs to a monetary scale and, even with it, the results are derived from the wage scale that the organization currently uses. In general, job evaluation cannot be used to set the wage rate; however, it provides the basis for this determination. To ensure that external factors such as labor market conditions, prevailing wage

Figure 10–6 Comparison of basic job evaluation methods

Method	Basis for comparison	Scope of comparison
Point	Predetermined scale	Compensable factors (quantitative)
Factor comparison	Other jobs	Compensable factors (quantitative)
Job classification	Predetermined classes of jobs	Job as a whole (nonquantitative)
Job ranking	Other jobs	Job as a whole (nonquantitative)

rates, and living costs are recognized in the wage scale, information about these factors must be gathered.

Wage surveys

Wage surveys are performed to collect reliable information on the policies, practices, and methods of wage payment from selected organizations in a given geographic location or particular type of industry so that comparisons can be made.[9] Wage surveys are the primary method used to ensure external equity in an organization's wage and salary system. Data may be gathered from a variety of sources. The Bureau of Labor Statistics of the U.S. Department of Labor regularly publishes wage data broken down by geographic area, industry, and occupation. Industry and employee associations sometimes conduct surveys and publish their results. Trade magazines also may contain wage survey information.

In addition to using these sources, many organizations design and conduct their own surveys. To design a wage survey, the jobs, area and organizations to be studied must be determined, as must the method used in gathering data. If the wage survey is done in conjunction with either the point or factor comparison method of job evaluation, the key jobs selected for these methods are normally the ones that are surveyed. With the classification or ranking method, the same guidelines used for selecting key jobs with the point and factor comparison methods should be applied in choosing the jobs to be surveyed.

A geographic area, an industry type, or a combination of the two may be surveyed. The size of the geographic area, the cost-of-living index for the area, and similar factors must be considered when defining the scope of the survey. The organizations to be surveyed are normally competitors or others who employ similar types of workers. The most important and most respected organizations in the area should be chosen from among those that are willing to cooperate.

The three basic methods of collecting wage data are personal interviews, telephone interviews, and mailed questionnaires. The most reliable and most expensive method is the personal interview. Mailed questionnaries are probably most frequently used. However, questionnaires should only be used to survey jobs that have a uniform meaning throughout the industry. If there is any doubt concerning the definition of a job, the responses to a questionnaire may be unreliable. Another potential problem with mailed questionnaires is that they can be answered by someone who is not thoroughly familiar with the wage structure. The telephone method, which is quick but often yields incomplete information, may be used to clarify responses to mailed questionnaires. Figure 10–7 lists a sampling of topics that might be covered in a wage survey.

Wage curves

Wage curves graphically show the relationship between the relative worth of jobs and their wage or salary rates. In addition, these curves can be used to indicate pay classes and ranges for the jobs. Regardless of the job evaluation method used, a wage curve plots the jobs in ascending level of difficulty along the abscissa (X-axis) and the wage rate along the ordinate (Y-axis). If the point method is used for evaluation, the point totals are plotted against their corresponding wage rates to produce a general trend, as shown in Figure 10–8.

To ensure that the final wage structure is consistent with both the job evaluations and the wage survey data, it is sometimes desirable to construct one wage curve based on present wages and one based on the survey data and compare the two. Any discrepancies can be quickly detected and corrected. Points on the graph that do not follow the general trend indicate that the wage rate for that job is too low or too high or that the job has been inaccurately evaluated. Underpaid jobs are sometimes called green circle jobs; when wages are overly high, the positions are known as red circle jobs. These discrepancies can be

Figure 10–7   Possible topics in a wage survey

Length of workday	Vacation practices
Normal workweek duration	Holiday practices
Starting wage rates	Cost-of-living clauses
Base wage rates	Where paid
Pay ranges	How often paid
Incentive plans	Policy on wage garnishment
Shift differentials	Description of union contract
Overtime pay	

Figure 10–8 Wage curve using the point method

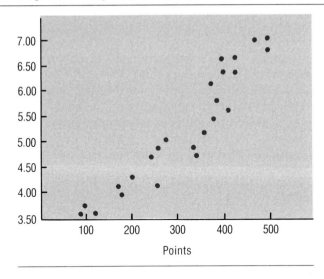

Points

remedied by granting either above- or below-average pay increases for the jobs.

Pay grades/ranges

To simplify the administration of a wage structure, similar jobs are often grouped into classes or grades for pay purposes. If the point method is used for evaluating jobs, classes are normally defined within a certain point spread. Similarly, a money spread can be used for defining grades if the factor comparison method is used. Figure 10–9 illustrates how grades might be formed for the jobs shown in Figure

Figure 10–9 Establishing wage grades

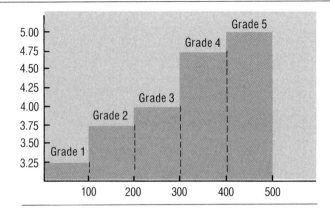

Figure 10–10   Establishing pay ranges within grades

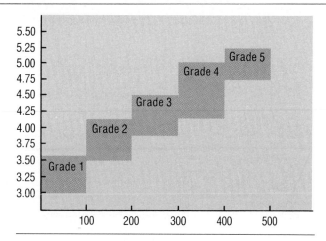

10–8. Usually at the same time that wage grades are established pay ranges are determined for each grade. The two possible alternatives are to have a relatively large number of grades with identical rates of pay for all jobs within each grade, or to have a small number of grades with a relatively wide dollar range for each grade. Most pay structures fall somewhere between these extremes. Ranges within grades are set up so that distinctions can be made among individuals within grades. Ideally, the placement of individuals within pay grades should be based on performance or merit. In practice, however, the distinction is often based solely on seniority. Figure 10–10 illustrates how pay ranges might be structured for the jobs in Figure 10–8.

On reaching the top of the range for a given grade, an individual can increase his or her pay only by moving to a higher grade. As shown in Figure 10–10, it is not abnormal for the ranges of adjacent pay grades to overlap. Under such circumstances, it is possible for an outstanding performer in a lower grade to make a higher salary than a below-average performer in a higher grade.

**BASE
WAGE/SALARY
STRUCTURE**

Figure 10–11 summarizes how the various segments of the compensation process fit together to establish the base wage or salary structure for an organization. Compensation policies are shown on all sides of Figure 10–11 to emphasize the fact that each step in the process is influenced by the organization's current compensation policies. Ideally an organization's compensation system should produce a base wage/salary structure that is both internally and externally equitable. The job evaluation process should ensure internal equity, while wage

Figure 10–11   Developing the base wage/salary structure

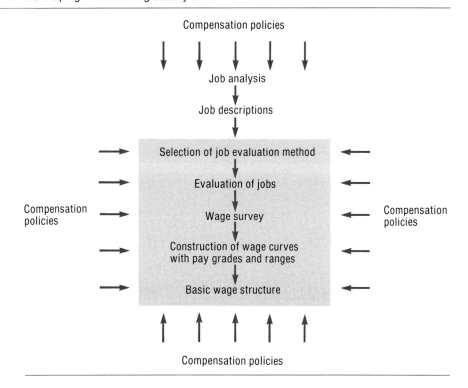

surveys should ensure external equity. The performance appraisal process, which is discussed in Chapter 13, is then used to position an individual employee within the established range.

SUMMARY

Compensation is usually composed of the base wage or salary, any incentives or bonuses, and any benefits. An organization's compensation system consists of the policies, procedures, and rules that it follows in determining employee compensation.

Pay dissatisfaction can influence an individual's feelings about his or her job in two ways: (1) it can increase the desire for more money, and (2) it can lower the attractiveness of the job. The question of fair pay involves both internal and external equity. Internal equity refers to what an employee is being paid for doing his or her job compared to what other employees are being paid to do their jobs in the same organization. External equity refers to what employees in other organizations are being paid for performing similar jobs.

Certain policies must be formulated before a successful compensation system can be developed and implemented. The effects of environmental factors such as government legislation and union contracts must be considered when formulating compensation policies. The Fair Labor Standards Act, the Davis-Bacon Act, the Walsh-Healey Public Contracts Act, the Federal Wage Garnishment Law, and the Equal Pay Act were all discussed in this chapter.

Nonexempt employees are covered by the Fair Labor Standards Act; they must be paid overtime and are subject to a minimum wage. Exempt employees are not covered by the act.

Job evaluation is a systematic determination of the value of each job in relation to other jobs in the organization. Most job evaluation plans are classified as either variations or combinations of four basic methods: the point, the factor comparison, the job classification, or the job ranking method. The point and factor comparison methods are referred to as quantitative plans because a number or dollar value is ultimately assigned to each job being evaluated. The job classification and ranking methods are called nonquantitative techniques and compare whole jobs.

In wage surveys, information is collected on the compensation policies, practices, and methods of wage payments of other organizations in the same or a related industry or in a given geographic area. The three basic methods for conducting a wage survey are personal interviews, telephone interviews, and mailed questionnaires.

Wage curves are used to develop a wage structure by combining the results of the job evaluation plan with wage surveys. These curves also help identify pay grades and pay ranges within grades.

REVIEW QUESTIONS

1. Define the three basic compenents of compensation and give examples for each.
2. Describe some of the potential consequences of pay dissatisfaction.
3. Distinguish between exempt and nonexempt personnel.
4. What is job evaluation?
5. What are the four basic methods of job evaluation?
6. What are compensable factors? subfactors? degrees?
7. What are wage surveys and how might they be conducted?
8. What is the purpose of wage curves?
9. What are job grades and ranges?

DISCUSSION QUESTIONS

1. Suppose your organization's recently completed wage survey showed that pay rates of several jobs were either less than or more than they should be. How might you bring these jobs "into line"?
2. The basic theory behind wage/salary administration is to pay people commensurate with their contributions. What should an organization do if an

individual's contributions to it are not in line with those of others in the same type of job? For example, suppose the company accountant's contributions are deemed to be far in excess of what is usual for someone earning an accountant's pay.

3. The choice of compensable factors is critical to job evaluation. How would you suggest that a job evaluator go about selecting such factors?

REFERENCES AND ADDITIONAL READINGS

1. E. Jacques, *Equitable Payment* (New York: John Wiley & Sons, 1961), p. 142.
2. Much of this section is drawn from R. I. Henderson, *Compensation Management,* 3d ed. (Reston Va.: Reston Publishing, 1979), pp. 264–65.
3. Ibid. p. 264.
4. This law is actually Title III of the Consumer Credit Protection Act. *The Federal Wage Garnishment Law, Wages and Hours,* Bureau of National Affairs, Policy and Practice Series (Washington, D.C., 1976), pp. 95:108b–108g.
5. P. Thompson and J. Pronsky, "Secrecy or Disclosure in Management Compensation," *Business Horizons,* June 1975, pp. 67–74.
6. E. E. Lawler III, "Managers' Perceptions of their Superiors' Pay and their Supervisors' Pay," *Personnel Psychology,* Winter 1965, p. 413; and Lawler, "Should Managers' Compensation Be Kept Under Wraps?" *Personnel,* January–February. 1965, p. 17.
7. C. W. Brennan, *Wage Administration,* rev. ed. (Homewood, Ill.: Richard D. Irwin, 1963), p. 143; and H. D. Janes, "Issues in Job Evaluation; The Union View," *Personnel Journal,* September 1972, p. 676.
8. Henderson, *Compensation Management,* p. 123.
9. Brennan, *Wage Administration,* p. 204.

Case 10–1

FAIR PAY FOR PECAN WORKERS

The Cloverdale Pecan Company is one of the country's largest processors of pecans. Located in a medium-sized southern town, it employs approximately 1,350 poeple. Although Cloverdale does own a few pecan orchards, the great majority of the nuts it processes are bought on the open market. The processing involves grading the nuts for both size and quality, shelling, packaging, and shipping them to customers. Most buyers are candy manufacturers.

Cloverdale, which was started 19 years ago by the family of Jackson C. Massie, its president, has been continually expanding since its inception. As do most growing companies, Cloverdale has always paid whatever was necessary to fill a vacancy without having a formal wage and salary system. Jackson Massie suspected that some wage inequities had developed over the years. His speculation was supported by complaints about such inequities from several good, long-term employees. Therefore, Jackson hired a group of respected consultants to do a complete wage and salary study of all the nonexempt jobs in the company. The study, which took five months to complete, confirmed Jackson's suspicion. Wages of several jobs were found to vary from the norm. Furthermore, the situation was complicated by several factors. First, many of the employees earning too much were being paid according to union wage scales. Cloverdale is not unionized, but most of its competitors are. Second, many of those in underpaid jobs were being paid at rates equal to similar positions in other companies in Cloverdale's geographic area. Third, because of a tight labor market, many new employees had been hired at the top of the range for their respective grades. The study also revealed that the nature of many jobs has changed so much that they needed to be completely reclassified.

1. *What should Cloverdale do to correct the existing wage inequities?*
2. *How could the company have prevented these problems?*
3. *If it is recommended that some jobs be placed in a lower pay grade, how might Cloverdale implement these adjustments?*

Case 10–2   **A DEAD-END STREET?**

Early in December, Roger Tomlin was called in for his annual salary review. Roger was a staff engineer for the Zee Engineering Company whom he had been with for just over ten years. In the past, Roger had usually received what he considered to be a fair pay raise. During this salary review, his manager, Ben Jackson, informed Roger that he was recommending a 10 percent raise. Ben went on to extoll the fine job Roger had done in the past year and to explain that Roger should be especially proud of the above-average pay raise he would be getting. Upon reflection, Roger was rather proud; in ten years, he had been promoted twice and his annual salary had gone from $17,000 to $32,000.

Things were rocking along just fine for Roger until he discovered a few weeks later that a new engineer right out of college had just been hired by Zee at a starting salary of $31,000. It really upset Roger to think that a new, unproven engineer would be starting at a salary almost equal to his.

Roger's first move was to talk to several of his colleagues. Most of Roger's fellow employees were aware of the situation and they didn't like it either. Luke Johnson, who had been an engineer with Zee for over 12 years, asked Roger if he realized that he was probably making less money, in actual dollars, than when he stated at Zee. This really floored Roger. Roger realized that inflation had eaten into everyone's paycheck, but he had never even considered the possibility that he had not kept up with inflation. That evening on the way home from work Roger stopped by the local library and looked up the consumer price index (CPI) for the past ten years. According to Roger's figures, had his pay kept up exactly with inflation, he would be making $30,500!

After a very restless night, the first thing Roger did upon arriving at work the next day was go straight to the personnel manager, Joe Dixon's office. After presenting his case about the new employee and about how inflation had eroded his pay, Roger sat back and waited for Dixon's reply.

Joe started out by explaining that he understood just how Roger felt. At the same time, however, Joe stated that Roger had to consider the situation from the company's standpoint. The current supply and demand situation dictated that Zee had to pay $31,000 to get new engineers who were any good at all! Roger explained that he could understand that, but what he couldn't understand was why the company couldn't pay him and other senior engineers more money. Joe again sympathized with Roger but then went on to explain that it was a supply and demand situation. The fact of the matter was that senior engineers just didn't demand that much more pay than engineers just starting!

1. *Do you think Roger is being fairly paid?*
2. *If you were Roger, how would you react to Joe's explanation?*
3. *Do you think a wage survey might help in this situation?*

Chapter 11

Incentive pay systems

Objectives

1. To develop an understanding of incentive pay systems.
2. To describe individual, group, and organizational incentive plans.
3. To distinguish between incentive plans for management and nonmanagement personnel.

Outline

Requirements of incentive plans
Individual incentives
  Piece rate plans
  Plans based on time saved
  Plans based on commissions
  Individual bonuses
  Bonuses for managerial personnel
  Stock options for managerial personnel
    Stock appreciation rights (SARs)
    Phantom stock plans

Restricted stock plans
Suggestion systems
Group incentives
Organizationwide incentives
  Profit-sharing plans
  Employee stock ownership plans (ESOP)
    TRASOPs/PAYSOPs
  Scanlon type plans
Making incentive plans work

Glossary of terms

Bedaux plan Incentive plan under which the incentive payment is based on a standardized unit of measurement, called a B. Incentive pay is determined by the number of Bs earned over standard in a given time period.

Bonus Reward that is offered on a one-time basis for high performance.

Commission plan Incentive plan which rewards employees, at least in part, based on their sales volume.

Differential piece rate plan Piece rate plan devised by Frederick W. Taylor that pays one rate for all acceptable pieces produced up to some standard and then a higher rate for all pieces produced if the output exceeds standard.

Employee stock option plan (ESOP) Form of stock option plan in which an organization provides for purchase of its stock by employees at a set fee for a set time period based on the employee's length of service and salary and the profits of the organization.

Group incentives Incentives based on group, rather than individual, performance.

Halsey premium plan Incentive plan under which the employee is paid a guaranteed hourly wage plus a premium for any time saved for producing a given quantity in less than standard time.

Incentive pay plans Pay plans designed to relate pay directly to performance or productivity; often used in conjunction with a base wage/salary system.

Incentive stock option (ISO) Form of qualified stock option plan made feasible by the Economic Recovery Tax Act of 1981.

Merit pay increase Reward that is based on performance, but which is also perpetuated year after year.

Organizationwide incentives Incentives that reward all members of the organization based on the performance of the entire organization.

PAYSOP Payroll-Based Stock Ownership Plan designed to replace the TRASOP (see below) as of January 1983. Under a PAYSOP, employer contributions are based on the pay of plan participants.

Phantom stock plan Special type of stock option plan which protects the holder if the value of the stock being held decreases and does not require the option holder to put up any money.

Profit-sharing plans Organization-wide incentive plans that generally divide a fixed percentage of net profits among employees.

Qualified stock options Stock options approved by the Internal Revenue Service for favorable tax treatment.

Restricted stock plans Plans under which a company gives shares of stock to participating managers subject to certain restrictions. The major restriction of most plans is that the shares are subject to forfeiture until they are "earned out" over a stipulated period of continued employment.

Rowan plan Incentive plan under which an employee is paid a guaranteed hourly wage plus a premium based directly on any time saved.

Scanlon plan Organizationwide incentive plan that provides employees with a bonus based on tangible savings in labor costs.

Stock appreciation rights (SARs) Type of nonqualified stock option in which an executive has the right to relinquish a stock option and receive from the company an amount equal to the appreciation in the stock price from the date the option was granted. Under an SAR, the option holder does not have to put up any money as would be required in a normal stock option plan.

Suggestion systems Most suggestion systems offer cash incentives for employee suggestions that result in either increased profits or reduced costs.

TRASOP Tax Reduction Act Ownership Plan established by the Tax Reduction Act of 1975 as an incentive to stimulate capital investment.

Your people should be encouraged to earn as much bonus as they can and then spend it on clubs, limousines, other corporate luxuries, or save it, or give it to charity.
However, the choice should be theirs. Don't ask your people to subsidize the ego of fat cats at the top.

Robert Townsend *

Incentive pay plans attempt to relate pay to performance in an endeavor to reward above-average performance rapidly and directly. Although good performance can be rewarded through the base wage or salary structure either by raising an individual's pay within the range of his or her job or by promoting the individual into a higher pay grade, these rewards are often subject to delays and other restrictions. Therefore, such rewards often are not viewed by the recipients as being directly related to performance. Incentive pay plans attempt to strengthen the performance-reward relationship and, thus, motivate the affected employees.

Because of minimum wage laws and labor market competition, most incentive plans include a guaranteed hourly wage or salary. The guaranteed wage or salary is normally determined from the base wage or salary structure. Thus, incentive plans usually function in addition to and not in place of the base wage or salary structure discussed in Chapter 10.

Incentive systems can be categorized in more than one manner. Probably the most popular manner has to do with whether the plan is applied on an individual, group, or organizational level. Additionally, plans are sometimes classified according to whether they apply to nonmanagement or to professional and management personnel. This chapter classifies incentives as individual, group, or organizational and, where appropriate, distinguishes between nonmanagement and management personnel within these categories.

REQUIREMENTS OF INCENTIVE PLANS

There are two basic requirements if an incentive plan is to be effective.[1] The first concerns the procedures and methods used to appraise employee performance. If incentives are to be based on performance, then employees must feel that their performance and the performance of others is accurately and fairly evaluated. Naturally, performance is easier to measure in some situations than in others. For example, the performance of a commissioned salesperson is usually easy to measure. On the other hand, the performance of a middle manager is often difficult to measure. A key issue in performance measurement is the degree of trust in management. If the employees distrust management, then it is almost impossible to establish a sound performance ap-

---

*R. Townsend, *Up the Organization* (New York: Alfred A. Knopf, 1970), p. 82

praisal system. Performance appraisal is discussed at length in Chapter 13.

The second requirement is that the incentives (rewards) must be based on performance. This may seem like an obvious requirement, yet it is often violated. Employees must believe that there is a relationship between what they do and what they get. Individual-based incentive plans require that employees perceive a direct relationship between their own performance and their subsequent rewards. Group-based plans require employees to perceive a relationship between the group's performance and the subsequent rewards of the group's members. Furthermore, the group members must believe that their individual performance has an impact on the group's overall performance. Organizational-based plans have the same basic requirements as group plans. Employees must perceive a relationship between the organization's performance and their individual rewards. Additionally, employees must believe that their individual performance affects the performance of the organization.

INDIVIDUAL INCENTIVES

While there are many types of individual incentive plans, all are tied to the performance of the individual as opposed to the performance of a group or the organization. The primary advantage of individual incentive systems is that the employee can readily see the relationship between what he or she does and what he or she gets. With group- and organization-based plans, this relationship is often not so clear. It is because of this advantage that individual incentives are the most frequently used type of plan. At the same time, individual incentives can have certain disadvantages. Competition among employees can reach the point of producing negative results. For example, salespeople might not share their ideas with one another for fear that their peers might win a prize that is being offered to the top salesperson. Quality is also sometimes sacrificed for quantity to reach an incentive.

Piece rate plans

As early as 1833, many cotton mills in England used individual piece rate incentives.[2] Piece rate plans are the simplest and most common type of incentive plan. Under such a plan, an employee is paid a certain amount for every unit he or she produces. In other words, an individual's wage is figured by multiplying the number of units produced times the rate of pay for each unit. The rate of pay for each unit is usually based on what a fair wage should be for an average employee. For example, if a fair wage for an average machine operator is determined to be $60 per day and it is also determined that the average machine operator should be able to produce 30 units per day, then the unit rate of pay would be $2 per unit.

Several variations of the straight piece rate plan have been developed. In 1895, Frederick W. Taylor proposed his differential piece rate plan. Under Taylor's plan one rate is paid for all acceptable pieces produced up to some standard, or set amount, and then a higher rate for all pieces produced if the output exceeds standard. Thus, if the standard were 30 units per day, an employee producing 30 units or less might receive $1.50 per unit. However, if the employee produced 31 units, he or she might receive $2 for all 31 units produced for a total of $62. Other plans pay a higher rate only for those units produced above standard.

Plans based on time saved

Incentive plans based on time saved give an employee a bonus for reaching a given level of production or output in less than standard time. Three common plans of this type are the Halsey premium plan, the Rowan plan, and the Bedaux plan. In the Halsey premium plan, the employee is paid a guaranteed hourly wage plus a premium for any time saved for producing a given quantity in less than standard time. For example, if an individual produces an hour's standard output in 45 minutes, he or she is paid the regular hourly rate plus a fixed percentage of the value of the 15 minutes saved. The Rowan plan differs from the Halsey premium plan in that the percentage paid for time saved is not fixed but is determined by the percentage of time saved. For example, if an individual produces standard output in 75 percent of the specified time, he or she would receive a 25 percent bonus on wages. With the Bedaux plan, payment is based on a standardized unit of measurement, called a B. Incentive pay is determined by the number of Bs earned over standard in a given time period.

Plans based on commissions

The previously discussed incentive plans are primarily applicable to blue-collar employees. However, there are incentive plans that apply to other groups of employees. One of the most prevalent types is based on commission. Many salespeople work under some type of commission plan. Although a variety of such plans exist, they all reward employees, at least in part, based on sales volume. Some salespeople work on a straight commission basis whereby their pay is entirely determined by their volume of sales. Others work on a combination of salary plus commission. Under this type of plan, a salesperson is paid a guaranteed base salary plus a commission on sales. Under a third type of commission plan, salespeople are paid a monthly draw which is later subtracted from their commissions. The purpose of the draw is to provide salespeople with enough money on a monthly basis to cover their basic expenses. The difference between a draw plan and the guaranteed salary plus commission plan is that the draw is really an advance against future commissions which must be repaid. The draw plan is especially useful for salespeople whose sales tend to fluctuate dramatically from month to month or season to season.

A commission plan has the advantage of relating rewards directly to performance. A salesperson on a straight commission knows that if her or she does not produce, then he or she will not be paid. A major disadvantage of commission plans is that things beyond the control of the individual can adversely affect sales. For example, a product might be displaced almost overnight by a technological breakthrough. Other environmental factors such as the national economy, the weather, and consumer preferences can affect a person's sales.

Individual bonuses

A bonus is a reward that is offered on a one-time basis for high performance. It should not be confused with a merit pay increase. A merit increase is a reward that is based on performance but which is also perpetuated year after year. A bonus may be in cash or in some other form. For example, many sales organizations periodically offer prizes, such as trips, for their top salespeople.

One potential problem with bonuses is that they can become an extension of salary. This occurs when awarding the bonus becomes practically guaranteed because the bonus is not tied to profits or some other measure of performance. In such circumstances, the recipients begin to expect the bonus. They do not view it as resulting from their individual performance or from the profits of the organization. Serious dissatisfaction can result if the expected bonus is not granted because of a decline in profits or for any other legitimate reason.

Bonuses for managerial personnel

By far the most common type of incentive for managerial personnel is the "annual" bonus.[3] A 1981–82 survey of 2,053 companies by the American Management Association reported that over 61 percent of the companies paid bonuses to managerial personnel.[4] Most plans provide a year-end bonus based on that year's performance, most often measured in terms of profits, but other measures may also be used. One company, Norton Simon, Inc., has tied their manager's annual bonuses to performance in the area of social responsibility.[5] Even though managerial bonuses are usually based on organizational or group performance, they are considered individual incentives because of the key roles that managers play in the success of organization. Typically, a bonus is paid in cash as a lump sum soon after the end of the performance year.[6] It is not unusual for executives to defer receiving some portion of a cash bonus until a later date for income tax purposes.

As can be seen from Table 11–1, the popularity of bonus plans grew

Table 11–1 Bonus plans, 1970 versus 1980

Type of business	Total companies	Percent with bonus plan	
		May, 1980	May, 1970
Manufacturing	419	90	65
Construction	65	89	no data
Retail trade	90	81	40
Commercial banking	248	55	19
Insurance	174	52	18
Gas and electric utilities	106	13	6

Source: H. Fox, *Top Executive Compensation* (New York: The Conference Board, 1980), p. 4.

substantially from 1970 to 1980. Bonuses often make up a substantial portion of total compensation. The American Management Association survey referenced earlier reported that bonuses composed 26.5 percent of the total compensation received by managers (See Table 11–2). Another interesting finding of this survey was that for higher-level managers the percentage was even greater (see Table 11–3). Table 11–4 shows the 1981 salaries and bonuses of some of the highest paid executives in the country.

Stock options for managerial personnel

Stock option plans are generally designed to give managers an option to buy company stock at a predetermined, fixed price. If the price of the stock goes up, the individual exercises the option to buy the

Table 11–2 Bonuses as a percent of total compensation and salaries

Industry	Number of companies	Percent paying bonuses	Percent of total compensation	Percent of salaries of recipients
Manufacturing				
Durable goods	800	65.5%	26.0%	35.2%
Nondurable goods	436	64.2	24.5	32.5
Petroleum and natural gas	40	57.5	26.6	36.2
Wholesale and retail trade	122	52.4	25.9	34.9
Utilities	119	21.8	21.0	26.6
Construction	37	72.9	24.2	32.0
Finance and insurance	201	49.7	23.1	30.1
Billion-dollar companies	294	73.0	29.1	41.1
U.S. Total	2,053	61.3	26.5	36.1

Source: *Executive Compensation Service Top Management Report*, 32nd ed. (New York: American Management Association, 1981), p. 14.

Table 11–3　　　　Bonuses as a function of managerial level

Position	Percent bonus to salary
Chief executive officer	44.2%
Chief operating officer	42.7
Executive vice president	38.6
Administrative vice president	38.3
Top marketing and sales executive	30.4
Top manufacturing or production executive	31.4
Top financial executive	35.2
All other positions	30.5

Source: *Executive Compensation Service Top Management Report*, 32nd ed. (New York: American Management Association, 1981), p. 14.

Table 11–4　　　　Salaries and bonuses of top U.S. executives

	Salary	Bonus	Total
David Tendler, co-chairman, Phibro	$1,285,000	$1,383,500	$2,668,500
Hal H. Beretz, president, Phibro	1,160,000	1,060,871	2,220,871
Steven J. Ross, chairman, Warner Communications	350,000	1,604,136	1,954,136
Sidney Sheinberg, president, MCA	330,000	1,382,918	1,712,918
J. Peter Grace, chairman, W. R. Grace	486,000	1,000,000	1,486,000
Rawleigh Warner, Jr., chairman, Mobil	590,786	887,000	1,477,786
Clifton Garvin, chairman, Exxon	716,667	713,745	1,430,412
Fred L. Hartley, chairman, Union Oil of California	508,333	823,074	1,331,407
Robert Anderson, chairman, Rockwell	—	—	1,309,666
William A. Marquard, chairman, American Standard	721,667	541,659	1,263,326
William Tavoulareas, president, Mobil	485,446	737,000	1,252,446
Paul Thayer, chairman, LTV	—	—	1,247,377
Harry J. Gray, technician, United Technologies	545,000	690,391	1,235,391
F. Ross Johnson, president, Nabisco Brands	410,000	793,900	1,203,900
Rand V. Araskog, chairman, ITT	497,500	650,582	1,148,082

Source: *U.S. News & World Report*, 24 May 1982, p. 60.

Minus numbers:
Math, science teachers are in short
supply; One solution: Money

To compete with industry, Houston urges
bonus plan and fills most vacancies

Houston—If any frontier is left in America, Robert Fliess believes that it exists in a cramped, wooden classroom, one of several barracks-like temporary structures on the lawn of Sharpstown High School.

Every weekday, Fliess works in this room, trying to teach basic chemistry and physics to five classes of ninth-graders.

And work it is. The other day, for example, a tall, blond-haired boy sauntered into class late, demanded to know why Fliess hadn't given him a paper (passed out earlier) and then said he hadn't done his homework. When Fliess said he would call in the boy's parents, the youth just laughed. His parents, he said, didn't care, either.

But Fliess cares very much. A stocky, balding 56-year-old with a spade-shaped beard, he views himself—perhaps with some justification—as akin to Uncas in *The Last of the Mohicans*. In a nation where science and math teachers are becoming a vanishing tribe, where test scores show a general decline in students' learning and analytical capabilities over two decades, Fliess decided last year to leave private employment and go back to teaching.

Widespread shortages

He picked a good time to do it. Last year, the National Science Teachers Association says, 43 states reported shortages of math teachers, 42 were short of physics teachers, and 25 percent of the math and science teachers surveyed by the association said they were planning to leave teaching for better-paying jobs in industry.

And Fliess also picked a good place to go back to teaching. Worried by the shortage of math and science teachers, Houston is attacking the problem with a tradition breaking, controversial approach. It's called money.

According to Billy Reagan, general superintendent of the Houston Independent School District, teachers with critical skills, such as science and math teachers, will be paid bonuses of $2,000 a year. If they agree to teach in some of the city's poorer neighborhoods, they get an addition $2,000. Then, if they are absent less than five days a year and if they teach in a school where test scores rise above the anticipated norm, they get another $1,300.

Considerable incentive

Because the average U.S. teacher makes about $19,000 for the school year, those bonuses can add up to a considerable incentive. They have reduced the Houston school system's teaching vacancies to 54 out of 10,000 teaching jobs, the lowest level in a dozen years. Only four of the vacancies are math or science positions.

Fliess's base pay is $20,000 a year, and evidently he is eligible for bonuses totaling $3,300 more. Still, he insists that he didn't come back just for the money. He loves teaching, and last year, after hearing Superintendent Reagan mention on a local radio show the urgent need for science teachers, Fliess talked to his wife about it. "For some foolish reason, she thinks there is prestige in teaching," Fliess says. Pretty soon, he adds, "I was hooked."

And so, after 15 years in the textbook-publishing and employment-agency businesses, Fliess stepped back into a classroom. Compared with the students he remembers teaching in a Long Island, N.Y., public-school system during the late 1950s and early 1960s, today's students seem to Fliess to have "much less" background in science. Some days, he finds that depressing, but he is approaching the problem with the attitude that "teaching has to be rigorous for it to be of any value" and the satisfaction that now he is in a position to try to do something about students' deficiencies. He considers this effort important.

"If there is no correction to this problem, we (as a nation) are going to go downhill so far that we aren't ever going to go uphill again," he predicts.

stock at the fixed price and realizes a profit. If, on the other hand, the price of the stock goes down, the stock option is said to be "underwater" and the manager does not purchase the stock. The theory behind such plans is providing an incentive for managers to work hard and increase company profits, thus increasing the price of the stock.

Before the passage of the Tax Reform Act of 1976, two major forms of stock options were available: qualified and nonqualified. Qualified stock options were those approved by the Internal Revenue Service (IRS) for favorable tax treatment. A qualified option was not taxed until the option was exercised and, in the interim, the option was treated as a capital asset. Income realized from the eventual sale of the stock usually was taxed as a long-term capital gain. To qualify for tax advantages, the stock option plan and the recipient had to adhere to certain conditions prescribed by the IRS. These conditions centered primarily around the length of time that the executive was required to hold the option before purchasing and selling the stock, and the basis for establishing the price that the executive paid for it. Nonqualified options are similar to qualified options except that they are not subject to as favorable a tax rate, but they also are not subject to the same restrictions.

As a result of the Tax Reform Act of 1976, with a few exceptions, no new qualified stock options were created after May 20, 1976. In addition, the act ordered that all qualified options in existence prior to the passage of the act had to be exercised before May 21, 1981. It also affected nonqualified options by increasing the period for which an exercised stock option had to be held to enjoy long-term capital gains tax rates.

Table 11–5 shows the increase in nonqualified stock option plans. The data reflect measurable gains in the adoption of such plans among manufacturers, retailers, and banks, but little change among the other categories listed. However, with the adoption of the Economic Recovery Tax Act of 1981, the qualified stock option was resurrected under the new name of incentive stock option (ISO).[7] Under an ISO, a manager does not have to pay any tax until he or she sells the stock, and

Table 11–5 Companies using nonqualified stock option plans

Type of business	Total companies	Percent with plan		
		May 1980	May 1978	May 1976
Manufacturing	478	68%	55%	56%
Retail trade	90	43	38	33
Commercial banking	248	23	17	13
Insurance (stock companies) . .	94	18	18	23
Gas and electric utilities	106	8	9	8
Construction (publicly held) . . .	20	55	56	n.a.*

*Not available.

Source: H. Fox, *Top Executive Compensation* (New York: The Conference Board, 1980), p. 6.

then up to $100,000 of the gain is taxed at the capital gains rate of 20 percent. The major drawback to ISOs is that the company granting such options does not get tax deductions, as it does with nonqualified options. Not surprisingly, managers are in favor of ISOs; but many compensation consultants have doubts about its benefits to the corporation because of the lost tax deduction.[8] At any rate, many companies, such as Exxon, Eastman Kodak, IBM, Tenneco, and United Airlines, have adopted ISOs in some measure.

Stock options often represent the largest portion of an executive's total compensation. For example, in 1981 Roland Genin, executive vice president of operations at Schlumberger received nearly $5.7 million in total compensation. Of this total only $438,000 was in the form of salary and bonuses; the rest came primarily from stock options. Table 11–6 shows the salary, bonuses, and long-term income for many of the country's top paid executives in 1981. The long-term income is primarily composed of stock options.

Stock appreciation rights (SARs) The most obvious trend among nonqualified stock options is the growth of *stock appreciation rights* (SARs).[9] Under an SAR, an executive has the right to relinquish a stock option and receive from the company an amount equal to the appreciation in the stock price from the date the option was granted. Table 11–7 shows how SARs have grown in popularity since 1976. The advantage of SARs is that the receiver does not have to put up any money to exercise the option, as he or she would with a normal stock option plan. Holders of SARs may have as long as 10 years to exercise their rights.

Phantom stock plans Phantom stock plans, also called performance share plans, can work in several ways. One is for the company to award stock as a part of its normal bonus plan. The receiver then defers this "phantom" stock until retirement. At retirement, the holder receives

Table 11–6 Salary, bonus, and long-term income of top paid executives (thousands)

	Salary	Bonus	Salary plus bonus	Long-term income	Total compensation
Roland Genin, executive vice-president, operations, Schlumberger	—	—*	$ 438	$5,220	$5,658
Frank G. Hickey, chairman, president and chief executive officer, General Instrument	$300	$ 324*	624	4,637	5,261
John W. Kluge, chairman and president, Metromedia	400	460	860	3,371	4,231
Jean Riboud, chairman and president, Schlumberger	—	—	700	2,329	3,029
Harry J. Gray, chairman, president and chief executive officer, United Technologies	545	480	1,025	1,946	2,971
Ray C. Adam, chairman and chief executive officer, NL Industries	400	421	821	2,083	2,904
Robert Cizik, president and chief executive officer, Cooper Industries	—	—	658	2,103†	2,761
David Tendler, co-chairman, president and chief executive officer, Phibro	—	—	2,125‡	544	2,669
August A. Busch III, chairman and president, Anheuser-Busch	—	—	721	1,896	2,617
Fred L. Hartley, chairman and president, Union Oil	508	1,033§	1,541	798	2,339
V. R. McLean, executive vice-president, NL Industries	160	143	303	1,944	2,247
Hal H. Beretz, president, chief operating officer and deputy chairman, Phibro	—	—	1,830	391	2,221
Robert Anderson, chairman and chief executive officer, Rockwell International	460	655	1,115	1,055	2,170
David S. Lewis, chairman and chief executive officer, General Dynamics	420	—‖	420	1,699	2,119
Daniel G. Schuman, chairman (retired), Bausch & Lomb	—	—	442	1,404	1,846
James R. Lesch, president and chief executive officer, Hughes Tool	—	—	501	1,334	1,835
J. Robert Fluor, chairman, president and chief executive officer, Fluor	—	—	984	733	1,717
Lester Crown, executive vice-president, General Dynamics	201	—‖	201	1,505	1,706
Ludwig Jesselson, executive vice-president and chairman, Philipp Brothers Division, Phibro	—	—	1,160	514	1,674
Robert T. Grohman, president and chief executive officer#, Levi Strauss	276	125	401	1,256	1,657
William M. Agee, chairman and chief executive officer,# Bendix	—	—	971	679	1,650
Richard L. Gelb, chairman, Bristol-Myers	510	350	860	633	1,493
Henry Rothschild, executive vice-president, Phibro	—	—	1,110	364	1,474
Chris J. Witting, vice-chairman, Cooper Industries	—	—	475	987	1,462
Rawleigh Warner Jr., chairman, Mobil	562	460	1,022	427	1,449

*Excludes deferred bonus awards.
†Includes value of unrestricted stock on which restrictions lapsed in 1981.
‡Includes special bonus for efforts toward company reorganization.
§Includes deferred amounts.
‖Not yet determined.
#Officer did not hold stated position for the entire year.

Source: *Business Week,* 10 May 1982, pp. 76–77.

Table 11–7 Growth in nonqualified stock option plans with stock appreciation rights (SARs)

Type of business	Nonqualified plans	Percentage of SARs		
		May, 1980	May, 1978	May, 1976
Manufacturing	320	61%	47%	21%
Retail trade	39	54	33	3
Insurance (stock companies)	17	53	44	9
Commercial banking	56	37	37	14
Gas and electric utilities	9	56	73	15
Construction (publicly held)	11	36	7	n.a.*

*Not available.

Source: H. Fox, *Top Executive Compensation* (New York: The Conference Board, 1980), p. 6.

the accumulated shares of stock or the equivalent value. The second form of phantom stock is very similar to SARs. The receiver is credited with phantom stock. After a stipulated period of time, usually three to five years, the receiver is paid in cash or equivalent shares, an amount equal to the appreciation in the stock. The major advantage of phantom stock plans is that the receiver does not have to put up any money at any point in the process. Also, if the value of the stock decreases, the holder does not lose any money.

Restricted stock plans Under a restricted stock plan, a company gives shares of stock, subject to certain restrictions, to participating managers.[10] The major restriction of most plans is that the shares are subject to forfeiture until they are "earned out" over a stipulated period of continued employment. As with SARs and phantom stock plans, the receivers do not put up or risk any of their own money. An advantage from the organization's viewpoint is that restricted stock plans provide an incentive for executives to remain with the organization.

Suggestion systems

The National Association of Suggestion Systems (NASS) estimates that approximately 6,000 formal suggestion systems and possibly an equal number of semiformal ones are in existence today.[11] Most suggestion plans offer cash incentives for employee suggestions that result in either increased profits or reduced costs. For example, Northern Natural Gas Company (NNG), a division of Inter North, Inc. reported suggestion-related savings in excess of $890,000 in 1980. Any ideas that are used are eligible for cash awards which can vary from a minimum of $20 to a maximum of $5,000.[12] In addition to the obvious potential cost savings that can result, suggestion plans can provide a means for making employees feel a part of the organization. A third potential benefit is improved communication between management and the employees.

Figure 11–1   Implementing a suggestion plan

Ownership life—How long the individual retains ownership of the idea

Award policy—How the amount or kinds of awards are determined and given out

Eligibility of subject matter—What is eligible for submission and evaluation and what is eligible for an award. (Some ideas may be eligible for evaluation, but may not be eligible for an award, depending on company philosophy.)

Eligibility of award compensation—The eligibility of an individual to receive an award is generally based on job responsibility in relation to the subject of the idea. Some systems do not permit management to receive awards. The highest eligibility level for award compensation is often the first-line supervisor.

Acceptable suggestions—After the purpose of the suggestion program has been determined by management, then guidelines and rules are developed which address the program's goals and philosophies, including acceptable areas for suggestions. For instance, some programs may be strictly concerned with cost reduction, so that suggestions on safety, housekeeping or public relations would not be eligible for an award.

Role of suggestion committee—If the suggestion program has a committee, then the rules which determine the authority, composition and other factors of the committee must be laid out. As an example, sometimes the suggestion committee is an awards committee awarding suggestions subsequent to implementation; sometimes it is a policy committee outlining acceptable suggestions and procedures and the philosophy governing the suggestion program; and sometimes the committee is a review or working committee which comments on, evaluates and acts on suggestions, basing their decisions on the guidelines of the policy committee.

Changes in the system—Each suggestion system plan should have a termination clause which states that the program can be terminated without notice at any time. However, if the plan is terminated, the company is still bound by the original contract regarding accepted suggestions and those still under review. This grandfather clause protects employees' suggestions and rights.

Property rights—For patentable ideas, the suggestion program should spell out ownership rights concerning patentability. Generally, these "property rights" belong to the company.

Administration—This covers such items as how to submit suggestions; when to submit them; what forms to use; appeal processes, if any; and other factors.

Source: Noyles, D. S. "Suggestion Systems: An Answer to Perennial Problems," *Personnel Journal,* July 1980, pp. 553–54.

Most suggestion plans have progressed far beyond the early 1950s "complaint box" on the wall. Modern suggestion plans generally involve specific procedures for submitting ideas and utilize committees to review and evaluate the suggestion. Figure 11–1 summarizes some general rules to be followed when implementing a suggestion plan.

GROUP INCENTIVES

Because jobs can be interdependent, it is sometimes difficult to isolate and evaluate individual performance. In these instances, it is often wise to establish incentives based on group performance. For example, an assembly line operator must work at the speed of the line. Thus, everyone working on the line is dependent on everyone else. With group incentives, all group members receive incentive pay based on the performance of the entire group. Many group incentive plans are based on such factors as profits or reduction in costs of operations.

Group incentive plans are designed to encourage employees to exert peer pressure on group members to perform. For instance, if a group member is not performing well, and thus lowering the production of the entire group, the group will usually pressure the individual to improve, especially if a group incentive plan is in operation. A disadvantage of group incentives is that the members of the group may not perceive a direct relationship between their individual performance and that of the group. The size and cohesiveness of the group are two factors that affect this relationship. Usually, smaller groups are more cohesive, because more individuals are likely to perceive a relationship between their performance and that of the group. Another potential disadvantage is that different groups can become overly competitive with each other to the detriment of the entire organization.

ORGANIZATION-WIDE INCENTIVES

Organizationwide incentives reward members based on the performance of the entire organization. With such plans, the size of the reward usually depends on the salary of the individual. Most organizationwide incentive plans are based on establishing cooperative relationships among all levels of employees. One of the first and most successful organizationwide incentive plans was the Lincoln Electric plan, developed by James F. Lincoln.[13] In addition to providing many other benefits, this plan calls for a year-end bonus fund for employees based on the profits of the company. Thus, the plan encourages the employees to unite with management to reduce costs and increase production so that the bonus fund will grow. Some of the most common organizationwide incentive plans include profit-sharing plans, employee stock ownership plans (ESOPs), and Scanlon type plans.

Profit-sharing plans

Profit-sharing plans generally divide a fixed percentage of net profits among employees. The percentage of the profits distributed can vary widely from company to company, but 20 to 30 percent is not uncommon. The division of these profits, which are given in addition to normal wages and salaries, usually is based on an employee's base salary or job level. However, many variations are possible including plans which give all employees the same amount, plans based on seniority, and plans based on individual performance. One potential drawback to profit-sharing plans is that the average employee may not perceive a direct relationship between his or her output and the performance of the entire organization. However, it is not unusual for executives and top managers to have a significant amount of their total compensation based on the profits of the company.

Employee stock
ownership plans
(ESOP)

An employee stock ownership plan (ESOP) is a form of stock option plan in which an organization provides for purchase of its stock by employees at a set fee for a set time period based on their length of service and salary and the profits of the organization. An ESOP is established when the company sets up a trust, called an employee stock ownership trust (ESOT), to acquire a specified number of shares of its own stock for the benefit of participating employees. The trust borrows a sum of money to purchase a specified number of shares of the adopting company's stock. Generally, the loan is guaranteed by the adopting company. Then, the company annually pays into the trust an agreed-upon sum necessary to amortize and pay the interest on the loan. As the stock is paid for and received by the trust, it is credited to an account which is established for each employee on the basis of his or her salary, in proportion to the total payroll of the participating employees. When the employee retires or leaves the company, the stock is either given to the employee or purchased by the trust under a buy-back arrangement.

The amount contributed to ESOP plans is limited to 15 percent of the total payroll of covered employees or up to 25 percent for plans in which stock bonus and other annuity plans are combined. The contribution of individuals is limited to the lesser of $30,000 or 25 percent of their annual compensation. One appealing feature of ESOPs is that they do have specific tax advantages for both the organization and the employees. For example, the organization can use pretax dollars to pay back the loan used to purchase the stock. Employees benefit by being able to defer any capital gains until the stock is actually distributed. Figure 11–2 summarizes the primary benefits of ESOPs for the organization, the employees, and the stockholders. It can be argued that ESOPs have a limited effect as incentives. The underlying assumption is that "having a piece of the action" will cause employees to take more interest in the success of the company. This assumption is often invalid simply because of the small amount of stock a given employee might have. Also, it is possible that the price of the stock may go down rather than up. Thus, some people view an employee stock option plan as more of a benefit than an incentive.

TRASOPs/PAYSOPs The Tax Reduction Act Stock Ownership Plan (TRASOP) was established by the Tax Reduction Act of 1975 as an incentive to stimulate capital investment. With a TRASOP, a company could establish a tax-qualified trust for employees and contribute stock

Figure 11–2   Major benefits of employee stock ownership plans

Organization	Employees	Stockholders
Allows use of pretax dollars to finance debt.	Favorable tax treatment of lump sum distribution, deferment of tax until distribution, and gift and estate tax exemptions.	Provides ready market to sell stock.
Increases cash flow.		Establishes definite worth of shares for estate purposes.
Provides a ready buyer for stock.		
Provides a counter to unwanted tender offers.	Allows employees to share in the successes of the company.	Maintains voting control of company.
Protects the company from estate problems.	Provides a source of capital gains income for employees.	Protects the company from having to come up with large sums of money to settle an estate.
Can result in substantial tax savings.		Can result in preferential consideration for a government guaranteed loan.

equal in value to up to 10 percent of the amount taken by the company as an investment tax credit. The primary advantage of a TRASOP was that company contributions were not charged against company earnings, but were treated as a tax credit.[14]

The Payroll-Based Stock Ownership Plan (PAYSOP) replaced the TRASOP in January 1983. Under a PAYSOP, employer contributions are based on the pay of plan participants rather than on the amount of the company's capital investments.[15] Most other provisions of TRASOPs apply to PAYSOPs. The PAYSOP is expected to grow in popularity over the next several years.

Scanlon type plans

The Scanlon plan was developed by Joseph Scanlon in 1927 and introduced at the LaPointe Machine Tool Company in Hudson, Massachusetts.[16] The Scanlon plan provides employees with a bonus based on tangible savings in labor costs, and is designed to encourage employees to suggest changes that might increase productivity. Departmental committees composed of management and employee representatives are established to discuss and evaluate proposed labor-saving techniques. Usually the bonus paid is determined by comparing actual productivity to a predetermined productivity norm. Actual productivity is measured by comparing the actual payroll to the sales value of production for the time period being measured. Any difference between actual productivity and the norm is placed in a bonus fund. The bonus fund is then shared by the employees and the company. Most Scanlon plans pay 75 percent of the bonus fund to employees and 25 percent to the company. Under the Scanlon plan, any cost savings are paid to all employees and not just to the individual who made the suggestions. Some companies have found that it is beneficial to review and modify their Scanlon plans periodically to take into account changes that might have occurred.[17]

NZ Forest Products Ltd. in New Zealand has introduced an incentive system similar to the Scanlon plan in that incentives are awarded on the basis of a "total productivity index."[18] Total inputs—labor, materials, and capital—and outputs of each production unit are constantly measured against a fixed standard. Employee incentives are then based on any improvements in total productivity. The interesting thing about the NZ plan is that employees are rewarded even when productivity improves solely through the introduction of more efficient machinery.

Figure 11–3 summarizes and categorizes the different incentive plans that have been discussed.

MAKING INCENTIVE PLANS WORK

Incentive plans have been in existence in one form or another for a long time. New plans are periodically developed, often as a result of changes in tax laws. As several examples in this chapter demonstrated, incentive compensation can make up a significant portion of an indi-

Figure 11–3   Summary of most used incentive plans

	Individual	Group	Organizational

Nonmanagers	Piece rate plans
	Plans based on time saved
	  Rowan plan
	  Halsey premium plan
	  Bedaux plan
	Commission plans
	Bonuses based on individual performance
	Suggestion systems
		Bonuses based on group performance	Lincoln Electric Plan
			Profit-sharing plans
			Employee stock ownership plans (ESOPs)
			  TRASOPs
			  PAYSOPs
			Scanlon type plans

Managerial	Bonuses based on organizational performance
	Stock option plans
	  Stock appreciation rights (SARs)
	  Phantom stock plans
	  Restricted stock plans
	Suggestion systems
		Bonuses based on group performance	Lincoln Electric Plan
			Profit-sharing plans
			Employee stock ownership plans (ESOPs)
			  TRASOPs
			  PAYSOPs
			Scanlon type plans

vidual's total compensation. This is especially true in the case of executives. If an incentive plan is to function as it is intended and generate higher performance among employees, it must be clearly communicated to employees and must be viewed as being fair. It is imperative that a clear explanation of all incentive plans be given to all affected employees. It also follows that the more employees understand an incentive plan, the more confidence and trust they will develop in the organization.

SUMMARY

Incentive pay plans attempt to relate pay to performance in an endeavor to reward above-average performance rapidly and directly. Most incentive plans function in addition to and not in place of the base wage or salary structure. Incentive systems can be categorized as individual, group, or organizational.

Two basic requirements are essential if an incentive plan is to be effective. The first is that employee performance be fairly and accurately evaluated. The second is that the incentives must be awarded on the basis of performance.

While there are many types of individual incentive plans, all are tied to the performance of the individual as opposed to the performance of a group or the organization. The primary advantage of individual incentive systems is that employees can readily see the relationship between what they do and what they get. Piece rate plans, plans based on time saved (Halsey premium plan, Rowan plan, Bedaux plan), plans based on commissions, individual bonuses, and suggestion plans are the major types of individual incentive plans in use today.

Bonuses for managerial personnel can and often do comprise a significant part of total compensation. Stock option plans for managers are generally designed to give managers an opportunity to buy company stock at a predetermined, fixed price. The theory behind managerial stock options is providing an incentive for managers to work hard and increase company profits, thus increasing the price of the stock. Under stock appreciation rights (SARs), a manager has the right to relinquish a stock option and receive from the company an amount equal to the appreciation in the stock price from the date it was granted. Phantom stock plans, also called performance share plans, and restricted stock plans are other special types of stock options designed for managerial personnel.

Because jobs can be interdependent, it is sometimes difficult to isolate and evaluate individual performance. In these instances, it is often wise to establish incentives based on group performance. Group incentive plans are designed to encourage employees to exert peer pressure on group members.

Organizationwide incentives reward members of the organization based on the performance of the entire organization. Some of the most common types of organizationwide arrangements include profit-sharing plans, employee stock ownership plans (ESOPs), and Scanlon plans.

REVIEW QUESTIONS

1. What are two essential requirements for an incentive plan to be effective?
2. Outline the advantages and disadvantages of individual incentive plans.
3. What is a piece rate plan?
4. What is an incentive plan based on time saved? Describe three common plans of this type.
5. Describe an incentive plan based on commission.
6. Define a stock option plan.
7. What is a suggestion plan?
8. Name the advantages and disadvantages of a group incentive plan.
9. Describe the most common types of organizationwide incentive plans.

DISCUSSION QUESTIONS

1. It has been said that "incentive plans only work for a relatively short time." Do you agree or disagree? Why?
2. If you were able to choose the type of incentive pay system your company would offer you, would you choose an individual, group, or organizational incentive plan? Why?
3. If you were president of Ford Motor Company and could design and implement any type of incentive plan, what general type would you recommend for top management? for middle management? for production employees?
4. Do you think that incentive plans are likely to increase or decrease in use over the next several years? Why?

REFERENCES AND ADDITIONAL READINGS

1. J. G. Goodale and M. W. Mouser, "Developing and Auditing a Merit Pay System," *Personnel Journal*, May 1981, p. 391.
2. S. Pollard, *The Genesis of Modern Management: A Study of the Industrial Revolution in Great Britain* (Cambridge, Mass: Harvard University Press, 1965), p. 190.
3. H. Fox, *Top Executive Compensation* (New York: The Conference Board, 1980), p. 4.
4. *Executive Compensation Service Top Management Report*, 32nd ed. (New York: American Management Association, 1981), p. 14.
5. D. Clutterbach, "Bonus Pay-Outs Linked to Social Responsibility," *International Management*, August 1978, pp. 49–52.
6. Fox, *Top Executive Compensation*, p. 4.

7. "No Sign of Recession in Pay at the Top," *Business Week*, 10 May 1982, pp. 76–77.

8. "New Game In Stock Options," *Dun's Business Monthly*, March 1982, p. 82.

9. Fox, *Top Executive Compensation*, p. 6.

10. Ibid., p. 7.

11. "Suggestion Systems, An Answer to Perennial Problems," *Personnel Journal*, July 1980, p. 553.

12. M. Olsen, "Implementing a Successful Suggestion System," *Personnel Administrator*, May 1982, p. 75.

13. C. W. Brennan, *Wage Administration*, rev. ed. (Homewood, Ill.: Richard D. Irwin, 1963), pp. 288–89.

14. "This Bonus Is a Real Incentive," *Business Week*, 14 March 1977, p. 54.

15. F. W. Rumack and R. E. Wallace, "The PAYSOP: A Gift From ERTA," *Personnel Administrator*, January 1983, pp. 66–69.

16. Brennan, *Wage Administration*, p. 299.

17. J. Ramquist, "Labor-Management Cooperation—The Scanlon Plan at Work," *Sloan Management Review*, Spring 1982, pp. 49–55.

18. S. Salmons, "Total Productivity Bonus Increases Involvement," *International Management*, September 1978, pp. 35–41.

Case 11–1 **REWARDING GOOD PERFORMANCE IN A BANK**

The performance of a bank branch manager often is difficult to measure. Evaluation can include such variables as loan quality, deposit growth, employee turnover, complaint levels, or audit results. However, many other factors that influence performance are beyond the branch manager's control, such as the rate structure, changes in the market area served by the branch, and loan policy as set by senior management. The appraisal system presently used by the First Trust Bank is based on points. Points are factored in for a manager's potential productivity and for the actual quality and quantity of his or her work. In this system, the vast majority of raises are between 4 and 10 percent of base salary.

Sales growth is a major responsibility of a branch manager. Although many salespeople are paid a salary plus bonuses and commissions, no commissions are paid on business brought in by a branch manager. Therefore, one problem for the bank has been adequately rewarding those branch managers who excel at sales.

In May 1976, the First Trust Bank opened a new branch on Northside Parkway, located in a high-income area. Three competing banks had been in the neighborhood for some 15 years. Jim Bryan, who had grown up in the Northside Parkway area, was selected as branch manager. In addition to Jim, the branch was staffed with five qualified women. Senior executives of the bank had disagreed about the feasibility of opening this branch. However, it was Jim's responsibility to get the bank a share of the market, which consisted at that time of approximately $28 million in deposits.

The result, after one year of operation, was that this branch had the fastest growth of any ever opened by the First Trust Bank. In 12 months, deposits grew to $6 million, commercial loans to $1 million, and installment loans to $.5 million. As measured by federal reserve reports, the new branch captured 50 percent of the market growth in deposits over the 12 months. The customer service provided for previously enrolled and new customers was extremely good, and branch goals for profit were reached ahead of schedule. Aware of the success, Jim looked forward to his next raise.

The raise amounted to 10 percent of his salary. His boss said that he would like to have given Jim more, but the system wouldn't allow it.

1. *Should Jim have been satisfied, since this was the maximum raise he could be given under the system?*
2. *Do you think the bank is currently offering adequate sales incentives to its branch managers? If not, what would you recommend?*

Case 11–2   **PART-TIME POOL PERSONNEL**

The Crystal Clear Pool Company builds and maintains swimming pools in a large midwestern city. Pool maintenance is handled through a contractual arrangement between Crystal Clear and the owners of the pools. Although individualized maintenance plans are available at a premium, the basic contract calls for Crystal Clear to vacuum the pools and adjust their chemical balance once a week. For 80 percent of the maintenance customers, the standard contract covers the months of May through September. The remaining 20 percent, who have either indoor or covered pools, require service year-round. Because of the seasonal nature of the work, Crystal Clear hires many students during the summer.

The maintenance staff is divided into three-person crews, each of which is assigned to service six pools per day. In the summer, one permanent employee and two student workers compose a team, with the permanent staffer responsible for training the students. All maintenance crews are paid on a straight hourly basis.

The present system has been in force for several years, but it has produced at least two problems that seem to be getting more serious each year. The first is that the students hired for the summer demand to be paid the same wage rates that apply to the permanent employees. This is because the college students can get other summer jobs at these rates and are simply not willing to work for less. Naturally, the permanent employees resent the idea of their pay being the same as the students. The second major problem involves the assignment of the pools, which vary in size and geographic location. The employees claim that this is unfair because of the travel time required and differences in pool size. Some pools take three or four times as long to clean as others. Thus, on a straight hourly wage, some teams must work harder than others to service the six assigned pools.

1. *What suggestions do you have for Crystal Clear to help remedy their compensation problems?*
2. *Can you think of any way to implement an incentive program at Crystal Clear? Do not ignore the scheduling problems that might be created by such a system.*
3. *In general, how do you think the problem of having to pay new employees the same rate as old employees can be resolved?*

Chapter 12

Employee benefits

Objectives

1. To discuss employment benefits mandated by law with special emphasis on social security.
2. To describe benefits that are provided voluntarily by organizations.
3. To stress the importance of clearly communicating employee benefits.

Outline

What are employee benefits?
Growth in employee benefits
Communicating the benefit package
Employee preferences among benefits
Flexible benefits
  Why are flexible plans attractive?
  Problems with flexible plans
Legally required benefits
  Social security
    Retirement benefits under social security
    Disability benefits
    Health insurance
    Problems facing social security
  Unemployment compensation
  Worker's compensation
Retirement-related benefits
  Pension plans
    Calculating benefits
    Pension rights
    ERISA
    Early retirement
    Mandatory retirement

Employees not covered by pension plans
Preretirement planning
Insurance-related benefits
  Health insurance
  Health maintenance organizations (HMOs)
  Dental insurance
  Supplemental medical and dental insurance
  Life insurance
  Accident and disability insurance
Payment for time not worked
  Paid holidays
  Paid vacations
Other benefits
The benefit package

Cafeteria plan of compensation and benefits Employees have the opportunity to choose how, from among a wide range of alternatives, their direct compensation and benefits will be distributed.

Disability insurance Designed to protect the employee if he or she experiences a long-term or permanent disability.

Employee benefits (fringe benefits) Rewards that an organization provides to employees for being a member of the organization, usually not related to employee performance.

Employee Retirement Income Security Act of 1974 (ERISA) Federal law passed in 1974 designed to give employees increased security for their retirement and pension plans.

Floating holiday Holiday that may be observed at the discretion of the employee.

Health maintenance organization (HMO) A health-service organization that contracts with companies to provide certain basic medical services around the clock, seven days a week, for a fixed cost.

Individual retirement account (IRA) Individual pension plan for employees not covered by private pension plans.

Keogh plan Pension plan for self-employed persons.

Private pension plans Employee benefit which provides a source of income to people who have retired; funded either entirely by the organization or jointly by the organization and employee during his or her employment.

Social security Federally administered insurance system designed to provide funds upon retirement or disability or both and to provide hospital and medical reimbursement to people who have reached reitrement age.

Unemployment compensation Form of insurance designed to provide funds to employees who have lost their jobs and are seeking other jobs.

Vesting The rights of individuals to receive the money paid into a pension or retirement fund on their behalf by their employer if they should leave the organization prior to retirement.

Worker's compensation Form of insurance that protects employees from loss of income and extra expenses associated with job-related injuries or illness.

The very expensive but often forgotten stepchild of the total compensation package is that segment frequently called *fringe benefits*. These benefits are primarily the in-kind payments employees receive in addition to the payments they receive in the form of money. At one time, fringe benefits were of marginal importance, but this is no longer true. In many organizations today, they account for at least 35 percent of the total compensation cost for each employee, and possibly in the next decade they will reach 50 percent. (Some organizations have already exceeded this point.) When an element of the compensation package reaches this proportion, it is no longer marginal. The fringe benefits of yesterday have evolved into the employee benefits and services of today.

Richard I. Henderson *

Employee benefits, sometimes called fringe benefits, are those rewards that organizations provide to employees for being a member of the organization. Unlike wages, salaries, and incentives, benefits are usually not related to employee performance. Figures compiled by the U.S. Chamber of Commerce show that payments by organizations for employee benefits in 1981 averaged slightly over $6,600 per year per employee.[1] These same figures indicated that benefit payments varied widely among the reporting companies, ranging from under $3,000 to more than $11,000 per year per employee. The average of slightly over $6,600 represents approximately 37 percent of total compensation received by the average employee.

The term "fringe benefits" was coined over 40 years ago by the War Labor Board.[2] Reasoning that employer-provided benefits such as paid vacations, holidays, and pensions were "on the fringe of wages" the agency exempted them from pay controls.[3] It has been argued that this action, more than any single event, led to the dramatic expansion of employee benefits that has since occurred. However, because of the significance of benefits to total compensation, the word "fringe" has been dropped by many employers for fear that it has a minimizing effect.[4]

WHAT ARE EMPLOYEE BENEFITS?

Figure 12–1 presents a listing of potential employee benefits. In general, these can be grouped into five major categories: (1) legally required, (2) retirement related, (3) insurance related, (4) payment for time not worked, and (5) other. Figure 12–2 categorizes many of the most common employee benefits.

Table 12–1 shows approximately how total benefit expenditures are allocated among the major categories. It should also be pointed out that most benefits apply to all members of the organization; however, some are reserved solely for executives. It is interesting to note that some of the examples listed in Figure 12–1 are now taken for granted by many employees.

---

*R. I. Henderson *Compensation Management: Rewarding Performance,* 3d ed. (Reston, Va.: Reston Publishing, 1979), p. 308.

Figure 12–1   Possible employee benefits

Accidental death, dismemberment insurance	Opportunity for travel
Birthdays (vacation)	Outside medical services
Bonus eligibility	Paid attendance at business, professional, and other outside meetings
Business and professional memberships	Parking facilities
Cash profit sharing	Pension
Club memberships	Personal accident insurance
Commissions	Personal counseling
Company medical assistance	Personal credit cards
Company-provided automobile	Personal expense accounts
Company-provided housing	Physical examinations
Company-provided or subsidized travel	Political activities (time off)
Day-care centers	Price discount plan
Deferred bonus	Private office
Deferred compensation plan	Professional activities
Deferred profit sharing	Psychiatric services
Dental and eye-care insurance	Recreation facilities
Discount on company products	Resort facilities
Education costs	Retirement gratuity
Educational activities (time off)	Sabbatical leaves
Employment contract	Salary
Executive dining room	Salary continuation
Free checking account	Savings plan
Free or subsidized lunches	Scholarships for dependents
Group automobile insurance	Severance pay
Group homeowners' insurance	Shorter or flexible workweek
Group life insurance	Sickness and accident insurance
Health maintenance organization fees	Social security
Holidays (extra)	Social service sabbaticals
Home health care	Split-dollar life insurance
Hospital-surgical-medical insurance	State disability plans
Incentive growth fund	Stock appreciation rights
Interest-free loans	Stock bonus plan
Layoff pay (S.U.B.)	Stock option plans (qualified, nonqualified, tandem)
Legal, estate-planning, and other professional assistance	Stock purchase plan
Loans of company equipment	Survivors' benefits
Long-term disability benefit	Tax assistance
Matching educational donations	Training programs
Nurseries	Vacations
Nursing-home care	Wages
	Weekly indemnity insurance

Source: D. J. Thomsen, "Introducing Cafeteria Compensation in Your Company," *Personnel Journal*, March 1977, p. 125. Reprinted with permission.

GROWTH IN EMPLOYEE BENEFITS

Prior to the passage of the Social Security Act in 1935, employee benefits were not widespread. The act not only mandated certain benefits, but its implementation greatly increased the general public's awareness of the area of employee benefits. By this same time, unions had grown in strength and had begun to demand more benefits in their contracts. Thus, the 1930s are generally viewed as the birth years for employee benefits of any widespread significance.

Figure 12–2   Examples of benefits by major category

Legally required	Retirement related	Insurance related	Payment for time not worked	Other
Social security	Pension fund	Medical insurance	Vacation	Company discounts
Unemployment compensation	Annuity plan	Accident insurance	Holidays	Meals furnished by company
Worker's compensation	Early retirement	Life insurance	Sick leave	Moving expenses
State disability insurance	Disability retirement benefits	Disability insurance	Military leave	Severance pay
	Retirement gratuity	Dental insurance	Election day	Tuition refunds
		Survivor benefits	Birthdays	Credit union
			Funerals	Company car
			Paid rest periods	Legal services
			Lunch periods	Financial counseling
			Wash-up time	Recreation facilities
			Travel time	

Table 12–1   Benefit expenditures by major categories

Legally required benefits (employer's share only)	25%
Retirement related	15
Insurance related	19
Payment for time not worked	37
Other	4
Total	100%

Source: Based on figures from U.S. Chamber Survey Research Center, *Employee Benefits, 1980* (Washington, D.C.: Chamber of Commerce of the United States, 1981), p. 8.

As productivity continued to increase through and after World War II, more and more employee benefits came into existence. Benefits have continued to expand since World War II. The U.S. Chamber of Commerce researched how benefit coverage had changed in 186 companies from 1959 to 1980. Although the categories used are different from those described earlier, Figure 12–3 shows how employee benefits have grown from 24.7 percent of payroll in 1959 to 41.4 percent of payroll in 1980.

COMMUNICATING THE BENEFIT PACKAGE

Although most organizations provide some form of benefits to their employees, the average employee often has little idea of what he or she is receiving.[5] Why are employees often not aware of their benefits? One explanation is that organizations don't make much of an effort to

Figure 12–3   Comparison of employee benefits for 186 companies (1959–1980)

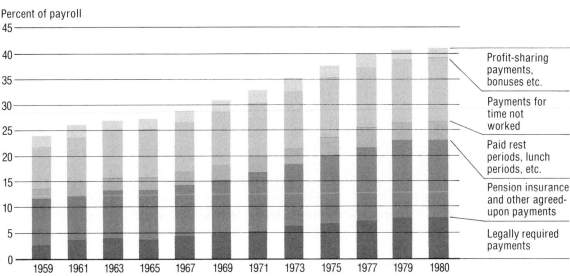

Percent of payroll

Profit-sharing payments, bonuses etc.

Payments for time not worked

Paid rest periods, lunch periods, etc.

Pension insurance and other agreed-upon payments

Legally required payments

Source: U.S. Chamber Survey Research Center, *Employee Benefits, 1980* (Washington, D.C.: Chamber of Commerce of the United States, 1981), p. 28. Reprinted with permission.

communicate their employee benefits. A survey conducted in 1978 reported that a majority of the companies studied spent no more than $10 per employee per year on communicating their benefits.[6] It is interesting that more than half of these companies reported placing a "high priority" on benefit communications. Another possible explanation of why employees are not aware of their benefits is that descriptive material on benefits, when available, is often not easily understood by employees. One provision of the Employment Retirement Income Security Act of 1974 (ERISA) requires an employer at specified intervals to communicate certain types of benefit information in a manner employees can understand. Several methods can be used to evaluate the readability of written documents. Generally, in these methods, the number of words per sentence and the percentage of difficult, polysyllabic words in the passage are counted in a readability index that is related to a school grade reading level.[7] The basic goal is to match the readability index of the benefit description to the educational level of the organization's employees.

The method used in communicating the benefit package is as important as the readability of the document. One successful method of communication is a personalized statement that is sent periodically to each employee. The "Employee Earnings and Benefits Letter" shown in Figure 12–4 is an example of such a statement. For organizations

Figure 12–4   Sample employee earnings and benefits letter

Company name
Address
Date

Employee's Name
Address

Dear

Enclosed are your W-2 forms showing the amount of taxable income that you received from _____ during 19__. Listed below in Section A are your gross wages and a cost breakdown of various fringe benefit programs that you enjoy. In addition to the money you received as wages, the company paid benefits for you which are not included in your W-2 statement. These are fringe benefits that are sometimes overlooked. In an easy-to-read form, here's what _____ paid to you in 19__:

Section A—Paid to you in your W-2 earnings

Cost-of-living allowance	_____
Shift premium	_____
Service award(s)	_____
Vacation pay	_____
Holiday pay	_____
Funeral pay	_____
Jury Duty pay	_____
Military pay	_____
Accident & sickness benefits	_____
Regular earnings	_____
Overtime earnings	_____
Alowances	_____
Gross wages	_____

Section B—Paid for you and not included in your W-2 earnings:

Company contribution to pension plan	
Company cost of your hospitalization payments	_____
Company cost of your life & accidental death insurance	_____
Company cost for social security tax on your wages	_____
Company cost of the premium for your workers compensation	_____
Company cost for the tax on your wages for unemployment compensation	_____
Company cost for tuition refund	_____
Company cost for safety glasses	_____
Total cost of benefits not included in W-2 earnings	_____

Total _____ paid
for your services in 19__   _____

You have earned the amount on the bottom line, but we want to give you a clearer idea of the total cost of your services to the company, and the protection and benefits that are being purchased for you and your family.

Sincerely,

Personnel Manager

Source: Adapted from J. C. Claypool and J. P. Cargemi, "The Annual Employee Earnings and Benefits Letter," *Personnel Journal*, July 1980, p. 564.

that use a computerized payroll system, some benefit information can easily be printed on each employee's check stub. Other methods for communicating benefit information include posters and visual presentations, such as movies, slide shows, and flip charts. Meetings and conferences can also be used to explain an organization's benefits.

EMPLOYEE PREFERENCES AMONG BENEFITS

If an organization expects to get the maximum return from its fringe benefit package in terms of such factors as motivation, satisfaction, low turnover, and good relations with unions, the benefits should be those most preferred by its employees. Ironically, however, organizations traditionally have done little to ensure that this is the case. Historically, they have offered uniform benefit packages selected by the personnel department and top management. Only on rare occasions are employees consulted concerning their benefit preferences.

Organizations that provide benefits without input from employees are assuming that management always knows what is best for the employees and that all employees need and desire the same benefits. A recent study found that sex, age, marital status, number of dependents, years of service, and job title generally appeared to influence benefit preferences.[8] For example, older employees wanted pension increases more than did younger employees. Thus, the problem of determining employee preferences is compounded by the fact that different groups of employees often have different preferences.

FLEXIBLE BENEFITS

Because different employees have different benefit needs and preferences, some organizations have begun to offer flexible benefit plans. Flexible compensation is a system under which each individual has some choice as to the form of all or a portion of his or her total compensation.[9] Employees select from among several options the distribution of their direct compensation and benefits. The idea is to allow employees to select benefits most appropriate to their individual needs and lifestyles.[10] For example, a middle-aged employee with several children in school might choose to take a different set of benefits from those chosen by a young, single employee. Flexible plans are also called "cafeteria plans" because they provide a "menu," or choice of benefits from which employees select.[11] The possibilities for choice within a flexible benefit plan may vary considerably from plan to plan. Some plans limit the choices to only a few types of coverages such as life insurance and health insurance.[12] Others allow employees to choose from a wide range of options.

American Can Company and North American Van Lines (a subsidiary of PepsiCo) are two companies that have successfully implemented flexible benefit plans on a large scale. At American Can, the plan has been expanded to 9,000 employees and at North American Van Lines over 2,000 employees are covered.[13] Approximately 92 percent of the American Can employees reported that they felt they had substantially improved their benefit program with the flexible plan.[14] Other studies have shown that flexible plans have also been well received in small firms.[15]

Why are flexible plans attractive?

Several reasons explain why flexible plans might be of interest to organizations:[16]

1. Employee benefits are an increasing component of overall compensation. Thus, benefits are taking on more and more significance.
2. Lifestyles have changed in the past several years, causing employees to reevaluate the need for certain traditional benefits. For example, in a family where both spouses work and receive family medical insurance, one coverage is sufficient.
3. Benefits can be useful in recruiting and retaining employees. However, when a mandatory benefit package is largely unresponsive to a prospective employee's needs or to the retention of present employees, the organization is wasting money.
4. The increasing cost of benefits is causing organizations to try to effectively communicate the real costs to the employee. By making specific benefit choices, the employee becomes intimately familiar with the costs associated with each benefit.
5. Because certain benefits are taxable and others are not, different benefit mixes can be attractive to different employees. Figure 12–5 summarizes some of the more common taxable and nontaxable benefits. Some people have suggested limiting flexible benefits only to those that are nontaxable.[17] This keeps the organization from having to value the taxable benefits for IRS purposes.
6. A flexible plan can have a positive impact on employee attitudes and behavior.

Problems with flexible plans

Unfortunately, flexible plans are not without their difficulties. The major difficulties are summarized below.[18]

1. A flexible plan requires more effort to administer.
2. Unions generally oppose flexible plans because they are required to give up control over the program details or they may lose some of their previously negotiated benefit improvements.
3. Employees may not choose those benefits that are in their own best interests.
4. Tax laws limit the amount of individual flexibility. For example, the 1978 Tax Reform Act specifically prohibits deferred compensation plans from being included in a flexible benefits program.

Figure 12–5   Taxable and nontaxable benefits

Taxable income to employee

Group term life insurance greater than $50,001   Pension plan contributions
Whole life insurance   Legal services
Additional vacation days   Employee vehicle
Cash   Employer contributions to savings fund
Day-care facilities   Group auto insurance
Bonus eligibility   Homeowner's insurance
Education costs   Housing
Extra holidays   Free checking account
Employee selected travel   Nursing-home care
Resort facilities   Personal expense account
Salary increase   Retirement gratuity
Personal liability insurance   Stock bonus plan

Nontaxable income to employee

Group term life insurance less than $50,000   Disability insurance
Hospital and major medical insurance   Accident insurance
Dental care   Uniform allowance
Optical care   Business membership
Executive dining room   Discounts on company products
Interest-free loans   HMO
Parking facilities   Matching charitable contributions
Flexible workweek   Private office
Tax assistance   Stock purchase
                                                      Vision care

Source: R. B. Cockrum, "Has the Time Come for Employee Cafeteria Plans?" *Personnel Administrator*, July 1982, p. 68.

Although implementation of a flexible type of compensation and benefits system is not simple, the potential gains from it are attractive enough to merit consideration.

LEGALLY REQUIRED BENEFITS

As discussed earlier, certain benefits have been mandated by law. The purpose of this section is to discuss these.

Social security

Social security is a federally administered insurance system. Under federal laws in force at the present time, both an employer and employee must pay into the system. Currently, a certain percentage of the employee's salary is paid up to a maximum limit. Table 12–2 shows how social security costs have changed over the past several years and how they are scheduled to change through 1990. In 1984, the tax rate is scheduled to be 7 percent and the maximum taxable pay is scheduled to be $36,000; thus, the most that any employee would pay into social security would be $2,520. With few exceptions, social security is mandatory for employees and employers. The most noteworthy exceptions are state and local government employees. For these employ-

Table 12–2   Changes in social security costs

Year	Percentage paid by employee	Maximum taxable pay	Maximum tax
1978	6.05	$17,700	$1,071
1979	6.13	22,900	1,404
1980	6.13	25,900	1,588
1981	6.65	29,700	1,975
1982	6.70	32,400	2,171
1983	6.70	35,700	2,392
1984	7.00	36,000*	2,520
1985	7.05	38,100*	2,686
1986	7.15	40,000*	2,874
1987	7.15	42,600*	3,046
1988	7.51	n.a.†	n.a.
1989	7.51	n.a.	n.a.
1990	7.65	n.a.	n.a.

*These figures are subject to being raised by Congress.
†Not available.

ees to become exempt, a majority must vote to do so and another retirement system must be substituted. Self-employed persons are required to contribute to social security at a rate higher than that paid by a normal employee but less than the combined percentage paid by both employer and employee. The payments distributed under social security can be grouped into three major categories: retirement benefits, disability benefits, and health insurance.

Retirement benefits under social security To be eligible for periodic payments through social security, a person must have reached retirement age, must actually be retired, and must be fully insured under the system. The full periodic allotment to which the retiree is entitled may begin at age 65 (this is scheduled to increase to age 67 by 2027); those who retire as early as age 62 receive lesser amounts. A person is considered fully retired if he or she is earning from gainful employment less than a prescribed amount of money.[19] In 1983, this was $6,600 for people aged 65 and over; however, the amount changes almost every year. Money earned from gainful employment does not include income from investments, pensions, or other retirement programs. In 1984, one half of an individual's social security benefits will be taxed if his or her gross income is over $25,000 or over $32,000 for spouses filing a joint tax return. Persons 70 and older are eligible for full retirement benefits regardless of their level of earned income.

To become fully insured, an employee must have at least as many quarters of coverage as the number of years elapsing between 1950 (or the year that he or she reached age 21, if later than 1950) and the year the person reached age 65 for men and 62 for women. However, a

Table 12–3

Calculating fully insured requirements

Date of birth	Year eligibility was calculated	Number of quarters required to be fully insured
1920	1984	1984 − 1950 = 34
1940	1984	1984 − (1940 + 21) = 23

person with 40 quarters of coverage is fully insured for life and needs no additional covered employment to qualify for retirement benefits. Table 12–3 gives some examples of how to calculate the requirements for being fully insured. A person who earns wages covered by social security of at least $50 in a three-month calendar quarter is credited with one quarter of coverage. Self-employed persons who earn at least $400 in a full calendar year are credited with four quarters of coverage.

The size of the retirement benefit varies among individuals according to average earnings under covered employment. However, there is a maximum and minimum limit to what eligible individuals and their dependents can receive. Figure 12–6 lists dependents who may be eligible for retirement benefits if an eligible employee should die.

Disability benefits Pensions may be granted under social security to eligible employees who have a disability that is expected to last at least 12 months. To be eligible, a person must have worked in a job covered by social security for at least 5 out of the 10 years before he or she became disabled. These pensions are calculated with basically the same methods used for calculating retirement benefits.

Health insurance Health insurance under social security, commonly known as Medicare, provides partial hospital and medical reimbursement for persons over 65. Hospital insurance, which is known as part A, is financed through the regular social security funds. Most hospital expenses and certain outpatient, posthospital, and home nursing ex-

Figure 12–6

Dependents eligible for retirement benefits in the event of death of a covered employee

Widow or widower at age 65, or age 60 if reduced benefits are chosen.

Widow or widower at any age, if she or he is caring for a child of the deceased. The child must be entitled to social security and be either disabled or under 18.

Disabled widow or widower 50 or older.

Unmarried children under 18, or 22 if full-time students, and those 18 or over who became disabled before reaching 22.

Dependent parents 62 or older.

Divorced wife if she is not married and is (1) caring for a child who is under 18 or disabled and who is entitled to social security benefits, or (2) age 62 and was married to the deceased for 10 years.

penses are covered by part A of Medicare. The medical insurance, known as part B, helps a participant pay for a number of different medical procedures and supplies that are completely separate from hospital care. For example, normal outpatient visits and checkups would fall under part B. Participation in the medical insurance program (part B) of Medicare is voluntary and requires the payment of a monthly fee by those wishing to receive coverage.

Problems facing social security Most everyone is aware of the financial crisis faced by social security stemming from major demographic changes that have taken place since the system was established. The basic problem is that fewer and fewer people are and will be working to support more and more retirees as the "baby boom" generation reaches retirement age. Several changes have been and probably will continue to be legislated to keep social security financially sound.

Unemployment
compensation

Unemployment insurance is designed to provide funds to employees who have lost their jobs and are seeking other positions. Title IX of the Social Security Act of 1935 requires employers to pay taxes for unemployment compensation. However, the law was written in such a manner as to encourage individual states to establish their own unemployment systems. If a state established its own unemployment compensation system according to prescribed federal standards, the proceeds of the unemployment taxes paid by an employer go to the state. By 1937, all states and the District of Columbia had adopted acceptable unemployment compensation plans.

To receive unemployment compensation, an individual must submit an application through the state employment office and must meet three eligibility requirements. First, he or she must have been covered by social security for a minimum number of weeks. Second, he or she must have been laid off. In some states, discharged employees may qualify. Third, he or she must be willing to accept any suitable employment offered through the state unemployment compensation commission. Many disputes have arisen regarding "suitable employment."

Generally, unemployment compensation is limited to a maximum of 26 weeks. The amount received, which varies from state to state, is calculated on the basis of the individual's wages or salary received in the previous period of employment.

Unemployment compensation is usually funded through taxes paid by employers; however, in some states, employees also pay a portion of the tax. To encourage organizations to minimize layoffs and discharges, the system provides that a lesser unemployment tax may be paid by those organizations that maintain stable employment.

Worker's
compensation

Worker's compensation is meant to protect employees from loss of income and extra expenses associated with job-related injuries or illnesses. Figure 12–7 summarizes the types of injuries and illnesses covered by most worker's compensation laws. Although some form of worker's compensation is available in all 50 states, the specific requirements, payments, and procedures vary among states. However, there are certain features which are common to virtually all programs:

1. The laws generally provide for replacement of lost income, medical expense payment, rehabilitation of some sort, death benefits to survivors, and lump-sum disability payments.
2. The worker does not have to sue the employer to get compensation—in fact, covered employers are exempt from such lawsuits.
3. The compensation is normally paid through an insurance program, financed through premiums paid by employers.
4. Worker's compensation insurance premiums are based on the accident and illness record of the organization. A large number of paid claims results in higher premiums.
5. An element of coinsurance exists in the workers' compensation coverage. Coinsurance is insurance under which the beneficiary of the coverage absorbs part of the loss. In automobile collision coverage, for example, there is often coinsurance in the amount of a $100 deductible for each accident. In workers' compensation coverage, there is coinsurance in that the worker's loss is usually not fully covered by the insurance program. For example, most states provide for a maximum payment of only two thirds of wages lost due to the accident or illness.
6. Medical expenses, on the other hand, are usually covered in full under workers' compensation laws.
7. It is a no-fault system; all job-related injuries and illnesses are covered, regardless of whose negligence caused them.[20]

Figure 12–7   Job-connected injuries usually covered by worker's compensation

Accidents in which the employee does not lose time from work.
Accidents in which the employee loses time from work.
Temporary partial disability.
Permanent partial or total disability.
Death.
Occupational diseases.
Noncrippling physical impairments such as deafness.
Impairments suffered at employer-sanctioned events such as social events or during travel related to organizational business.
Injuries or disabilities attributable to an employer's gross negligence.

Source: Reprinted by permission from *Personnel Administration and the Law* 2nd ed., by Greenman, Russell L., and Eric J. Schmertz, Copyright © 1979 by The Bureau of National Affairs, Inc., Washington, D.C. 20037, pp 190–191.

It should be pointed out that worker's compensation coverage is compulsory in all states except South Carolina, New Jersey, and Texas. In these states, it is elective for the employer. When elective, any employers who reject the coverage also give up certain legal protections.

One major criticism of worker's compensation involves the extent of coverage provided by different states.[21] The amounts paid, the ease of collecting, and the likelihood of collecting all vary significantly from state to state.

RETIREMENT-RELATED BENEFITS

In addition to the benefits required under social security, many organizations provide additional retirement benefits in the form of private pensions and retirement plans.

Pension plans

Pension and retirement plans, which provide a source of income to people who have retired, represent money paid for past services. Private pension plans can be funded entirely by the organization or jointly by the organization and the employee during his or her employment. Plans requiring employee contributions are called contributory plans; those that do not are called noncontributory plans. Funded pension plans are financed by money that has been set aside previously for that specific purpose. Nonfunded plans make payments to recipients out of current contributions to the fund.

A survey reported by the Conference Board in 1981 found that 88 percent of the participants had pension plans.[22] While the percentage having private pension plans had not changed from a 1973 study, the proportion of noncontributory plans had increased from 80 percent to 91 percent. A similar 1981 study by the Bureau of National Affairs (BNA) found that all but 7 out of 246 employers surveyed sponsored some type of pension or retirement plan.[23] This can be compared with the fact that less than one sixth of the nonagricultural work force was covered by private pension plans prior to 1948.

Calculating benefits One issue of concern for individuals covered by a pension plan is how much they will receive under the plan. Although there are numerous formulas for calculating benefits, the most popular approach has been the final average pay plan, in which the retirement benefit is based on average earnings in the years, generally five, immediately preceding retirement. The actual benefit sum is then computed as a function of the person's calculated average earnings and years of service. In another common approach, the flat-benefit plan, all participants who meet the eligibility requirements receive a fixed benefit regardless of their earnings. Plans affecting salaried employees

College retirement plans are told to pay men, women equally

New York—A federal appeals court ruled that two college retirement plans must pay men and women retirees equal benefits for equal contributions.

The decision affects the $20 billion Teachers Insurance and Annuity Association and the College Retirement Association and the College Retirement Equities Fund, the two principal retirement plans for about 3,400 colleges and universities, and other institutions. About 680,000 people are participants in the plans.

The ruling, the latest in a legal dispute that began in 1974, ordered the plans to cease calculating retirement benefits on sex-distinct mortality tables, retroactive to May 1, 1980.

The plans invest employee and employer contributions and, at retirement, provide annuities based on actuarial tables reflecting life expectancy. Because the plans have used separate tables for each sex, and because women as a group live longer than men, the same invested sum provides smaller monthly payments to women than to men. In some cases, the payment is about 11% greater for men.

The Second Circuit Court found that the separate mortality tables violate Title VII of the 1964 Civil Rights Act. It rejected arguments that the plans aren't covered by federal law because they are in the insurance business, which is exempt from federal regulation. A lower court had ruled Teachers Insurance was exempt from Title VII.

A spokesman for the two funds said an appeal of the latest ruling is expected. The issue of equal benefits involves the "entire insurance and pension industries," he said, noting that two related decisions from the Ninth Circuit have been appealed to the U.S. Supreme Court.

The case originally was filed by a female professor at Long Island University.

The decision affects people who retire after May 1, 1980. The court said the decision wouldn't require "the wholesale removal of money" from the funds' reserves, declaring that equal payments could be calculated without changing the total anticipated obligations of the funds. A decision that didn't affect past contributions, it said, "would effectively postpone full conversion to gender-neutral tables for as much as 30 to 40 years."

Source: *The Wall Street Journal,* 1 October 1982, p. 39. Reprinted by permission of The Wall Street Journal. © Dow Jones & Company, Inc. (1982). All rights reserved.

usually use the final average pay plan. Plans limited to hourly paid employees traditionally have used the flat-benefit plan. Where hourly and salaried employees are affected, a final average pay formula may be modified to provide a minimum dollar benefit for participants in the lower pay classifications. Many final average pay plans are currently being calculated with an offset or deduction for the employee's social security benefits. In these cases, the amount of social security that a person receives is taken into account when determining how much he or she will receive from the pension plan. The 1981 survey by the Conference Board reported that 64 percent of final average pay plans were offset by social security.[24]

Pension rights An inherent promise of providing security of some form exists in every pension plan. However, if the pension benefits are too low or the plan is seriously underfunded, this promise of security is breached. One result of this situation is that employees who have spent most of their working lives with companies that have pension plans do not receive an adequate, or in some cases any, pension. Another problem involves the vested rights of employees. Vesting refers to the rights of individuals to receive the dollars paid into a pension or retirement fund by their employer if they should leave the organization prior to retirement. For example, if an employee is vested, he or she can receive, at some later date, the funds invested by the employer. If an employee is not vested, he or she cannot receive the funds paid by the employer. A frequent approach is deferred full vesting, in which an employee, on meeting certain age and service requirements, enjoys full vested rights. A similar approach, called deferred graded vesting, gradually gives the employee an increasing percentage of benefits until he or she meets the age and service requirements for full vesting.

Vesting requirements historically have caused problems for both employees and employers. In many old plans, the employee who was terminated or quit before retirement age did not receive any pension benefits regardless of the number of years worked under the pension plan or how close he or she was to retirement. Even under plans that did provide vesting rights, the requirements were strict in terms of length of service. Requirements for vesting are often made stringent by employers in an effort to keep employees from leaving the organization, at least until their rights have become fully vested. On the other hand, employers have experienced the problem of employees quitting after they have been vested in the pension plan in order to draw out the funds credited to them. To counteract this, employers have incorporated provisions in their pension plans stating that funds other than those contributed by the employee will not be distributed until the employee reaches a certain age, even if he or she has left the organization.

ERISA In an effort to ensure the fair treatment of employees under pension plans, Congress in 1974, passed the Employee Retirement Income Security Act (ERISA). This law was designed to ensure the solvency of pension plans by restricting the types of investments that could be made with the plan's funds and providing general guidelines for fund management. Figure 12–8 summarizes the major provisions of ERISA. The act has been criticised as being too costly. In fact, it has been reported that many companies dropped their pension plans rather than comply with ERISA.[25] Another major complaint about ERISA has been that it causes an unwieldy amount of paperwork.

Figure 12–8   Major provisions of ERISA

Eligibility	Prohibited plans from establishing eligibility requirements of more than one year of service, or an age greater than 25, whichever is later
Vesting	Established new minimum standards; employer has three choices: **1** 100 percent vesting after 10 years of service. **2** 25 percent vesting after 5 years of service, grading up to 100 percent after 15 years. **3** 50 percent vesting when age and service (if the employee has at least 5 years of service) equal 45, grading up to 100 percent vesting 5 years later.
Funding	Required the employer to fund annually the full cost for current benefit accruals and amortize past service benefit liabilities over 30 years for new plans and 40 years for existing plans.
Plan termination insurance	Established a government insurance fund to insure vested pension benefits up to the lesser of $750 a month or 100 percent of the employee's average wages during his highest paid five years of employment; the employer pays an annual premium of $1 per participant and is liable for any insurance benefits paid up to 30 percent of the company's net worth.
Fiduciary responsibility	Established the "prudent man" rule as the basic standard of fiduciary responsibility; prohibits various transactions between fiduciaries and parties-in-interest; prohibits investment of more than 10 percent of pension plan assets in the employer's securities.
Portability	Permitted an employee leaving a company to make a tax-free transfer of the assets behind his vested pension benefits (if the employer agrees) or of his vested profit-sharing or savings plan funds to an individual retirement account.
Individual retirement accounts (IRAs)	Provided a vehicle for transfers as noted above and permits employees of private or public employers that do not have qualified retirement plans to deduct 15 percent of compensation, up to $1,500, each year for contributions to a personal retirement fund. Earnings on the fund are not taxable until distributed.
Reporting and disclosure	Required the employer to provide employees with a comprehensive booklet describing plan provisions and to report annually to the secretary of labor on various operating and financial details of the plan.
Lump-sum distributions	Changed the tax rules to provide capital gains treatment on pre–1974 amounts and to tax post–1973 amounts as ordinary income, but as the employee's only income and spread over 10 years.
Limits on contributions and benefits	**1** Limited benefits payable from defined benefit pension plans to the lesser of $75,000 a year or 100 percent of average annual cash compensation during the employee's three highest paid years of service. **2** Limited annual additions to employee profit-sharing accounts to the lesser of $25,000 or 25 percent of the employee's compensation that year.

Source: Adapted from D. G. Carlson, "Responding to the Pension Reform Law," *Harvard Business Review*, November–December 1974, p. 134.

Early retirement Most pension plans have special allowances for voluntary early retirement. Usually an employee's pension is reduced by a stated amount for every month that he or she retires before age 65. Popular early retirement ages are 62, 60, and 55. Most plans require that an individual must have worked a minimum number of years with the organization to be eligible for early retirement. Early retirement has grown in popularity, partially because of the pension benefits available. For example, the 1981 Conference Board report that was referenced earlier found that the median pension benefit for people retiring at age 62 was 91 percent of the normal benefit.[26] Presently, the earliest that an employee can receive reduced social security benefits is at age 62. While early retirement has become increasingly popular, inflation has proved to be a major obstacle for many.

Mandatory retirement The 1978 amendment to the Age Discrimination in Employment Act (ADEA) forbids mandatory retirement before age 70 for all companies employing 20 or more people in the private sector and at any age in federal employment. Prior to the effective date (January 1, 1979) of this amendment, employers could choose any age for mandatory retirement.

Several arguments can be made both for and against mandatory retirement. A major argument in its favor is that it makes jobs available for younger employees. A major argument against the practice is that many employees at retirement age are still capable of making significant contributions to the organization.

As an alternative to mandatory retirement, some organizations offer incentives to encourage early retirement. This method of reducing the work force is often viewed as a humanitarian way of reducing the payroll and rewarding long-tenured employees.[27] The types of incentives offered vary but usually include a lump-sum payment plus the extension of other benefits such as medical insurance. For example, more than 900 employees retired early under a plan offered by Sears, Roebuck which combined a cash payment plus profit sharing, a medical plan, life insurance, and a lifetime employee discount.[28]

Employees not covered by pension plans

In recent years, legislation has been enacted and updated to allow employees not covered by private pension plans to set up individual plans, called Individual Retirement Accounts (IRAs). With an IRA, an individual can make tax-exempt contributions to a maximum of $2,000 per year. In conjunction with a spouse-homemaker, a person can contribute up to $2,250 per year. A similar plan, called a Keogh plan, has been effected for self-employed persons. Under a Keogh plan, starting in 1984, self-employed persons can make tax-exempt contributions of up to $30,000 or 25 percent of net self-employment income, whichever is less. The major advantage of IRAs and Keogh plans is that they offer tax incentives for people to save toward retirement.

Preretirement
planning

A benefit which has recently evolved is preretirement planning. The purpose of such a planning program is to help employees prepare for retirement—both financially and psychologically. At the most basic level, preretirement planning provides employees with information about the financial benefits they will receive upon retirement.[29] Social security, pensions, employee stock ownership, and health and life insurance coverage are usually discussed. Other programs go beyond financial planning and into such topics as housing, relocation, health, nutrition, sleep, exercise, part-time work, second careers, community service, recreation, and continuing education.[30]

The rapid pace of change in today's world accentuated by volatile inflation and uncertainty concerning social security have enhanced the need for some type of preretirement planning. This need is not expected to be diminished in the near future.

INSURANCE-
RELATED
BENEFITS

Insurance programs of various types represent an important part of any benefit package. For example, the U.S. Chamber of Commerce reported that of 994 companies surveyed in 1981, all but five provided some form of medical insurance.[31] Company-sponsored medical insurance programs are designed so that the employer either pays the entire premium or a portion of it, with the employee paying the balance.

Health insurance

In addition to normal hospitalization and outpatient doctor bills, some plans now cover prescription drugs, and dental, eye, and medical-health care. Many health-care plans incorporate a deductible, which requires the employee to pay the first $50 or $100. The health insurance plan then pays the bulk of the remaining expenses. Some plans pay the entire cost of health insurance for both the employee and dependents, some plans require the employee to pay part of the cost only for dependents, and some plans require the employee to pay part of the cost for both him- or herself and dependents (see Figure 12–9). Two distinct plans have evolved over the years in health insurance; the "base plan" and the "major medical expense plan."[32] Base plans cover expenses for specified services within certain limits established for each kind of service. On the other hand, major medical plans define a broad range of covered expenses including all services that may be required for successful treatment. When used alone, a major medical plan is referred to as a comprehensive plan. Many organizations

Figure 12–9   Financing of employee and dependent health insurance

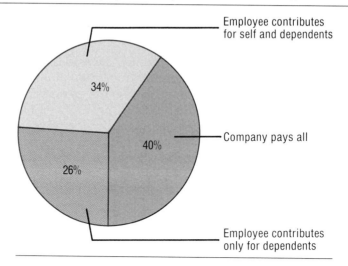

Source: Compiled based on data provided in Profile of Employee Benefits (New York: The Conference Board, 1981), p. 8.

supplement a base plan with a major medical expense plan. The reason for combining the two is usually to reduce the deductible amount for certain types of treatment. The precise coverage, size of the deductible, and other specifics vary considerably among plans.

Health maintenance organizations (HMOs)

    The Health Maintenance Organization Act of 1973 ushered in a new concept of one-stop, prepaid medical services as an alternative to traditional insurance programs. With this arrangement, organizations contract with an approved HMO to provide certain basic medical services for the organization's employees for a fixed price. Advantages to HMOs include emphasis on prevention of health problems and costs that are usually cheaper than traditional coverage. The major disadvantage, from the employees' viewpoint, is that they must use physicians employed or approved by the HMO, not the doctors of their choice. While HMOs are growing in popularity, they still are not widely accepted and used by employees as illustrated by the following quote:

    Among the 1,368 companies reporting in this study, 41 percent have offered employees the option of membership in Health Maintenance Organizations (HMOs). Where offered, only a small part of the work force usually participates; the median company reports that about 3 percent of its employees do so. No one participates in 14 percent of the offering companies, but somewhat over 2 percent note that half or more of the work force is [in] an HMO.[33]

Dental insurance

Dental insurance has been one of the fastest growing types of employee benefits in recent years. For example, surveys conducted by the Conference Board show the number of companies providing dental plans have grown from 8 percent in 1973 to 19 percent in 1975 to 41 percent in 1981.[34] Some major medical expense plans include dental treatment, but most dental insurance is provided as a separate plan. The majority of dental plans specify a deductible.

Supplemental medical and dental insurance

Many organizations offer to their executives medical and dental coverage to supplement the coverage provided for all employees. Such plans normally reimburse the executive for all medical and dental costs, including deductibles, not covered in the regular plan. The advantage of this benefit is that the coverage is tax deductible to the organization and yet does not have to be reported by the recipient as income.

Life insurance

Life insurance is a benefit commonly available from organizations. When provided for all employees, it is called group life insurance. Costs of this type of insurance, based on the characteristics of the entire group covered, typically are the same per dollar of insurance for all employees. Generally, the employer provides a minimum of coverage, usually $10,000 to $20,000. Employees often have the option of purchasing more insurance at their own expense. A physical examination is usually not required for coverage. Presently, employers can provide up to a maximum of $50,000 worth of life insurance for an employee without the cost of the policy being considered as income to the individual.

Accident and disability insurance

In addition to health, dental, and life insurance, many organizations provide some form of accident or disability insurance, or both. Most accident insurance is designed to provide funds for a limited period of time, usually up to 16 weeks. The amount of the benefit is often some percentage of the accident victim's weekly salary. Disability insurance is designed to protect the employee if he or she experiences a long-term or permanent disability. Normally, a one- to six-month waiting period is required following the disability before the employee becomes eligible for benefits. As with accident insurance, disability insurance benefits are usually calculated as a percentage of wages or salary.

PAYMENT FOR TIME NOT WORKED

It is now standard practice for organizations to pay employees for certain times when they do not work. Rest periods, lunch breaks, and wash-up time represent times not worked that are almost always taken for granted as part of the job. Recognized holidays, vacations, and days missed because of sickness, jury duty, and funerals represent other compensated times that are not worked.

Paid holidays

The number of paid holidays has somewhat stabilized over the last several years. One relatively new concept is the *floating holiday* that is observed at the discretion of the employee. A recent survey conducted by the Bureau of National Affairs (BNA) revealed the following facts: [35]

Employers surveyed grant a median of 10 paid holidays a year, with policies ranging from 6 to 16 holidays in individual firms.

Christmas, New Year's Day, Thanksgiving, Labor Day, and the Fourth of July are paid holidays in *all* of the responding organizations, and Memorial Day is observed as a holiday in 95 percent of the companies.

Nearly half of the surveyed companies have floating holidays, which are observed on different days from year to year, either taken at the individual employee's option or designated by management or through union agreement for all employees.

Regular, full-time employees typically receive their usual rate of pay for holidays, but in over half of the firms, eligibility for holiday pay is contingent on the employees working the scheduled days before and after the holiday or being on approved absence.

Employees who are required to work on a holiday receive holiday pay plus time and a half for the hours they work in 42 percent of the responding firms, holiday pay plus double time in 16 percent, and holiday pay plus straight time in 15 percent.

The majority of surveyed companies observe Sunday holidays on the following Monday (87 percent) and Saturday holidays on the preceding Friday (69 percent), and they give employees another day off with pay when a holiday occurs during their scheduled vacations (84 percent).

Table 12–4 shows the frequency with which certain holidays are observed by the participants in the BNA survey.

Paid vacations

Normally, certain length of service requirements must be met before an employee becomes eligible for a paid vacation. Also, the time allowed in paid vacations generally depends on the employee's length of service. Unlike holiday policies that usually affect everyone in the same manner, vacation policies may differ between categories of employees. The BNA survey reported the following information with regard to paid vacations: [36]

Table 12–4   Holidays observed

| | Percent of companies | | | | | |
| | By industry | | | By size | | |
	Manu-facturing	Nonmanu-facturing	Non-business	Large	Small	All companies
Christmas Day	100	100	100	100	100	100
New Year's Day	100	100	100	100	100	100
Thanksgiving Day	100	100	100	100	100	100
Fourth of July	100	100	100	100	100	100
Labor Day	100	100	100	100	100	100
Memorial Day	98	92	95	95	96	95
Day after Thanksgiving	77	34	36	45	60	54
Good Friday—full or half day	65	34	31	38	54	48
Washington's Birthday	23	60	54	36	45	42
Christmas Eve	57	22	13	32	39	36
Veterans Day	10	35	44	22	27	25
Columbus Day	10	31	41	22	24	23
Employee's birthday	14	28	36	31	18	23
New Year's Eve	26	5	8	12	17	15
Half day, Christmas Eve	14	20	5	16	13	14
State/local holiday	7	20	10	14	11	12
Election Day	2	14	13	11	7	8
Half day, New Year's Eve . . .	10	9	3	11	7	8
Martin Luther King's Birthday	1	3	15	1	7	5
Easter Monday	4	0	8	3	4	4
Lincoln's Birthday	0	6	5	5	2	3

Source: From *Paid Holidays and Vacation Policies*, (Washington, D.C., Bureau of. National Affairs, Personnel Policies Forum Survey no. 130 (Washington, D.C., copyright 1980), p. 4. Reprinted by permission.

The most common patterns in vacation eligibility requirements for employees of surveyed companies are: one week's vacation after six months of service for office/clerical and management employees and one week after a year for production/maintenance workers; two weeks after one year for all employee groups; three weeks after 5 or 10 years; four weeks after 15 years; five weeks after 20 or 25 years; and six weeks after 30 years. Over half of the companies have no five-week vacations, however, and close to 90 percent have no six-week vacations.

Vacations generally are scheduled during a shutdown of operations in about a fifth of the responding companies—nearly all manufacturers. In situations where a shutdown is not involved in the scheduling decision, preference for vacation time is most frequently determined by work requirements in the employee's department (70 percent of companies) and the employee's length of service (62 percent).

In the majority of responding companies, employees may take their vacations a week at a time, a day at a time, or all at one time, regardless of the amount of time they have accrued.

OTHER BENEFITS In addition to the previously discussed major benefits, organizations may offer a wide range of additional benefits, including food services, health and first aid services, financial and legal advice, counseling services, educational and recreational programs, day care services, and purchase discounts. Employee assistance programs, a type of general service related to employee health, are discussed in Chapter 18.

The extent and attractiveness of these benefits vary considerably among organizations. For example, purchase discounts would be especially attractive to employees of a major retail store or an airline. A 1981 survey by BNA reported the following facts regarding services and other benefits: [37]

More than 9 out of 10 organizations have vending machines at the workplace, and the majority have some facilities for employees who bring meals from home—89 percent have lunchrooms, 81 percent have food-heating or cooking facilities, and 74 percent have refrigerators for employee use.

The vast majority of surveyed organizations—88 percent—have a parking lot or a garage for all or most employees to use.

Manufacturing plants have somewhat greater concern with first aid than do the other industries. Nine out of 10 manufacturers have first aid stations, compared to 7 out of 10 nonbusiness organizations and a little over half of the nonmanufacturing businesses. Nonbusiness organizations include establishments such as hospitals, educational institutions, and government agencies. Similarly, 46 percent of manufacturers have first aid specialists on the staff compared to 31 percent of nonmanufacturers and 26 percent of nonbusiness employers. More than two thirds of all the surveyed companies, however, provide CPR or first aid training to at least some employees.

The financial and/or legal services most commonly offered by surveyed employers are: notary public (69 percent), company credit union (57 percent), and direct deposit of paychecks in employees' bank accounts (52 percent).

Less than 20 percent of the firms provide any one of the following recreational services: outdoor playing fields, showers and/or lockers for sports, conditioning facilities, indoor sports facilities, or recreation parks. Employees in 19 percent of the companies have access to outdoor playing fields, and in 16 percent of the companies they may use company shower and locker facilities for sports activities. A substantially greater proportion of nonbusiness organizations offers all of these services, compared to the other industry categories.

Of the 313 responding employers, just 18—mostly nonbusiness organizations—have day-care arrangements for employees' children. Eight of those organizations operate their own child-care centers at the workplace, and six have on-premises centers operated by an outside service.

Half of the surveyed firms give employees discounts on the products the company manufactures or on the services it provides, and nearly 3 out of 10 (28 percent) arrange for employees to purchase other companies' products or services at a discounted rate.

THE BENEFIT PACKAGE

Unfortunately, there is ample evidence to show that "most benefit packages are thrown together piecemeal, are not well-balanced, and don't show sufficient regard for holes or overlap within the total package."[38] There are many reasons benefit packages are often not well integrated. The major problem is that new benefits are often added or deleted without examining their impact on the total package. Also, benefits are added or deleted for all the wrong reasons: because of a whim of a top manager, because of union pressures, or because of a fad. The key to any successful benefit package is to plan the package and to integrate all of the different components. Such an approach ensures that any new benefit additions or deletions will fit in with the other benefits that are currently being offered.

SUMMARY

Employee benefits, sometimes called fringe benefits, are those rewards that organizations provide to employees for being a member of the organization. Employee benefits can be grouped into five major categories: (1) legally required, (2) retirement related, (3) insurance related, (4) payment for time not worked, and (5) other. Employee benefits have grown substantially in the years since World War II. Currently, employee benefits make up over 40 percent of total payroll costs.

Although most organizations provide substantial benefits to their employees, the average organization does a poor job of communicating these benefits. Providing employee benefits is complicated by the fact that different groups of employees often have different preferences and needs, causing some organizations to offer flexible or cafeteria benefit plans. Under this approach, employees can select from among several options how they would like their direct compensation and benefit dollars distributed.

Legally required benefits include social security, unemployment compensation, and worker's compensation. The benefits of social security can be grouped into three major categories: retirement benefits, disability benefits, and health insurance. Unemployment compensation is designed to provide funds to employees who have lost their jobs and are seeking other jobs. Worker's compensation is a form of protection for employees from loss of income and extra expenses associated with job-related injuries.

In addition to the benefits required under social security, many organizations provide additional retirement benefits in the form of private pensions and retirement plans. Private pension plans can be funded entirely by the organization or jointly by the organization and the employee during his or her employment. In recent years, legislation has been enacted and updated to allow employees not covered by private pension plans to set up individual plans, called individual retirement accounts (IRAs). A similar plan, called a Keogh plan, has been effected for self-employed persons.

Insurance-related benefits include health insurance, dental insurance, life insurance, and accident and disability insurance. The Health Maintenance Organization Act of 1973 ushered in a new concept of one-stop, prepaid medical services. Under this concept, organizations contract with an approved HMO to provide certain basic medical services for their employees for a fixed price.

It is now standard practice for organizations to pay employees for certain times when they do not work. Rest periods, lunch breaks, and wash-up time represent compensated times that are not worked. Recognized holidays, vacations, and days missed because of sickness, jury duty, and funerals represent other compensated times that are not worked.

In addition to the previously mentioned major benefits, organizations may offer a wide range of additional benefits, including food services, health and first aid services, financial and legal advice, counseling services, educational and recreational programs, day-care services, and purchase discounts.

REVIEW QUESTIONS

1. Why are many employees unaware of some of the benefits provided by their organizations?
2. What is the flexible approach to compensation and benefits?
3. What are the advantages and disadvantages with flexible plans?
4. What is social security? Describe the three major categories of social security.
5. Briefly explain how unemployment compensation works.
6. What types of injuries and illnesses are covered by worker's compensation?
7. What was the overriding purpose of the Employee Retirement Income Security Act (ERISA)?
8. Mandatory retirement is forbidden by law in most organizations before what age?

9. What are the two alternatives for individuals not covered by private pension plans?

10. Discuss some of the insurance programs offered to employees by organizations.

11. What is a health maintenance organization (HMO)?

DISCUSSION QUESTIONS

1. If an average production employee is given the option of having an additional $100 per month in salary or the equivalent of $200 per month in voluntary benefits, which do you think he or she would choose? Why? What are the implications of your answer for management?

2. Develop and discuss at least two arguments in support of social security. Compare and contrast your arguments.

3. If you were offered an option of joining an HMO by your employer, would you be interested? Why or why not?

4. Many people feel that employers use pension vesting requirements solely for the purpose of retaining employees. If this is true, or even partially true, do you think that such behavior is ethical?

REFERENCES AND ADDITIONAL READINGS

1. U.S. Chamber Survey Research Center, *Employee Benefits* (Washington, D.C.: Chamber of Commerce of the United States, 1981), p. 5.

2. R. M. McCaffery, "Employee Benefits: Beyond the Fringe?" *Personnel Administrator*, May 1981, p. 26.

3. Ibid.

4. Ibid.

5. W. H. Holley, Jr. and E. Ingram, II, "Communicating Fringe Benefits," *The Personnel Administrator*, March–April 1973, pp. 21–22; and R. C. Huseman, J. D. Hatfield, and R. W. Driver, "Getting Your Benefit Programs Understood and Appreciated," *Personnel Journal*, October 1978, pp. 560–66.

6. Huseman, Hatfield, and Driver, "Getting Your Benefits Programs," p. 563.

7. R. L. Kagerer, "Do Employees Understand Your Benefits Program?" *The Personnel Administrator*, October 1975, pp. 29–31.

8. J. B. Chapman and R. Ottemann, "Employee Preference for Various Compensation and Fringe Benefit Options," *The Personnel Administrator*, November 1975, p. 31.

9. C. Seltz and D. L. Gifford, *Flexible Compensation: A Forward Look* (New York: American Management Association, 1982), p. 14.

10. A. Cole, Jr., "Flexible Benefits are a Key to Better Employee Relations," *Personnel Journal*, January 1983, p. 49.

11. Ibid.

12. Ibid.

13. R. B. Cockrum, "Has the Time Come for Employee Cafeteria Plans?" *Personnel Administrator*, July 1982, p. 67.

14. B. S. Maskal, "More Flexibility in Benefit Plans," *Industry Week*, 7 January 1980, p. 110.

15. Cockrum, "Has the Time Come."

16. The first four of these reasons were adapted from Ibid.

17. Ibid., p. 72.

18. Adapted from J. H. Shea, "Cautions About Cafeteria—Style Benefit Plans," *Personnel Journal*, January 1981, pp. 37–38.

19. R. L. Greenman and E. J. Schmertz, *Personnel Administration and the Law* (Washington, D.C.: Bureau of National Affairs, 1972), p. 130.

20. S. Ledvinka, *Federal Regulation of Personnel and Human Resource Management* (Boston: Kent Publishing, 1982) p. 144.

21. Ibid., p. 145.

22. *Profile of Employee Benefits* (New York: The Conference Board, 1981), p. 27.

23. *Pensions and Other Retirement Benefit Plans* (Washington, D.C.: Bureau of National Affairs, 1982), p. 1.

24. *Profile of Employee Benefits*, p. 28.

25. P. S. Greenlaw and W. D. Biggs, *Modern Personnel Management* (Philadelphia: W. B. Saunders, 1979) p. 513.

26. *Profile of Employee Benefits*, p. 29.

27. L. B. Baenen and R. C. Ernest, "An Argument for Early Retirement Incentive Planning," *Personnel Administrator*, August 1982, p. 63.

28. Ibid., p. 64.

29. W. Arnone, "Preretirement Planning: An Employee Benefit that Has Come of Age," *Personnel Journal*, October 1982, p. 761.

30. Ibid.

31. Survey Research Center, *Employee Benefits*, p. 17.

32. *Profile of Employee Benefits*, p. 6.

33. Ibid., p. 9.

34. Ibid., p. 13.

35. *Paid Holidays and Vacation Policies*, Bureau of National Affairs, Personnel Policies Forum Survey no. 130 (Washington, D.C., 1980), p. 1.

36. Ibid., pp. 1–2.

37. *Services for Employees*, Bureau of National Affairs, Personnel Policies Forum Survey no. 133 (Washington, D.C., 1981), pp. 1–2.

38. R. B. Dunham and R. A. Formisano, "Designing and Evaluating Employee Benefit Systems," *Personnel Administrator*, April 1982, p. 29.

Case 12–1

WHO IS ELIGIBLE FOR RETIREMENT BENEFITS?

Preston Jones, 51, had been an hourly worker in the machine shop of the Armon Company for 21 years and 4 months.

On a Christmas holiday, he suffered a severe heart attack and was hospitalized for three weeks. At his release, his doctor said he was to rest at home for a couple of months. After this recuperation period, his doctor, along with Armon Company's physicians, was to decide whether or not Preston should be retired for disability reasons. They never got the opportunity to make this decision—in February, Preston died of a second heart attack.

He left a wife, four sons, two daughters, and two daughters-in-law. Mrs. Jones still had four children at home.

As a part of Preston's estate, his wife received the normal group insurance payments, the balance in his savings plan account, and the other benefits due her. However, she did not receive a pension from Armon as a survivor of an eligible employee.

When Mrs. Jones and the company representatives had discussed the settlement, she had inquired about her husband's pension and about her right to receive it. The personnel department had stated that since contributions to this fund were made only by the company, no survivors benefits were provided.

1. *What do you think Mrs. Jones should do at this point?*
2. *Does the Employment Retirement Income Security Act of 1974 have anything to say about this issue?*

Case 12–2   **FRINGE BENEFITS FOR PROFESSIONALS**

LJT, Architect is a small architectural firm, organized as a sole proprietorship, that serves clients in the New York metropolitan area. Anticipating a good year, Len Elmore, the principal, hopes for a gross of between $300,000 and $400,000.

In an architectural practice, revenue is produced by providing a variety of services that range from creating a design and generating the construction documents used by a contractor to execute the project to visiting the site periodically to verify that construction is progressing according to specifications. An architect is also responsible for coordinating his or her work with that of the engineers and other consultants associated with the project.

Many small architectural firms such as LJT, Architect, have no permanent employees. Workers are hired for a particular project with the understanding that they might remain after a particular phase of the project is completed, but that they might be laid off. Employees are usually needed for the function of design, development, and production of construction documents, which includes approximately 50 to 70 percent of the services provided under a standard architectural agreement.

The personnel needed for these projects are acquired in several ways. They can be hired on a full-time permanent or temporary basis or on a part-time basis to "moonlight," that is as a second job. An employee might also be borrowed from another firm whose contracted work has been completed, with no new work foreseen immediately. Len feels that hiring full-time temporary or permanent employees gives him more control over the production aspect of his practice.

At this time, Len does not follow any formal personnel policies. He prefers to "work things out" as issues and problems arise.

When hiring, he will agree verbally to certain broad terms of employment, compensation, and benefits common to local professional offices, such as two weeks' vacation per year. He usually insists on a two-week to one-month probationary period during which the salary paid is slightly less than normal. A spot check of some of his colleagues leads him to believe that his salary rates are comparable with those of similar employers. Because the nature of the employment tends to be temporary, Len suggests a "contract arrangement" with his employees in which no taxes are withheld and no government-required benefits are provided.

Len's plans for expansion include adding employees until his staff numbers 10. For him, this is the best staff size to provide high-quality professional services. However, the employment situation is easing for workers in architectural firms; more newspaper ads seek applicants and fewer callers contact Len for jobs. Those coming for interviews have more questions than, "When do I start?" Many ask about vacation, sick leave, paid holidays, medical insurance, and profit-sharing plans. Others want to know about the possibilities of advancement with LJT, Architect, and about such long-range benefits as pensions and education leave.

In view of the situation, Len has decided to look into the possibility of providing his employees with a fringe benefit package. At the same time, however, he fears that his practice may be too small to begin providing these benefits, which may prove to be extremely expensive. He has set aside money from his own earnings to provide these extras for himself and has difficulty in understanding why his employees cannot do the same.

1. *What recommendations would you make to Len?*
2. *How much do you think your recommendations would cost?*

WHERE TO CUT BACK?

Leon Hart, president of Star Chemical Company, learned from the midyear financial figures that his company's situation was far worse than previously believed. Sales for the past quarter had been 25 percent lower than for the comparable period last year. In fact, sales had slumped so badly that the company was now operating at a loss.

This loss was unusual because Star Chemical had grown at rates averaging 22 percent year for the past eight years. The current recession was hurting the entire industry, but Leon knew that its effect was not the entire problem. Star had a reputation of providing a good line of products with fewer defects than those of its competitors—that is, until two years ago. At that time, rapid growth had forced a quick expansion of production capability. This had resulted in some new equipment being incorrectly used, which had caused quality problems. The product defects, which could not be detected by normal quality control procedures, showed up only after use. Of course, the company had replaced all defective merchandise at no charge.

By winter, these problems seemed to be over. However, raw material shortages then hit the chemical industry. Star, like its competitors, was forced to formulate many products quickly, often without adequate testing. As a result, the entire industry was afflicted with quality problems, but Star suffered more than the average company because its customers remembered its previous difficulties. Finally, as this situation began to improve, bacteria in a tank car of raw material caused large quantities of the product that Star made from it to fail a short time after shipment. Even though quality control measures could not have detected the problem and the company that sold the material to Star was liable for the loss, some of Star's major customers decided that a third crisis was too much. They cancelled their future orders.

Leon was dismayed; as quickly as one problem had been solved, another had erupted. The sales force and the customers had been reassured that one problem was solved only to be forced to deal with a new one. The marketing director and the sales manager were depressed, and the entire sales force was demoralized. All salespeople worked on straight commission, and naturally their pay had decreased with sales. In fact, two of Star's top salespeople had left within the last month. Because the future of the company was at stake, Leon knew that something had to be done, and quickly.

Leon met with his entire management team to review the midyear sales and profit figures. All agreed that confidence would have to be restored dramatically among the customers and sales force. One manager, Barney Blue, even suggested that they talk to employees about a temporary reduction in wages. His argument was based on the fact that Star had always paid at the top of the industry scale. Most observers felt that Star's relatively high wage scale was the primary reason that Star had never been seriously threatened with unionization. In fact, the last time that a unionization effort took place, union officials were not able to get enough employee signatures to even hold an election. As a matter of record, for the past eight years, Star had always granted pay raises before its major competitors, all of which were unionized. Barney Blue reasoned that the employees, once they realized the situation, would gladly accept a small pay cut to put the company back on its feet.

Chet Hoover, the personnel manager, was quick to take exception to Barney's ideas. Chet strongly believed that any pay cut, regardless of how small, would be disastrous to employee relations. Chet stated that he believed a pay cut would be the worst possible alternative and that even if it didn't open the door to the union, it would certainly adversely affect employee motivation.

Tom Moore, the sales manager, suggested that they consider reducing employee benefits. According to recent figures, benefits made up almost 40 percent of total compensation costs. As with wages, Star was tops in the industry when it came to benefits. Full health and dental insurance, term insurance, an employee stock option plan, paid vacations, a liberal sick leave policy, and a good pension plan were among Star's benefits. In addition, Star even had a day-care center and a small, but well-equipped exercise room. Tom asked the group whether it would not be better to cut benefits than wages. His reasoning was that any cut in benefits would not be felt as directly as a cut in wages.

Once again, Chet Hoover disagreed. Chet's argument was similar to his earlier one. He felt that reducing any part of employee compensation would tear down everything they had accomplished in employee relations. Chet then suggested that the group consider reducing bonuses, especially for managerial personnel. Chet pointed out that, even in an off year like the present one, Star paid out considerable sums in the form of managerial bonuses. Chet felt that all managers would be much more understanding and ready to accept some type of compensation cut than would nonmanagerial employees. Chet backed up his argument by stating that in any company, the managers were ultimately responsible for the performance of the company.

Knowing that all the options presented had both good and bad points, Leon was still not convinced as to what should be done. However, he did know one thing for sure, and that was that something had to be done quickly.

Guiding and directing employees

Chapter 13

Performance appraisal systems

Objectives

1. To describe several methods used for conducting performance appraisals.
2. To explore some common errors made in conducting performance appraisals and to present methods for overcoming these errors.
3. To discuss equal employment opportunity considerations in the performance appraisal process.

Outline

Glossary of terms

Behaviorally anchored rating scale (BARS) Method of performance appraisal which determines an employee's level of performance based on whether or not certain specifically described job behaviors are present.

Central tendency Tendency of a manager to rate all or most of his or her employees in the middle of the rating scale.

Checklist Method of performance appraisal in which the rater answers a series of questions about the behavior of the individual being rated with a yes or no.

Critical incident Method of performance appraisal in which the rater keeps a written record of incidents that illustrate both positive and negative behavior of the employee; the rater then uses these incidents as a basis for evaluating the employee's performance.

Essay appraisal Method of performance appraisal in which the rater prepares a written statement describing an individual's strengths, weaknesses, and past performances.

Forced-choice rating Method of performance appraisal that requires the rater to rank a set of statements describing how an employee carries out the duties and responsibilities of his or her job.

Graphic rating scale Method of performance appraisal that requires the rater to indicate on a scale where the employee rates on factors such as quantity of work, dependability, job knowledge, and cooperativeness.

Halo effect Occurs when a manager allows his or her general impression of an employee to influence his or her judgment on each separate item on the performance appraisal.

Leniency Occurs in performance appraisals when a manager's ratings are grouped at the positive end instead of being spread throughout the performance scale.

Performance The degree of accomplishment of the tasks that make up an individual's job.

Performance appraisal Process of determining and communicating to an employee how he or she is performing on the job and, ideally, establishing a plan of improvement.

Ranking methods Methods of performance appraisal in which the performance of an individual is ranked relative to the performance of others.

Work standards approach Method of performance appraisal that involves setting a standard or expected level of output and then comparing each employee's level to the standard.

It meant also informing the men each day just what they had done the day before and just what they were to do that day. In order to do that, as each man came in the morning he had to reach his hand up to a pigeonhole (most of them could not read or write, but they could all find their pigeonholes) and take out two slips of paper. One was a yellow slip and one was a white slip. If they found the yellow slip, those men who could not read and write knew perfectly well what it meant; it was just the general information: "Yesterday you did not earn the money that a first-class man ought to earn. We want you to earn at least 60 percent beyond what other laborers are paid around Bethlehem. You failed to earn that much yesterday; there is something wrong."

*Frederick W. Taylor**

In modern organizations, performance appraisal systems have undergone major changes from the rather simple method described in the above quote. Today's systems require a coordinated effort between the human resource department and the managers of the organization who are responsible for conducting performance appraisals. Generally, the responsibilities of the human resource department are to:

1. Design the formal performance appraisal system and select the methods and forms that are to be used for appraising employees.
2. Train managers in how to conduct performance appraisals.
3. Maintain a reporting system to ensure that appraisals are conducted on a timely basis.
4. Maintain performance appraisal records for individual employees.

The responsibilities of managers in performance appraisals are to:

1. Evaluate the performance of employees.
2. Complete the forms used in appraising employees and return them to the human resource department.
3. Review appraisals with employees.

The purpose of this chapter is to describe in detail the performance appraisal process.

UNDERSTANDING PERFORMANCE

Performance refers to the degree of accomplishment of the tasks that make up an individual's job. It reflects how well an individual is fulfilling the requirements of a job. Often confused with effort, which refers to energy expended, performance is measured in terms of results. For example, a student may exert a great deal of effort in preparing for an examination and still make a poor grade. In such a case, the effort expended is high yet the performance is low.

---

*F. W. Taylor, *Addresses and Discussions at the Conference on Scientific Management*, Hanover, N.H.: Dartmouth College, 1911, pp. 39–40.

Determinants of
performance

Job performance has been described as being "the net effect of a person's effort as modified by his abilities and traits and by his role perceptions."[1] This definition implies that performance in a given situation can be viewed as resulting from the interrelationships between effort, abilities, and role (or task) perceptions.

Effort, which results from being motivated, refers to the amount of energy (physical and/or mental) used by an individual in performing a task. Abilities are personal characteristics used in performing a job. Abilities usually do not fluctuate widely over short periods of time. Role or task perceptions refer to the direction(s) in which individuals believe they should channel their efforts on their jobs. The activities and behavior that people believe are necessary in the performance of their jobs define their role perceptions.

To attain an acceptable level of performance, a minimum level of proficiency must exist in each of the performance components. Similarly, the level of proficiency in any one of the performance components can place an upper boundary on performance. If individuals put forth tremendous effort and have excellent abilities but lack a good understanding of their roles, performance will probably not be good in the eyes of their managers. A lot of work will be produced, but it will be misdirected. Likewise, an individual who puts forth a high degree of effort and understands the job, but lacks ability, probably will rate low on performance. A final possibility is the individual who has good ability and understands his or her role but is lazy and expends little effort. This person's performance will also probably be low. Of course, an individual can compensate up to a point for a weakness in one area by being above average in one or both of the other areas.

Environmental
factors as
performance
obstacles

Other factors beyond the control of the subordinate can also stifle performance. Although such potential obstacles are sometimes used merely as excuses, they are often very real and should be recognized.

Some of the more common potential performance obstacles include a lack of time or conflicting demands on the subordinate's time, inadequate work facilities and equipment, restrictive policies that affect the job, lack of cooperation from others, type of supervision, timing, and even luck.[2]

Environmental factors should not be viewed as direct determinants of individual performance but as modifying the effects of effort, ability, and direction (see Figure 13–1). For example, poor ventilation or worn-out equipment might very easily affect the effort exerted by an individual. Unclear policies or poor supervision can also produce misdirected effort. Similarly, a lack of training could result in underutil-

Figure 13–1   Environmental factors that modify performance

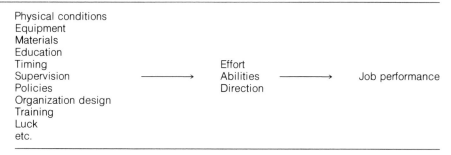

ized abilities. One of management's greatest responsibilities is to provide employees with adequate working conditions and a supportive environment to eliminate or minimize performance obstacles.

PERFORMANCE APPRAISAL— DEFINITION AND USES

Performance appraisal is a process that involves determining and communicating to an employee how he or she is performing the job and, ideally, establishing a plan of improvement. When properly conducted, performance appraisals not only let the employee know how well he or she is performing, but should also influence the employee's future level of effort and task direction. Effort should be enhanced if the employee is properly reinforced. The task perception of the employee should be clarified through the establishment of a plan for improvement.

One of the most common uses of performance appraisals is for making administrative decisions about employees relating to salary increases, promotions, transfers, and sometimes demotions or terminations.[3] For example, the present job performance of an individual is often the most significant consideration for determining whether to promote the person. While successful performance by an individual in his or her present job does not necessarily mean that he or she will be an effective performer in a higher level job, performance appraisals do provide some predictive information.[4]

Performance appraisal information can also provide needed input for determining both individual and organizational training and development needs. For example, it can be used to identify individual strengths and weaknesses. These data can then be used to help determine the organization's overall training and development needs. For an individual employee, a completed performance appraisal should include a plan outlining his or her specific training and development needs.

A final and most important use of performance appraisals is to encourage performance improvement. In this regard, performance appraisals are used as a means of communicating to an employee how he or she is doing and suggesting needed changes in behavior, attitude, skill, or knowledge. This type of feedback clarifies for the employee the job expectations of the manager. Often this feedback must be followed by coaching and training by the manager to guide an employee's work efforts.

A concern in organizations is how often performance appraisals should be conducted. One study indicated that annual performance appraisals are most common.[5] However, there seems to be no real consensus on the question of how frequently performance appraisals should be done. The answer seems to be as often as necessary to let the employee know what kind of job he or she is doing and, if performance is not satisfactory, the measures that must be taken for improvement. For many employees, this cannot be accomplished through one annual performance appraisal. Therefore, it is recommended that informal performance appraisals be conducted two or three times a year in addition to the annual performance appraisal for most employees.

PERFORMANCE APPRAISAL METHODS

The most commonly used performance appraisal methods include:

1. Essay appraisal.
2. Graphic rating scale.
3. Behaviorally anchored rating scale (BARS).
4. Checklist.
5. Forced-choice rating.
6. Critical incident appraisal.
7. Work standards approach.
8. Ranking methods.
9. Management by objectives.

Each of these methods is discussed in the following sections.

Essay appraisal

The essay appraisal method requires that the rater describe an individual's performance in written narrative form. Instructions are often provided to the rater as to the topics that should be covered. A typical essay appraisal question might be phrased as follows: "Describe in your own words, this employee's performance, including quantity and quality or work, job knowledge, and ability to get along with other employees. What are his or her strengths and weaknesses?"[6] The primary problem with essay appraisals is that their length and content can vary considerably, depending on the rater. For instance, one rater may write a lengthy statement describing an individual's potential and little about his or her past performance. On the other hand, another rater might concentrate on the individual's past performance. Thus, essay appraisals are difficult to compare. The writing skill of the appraiser can also affect the appraisal. An effective writer can make an average employee look better than his or her actual performance warrants.

Graphic rating scale   One of the most popular methods used in performance appraisals is the graphic rating scale. With this method, the rater assesses an individual on factors such as quantity of work, dependability, job knowledge, attendance, accuracy of work, and cooperativeness. Graphic rating scales include both numerical ranges and written descriptions. Figure 13–2 gives an example of some of the items that might be included on a graphic rating scale that uses written descriptions.

The graphic rating scale method is subject to some serious weaknesses. One potential weakness is that all raters are unlikely to inter-

Figure 13–2   Sample items that might be included on a graphic rating scale evaluation form

Quantity of work—is the amount of work an individual does in a workday.

( )	( )	( )	( )	( )
Does not meet minimum requirements.	Does just enough to get by.	Volume of work is satisfactory.	Very industrious, does more than is required.	Superior work production record.

Dependability—the ability to do required jobs well with a minimum of supervision.

( )	( )	( )	( )	( )
Requires close supervision; is unreliable.	Sometimes requires prompting.	Usually completes necessary tasks with reasonable promptness.	Requires little supervision, is reliable.	Requires absolute minimum of supervision.

Job knowledge—information on work duties that an individual should have for satisfactory job performance.

( )	( )	( )	( )	( )
Poorly informed about work duties.	Lacks knowledge of some phases of job.	Moderately informed, can answer most questions about the job.	Understands all phases of job.	Has complete mastery of all phases of job.

Attendance—faithfulness in coming to work daily and conforming to work hours.

( )	( )	( )	( )	( )
Often absent without good excuse or frequently reports for work late, or both.	Lax in attendance or reporting for work on time, or both.	Usually present and on time.	Very prompt, regular in attendance.	Always regular and prompt, volunteers for overtime when needed.

Accuracy—the correctness of work duties performed.

( )	( )	( )	( )	( )
Makes frequent errors.	Careless, often makes errors.	Usually accurate, makes only average number of mistakes.	Requires little supervision, is exact and precise most of the time.	Requires absolute minimum of supervision, is almost always accurate.

pret written descriptions in the same manner due to differences in background, experience, and personality.

Another potential problem relates to the choice of rating categories. It is possible to choose categories which have little relationship to job performance or to omit categories which have a significant influence on job performance. Regardless of these criticisms, however, a study of major national and international companies found that graphic rating scales were the primary appraisal technique used by these organizations.[7]

Behaviorally anchored rating scale (BARS)

The behaviorally anchored rating scale (BARS) method of performance appraisal is designed to assess behaviors that are required in successfully performing a job. To understand the use and development of BARS, several key terms must be clearly understood. First, most BARS use the term job dimension to mean those broad categories of duties and responsibilities that make up a job. In terms of the definitions given earlier in Chapter 2, a job dimension is the same as a job task. Each job is likely to have several job dimensions and separate scales must be developed for each. Figure 13–3 is an example of a BARS written for the job dimension found in many managerial jobs of planning, organizing, and scheduling project assignments and due dates. Scale values appear on the left-hand side of Figure 13–3 and define specific categories of performance. Anchors, which appear on the right-hand side of Figure 13–3, are specific written statements of actual behaviors that, when they are exhibited on the job, indicate the level of performance on the scale opposite that particular anchor.[8] As the anchor statements appear beside each of the scale values, they are said to "anchor" each of the scale values along the scale.

Rating performance using BARS requires the rater to read the list of anchors on each scale until he or she finds the group of anchors that best describes the employee's job behavior during the period being reviewed. The scale value opposite that group of anchors is then checked. This process is followed for all the identified dimensions of the job. A total evaluation is obtained by combining the scale values checked for all the different job dimensions.

BARS are normally developed through a series of meetings attended by both managers and job incumbents. The steps outlined below are usually followed:

1. Managers and job incumbents identify the relevant job dimensions for the job.
2. Managers and job incumbents write behavioral anchors for each of the job dimensions. As many anchors as possible should be written for each dimension.

Figure 13–3   Example of behaviorally anchored rating scale

Scale values	*Anchors*
7 [ ] Excellent	Develops a comprehensive project plan, documents it well, obtains required approval, and distributes the plan to all concerned.
6 [ ] Very good	Plans, communicates, and observes milestones; states week by week where the project stands relative to plans. Maintains up-to-date charts of project accomplishments and backlogs and uses these to optimize any schedule modifications required.
	Experiences occasional minor operational problems, but communicates effectively.
5 [ ] Good	Lays out all the parts of a job and schedules each part; seeks to beat schedule and will allow for slack.
	Satisfies customers' time constraints; time and cost overruns occur infrequently.
4 [ ] Average	Makes a list of due dates and revises them as the project progresses, usually adding unforeseen events; instigates frequent customer complaints.
	May have a sound plan, but does not keep track of milestones; does not report slippages in schedule or other problems as they occur.
3 [ ] Below average	Plans are poorly defined, unrealistic time schedules are common.
	Cannot plan more than a day or two ahead, has no concept of a realistic project due date.
2 [ ] Very poor	Has no plan or schedule of work segments to be performed.
	Does little or no planning for project assignments.
1 [ ] Unacceptable	Seldom, if ever, completes project because of lack of planning and does not seem to care.
	Fails consistently due to lack of planning and does not inquire about how to improve.

Source: C. E. Schneier and R. W. Beatty, "Developing Behaviorally Anchored Rating Scales (BARS)," *The Personnel Administrator*, August 1979, p. 60.

3. Managers and job incumbents reach a consensus concerning the scale values that are to be used and the grouping of anchor statements for each scale value.

The use of BARS can result in several advantages. First, BARS are developed through the active participation of managers and job incumbents. This participation increases the likelihood that the method will be accepted. A second advantage is that the anchors are developed from the observations and experiences of employees who actually perform the job. Finally, BARS can be used for providing specific feedback concerning an employee's job performance.

One of the major drawbacks to the use of BARS is that they take considerable time and commitment to develop. Furthermore, separate forms must be developed for different jobs.[9]

Figure 13–4   Sample checklist questions

	Yes	No
1. Does the individual lose his or her temper in public?	_____	_____
2. Does the individual play favorites?	_____	_____
3. Does the individual praise employees in public when they have done a good job?	_____	_____
4. Does the employee volunteer to do special jobs?	_____	_____

Checklist

In the checklist method, the rater makes yes-or-no responses to a series of questions concerning the employee's behavior. Figure 13–4 lists some typical questions. The checklist can also have varying weights assigned to each question.

Normally the scoring key for the checklist method is kept by the human resource department. The rater is generally not aware of the weights associated with each question, but because he or she can see the positive or negative connotation of each question, bias can be introduced. Additional drawbacks to the checklist method are that it is time-consuming to assemble the questions for each job category, a separate listing of questions must be developed for each different job category, and the checklist questions can have different meanings to different raters.

Forced-choice rating

Many variations of the forced-choice rating method exist. However, the most common practice requires the rater to rank a set of statements describing how an employee carries out the duties and responsibilities of his or her job. Figure 13–5 illustrates a group of forced-choice statements.

The statements are normally weighted, and the weights are not generally known to the rater. After the rater ranks all of the forced-choice

Figure 13–5   Sample forced-choice item

Instructions: Rank the following statements according to how they describe the manner in which this employee carries out his/her duties and responsibilities. Rank 1 should be given to the most descriptive and Rank 4 to the least descriptive. No ties are allowed.

Rank

_____ Has complete mastery of all phases of his/her job.

_____ Shows superior ability to express himself/herself.

_____ Requires close supervision.

_____ Careless and makes recurrent errors.

statements, the human resource department applies the weights and computes a score.

This method attempts to eliminate rater bias by forcing the rater to rank statements that may be seemingly indistinguishable or unrelated. However, it has been reported that the forced-choice method tends to irritate raters who feel they are not being trusted. Furthermore, the results of the forced-choice appraisal can be difficult to communicate to employees.

Critical incident appraisal

This appraisal method requires the rater to keep a written record of incidents, as they occur, involving job behaviors that illustrate both satisfactory and unsatisfactory performance of the person being rated. The incidents as they are recorded over time provide a basis for evaluating performance and providing feedback to the employee.

The main drawback to this approach is that the rater is required to jot down incidents regularly; this can be burdensome and time-consuming. Also, the definition of a critical incident is unclear and may be interpreted differently by different people. It is felt that this method can lead to friction between the manager and his or her employees when the employees feel that the manager is keeping a "book" on them.

Work standards

This method involves setting a standard or expected level of output and then comparing each employee's level to the standard. Generally speaking, work standards should reflect the normal output of a normal person. Work standards attempt to answer the question: What is a fair day's output? The work standards approach is most frequently used for production employees.

Several methods can be used for setting work standards. Some of the more common methods are summarized in Figure 13–6.

An advantage of the work standards method is that the performance review is based on factors that are highly objective. Of course, to be effective, the standards must be viewed as being fair by the affected employees. The most serious criticism of work standards is a lack of comparability of standards for different job categories.

Ranking methods

When it becomes necessary to compare the performance of two or more individuals, ranking methods can be used. Three of the more commonly used ranking methods are alternation, paired comparison, and forced distribution.

Alternation ranking Using this ranking method, the names of the individuals who are to be rated are listed down the left-hand side of a

Figure 13–6   Frequently used methods for setting work standards

Methods	Areas of applicability
Average production of work groups	When tasks performed by all individuals are the same or approximately the same.
Standards based on the performance of specially selected individuals	When tasks performed by all individuals are basically the same and it would be cumbersome and time-consuming to use the group average.
Time study	Jobs involving repetitive tasks.
Work sampling	For noncyclical types of work where many different tasks are performed, there is no set pattern or cycle.
The use of expert opinion	When none of the more direct methods (described above) applies.

sheet of paper. The rater is then asked to choose the "most valuable" employee on the list, cross his or her name off the left-hand list, and put it at the top of the column on the right-hand side of the paper. The rater is then asked to select and cross off the name of the "least valuable" employee from the left-hand column and move it to the bottom of the right-hand column. The rater then repeats this process for all of the names on the left-hand side of the paper. The resulting list of names in the right-hand column gives a ranking of the employees from most to least valuable.

Paired comparison ranking This method is best illustrated with an example. Suppose a rater is to evaluate six employees. The names of these individuals are listed on the left-hand side of a sheet of paper. The rater then compares the first employee with the second employee on a chosen performance criterion, such as quantity of work. If the rater feels that the first employee has produced more work than the second employee, a check mark would be placed by the first employee's name. The first employee would then be compared to the third, fourth, fifth, and sixth employee on the same performance criterion. A check mark would be placed by the name of the employee who had produced the most work in each of these paired comparisons. The process is repeated until each worker is compared to every other worker on all of the chosen performance criteria. The employee with the most check marks is considered to be the best performer. Likewise, the employee with the least number of check marks is the lowest performer. One major problem with the paired comparison method is that it becomes unwieldy when comparing large numbers of employees.

Forced distribution This method requires the rater to compare the performance of employees and place a certain percentage of employees

Figure 13–7   Forced distribution curve

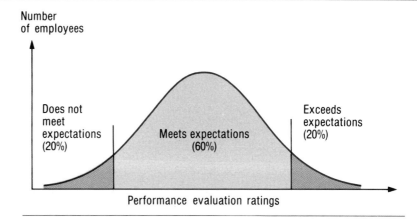

Number
of employees

Does not
meet
expectations
(20%)

Meets expectations
(60%)

Exceeds
expectations
(20%)

Performance evaluation ratings

at various performance levels. This method assumes that the performance level in a group of employees will be distributed according to a bell-shaped or "normal" curve. Figure 13–7 illustrates how the forced distribution method works. The rater is required to rate 60 percent of the employees as meeting expectations, 20 percent as exceeding expectations, and 20 percent as not meeting expectations. One problem with the forced distribution method is that in small groups of employees, a bell-shaped distribution of performance may not be applicable. Also, whereas the distribution may approximate a normal curve, it is probably not a perfect curve. This means that some employees will probably not be rated accurately.

Management by objectives (MBO)

The management by objectives (MBO) approach to performance appraisal is more commonly used with professional and managerial employees. Other names for MBO include management by results, performance management, results management, and work-planning and review program.

The process of MBO typically consists of: (1) establishing clear and precisely defined statements of objectives for the work that is to be done by an employee, (2) developing an action plan indicating how these objectives are to be achieved, (3) the employee implementing this action plan, (4) measuring objective achievement, and (5) taking corrective action, when necessary, and (6) establishing new objectives for the future. If an MBO system is to be successful, several requirements must be met. First, objectives should be quantifiable and measurable. Objectives whose attainment cannot be measured or at least verified should be avoided where possible. Objectives should be challenging and yet achievable. Finally, objectives should be in writing

Figure 13–8   Example objectives for MBO
_____

To answer all customer complaints in writing within three
    days of receipt of complaint.
To reduce order processing time by two days within the
    next six months.
To implement the new computerized accounts receivable system
    by August 1.
_____

and should be expressed in clear, concise, and unambiguous language. Figure 13–8 lists some sample objectives that meet these requirements.

MBO also requires that employees have considerable input into the
objective-setting process. Active participation by the employee in developing the action plan is also essential in MBO. Managers who set
an employee's objectives without input and then ask the employee,
"You agree to these, don't you?" are unlikely to get high levels of
employee commitment.

A final requirement for the successful use of MBO is that the objectives and action plan must serve as a basis for regular discussions between the manager and employee concerning the employee's performance. These regular discussions provide an opportunity for the
manager and employee to modify objectives when necessary and discuss progress.

**POTENTIAL
ERRORS IN
PERFORMANCE
APPRAISALS**

Several common errors have been identified in performance appraisals. _Leniency_ is grouping ratings at the positive end instead of spreading them throughout the performance scale. _Central tendency_ is rating
all or most employees in the middle of the scale. Leniency and central
tendency errors make it difficult, if not impossible, to separate the
good performers from the poor performers. In addition, these errors
make it difficult to compare ratings from different raters. For example,
it is possible for a good performer who is evaluated by a manager
committing central tendency errors to receive a lower rating than a
poor performer who is rated by a manager committing leniency errors.

Another common error in performance appraisals is the _halo effect_.
This occurs when a manager allows general impressions of an employee to influence his or her judgment on each separate item in the
performance appraisal. This often results in the employee receiving
approximately the same rating on every item. An employee should not
necessarily be evaluated at the same level on all items in the performance appraisal.

Personal preferences, prejudices, and biases can also cause errors in performance appraisals. Managers with biases or prejudices tend to look for employee behaviors that tend to conform to his or her biases. Appearance, social status, dress, race, and sex have influenced many performance appraisals. Managers have also allowed first impressions to influence later judgments of an employee. First impressions are only a sample of behavior; however, people tend to retain these impressions, even when faced with contradictory evidence.[10]

OVERCOMING ERRORS IN PERFORMANCE APPRAISALS

As can be seen from the previous section, the potential for errors in performance appraisals is great. One approach to overcoming these errors is to make refinements in the design of appraisal methods. For example, it could be argued that the forced distribution method of performance appraisal attempts to overcome the errors of leniency and central tendency. In addition, behaviorally anchored rating scales are designed to reduce halo, leniency, and central tendency errors because managers have specific examples of performance against which an employee is to be evaluated. Unfortunately, refined instruments frequently do not overcome all the obstacles.[11] Thus, it does not appear likely that refining appraisal instruments will totally overcome errors in performance appraisals.

A more promising approach to overcoming errors in performance appraisals is to improve the skills of raters. Several studies have shown that certain appraisal errors can be reduced through training programs for the raters.[12] Suggestions on the specific training that should be given to raters is often vague, but normally emphasizes that raters should be given training to observe behavior more accurately and judge it fairly. One study found that training raters in how to keep a diary of critical incidents significantly reduced leniency and halo errors.[13] At this point, more research is needed before a definitive set of topics for rater training can be established. However, at a minimum, raters should receive training in the performance appraisal method(s) used by the company, the importance of the rater's role in the total appraisal process, and the communication skills necessary to provide feedback to the employee.

PROVIDING FEEDBACK THROUGH THE APPRAISAL INTERVIEW

After one of the previously discussed methods for developing an employee's performance appraisal has been used, the results must be communicated to the employee. Unless this interview is properly conducted, it can and frequently does result in an unpleasant experience for the manager and the employee.

Many research studies have been conducted concerning the conditions associated with the success or failure of appraisal interviews. Some of the conclusions reached are summarized as follows:

Sybron trains managers to improve performance appraisals

Like many other companies, the Sybron Corporation was not satisfied with its existing performance evaluation system.

"Many managers still did not know how to set measurable objectives," explains Ben Harper, training coordinator at Sybron, headquartered in Rochester, New York. "Nor did they know how to evaluate subordinates effectively and objectively."

The human resources staff reviewed the company's performance evaluation system and concluded that the problem was not in the system itself but in the area of management training.

"The system was good," says Franklin Rubenstein, executive vice president of Mohr Development, management consultants based in Stamford, Connecticut, who were called in by Sybron. "But it was so sophisticated that few managers had the skills to use it effectively. Lack of skills and confidence can result in performance appraisals being completed in a matter of minutes."

"It became obvious that we needed to develop a training program that would incorporate our views on goal setting, performance appraisal, and wage and salary administration," says Harper.

Sybron and the consultants designed a training program to provide the managers with the necessary skills and motivation to set objectives and assess subordinates' performance. In addition, the program is designed to train managers to encourage their employees to work to their full potential, through a systematic approach to employee goal setting, and to create a work atmosphere where employees will excel.

Interpersonal pointers

In the first part of the program, managers are taught the interpersonal skills and procedures for setting reviews, substantiating goals, and carrying out performance and salary reviews. They are given pointers, which are then demonstrated by a Sybron manager on a videotape. Each manager then practices the skill and receives the necessary feedback, including the opportunity to view himself on videotape. The managers are then asked to use the newly learned skills on the job and subsequently report back to their group on their progress.

The second part of the training course provides the managers with five general principles intended to help them change their behavior. The managers are asked to use these five principles to get better performance from subordinates as well as their peers and even customers and suppliers:

1. Maintain and enhance self-esteem.
2. Focus on behavior, not personality.
3. Use reinforcement techniques to shape behavior.
4. Active listening.
5. Maintain communication and set specific follow-up dates.

So far more than 250 Sybron managers have been through the program, starting from the top and moving through each successive level of management.

Source: Adapted from "Sybron Trains Managers to Improve Performance Appraisals," *Management Review,* January 1981, pp. 32–33. Published by: AMA-COM, American Management Association, 135 West 50th St., New York, N.Y. 10020.

1. The more the employee participates in the appraisal process, the more satisfied he or she is with the appraisal interview and with the manager, and the more likely are performance improvement objectives to be accepted and met.
2. The more a manager uses positive motivational techniques (e.g., recognizing and praising good performance), the more satisfied the employee is likely to be with the appraisal interview and with the manager.
3. The mutual setting by the manager and the employee of specific performance improvement objectives results in more improvement in performance than does a general discussion or criticism.
4. Discussing and solving problems that may be hampering the employee's current job performance improve the employee's performance.
5. Areas of job performance needing improvement that are most heavily criticized are less likely to be improved than similar areas of job performance that are less heavily criticized.
6. The more employees are allowed to voice their opinions during the interview, the more satisfied they feel with the interview.
7. The amount of thought and preparation employees independently devote before the interview increases the benefits of the interview.
8. The more employees perceive that performance appraisal results are tied to organizational rewards, the more beneficial is the interview.[14]

Many of the variables that have been identified and associated with positive outcomes from performance appraisal interviews are behaviors and skills that can be taught to those managers who are responsible for conducting the interviews. The human resource department should play a key role in the development and implementation of these programs.

PERFORMANCE APPRAISAL AND EQUAL EMPLOYMENT OPPORTUNITY

Title VII of the Civil Rights Act, which was discussed in depth in Chapter 4, permits the use of a bona fide performance appraisal system. Performance appraisal systems are not generally considered to be bona fide when their application results in adverse effects on minorities, women, or older employees.

A number of court cases have ruled that performance appraisal systems used by organizations were discriminatory and not job related. In one case involving layoffs, *Brito, et al.* v. *Zia Company*,[15] Spanish-surnamed workers were reinstated with back pay because the company had used a performance appraisal system of unknown validity in an uncontrolled and unstandardized manner. In *Mistretta* v. *Sandia Corporation*, performance appraisals were used as the main basis of layoff decisions affecting a disproportionate number of older employees.[16] The judge awarded the plantiffs double damages plus all court costs. One review of court decisions relating to performance appraisal systems concluded that the use of such systems may be illegal if the method of appraisal is not job related, performance standards are not derived through careful job analysis, the number of performance observations is inadequate, ratings are based on an evaluation of subjective or vague factors, raters are biased, or rating conditions are uncontrolled or unstandardized.[17]

Many suggestions have been offered for making performance appraisal systems more acceptable from a legal point of view. Some of these include: (1) providing written instructions to raters for the completion of evaluations; (2) deriving the content of the appraisal system from job analysis; and (3) ensuring that the results of the appraisals are reviewed by employees.[18] Unfortunately, it appears that appraisal systems in many organizations lag behind these requirements.[19] Human resource departments must play a key role in the development and implementation of effective and legal performance appraisal systems.

SUMMARY

Performance refers to the degree of accomplishment of the tasks that make up an individual's job. Performance in a given situation results from the interrelationships between effort, ability, and role perceptions, as modified by environmental forces.

Performance appraisal is a process that involves determining and communicating to an employee how he or she is performing the job and, ideally, involves establishing a plan of improvement. Methods of performance appraisal include: essay, graphic rating scale, behaviorally anchored rating scale, checklist, forced-choice rating, critical incident, work standards approach, ranking methods, and management by objectives. Each of these methods was discussed in this chapter.

Several common errors have been identified in performance appraisals. Leniency occurs when ratings are grouped at the positive end instead of being spread throughout the performance scale. Central tendency occurs when all or most employees are ranked in the middle of the rating scale. The halo effect occurs when a manager allows his or her general impression of an employee to influence judgment of each separate item in the performance appraisal. Two approaches to overcoming these errors are refining performance appraisal instruments and improving the skills of raters.

Many of the conditions associated with the success or failure of appraisal interviews were described in this chapter. Finally, the requirements of equal employment opportunity regarding performance appraisal systems were described.

REVIEW QUESTIONS

1. What is performance? What factors influence an employee's level of performance?
2. Define performance appraisal.
3. Give at least three uses of performance appraisal information.
4. Describe the following methods used in performance appraisal:
   a. Essay.
   b. Graphic rating scale.
   c. Behaviorally anchored rating scale.
   d. Checklist.
   e. Forced-choice rating.
   f. Critical incident.
   g. Work standards.
   h. Ranking methods.
   i. Management by objectives.
5. Define the following types of performance appraisal errors:
   a. Leniency.
   b. Central tendency.
   c. Halo effect.
6. Outline some of the conditions associated with the success or failure of appraisal interviews.
7. Describe some of the conditions which might make a performance appraisal system illegal.

DISCUSSION QUESTIONS

1. How often do you think that performance reviews should be conducted?
2. Describe your thoughts on discussing salary raises and promotions during the performance appraisal interview.
3. What technique do you believe would best apply to the evaluation of a college professor?
4. Was your last exam a performance appraisal? Use your last exam to discuss both the reasons for using performance appraisals and their limitations.

REFERENCES AND ADDITIONAL READINGS

1. L. W. Porter and E. E. Lawler, III, *Managerial Attitudes and Performance* (Homewood, Ill.: Dorsey Press, 1968), p. 28.
2. C. N. Greene, "The Satisfaction—Performance Controversy," *Business Horizons,* October 1972, p. 36. Copyright 1972, by the Foundation for the School of Business at Indiana University. Reprinted by permission.
3. D. McGregor, "An Uneasy Look at Performance Appraisal," *Harvard Business Review,* May–June 1975, pp. 89–94.
4. D. Yoder and H. Henneman, *Handbook of Personnel and Industrial Relations* (Washington, D.C.: Bureau of National Affairs, 1979), p. 4-168.
5. *Management Performance Appraisal Programs,* Bureau of National Affairs PPF Survey no. 104 (Washington, D.C. 1974), p. 13.
6. Ibid. p. 4-168.
7. K. S. Teel, "Performance Appraisal: Current Trends, Persistent Progress," *Personnel Journal,* April 1980, pp. 296–301.

8. C. E. Schneier and R. W. Beatty, "Developing Behaviorally Anchored Rating Scales (BARS)," *The Personnel Administrator,* August 1979, p. 63.

9. For a further discussion of BARS, see P. O. Kingstrom and A. R. Bass, "A Critical Analysis of Studies Comparing Behaviorally Anchored Rating Scales (BARS) and Other Rating Formats," *Personnel Psychology* 34 (1981), pp. 263–89.

10. For additional discussion of appraisal errors, see W. F. Cascio, *Applied Psychology in Personnel Management* (Reston, Va.: Reston Publishing, 1978), pp. 320–22.

11. See, for instance, D. P. Schwab, H. G. Henneman, and T. A. DeCatiris, "Behaviorally Anchored Rating Scales: A Review of the Literature," *Personnel Psychology* 28 (1975), pp. 549–62.

12. See J. M. Ivancevich, "A Longitudinal Study of the Effects of Rater Training on Psychometric Errors in Ratings," *Journal of Applied Psychology* 64 (1979), pp. 502–508; and H. J. Bernardin and D. S. Walter, "Effects of Rater Training and Diary-Keeping on Psychometric Error in Ratings," *Journal of Applied Psychology* 62 (1977), pp. 64–69.

13. H. J. Bernardin and M. R. Buckley, "Strategies in Rater Training," *Academy of Management Review* 6 (1981), pp. 205–12.

14. R. J. Burke, W. Weitzel, and T. Weir, "Characteristics of Effective Employee Performance Review and Development Interviews: Replication and Extension," *Personnel Psychology* 31 (1978), pp. 903–19.

15. *Brito, et al.* v. *Zia Company,* 478 F.2d. 1200 (1973).

16. H. B. Winstanley, "Legal and Ethical Issues in Performance Appraisals," *Harvard Business Review,* November–December 1980, p. 188.

17. W. H. Holley and H. S. Field, "Performance Appraisal and the Law," *Labor Law Journal,* July 1975, p. 423.

18. H. S. Field and W. H. Holley, "The Relationship of Performance Appraisal System Characteristics to Verdicts in Selected Employment Discrimination Cases," *Academy of Management Journal,* June 1982, pp. 399–402.

19. Ibid., p. 403.

Case 13–1

THE COLLEGE ADMISSIONS OFFICE

Bob Luck was hired to replace Alice Carter as administrative assistant in the admissions office of Claymore Community College. Before leaving, Alice had given a month's notice to the director of admissions, hoping that this would allow ample time to locate and train her replacement. Alice's responsibilities included preparing and mailing transcripts at the request of students, mailing information requested by people interested in attending the college, answering the telephone, assisting students or persons interested in enrolling when they came to the office, and general supervision of the clerk-typists and student assistants in the office.

After interviewing and testing many people for the position, the director hired Bob, mainly because his credentials were good and he made a good impression. Alice spent many hours during the next 10 days training Bob. He appeared to be quite bright and seemed to pick up quickly the procedures involved in operating a college admissions office. When Alice left, everyone thought that Bob would do an outstanding job.

However, little time had elapsed before it was realized that Bob had not caught on to his job responsibilities. Bob seemed to have personal problems that were severe enough to stand in the way of his work. He asked questions about subjects that Alice had covered explicitly; he would have been able to answer these himself if he had comprehended her instructions.

Bob appeared to have other things on his mind constantly. He seemed to be preoccupied with such problems as his recent divorce, which he blamed entirely on his ex-wife, and the distress of his eight-year-old daughter, who missed her father terribly. His thoughts also dwelled on his search for peace of mind and some reason for all that had happened to him. The director of admissions was aware of Bob's preoccupation with his personal life and his failure to learn the office procedures rapidly.

1. *What would you do at this point if you were the director of admissions?*

2. *Describe how you might effectively use a performance appraisal in this situation.*

Case 13–2 **THE LACKADAISICAL PLANT MANAGER**

Plant manager Paul Dorn wondered why his boss, Leonard Hech, had sent for him. Paul, who thought that Leonard had been tough on him lately, was slightly uneasy at being asked to come to Leonard's office at a time when such meetings were unusual. "Close the door and sit down, Paul," invited Leonard. "I've been wanting to talk to you." After preliminary conversation was completed, Leonard said that because Paul's latest project had been finished, he would receive the raise that he had been promised on its completion.

Leonard went on to say that since it was time for Paul's performance appraisal, they might as well do that now. Leonard explained that the performance appraisal was based on four criteria: (1) amount of high-quality merchandise manufactured and shipped on time, (2) quality of relationships with plant employees and peers, (3) progress in maintaining employee safety and health, and (4) reaction to demands of top management. The first criterion had a relative importance of 40 percent, and the rest had a weight of 20 percent each.

On the first item, Paul received an excellent rating. Shipments were at an all-time high, quality was good, and few shipments had arrived late. On the second item, Paul also was rated excellent. Leonard said that plant employees and peers related well to Paul, that labor relations were excellent, and that there had been no major grievances since Paul had become plant manager.

However, on attention to matters of employee safety and health, the evaluation was below average. His boss stated that no matter how much he bugged Paul about improving housekeeping in the plant, he never seemed to produce results. Leonard also rated Paul below average on meeting demands from top management. He explained that Paul always answered yes to any request and then disregarded it, going about his business as if nothing had happened.

Seemingly surprised at the comments, Paul agreed that perhaps Leonard was right and that he should do a better job on these matters. Smiling as he left, he thanked Leonard for the raise and the frank appraisal.

As weeks went by, Leonard noticed little change in Paul. He reviewed the situation with an associate. "It's frustrating. In this time of rapid growth, we must make constant changes in work methods. Paul agrees, but can't seem to make people break their habits and adopt more efficient ones. I find myself riding him very hard these days, but he just calmly takes it. He's well liked by everyone. But somehow, he's got to care about safety and housekeeping in the plant. And when higher management makes demands he can't meet, he's got to say, 'I can't do that and do all the other things you want, too.' Now he has dozens of unfinished jobs because he refuses to say no."

As he talked, Leonard remembered something Paul had told him in confidence once. "I take Valium for a physical condition I have. When I don't take it, I get symptoms similar to a heart attack. But I only take half as much as the doctor prescribed." Now, Leonard thought, I'm really in a spot. If the Valium is what is making him so lackadaisical, I can't endanger his health by asking him to quit taking it. And I certainly can't fire him. Yet, as things stand, he really can't implement all the changes we must have to fulfill the goals we have set for the next two years.

1. *What would you do if you were in Leonard's place?*
2. *What could have been done differently during the performance appraisal session?*

Chapter 14

Career planning

Objectives

1. To develop an understanding of the increasing importance of career planning.
2. To outline the responsibilities of both the organization and the individual with regard to career planning.
3. To present a general approach to developing a career plan.
4. To refute several myths related to career planning and advancement.

Outline

Why is career planning necessary?
Who is responsible for career planning?
 The organization's responsibilities
 The manager's responsibilities
 The individual's responsibilities
Developing a career plan
 Individual assessment
 Assessment by the organization
  Communicating career options
  Career counseling
 Career pathing
Reviewing career progress
Career-related myths
 Myth 1: There is always room for one more person at the top
 Myth 2: The key to success is being in the right place at the right time
 Myth 3: Good subordinates make good superiors
 Myth 4: Career planning and development are a function of the human resource department
Myth 5: All good things come to those who work long, hard hours
Myth 6: Rapid advancement along a career path is largely a function of the kind of manager one has
Myth 7.: The way to get ahead is to determine your weaknesses and then work hard to correct them
Myth 8: Always do your best regardless of the task
Myth 9: It is wise to keep home life and work life separated
Myth 10: The grass is always greener on the other side of the fence
Dealing with career plateaus
Outplacement

Glossary of terms

Career pathing A sequence of developmental activities involving informal and formal education, training, and job experiences that help make an individual capable of holding a more advanced job in the future.

Career planning The process of analyzing an individual's situation, identifying his or her career objectives and developing the means for realizing these objectives.

Career plateau The point in an individual's career where the likelihood of an additional promotion is very low.

Deadwood Individuals in an organization whose present performance has fallen to an unsatisfactory level and who have little potential for advancement.

Learners Individuals in an organization who have a high potential for advancement but who are currently performing below standard.

Outplacement Benefit provided by an employer to help an employee leave the organization and get a job someplace else.

Solid citizens Individuals in an organization whose present performance is satisfactory but whose chance for future advancement is small.

Stars Individuals in an organization who are presently doing outstanding work and have a high potential for continued advancement.

"The emergence and decline of occupations will be so rapid," says economist Norman Anon, an expert in manpower problems, "that people will always be uncertain in them." The profession of airline flight engineer, he notes, emerged and then began to die out within a brief period of 15 years.

Alvin Toffler[*]

Not too many years ago, an individual would join an organization and would probably stay with it for his or her entire working career.[1] Gold watches and length-of-service pins were frequently given by organizations. The concept of organizational loyalty has faded in the decades since World War II. Under conditions prevailing in the 1980s, the average 20-year-old employee could be expected to change jobs approximately six or seven times during his or her lifetime. Consequently, instead of thinking in terms of remaining with one organization, many employees now expect to pursue different careers. The accelerated rate of change in today's world has significantly increased employee mobility. Even when an employee desires to remain with the same organization, changes in its environment may make this choice unfeasible. These environmental forces plus changes within the individual make career planning important for today's employees.

WHY IS CAREER PLANNING NECESSARY?

An individual's career goals are more likely to be reached if he or she develops a plan to reach these goals. Realistic career planning forces an individual to look at the available opportunities in relation to his or her abilities. For example, a person might strongly desire to be a history teacher until he or she discovers there are two history teachers available for every job.

With a career plan, a person is much more likely to experience satisfaction as progress is made along the career path. A good career plan identifies certain milestones along the way. When these milestones are consciously recognized and reached, the person is much more likely to experience feelings of achievement. Furthermore, these feelings increase the individual's personal satisfaction and motivation.

From the organization's viewpoint, career planning can reduce costs due to employee turnover. For example, one bank's career counseling program saved $1.95 million in a year through an estimated 65 percent reduction in turnover, an 85 percent improvement in performance, a 25 percent increase in productivity, and a 75 percent increase in promotability.[2] If a company assists employees in developing career plans, these plans are likely to be closely tied to the organization; therefore, employees are less likely to quit. The fact that an organization shows interest in an employee's career development also has a positive effect

*[*]A. Toffler, *Future Shock* (New York: Random House, 1970), pp. 94–95.

on the employee. Under these circumstances, employees feel that they are regarded by the company as part of an overall plan and not just as numbers.

From the organization's viewpoint, career planning has three major objectives:

1. To meet the immediate and future human resource needs of the organization on a timely basis.
2. To better inform the organization and the individual about potential career paths within the organization.
3. To utilize existing human resource programs to the fullest by integrating the activities which select, assign, develop, and manage individual careers with the organization's plans.[3]

WHO IS RESPONSIBLE FOR CAREER PLANNING?

What are the responsibilities of both the organization and the individual with regard to career planning and development? Which one has the primary responsibility? The answer is that successful career planning and development requires actions from three sources—the organization, the employee's immediate manager, and the individual.

The organization's responsibilities

The organization alone cannot and should not bear total responsibility for planning and developing an individual's career. The organization's responsibilities are to develop and communicate career options within the organization.[4] The organization should carefully advise an employee concerning the career paths (series of jobs) that he or she might take to achieve his or her career goals. The human resource department generally is responsible for ensuring that this information is kept current as new jobs are created and old ones are phased out. Working closely with both employees and their managers, human resource specialists should see that accurate information is conveyed and that interrelationships between different career paths are understood. Thus, rather than bearing the primary responsibility for preparing career plans, the organization should promote the conditions and create the environment that will facilitate employee career development.[5]

The manager's responsibilities

It has been said that "the critical battleground in career development is inside the mind of the person charged with supervisory responsibility."[6] Although not expected to be a professional counselor, the manager can and should play an important role in facilitating a subordinate's career planning. First and foremost, the manager should serve as the catalyst for the process. Figure 14–1 lists several roles that a manager might perform to assist subordinates in career planning.

Figure 14–1   Potential career planning roles of managers

Communicator
    Holds formal and informal discussions with employees.
    Listens to and understands an employee's real concern.
    Clearly and effectively interacts with an employee.
    Establishes environment for open interaction.
    Structures uninterrupted time to meet with employees.

Counselor
    Helps employee identify career-related skills, interests, values.
    Helps an employee identify a variety of career options.
    Helps employee evaluate appropriateness of various options.
    Helps employee design/plan strategy to achieve an agreed-upon career goal.

Appraiser
    Identifies critical job elements.
    Negotiates with employee a set of goals and objectives to evaluate performance.
    Assesses employee performance related to goals and objectives.
    Communicates performance evaluation and assessment to employee.
    Designs a development plan around future job goals and objectives.
    Reinforces effective job performance.
    Reviews an established development plan on an ongoing basis.

Coach
    Teaches specific job-related or technical skills.
    Reinforces effective performance.
    Suggests specific behaviors for improvement.
    Clarifies and communicates goals and objectives of work group and organization.

Mentor
    Arranges for an employee to participate in a high-visibility activity either inside or
        outside the organization.
    Serves as a role model in an employee's career development by demonstrating suc-
        cessful career behaviors.
    Supports employee by communicating to others in and out of organization employee's
        effectiveness.

Advisor
    Communicates the informal and formal realities of progression in the organization.
    Suggests appropriate training activities which could benefit employee.
    Suggests appropriate strategies for career advancement.

Broker
    Assists in bringing employees together who might mutually help each other in their
        careers.
    Assists in linking employees with appropriate educational or employment opportuni-
        ties.
    Helps employee identify obstacles to changing present situation.
    Helps employee identify resources enabling a career development change.

Referral agent
    Identifies employees with problems (e.g., career, personal, health).
    Identifies resources appropriate to an employee experiencing a problem.
    Bridges and supports employee with referral agents.
    Follows up on effectiveness of suggested referrals.

Advocate
    Works with employee in designing a plan for redress of a specific issue for higher
        levels of management.
    Works with employee in planning alternative strategies if a redress to management is
        not successful.
    Represents employee's concern to higher-level management for redress of specific
        issues.

Source: Z. B. Leibowitz and N. K. Schlossberg, "Training Managers for Their Role in A Career Development System," *Training and Development Journal*, July 1981, p. 74.

Unfortunately, many managers do not perceive career counseling as part of their managerial duties. It is not that they are opposed to this role, but rather that they have never considered it as part of their job. To help overcome this and other related problems, many organizations have designed training programs to help their managers develop the necessary skills in this area. Figure 14–2 presents a suggested chronology of topics that might be covered in such a program.

The individual's responsibilities

The ultimate responsibility for career planning and development rests with the individual. Only the individual knows what he or she really wants out of a career, and certainly these desires vary appreciably from person to person. If an individual leaves career-planning responsibilities entirely to the organization, he or she is lowering chances for achieving career goals.

Career planning requires a conscious effort on the part of the individual; it does not automatically happen. Although an individual may be convinced that developing a sound career plan would be in his or her best interest, finding the time to develop such a plan is often another matter. This is where the organization can help by providing trained specialists to encourage and guide the employee. This can best

Figure 14–2   Suggested chronology of topics for training managers in career planning

First day
A.M.   What is career planning and development?
             Common misconceptions about career planning and development.
             The manager's role in career planning.
             Self-assessment of current strengths and skills.
P.M.   Career planning and development.
             Stuck versus moving employees.
             Career anchors.
             Career stages.

Second day
A.M.   Career-planning process model.
             Communications skills presentation and practice.
P.M.   Identifying career-planning issues and action strategies.
             What's appropriate.
             Constraints, obstacles, and reality checks.
      Summary and homework

Half-day session (one or two weeks later)
      Sharing of experience.
        Dealing with problems.
        Review of skills and model.
        Additional practice and evaluation.

Source: Z. B. Leibowitz and N. K. Schlossberg, "Training Managers for Their Role in a Career Development System," *Training and Development Journal,* July 1981, p. 76.

be accomplished by alloting a few hours of company time each quarter to this type of planning.

While the individual is ultimately responsible for career planning and development, experience has shown that when people are not given some encouragement and direction, little progress is made. Successful career planning results from a joint effort by the individual, the immediate manager, and the organization; the individual does the planning, the immediate manager provides the guidance and encouragement, and the organization provides the resources and structure.

DEVELOPING A CAREER PLAN

Career planning is closely related to and dependent upon many human resource functions. Figure 14–3 summarizes how several of the basic human resource functions can be integrated into the career-planning process.

Although many variations are possible, the development of a career plan involves four basic steps: (1) an assessment by the individual of his or her abilities, interests, and career goals; (2) an assessment by the organization of the individual's abilities and potential; (3) communication of career options and opportunities within the organization; and (4) career counseling to set realistic goals and plans for their accomplishment.[7]

Individual assessment

Many people never stop to analyze their abilities, interests, and career goals. It isn't that most people don't want to analyze these factors, but rather that they simply never take the time. While this is not something an organization can do for the individual, the organization can provide the impetus and structure. A variety of self-assessment materials are available commercially and some organizations have developed tailor-made forms for the use of their employees.[8] Another option is to use some form of psychological testing.

An individual's self-assessment should not necessarily be limited by his or her current resources and abilities. Career plans normally require that the individual acquire additional training and skills. However, this assessment should be limited by reality. For the individual, the heart of this assessment involves identifying his or her personal strengths. These strengths include not only the individual's developed abilities, but also the financial resources available.

Assessment by the organization

Organizations have several potential sources of information that can be used for assessing employees. Traditionally, the most frequently used source has been the performance appraisal process. The assessment center, discussed in Chapter 8, can also be an excellent source of

Figure 14–3   Basic human resource functions and their relationship to the career development process

	Existing programs	*Essential elements*	*Integration with career development system*
	Human resource planning	Summary of existing management positions in all divisions. Listing of employees in those positions. Rating as to performance/promotability from supervisor's point of view.	To determine current status of existing employees and positions that may become open.
		Summary of the types and numbers of employees needed to accomplish the short-and-long-term goals and objectives of each division.	To determine future human resource needs of the organization, by division, to advise employees of future growth/reduction, typical turnover of positions and to adivse on the development of employees to meet future organization needs
	Performance review system	Objective evaluation of immediate past performance of individual job.	To counsel future development of employees based on current performance. To test the reality of individual's career goals in the organization.
	Organization charts, job descriptions and job specifications	Overall structure of organization. Types of positions in the organization. Essential skills, education and experience required for those positions.	To use as counseling tool to focus employee's options on types of positions available in organization and methods of preparation for those positions.
	Training and development programs	Summary of development programs available to include target audience and objectives of the programs.	To facilitate formal development of employees at appropriate points after development of career plan.
	Organization promotion policy	Stated procedure for filling internal openings.	To enable employee to have access to certain openings if in line with

Source: Adapted from B. C. Winterscheid, "A Career Development System Coordinates Training Efforts," *Personnel Administrator*, August 1980, p. 29.

Displaced executives try career change,
and some succeed in face of heavy
odds

When Robert Kemble joined Dart Industries Inc. in Los Angeles 14 years ago, he hoped to make his career there. But in 1980, Dart agreed to merge with Kraft Inc. and to move its headquarters to the Chicago area. The move changed the Dart vice president's plans.

"The day the merger was announced, my wife and I made the decision that if we were asked to move to Chicago, we would fulfill a fantasy and move to Maui," recalls Kemble, now 52. And move to Hawaii they did.

Executives like Kemble, displaced from seemingly secure posts, are finding unlikely jobs in unlikely places. Many are launching second careers that sometimes reduce their income but often stretch their minds and recharge their lives.

A career change, while difficult, has worked so far for Kemble. He and other such survivors are perhaps the one bright note in a year of gloom for many middle-aged executives. Recessionary layoffs and disruptive mergers have put thousands of managers out of work at what they had expected to be the peak of their careers. White-collar unemployment was at 5.6 percent in November, according to the Bureau of Labor Statistics. That is a higher rate than prevailed at any point in the 1973–75 recession.

Many displaced executives consider career changes, but most end up at jobs much like the ones they have left, experts say. "When someone is terminated, the natural reaction is, 'I'm going to stop doing this,' " says Harold B. Bray Jr., a Chicago job counselor. "Then they begin to get more objective and realize they have to go with what they've got."

One's own man

The sacrifice of taking a lower-level job—at less pay—proves too great for many executives accustomed to the perquisites of corporate life. But others like Kemble, cushioned by generous severance payments (a year's pay in his case), risk the change for peace of mind or the chance to be an entrepreneur.

"In today's climate, it's difficult to make career switches," says Joseph Jannotta of the Chicago outplacement firm that bears his name. Even so, more people are defying the odds and attempting to switch vocations, counselors say, though no one keeps statistics on managerial career changes. Of those who find new jobs, one in four fails at them, the experts estimate.

The Hawaiian

Outplacement services and job counselors often throw cold water on notions people have about running off to the tropics, or about going into their own business. Robert McCarthy, Kemble's outplacement counselor, remembers how he reacted to his client's plans. "Oh God, we've got another one," he thought to himself.

But the former vice president of personnel at Dart wouldn't settle for anything else. He was tired of the stress of corporate life, and his youngest son had just graduated from high school. "It was perfect timing," Kemble recalls.

Kemble decided to look for a small accounting and bookkeeping firm to buy. He found one. But before he took over, he worked his way through a high school bookkeeping text to brush up some of the accounting skills he had last used in graduate school. He taught himself to use an Apple computer. Then he rented a storefront office, and Lahaina Computer Services hung out its shingle. Instead of commuting 50 miles to Dart headquarters, as he had done, he now walks the half mile to work. "I'm sitting here in the office in a pair of shorts, bare feet and a blue plaid sport shirt," he says by telephone from Maui. "When I wrap things up, it is five minutes home to play tennis."

Kemble is drawing about a third of his previous salary, which he won't divulge, but he is building equity in a business that he hopes will pay off later. In the year ahead, however, Kemble says he expects the business will put food on the table and provide for one trip to California.

For the moment, the new Hawaiian isn't worried. He's still coasting on what remains of his severance pay.

information. Other potential sources include personnel records reflecting information such as education and previous work experience.

It is usually a good idea for an organization not to depend on any one source of information but rather to use as many as are readily available. Such an approach provides a natural system of checks and balances. The organization's assessment of an individual employee should normally be conducted jointly by the human resource department and the individual's immediate manager.

Communicating career options Before an individual can set realistic career goals, he or she must know the options and opportunities that are available. Several things can be done by the organization to make an individual aware of his or her options. Posting and advertising job vacancies is one activity that helps employees get a feel for their options. Clearly identifying possible paths of advancement within the organization is also helpful. This can be done as part of the performance appraisal process. Another good idea is to share human resource planning forecasts with employees.

Career counseling Career counseling is the activity that integrates the different steps in the career-planning process. Career counseling may be performed by an employee's immediate manager, a human resource specialist, or a combination of the two. In most cases, it is preferable to have the counseling conducted by the immediate manager with appropriate input from the human resource department. The immediate manager generally has the advantage of practical experience, knows the company, and is in a position to make a realistic appraisal of organizational opportunities.

Some managers are reluctant to attempt counseling for fear that they haven't been trained in the area. However, it is not necessary to be a trained psychologist to be a successful career counselor.[9] In fact, behavioral research and actual experience suggest that the characteristics that make people likable and effective are basically the same qualities that contribute to successful counseling.[10] Of course, the right type of training can be very beneficial to even accomplished career counselors.[11] Figure 14–4 presents a short quiz that can be used by managers to evaluate their skills in career counseling.

Generally, managers who are good in basic human relations are successful as career counselors. Developing a caring attitude and atmosphere toward the employee and his or her career is of prime importance. Being receptive to employee concerns and problems is another requirement. In addition to these general requirements, some specific suggestions for helping managers become better career counselors are offered below:[12]

> Recognize the limits of career counseling—Remember the manager and the organization serve as catalysts in the career development process. The primary responsibility for developing a career plan lies with the individual employee.
>
> Respect confidentiality—Career counseling is very personal and has basic requirements of ethics, confidentiality, and privacy.
>
> Establish a relationship—Be honest, open, and sincere with the subordinate. Try to be empathetic and see things from the subordinate's point of view.
>
> Listen effectively—Learn to be a sincere listener. A natural human tendency is to want to do most of the talking. It often takes a conscious effort to be a good listener.
>
> Consider alternatives—An important goal in career counseling is to help subordinates realize that there are usually a number of available choices. Help the subordinates to expand their thinking and not necessarily be limited by past experience.
>
> Seek and share information—Be sure the employee and the organization have completed their respective assessments of the employee's abilities, interests and desires. Make sure that the organization's assessment has been clearly communicated to the employee and that the employee is aware of potential job openings within the organization.
>
> Assist with goal definition and planning—Remember that the employee must make the final decisions. Managers should serve as "sounding boards" and help ensure that the individual's plans are valid.

Career pathing

Career pathing is a technique which addresses the specifics of progressing from one job to another in the organization. It can be defined as a sequence of developmental activities involving informal and formal education, training, and job experiences that help make an indi-

Figure 14–4   Examining a manager's knowledge of career counseling

How do you rate as a career counselor?

This quiz will help managers examine their knowledge of the career counseling function and help them to discover those areas in which some skill building may be necessary. Rate your knowledge, skill, and confidence as a managerial career counselor by scoring yourself on a scale of 0 (low) to 10 (high) on each of the following statements.

_____ 1. I am aware of how career orientations and life stages can influence a person's perspective and contribute to career-planning problems.

_____ 2. I understand my own career choices and changes and feel good enough about what I have done to be able to provide guidance to others.

_____ 3. I am aware of my own biases about dual career paths and feel that I can avoid these biases in coaching others to make a decision on which way to go with their careers.

_____ 4. I am aware of how my own values influence my point of view and recognize the importance of helping others to define their values and beliefs so they are congruent with career goals.

_____ 5. I am aware of the pitfalls of "shooting behind the duck," and try to keep myself well informed about my organization so I can show others how to "shoot ahead of the duck."

_____ 6. I know the norms existing within my own department as well as those within other departments and parts of the organization so I can help others deal with them effectively.

_____ 7. I understand the organizational reward system (nonmonetary) well enough to help others make informed decisions about career goals, paths, and plans.

_____ 8. I have access to a variety of techniques I can use to help others articulate their skills, set goals, and develop action plans to realize their career decisions.

_____ 9. I am informed on the competencies required for career success in this organization in both the managerial and technical areas, so I can advise others on the particular skills they need to build upon, and how to go about developing that expertise.

_____10. I feel confident enough about my own skills as a career counselor that I can effectively help my people with their problems and plans and make midcourse corrections when necessary.

Scoring
Add up your score and rate yourself against the following scale:

0–30	It might be a good idea if you found *yourself* a career counselor
31–60	Some of your people are receiving help from you . . . however, do you know how many and which ones are not?
61–80	You're a counselor! You may not be ready for the big league yet, but you are providing help for your people.
81–100	Others have a lot to learn from you. You understand the importance of career counseling and you know how to provide it.

Source: Adapted from P. R. Jones, B. Kaye, and H. R. Taylor, "You Want Me to Do What?" *Training and Development Journal*, July 1981, p. 62.

vidual capable of holding more advanced jobs.[13] Career pathing is most useful when used as a part of the overall career-planning process. For example, career pathing is helpful after an individual has determined the next job he or she would like to have. Figure 14–5 summarizes the basic steps involved in career pathing.

Figure 14–5   Basic steps of career pathing

Determine or reconfirm the abilities and end behaviors of the target job.
>   Because jobs tend to change over time, it is important to determine or confirm requirements and review them periodically.

Secure employee background data and review them for accuracy and completeness
>   Because interests and career objectives of people tend to shift, these also have to be confirmed. Also, it is often necessary to update the individual's records concerning skills, experience, etc.

Undertake a needs analysis comparison that jointly views the individual and the targeted job.
>   Determine if the individual and the targeted job tend to match. Surprisingly many organizations neglect to query individuals when questions arise concerning their backgrounds, potential abilities, and interests.

Reconcile employee career desires, developmental needs, and targeted job requirements with those of organizational career management.
>   Individuals formalize their career objectives or modify them as circumstances warrant.

Develop individual training work and educational needs using a time-activity orientation.
>   Identify the individual actions (work education and training experiences) necessary for the individual to progress to the targeted job.

Blueprint career path activities.
>   This is the process of creating a time-oriented blueprint or chart to guide the individual.

Source: Adapted from E. H. Burack and N. J. Mathys, *Career Management in Organizations: A Practical Human Resource Planning Approach* (Lake Forest, Il.: Brace-Park Press, 1979), pp. 79–80.

REVIEWING CAREER PROGRESS

Individual careers rarely go exactly according to plan. The environment changes, personal desires change, and other things also happen. However, if the individual periodically reviews his or her career plan and the situation, adjustments can be made so that career development is not impaired. If, on the other hand, the individual does not keep his or her career plan current, it rapidly becomes useless. Complacency is the greatest danger once a career plan has been developed. The plan must be changed as the situation and the individual change. Figure 14–6 presents a model which shows how the different parts of the career-planning process fit together.

CAREER-RELATED MYTHS

Many myths related to career planning and advancement have surfaced over the years and new ones are constantly being generated. These are summarized in Figure 14–7.[14] Frequently, these myths are misleading and can inhibit career planning and growth. The purpose of this section is to explore these myths and provide evidence disproving them.

Figure 14–6   Career development model

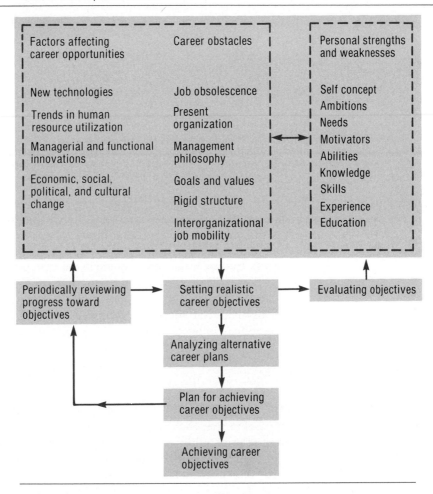

Factors affecting career opportunities

New technologies

Trends in human resource utilization

Managerial and functional innovations

Economic, social, political, and cultural change

Career obstacles

Job obsolescence

Present organization

Management philosophy

Goals and values

Rigid structure

Interorganizational job mobility

Personal strengths and weaknesses

Self concept

Ambitions

Needs

Motivators

Abilities

Knowledge

Skills

Experience

Education

Periodically reviewing progress toward objectives

Setting realistic career objectives

Evaluating objectives

Analyzing alternative career plans

Plan for achieving career objectives

Achieving career objectives

Source: Adapted from W. E. Reif, and J. W. Newstrom, "Career Development by Objectives," *Business Horizons*, October 1974, p. 8. Copyright 1974 by the Foundation for the School of Business at Indiana University. Reprinted by permission.

Myth 1: There is always room for one more person at the top   This myth is contradictory to the fact that structures of the overwhelming majority of today's organizations are shaped like a pyramid, with fewer positions available as one ascends the pyramid. Adherence to this myth fosters unrealistic aspirations and generates self-perpetuating frustrations. There is nothing wrong with wanting to become president of the organization; however, an individual must also be aware that the odds of attaining such a position are slim. For example, General Motors Corporation has approximately 748,000 employees and only one

Figure 14–7   Common myths related to career planning and development

---

Myth 1: There is always room for one more person at the top.
Myth 2: The key to success is being in the right place at the right time.
Myth 3: Good subordinates make good superiors.
Myth 4: Career planning and development are a function of the human resource department.
Myth 5: All good things come to those who work long, hard hours.
Myth 6: Rapid advancement along a career path is largely a function of the kind of manager one has.
Myth 7: The way to get ahead is to determine your weaknesses and then work hard to correct them.
Myth 8: Always do your best regardless of the task.
Myth 9: It is wise to keep home life and work life separated.
Myth 10: The grass is always greener on the other side of the fence.

---

president. The major lesson to be learned from Myth 1 is to pick career paths that are realistic and attainable.

Myth 2: The key to success is being in the right place at the right time Like all the career-related myths, this one has just enough truth to make it believable. One can always find a highly successful person who attributes all his or her success to being in the right place at the right time. People who adhere to this myth are rejecting the basic philosophy of planning: that a person, through careful design, can affect rather than merely accept the future. Adherence to Myth 2 is dangerous, because it can lead to complacency and a defeatist attitude.

Myth 3: Good subordinates make good superiors This myth is based on the belief that those employees who are the best performers in their current jobs should necessarily be the ones who are promoted. This is not to imply that good performance should not be rewarded, for it should. However, when an individual is being promoted, those making the decision should look carefully at the requirements of the new job in addition to the individual's performance in his or her present job. How many times has a star engineer or salesperson been promoted into a managerial role, only to fail miserably? Similarly, outstanding athletes are frequently made head coaches and everybody seems surprised when the former star fails in this job. Playing a sport and coaching require different talents and abilities. Because someone excels at one job does not mean that he or she will excel at all jobs.

Myth 4: Career planning and development are a function of the human resource department The ultimate responsibility for career planning and development belongs to the individual and not to the human resource department or the individual's manager. Personnel specialists can assist the individual and answer certain questions, but they cannot develop a career plan for the person. Only the individual can make his or her own career-related decisions.

Myth 5: All good things come to those who work long, hard hours People guided by this myth often spend 10 to 12 hours a day trying to impress their managers and move ahead rapidly in the organiza- tion. However, the results of these extra hours on the job often have little or no relationship to what the manager considers important, to the person's effectiveness on the job, and, most important in this con- text, to the individual's long-range career growth. Unfortunately, many managers reinforce this myth by designing activities "to keep every- one busy."

Myth 6: Rapid advancement along a career path is largely a function of the kind of manager one has A person's manager can affect an individ- ual's rate of advancement. However, those who adhere to this myth often accept a defensive role and ignore the importance of their own actions. Belief in this myth provides a ready-made excuse for failure. It is easy and convenient to blame failures on one's manager.

Myth 7: The way to get ahead is to determine your weaknesses and then work hard to correct them Successful salespeople do not emphasize the weak points of their products, rather, they emphasize the strong points. The same should be true in career planning and development. Indi- viduals who achieve their career objectives do so by stressing those things that they do uncommonly well. The secret is to capitalize first on one's strengths and then try to improve deficiencies in other areas.

Myth 8: Always do your best regardless of the task This myth stems from the Puritan work ethic. The problem is that believers ignore the fact that different tasks have different priorities. Since a person has only a limited amount of time, he or she should spend that time ac- cording to priorities. Those tasks and jobs that rank high in impor- tance in achieving one's career goals should receive the individual's "best" effort. Those tasks that do not rank high should be done, but not necessarily with one's best effort. The idea is for the individual to give something less than his or her best effort to unimportant tasks so that he or she will have time to give his or her best effort to the im- portant tasks.

Myth 9: It is wise to keep home life and work life separated An individ- ual cannot make wise career decisions without the full knowledge and support of his or her spouse. Working husbands and wives should share their inner feelings concerning their jobs so that their spouses understand the basic factors that weigh in any career decisions.

A healthy person usually has interests other than his or her job. Career strategy should be designed to recognize and support, not contradict, these other interests. Career objectives should be a subset of one's life objectives. Too often, however, career objectives conflict with rather than support life objectives.

Myth 10: The grass is always greener on the other side of the fence Regardless of the career path the individual follows, another one always seems a little more attractive. The fact is, however, that Utopia does not exist. More than likely, the job that John Doe holds involves many of the same problems that every working person might face. As the individual assumes more and more personal responsibilities, the price of taking that "attractive" job becomes high in terms of possibly relocating, developing a new social life, and learning new duties. This is not to say that job and career changes should not be made—however, one should avoid making such changes hastily.

DEALING WITH CAREER PLATEAUS

A career plateau is defined as "the point in a career where the likelihood of additional hierarchical promotion is very low."[15] Virtually all people reach a plateau in their careers. The difference is that some individuals reach their plateau earlier than others. Because it is inherently true that fewer positions are available as one moves up the hierarchical ladder, "plateauing" does not necessarily indicate failure. However, as will be shown in this section, the case of a "plateauee" may need to be handled differently in some situations from that of the employee still on the rise in the organization.

Fig 14–8 presents a model for classifying managerial careers. The four principal career states are described as:

Learners—Individuals with high potential for advancement who are performing below standard (for example, a new trainee).

Stars—Individuals presently doing outstanding work with a high

Figure 14–8 Classifying managerial careers

Current performance	Likelihood of future promotion	
	Low	High
High	Solid citizens (effective plateauees)	Stars
Low	Deadwood (ineffective plateauees)	Learners (comers)

Source: Adapted from T. P. Ference, J. A. F. Stoner, and E. K. Warren, "Managing the Career Plateau," *Academy of Management Review*, October 1977, p. 603.

potential for continued advancement; these are people on "fast track" career paths.

Solid citizens—Individuals whose present performance is satisfactory but whose chance for future advancement is small. (These people make up the bulk of the employees in most organizations.)

Deadwood—Individuals whose present performance has fallen to an unsatisfactory level; they have little potential for advancement.[16]

Naturally, organizations would like to have all "stars" and "solid citizens." The challenge, however, is to transform the learners into stars or solid citizens and to keep the current stars and solid citizens from slipping into the deadwood category. Furthermore, there is a tendency to overlook solid citizens. The learners, stars, and deadwood usually get most of the attention in terms of development programs and stimulating assignments. Neglect of the solid citizens may result in their slipping into the deadwood category.

Three actions can aid in managing the plateauing process: (1) prevent plateauees from becoming ineffective (prevent a problem from occurring): (2) integrate the relevant career-related information systems (improve monitoring so that emerging problems can be detected and treated early); and (3) manage ineffective plateauees and frustrated managers more effectively ("cure" the problem once it has arisen).[17] The first action basically involves helping plateauees adjust to the solid citizen category and helping them to realize that they have not necessarily failed. Available avenues for personal development and growth should be pointed out. The second suggestion can largely be implemented through a thorough performance appraisal system. Such a system should encourage open communication between the manager and the person being appraised. Possibilities for the third suggestion center around renewing the plateauee's interest through exposure to training and development programs and new experiences through varied job assignments.

OUTPLACEMENT

Outplacement "refers to a benefit provided by an employer to help an employee terminate and get a job someplace else."[18] Outplacement is a way of terminating employees that is of benefit to both the employee and the organization. The organization gains by terminating the employee before he or she becomes "deadwood." The employee gains by finding a new job, and at the same time preserving his or her dignity. Additionally, an outplacement program can have a very positive effect on employee morale. Sophisticated outplacement programs include assistance in resume preparation, job interviewing, and the generation of job interviews. The best approach to outplacement is to treat it as an alternative within the career-planning process.

SUMMARY

The increasing rate of change in the existing political, economic, technological, and social systems has made career planning and development much more important than it was in the past. As with any type of planning, one's chance of success is appreciably enhanced if career objectives have been clearly identified. In addition, a well-executed career plan can provide satisfaction to the individual as he or she progresses. From the organization's viewpoint, career planning can reduce employee turnover and its attendant costs.

Career planning and development is primarily the responsibility of the individual. However, the organization and the immediate manager should act as catalysts in the process.

Although many variations are possible, the development of a career plan involves four basic steps: (1) an assessment by the individual of his or her abilities, interests, and career goals; (2) an assessment by the organization of the individual's abilities and potential; (3) communication of career options and opportunities within the organization; and (4) career counseling to set realistic goals and plan for their accomplishment. Career pathing is a sequence of developmental activities involving informal and formal education, training, and job experience that help make an individual capable of holding more advanced jobs in the future. A career plan should be periodically evaluated and updated as changes occur in the work situation and in the individual.

Many myths related to career planning and advancement have surfaced over the years, and new ones are constantly being generated. Frequently, these myths are misleading and inhibit career growth.

A career plateau is defined as the point in an individual's career at which the likelihood of additional promotion is low. Almost everyone eventually reaches a plateau. The challenge in today's organizations is to keep "plateauees" from becoming "deadwood." Outplacement refers to a benefit provided by an employer to help an employee terminate and get a job somewhere else.

REVIEW QUESTIONS

1. Name at least two ways that career planning might benefit an individual.
2. What are the three major objectives of career planning from the organization's viewpoint?
3. Where does the primary responsibility for career planning belong?
4. What are the four basic steps for the development of a career plan?
5. What are some specific suggestions for helping managers become better career counselors?
6. What are the basic steps involved in career pathing?
7. How often should an individual review and revise his or her career plan?
8. Define the following categories of employees: learners, stars, solid citizens, and deadwood.
9. What is outplacement?

DISCUSSION QUESTIONS

1. Do you think that career planning can adversely affect organizational performance in that the process sometimes convinces the involved parties to change jobs?

2. Is the concept of career planning and development realistic in today's rapidly changing environment?

3. Discuss how the career-related myths can inhibit career planning and growth.

4. Is it better to tell a person that he or she has reached a plateau in the organization or to allow the person to maintain hope of eventual promotion?

REFERENCES AND ADDITIONAL READINGS

1. A. H. Soverwine, "Why Develop a Career Strategy?" *Management Review*, May 1977, p. 24.

2. M. Moravec, "A Cost-Effective Career Planning Program Requires a Strategy," *Personnel Administrator*, January 1982, p. 28.

3. B. C. Winterscheid, "A Career Development System Coordinates Training Efforts," *Personnel Administrator*, August 1980, pp. 28–32.

4. A. W. Hill, "Career Development—Who is Responsible?" *Training and Development Journal*, May 1976, p. 14.

5. Ibid., p. 15.

6. A. B. Randolph, "Managerial Career Coaching," *Training and Development Journal*, July 1981, pp. 54–55.

7. T. H. Stone, *Understanding Personnel Management* (Hinsdale, Il: Dryden Press, 1982), p. 324.

8. Ibid., p. 325.

9. N. T. Meckel, "The Manager as Career Counselor," *Training and Development Journal* July 1981, 65–69.

10. R. R. Carkhuff, *Helping and Human Relations: A Primer for Lay and Professional Helpers,* vol. I & II (New York: Holt, Rinehart & Winston, 1969).

11. For a suggested approach, see Z. B. Leibowitz, and N. K. Schlossberg, "Training Managers for Their Role in a Career Development System," *Training and Development Journal,* July 1981, pp. 72–79.

12. These suggestions are adapted from Meckel, "The Manager as Career Counselor," pp. 67–69.

13. E. H. Burack and N. J. Mathys, *Career Management in Organizations: A Practical Human Resource Planning Approach* (Lake Forest, Ill.: Brace-Park Press, 1979) p. 78.

14. The myths are adapted from the following sources: E. Staats, "Career Planning and Development: Which Way is Up?" *Public Administration Review,* January–February 1977; and A. H. Soverwine, "A Mythology of Career Growth," *Management Review,* June 1977, pp. 56–60.

15. T. P. Ference, J. A. F. Stoner, and E. K. Warren, "Managing the Career Plateau," *Management Review,* October 1977, p. 602.

16. Ibid., pp. 603–4.

17. Ibid., p. 607.

18. T. M. Camden, "Using Outplacement as a Career Development Tool," *Personnel Administrator*, January 1982, p. 35.

Case 14–1

THE UNHAPPY LINEMAN

John James had been a lineman for the telephone company for almost six years. Since the work kept him outdoors most of the day, he liked the job; the pay was good, and his fellow linemen were congenial. John had gone to work on this job right after high school graduation and had never considered doing anything else. Occasionally, through the years, his fellow linemen had been promoted into supervisory positions, had taken advantage of company-paid educational benfits, or had received recognition for outstanding service to the company.

John was close friends with Ross Bartlett, his partner on the line. Ross, who had been in his job about two years, was a good worker. About six months ago, Ross began to express dissatisfaction with the routine, monotonous work, saying that there had to be some better way to make a living.

Last week, John learned that the company would pay Ross's way to take college courses in business administration. That same day, John really began to feel some concern about himself and his status with the telephone company. He began having restless, sleepless nights as he thought back over the past six years—what he had done with his life, where he was now in his career, and where he was going. His thoughts became so muddled and confused that he realized he was going to need some help.

John had never set any personal goals for himself other than to live reasonably comfortably from day to day and month to month. He had come from a poor family and had received little encouragement or help from his family to develop ambitions when he was young. The one thing that his mother and father had insisted on was that someone in the family was going to be a high school graduate; luckily, John was that person. He never had any desire to go to college, because graduation from high school had proved to be extremely difficult for him. John could not think of spending four more years in school when he needed and wanted to be out making money for himself and the family.

Now, with people around him moving on in their careers and John's career at a standstill, he felt he was at a dead end. He realized suddenly that he needed to do something, but he was not sure just what.

1. *What advice might you give John?*
2. *Would a career plan help a person like John?*
3. *Is John's situation atypical of most employees?*

Case 14–2

"I DIDN'T KNOW YOU WANTED THE JOB"

Doris Martin had been an employee of the United States Central Bank for eight years. During this time, she had held the position of settlement clerk in the check collection department. Recently, Doris had risen to the position of senior settlement clerk and could not advance any further unless she moved into a supervisory job. Until just a short time ago, her superiors had no idea that Doris was interested in advancing beyond her present position.

Approximately eight months ago, a clerical position came open in the technical study unit of the check collection department. The position was not an upgrade for Doris; however, every clerk who had held the position had moved up in the department. Doris wanted the job badly.

Kathy Myers, a co-worker of Doris' was selected for the clerical post in the technical study unit. When Doris learned this, she became furious and stormed into the supervisor's office to tell him so. Bill Monk, her supervisor, was stunned.

"Doris, I had no idea that you were interested in the position. Kathy was the only person who applied for an intradepartmental transfer, so she was the only one considered."

"Intradepartmental transfer?" Doris cried. "What is that? Nobody told me about applications for transfers. How could I have known?"

"Now, Doris, don't get so angry," Bill said. "Management has decided to keep those transfers kind of quiet. You know, in the past six months, our department has lost over 15 people to job posting. If we start publicizing intradepartmental transfer opportunities, we won't have any experienced workers. I know what you mean, though. As soon as I get a chance, I'm going to get out of here. I've told my wife we might even have to take a cut in salary, but I don't care. This place is just driving me crazy."

Six months after that incident, Doris was still in her position in the settlement unit. She was, however, selected to attend a personal leadership program, a class run by the training and development unit and aimed at developing the skills of bank employees and their supervisors. A feedback instrument was developed in class by the participants, and if the participants were willing, the form was sent directly to their supervisors. Doris elected to send her form to her supervisor. On the form, Doris asked questions concerning such topics as career development, performance improvement, and skills development.

Bill Monk did not have the answers to Doris's questions, so he forwarded the form on to Sally Sugar, the departmental supervisor. Sally stopped by Doris's desk the next day and said, "Doris, don't pay any attention to what those training people say. I went to that supervisors' course and all they do is brainwash you. I wouldn't send anybody to that course unless I was forced to. Just forget about those questions on the form. You'll be a lot happier."

Doris was crushed. The questions she had listed on the form were important to her and she felt put down by Sally's remarks.

1. *What should Doris do?*
2. *Would a career plan help Doris?*

Chapter 15

Discipline and grievance handling

Objectives

1. To discuss the causes of disciplinary action.
2. To describe the organizational discipline process.
3. To discuss grievance procedures.
4. To define the concepts of just cause, due process, and fair representation.

Outline

Discipline defined
Causes of disciplinary actions
The discipline process
  Prediscipline recommendations
  Administering discipline
Legal restrictions and the discipline
    process
Discipline and unions
The grievance procedure
  Just cause
  Due process
  Fair representation
  Time delays in grievance
    procedures
Arbitration
Discipline in nonunionized
    organizations

Glossary of terms

Alexander* v. *Gardner-Denver
Supreme Court decision in 1974
which ruled that using the final and
binding grievance procedure in an
organization did not preclude an
aggrieved employee from seeking
redress through court action.

Arbitration Process whereby the
parties agree to settle a dispute
through the use of an independent
third party. Arbitration is binding on
the parties.

Discipline Action that is taken against
an employee when the employee
has violated an organizational rule
or when the employee's performance
has deteriorated to the point where
corrective action is needed.

Due process Right of an employee to
be dealt with fairly and justly during
the investigation of an alleged
offense and the administration of any
subsequent disciplinary action.

Enterprise Wheel Supreme Court
decision in 1960 which ruled that as
long as an arbitrator's decision
involved the interprétation of a
contract, the courts should not
overrule the arbitrator merely
because their interpretation of the
contract was different from that of
the arbitrator.

Fair representation Statutory duty of
a union to represent fairly all
employees in the bargaining unit,
whether or not they are union
members.

Grievance procedures Systematic
means of resolving disagreements
over the collective bargaining
agreement and providing assurance
that the terms and conditions agreed
to in negotiations are properly
implemented.

"Hot stove" rule Set of guidelines
used in administering discipline that
calls for quick, consistent, and
impersonal action, preceded by a
warning.

Just cause Requires that
management initially bears the
burden of proof of wrongdoing in
discipline cases and that the
severity of the punishment must
coincide with the seriousness of the
wrong.

NLRB* v. *Weingarten Supreme Court
decision in 1975 which held that an
employee has the right to refuse to
submit to a disciplinary interview
without union representation.

Vaca* v. *Sipes Supreme Court
decision in 1967 which held that a
union is not obligated to take all
grievances to arbitration, but rather
has the authority to decide whether
or not the grievance has merit. If
such a decision is made fairly and
nonarbitratily, the union has not
breached its fair representation duty.

It is not the duty of the disciplinarian to "take out anybody's grudge" against a man; it is his duty to adjust disagreements. He must remember constantly that his discipline must be of such a nature that the result will be for the permanent best interests of the one disciplined, his co-workers, his associates, and his family.

Lillian Gilbreth*

When a member of management must take action against an employee for violating an organizational work rule or for poor performance, the organization's disciplinary procedure is used to resolve the problem. When an employee has a complaint against the organization or its management, the grievance procedure is normally used to resolve the problem. Some organizations have very formal discipline and grievance procedures, others are less formal, and some organizations have no formal procedures at all. The purpose of this chapter is to describe typical discipline and grievance handling procedures.

DISCIPLINE DEFINED

Organizational discipline is action taken against an employee when the employee has violated an organizational rule or when the employee's performance has deteriorated to the point where corrective action is needed. Fifty years ago, a manager who objected to an employee's performance or behavior could simply say "You're fired!" and that was it. Justification often played little, if any, part in the decision. At that time managers had the final authority to effect discipline at will.

However, in applying organizational discipline, the primary question should be: Why are employees disciplined? Too many managers, when faced with a discipline problem in their organization, immediately think of "what" and "how much." What should the penalty be? And how severely should the employee be punished? Rather than being seen as an end itself, however, discipline should be viewed as a learning opportunity for the employee and as a tool to improve productivity and human relations.

The ultimate form of discipline is discharge or "organizational capital punishment," as it is frequently called. Organizations should use discharge in the case of repeated offenses or when the act committed is such that discharge is believed to be the only reasonable alternative.

CAUSES OF DISCIPLINARY ACTIONS

Generally, disciplinary actions are taken against employees for three types of conduct. First, poor job performance or conduct that negatively affects an employee's job performance. Absenteeism, insubordination, and negligence are examples of behaviors that can lead to

*L. Gilbreth, *The Psychology of Management* (New York: Sturgis & Walton, 1914), p. 72.

discipline. Second, employees are disciplined for actions that indicate poor citizenship. Examples include fighting on the job or theft of company property. The third area includes actions that negatively affect society in general, whether they occur on or off the job. An example of this might be any criminal or civil violation that negatively influences the employer's interests. Figure 15–1 summarizes many reasons that often lead to disciplinary actions or the discharge of employees.

THE DISCIPLINE PROCESS

The first step in the disciplinary process is the establishment of performance requirements and work rules. Performance requirements are normally established through the performance appraisal process discussed in Chapter 13. Work rules should be relevant to successful performance of the job. Because implementation of work rules partially depends on the employee's willingness to accept them, periodic re-

Figure 15–1   Reasons for discipline or discharge of employees

Absenteeism
Tardiness
Loafing
Absence from work
Leaving place of work (includes early quitting)
Sleeping on job
Assault and fighting among employees
Horseplay
Insubordination
Threat or assault of management representative
Abusive language to supervisor
Profane or abusive language (not toward supervisor)
Falsifying company records (including time records, production records)
Falsifying employment application
Dishonesty
Theft
Disloyalty to government (security risk)
Disloyalty to employer (includes competing with employer, conflict of interest)
Moonlighting
Negligence
Damage to or loss of machinery or materials
Incompetence (including low productivity)
Refusal to accept job assignement
Refusal to work overtime
Participation in prohibited strike
Misconduct during strike
Slowdown
Possession or use of drugs
Possession or use of intoxicants
Obscene or immoral conduct
Gambling
Abusing customers

Source: Adapted from F. and E. Elkouri, *How Arbitration Works*, 3d ed. (Washington, D.C.: Bureau of National Affairs, 1973), pp. 652–66.

view of their applicability is essential. In addition, it is often desirable to solicit employee input either directly or indirectly in establishing work rules. Work rules are more easily enforced when employees perceive them as being fair and relevant to the job.

The second step in the process is to communicate the performance requirements and work rules to employees. This is normally handled through the orientation and performance appraisal processes. Work rules are communicated in a variety of ways. Generally, when an employee is hired, he or she receives a manual which describes the work rules and policies of the organization. The human resource department normally explains these work rules and policies to the new employee during orientation. Furthermore, it is not unusual for new employees to be required to sign a document indicating that they have received and read the manual. In unionized organizations, work rules and the corresponding disciplinary action taken should an infraction occur are frequently part of the labor contract. Bulletin boards, company newsletters, and memos are also commonly used to communicate work rules. In the final analysis, management bears the responsibility for clearly communicating all work rules to employees.

The next step in the disciplinary process involves evaluation of employee work performance. Again, the performance appraisal process is used. Violations of work rules are usually identified by management through observation or problem situations. The final step in the disciplinary process is the application of corrective action (discipline), when necessary.

Prediscipline recommendations

Before an employee is disciplined, several steps can be taken to ensure that the action will be constructive and will not likely be rescinded by higher levels of management. The importance of maintaining adequate records cannot be overemphasized. Written records often have a significant influence on decisions to overturn or uphold a disciplinary action. Past rule infractions and overall performance should be recorded. Management bears the burden of proof when a decision to discipline an employee is questioned. In cases where the charge is of a moral or criminal nature, the proof required is usually the same as that required by a court of law (proof beyond a reasonable doubt). Adequate records are of utmost importance in cases of this type.

Another key responsibility of management is the investigation. That which appears obvious on the surface is sometimes completely discredited after investigation. Accusations against an employee must be supported by facts. Many decisions to discipline employees have been overturned due to an improper or less than thorough investigation. Undue haste in taking disciplinary action, taking the action when the manager is angry, and improper and incomplete investigations frequently cause disciplinary actions to be rescinded. An employee's work record should also be considered as part of the investigation. Good performance and a long tenure with the organization are considerations that should influence the severity of a disciplinary action. Naturally, the investigation must take place before any discipline is administered. A manager should not discipline an employee and then look for evidence to support the decision.

A normal step in the investigation of the facts is for management first to discuss the situation with the employee. Providing the employee an opportunity to present his or her side of the situation is essential if a disciplinary system is to be viewed positively by employees.

Employees who are represented by a union are allowed to have a union representative present during any disciplinary interview. This right is protected by the National Labor Relations Board (NLRB).[1] The most significant of the NLRB policies in this area was supported by a Supreme Court decision in 1975. In *NLRB* v. *Weingarten,*[2] an employee was investigated for allegedly underpaying for food purchased from the employer. The employee requested and was denied union representation at an interview which was held after the employee was charged with the underpayments. The union filed unfair labor practice charges against the company with the NLRB. The NLRB ruled that the employee had a right to refuse to submit to an interview without union representation, but also ruled that this right was available only if the employee requested union representation and applied only when disciplinary actions might reasonably be expected as a result of the interview. However, in a later case, *Baton Rouge Water Works,*[3] the NLRB ruled that an employee does not have the right to union representation when management meets with the employee simply to inform him or her of discipline which has been previously determined.

Thus, as the law presently stands, management must be prepared to allow the presence of a union representative in any investigatory meeting. This means that management must not only deal with the employee and his or her problem, but also must do so in the presence of a union representative who normally acts in the role of an adversary.[4]

Besides being involved in the investigation, the union should be kept informed on matters of discipline. Some organizations give unions advance notice of their intention to discipline an employee. Also, copies of warnings are sometimes sent to the union.

Administering discipline

Administering discipline should be analagous to the burn received when touching a hot stove. Often referred to as the "hot stove" rule, this approach emphasizes that discipline should be directed against the act rather than the person. Other key points of the hot stove rule are: immediacy, advance warning, and consistency. Figure 15–2 outlines the hot stove rule.

Immediacy refers to the length of time between the misconduct and the discipline. For discipline to be most effective, it must be taken as soon as possible but without involving an emotional, irrational decision.

Notation of rules infractions in an employee's record is not sufficient to support disciplinary action. An employee must be advised of the infraction for it to be considered a warning. Noting that the employee was warned about the infraction and having the employee sign a form acknowledging the warning are both good practices. Failure to warn an employee of the consequences of repeated violations of a rule is one reason often cited for overturning a disciplinary action.

A key element in discipline is consistency. Inconsistency lowers morale, diminishes respect for management, and leads to grievances. Striving for consistency does not mean that past infractions, length of service, work record, and other mitigating factors should not be considered when applying discipline. However, an employee should feel that any other employee under essentially the same circumstances would receive the same penalty. Similarly, management should take steps to ensure that personalities are not a factor when applying discipline. The employee should feel that the disciplinary action is a consequence of what he or she has done, and not caused by his or her personality. A manager should avoid arguing with the employee and

Figure 15–2　　　　　Hot stove rule for applying discipline

1. The hot stove burns immediately. Disciplinary policies should be administered quickly. There should be no question of cause and effect.
2. The hot stove gives a warning and so should discipline.
3. The hot stove consistently burns everyone that touches it. Discipline should be consistent.
4. The hot stove burns everyone in the same manner regardless of who they are. Discipline must be impartial. People are disciplined for what they have done and not because of who they are.

should administer the discipline in a straightforward, calm manner. Administering discipline without anger or apology and resuming a pleasant relationship aids in reducing the negative effects of discipline.

Discipline should also be administered in private. The only exception would be in the case of gross insubordination or flagrant and serious rule violations, where a public reprimand would help the manager regain control of the situation. Even in this type of situation, the objective should be to gain control and not to embarrass the employee.

Lower-level managers should be very reluctant to impose disciplinary suspensions and discharges. Usually, discipline of this degree is reserved for higher levels of management. Even if a lower-level manager does not have the power to administer disciplinary suspensions or discharges, he or she is nearly always the one who must recommend the action to higher management. Since discipline of this nature is more likely to be reviewed, is more costly to the organization, and is more likely to be reflected in overall morale and productivity, it is very important for the lower-level manager to know when it should be recommended. Observing the hot stove rule is essential for administering suspensions and discharges.

Management is expected to use corrective discipline whenever possible. There are, however, some offenses which may justify discharge, such as stealing, striking a member of management, and gross insubordination. Management must be able to show, generally beyond a reasonable doubt, that the offense was committed. Attention to the points covered in the prediscipline recommendations section discussed earlier are especially important in supporting a decision to discharge an employee.

As in any lesser discipline, but even more essential in suspension and discharge, the employee has the right to a careful and impartial investigation. This involves allowing the employee to state his or her side of the case, to gather evidence to support that side, and usually to question the accuser. In the case of very serious offenses, the employee may be suspended pending a full investigation. This may be necessary when an employee has been accused of a serious crime which could affect the safety or others.[5]

The suggestions outlined in the preceding paragraphs are designed to assist managers in applying discipline in a positive manner and with a minimum of application of the harsher forms of discipline. In applying the disciplinary procedure, observance of these suggestions should reduce the chance of a grievance, or if a grievance is filed, the chance of having the disciplinary action overruled. Figure 15–3 provides a checklist of rules which should be observed when applying discipline.

Figure 15–3   Considerations in disciplining or discharging employees

1. Avoid hasty decisions.
2. Document all actions and enter in personnel file.
3. Thoroughly and fully investigate the circumstances and facts of the alleged offense.
    a. Notify the employee of the nature of the offense.
    b. Obtain the employee's version of the circumstances, reasons for his or her actions, and the names of any witnesses.
    c. If suspension is required until the investigation is completed:
        (1) Inform the employee to return 24 to 72 hours later to receive the decision and that he or she will be reinstated with pay if the decision is in his or her favor. If it is not in his or her favor, the discipline to be imposed should be indicated.
    d. Interview all witnesses to the alleged misconduct. Obtain signed statements, if necessary.
    e. Check all alternative possible causes (e.g., broken machinery).
    (f). Decide whether the employee committed the alleged offense.
4. Determine the appropriate discipline.
    a. Considerations:
        (1) Personnel record: length of service, past performance, past disciplinary record, has corrective discipline ever been applied?
        (2) Nature of the offense.
        (3) Past disciplinary action for other employees in similar situations.
        (4) Existing rules and disciplinary policies.
        (5) Provisions in the labor contract if one exists.
5. Advise the employee of the nature of the offense, the results of the investigation, the discipline to be imposed, and the rationale behind the discipline.

LEGAL RESTRICTIONS AND THE DISCIPLINE PROCESS

The Civil Rights Act of 1964 and the Age Discrimination in Employment Act of 1967 as amended in 1978 changed an employer's authority in making decisions and taking actions involving employment conditions. Specifically, Title VII of the Civil Rights Act prohibits the use of race, color, religion, sex, or national origin as the basis of any employment condition. The Age Discrimination in Employment Act makes similar prohibitions involving persons between ages 40 and 70. Discipline is, of course, a condition of employment and is subject to these laws. Under these laws, employees have the right to appeal to the Equal Employment Opportunity Commission (EEOC) and the courts any disciplinary action that is considered discriminatory.

The landmark case guaranteeing employees this right was decided in 1974 by the Supreme Court in the *Alexander* v. *Gardner-Denver* case. In that case, the Supreme Court ruled that using the grievance procedure in an organization did not preclude the aggrieved employee from seeking redress through court action.[6] Basically, the Court decided that the Civil Rights Act guaranteed individuals the right to pursue remedies of illegal discrimination regardless of prior rejections in another forum.[7]

The courts have developed a concept of the shifting burden of proof in disciplinary cases where alleged discrimination has occurred. Initially, the burden of proof rests on the employee to establish that a

Discharge for violent attack on fellow employee

Rape attempt claimed as provocation for grievant's action

(Discharge was upheld in the case of an employee who, accompanied by her boyfriend, sought out and seriously wounded a fellow worker whom the grievant claimed had tried to rape her earlier in the evening. In the absence of evidence to prove that the fellow employee had attempted to rape the grievant, management was not guilty of "disparate treatment" in failing to discipline him.)

The violence in question occurred one evening while employees were at the company clubhouse preparing for the annual barbecue, turkey shoot, and dance that is sponsored by the employer. According to the grievant, a fellow worker tried to rape her while she was taking a nap in her boyfriend's van.

Several witnesses testified that the grievant pinpointed her fellow employee as the man who had tried to rape her and that she and her boyfriend advanced toward him. One witness to the incident stated that the grievant attacked the man with a knife and another witness testified that he saw her jump on his back. A police statement by another witness to the fight corroborated this testimony. The record showed that the victim of the assault was seriously injured by a cutting instrument and that his injuries were in part due to being hit by a liquor bottle wielded by the grievant's boyfriend. (The boyfriend, also an employee of the company, was discharged but did not file a grievance.)

"The union's contention that the grievant was not prosecuted as a result of her trial does not influence the arbitrator's opinion. Neither the company at the time of the investigation nor the arbitrator now are privy to the evidence and arguments presented at the trial. The company must make a decision to retain or discharge an employee based on its investigation of the evidence at the time of the incident." The evidence was "clear and convincing" that the grievant participated in the fight.

Company's obligation to discipline consistently

"Although the arbitrator did not believe that provocation of the type charged by the grievant defends her actions, it is a circumstance which should be investigated, especially considering the company's contractural obligation to discipline its employees consistently."

It appeared that the company conducted a thorough investigation in an attempt to determine the fellow employee's involvement in the case. A member of management and a sheriff's investigator independently talked to approximately 11 people who were at the clubhouse. Neither investigator found any evidence that there had been an attempted assault on the grievant. Instead, there was some evidence to indicate that she had not been the victim of a criminal assault. There was no evidence to link the victim of the physical attack to the alleged rape attempt, other than his being the object of the assault by the grievant and her boyfriend.

The grievant did not formally allege that she had been assaulted until some two months after the night in question. The grievance states that she was not involved in the attack on her fellow employee. Later, her testimony indicated that she and her boyfriend had been involved in the altercation but that they had been provoked into taking action.

The union noted that the grievant's fellow worker did not bring charges against her (criminal charges were brought by the state) and that he refused to talk about the incident during the grievance procedure. "The arbitrator must agree with the company that it is possible that a person who has sustained a grievous in-

(continued)

jury might not remember what had happened." Additionally, the evidence indicated that he was intoxicated on the night in question.

No disparate treatment

A "good hindsight observation" is the union's contention that the company might have obtained some information from the victim of the attack if he had been suspended. Had he returned to work shortly after the night in question, the company might have suspended him. "But, since he was away from work for approximately 30 days, a thorough investigation could and did take place during this time."

Under the circumstances, the grievant did not receive disparate treatment.

Although management contributed to the violence that occurred by permitting employees to consume alcohol and become intoxicated on company premises in violation of a plant rule, such negligence does not warrant "reinstatement of an employee who has exhibited as violent a nature as has the grievant."

Source: L. L. Byars, *Summary of Labor Arbitration Awards,* American Arbitration Association, Report no. 252, (New York, 1980), p. 4. American Arbitration Association 140 West 51st Street, New York, N.Y., 10020.

prima facie[8] case of discrimination exists. In discipline cases, prima facie can be established by producing evidence that the aggrieved employee's discipline was different from that applied to a similarly situated employee outside of the protected group. If a prima facie case is established, the employer must then prove that the discipline was applied in a nondiscriminatory manner. If the employer successfully shows that this was so, then the employee has the right to show that the reasons given by the employer are not legitimate.[9]

DISCIPLINE AND UNIONS

Management's authority to administer discipline has been greatly affected by unions. Central to the goals of unionism is the desire to protect employees from arbitrary and unfair treatment. The philosophy of unions has been that employees are economically dependent upon the employer and, as a result, are helpless against the whims of management. Therefore, disciplinary policy is viewed as being an integral part of the collective bargaining process. Union contracts contain provisions specifying how management can deal with employees accused of rule violations or misconduct. Figure 15–4 gives some sample rules for discipline from a typical union contract. While management usually reserves the right to make reasonable rules for employee performance and conduct, the union can often question management's application and the reasonableness of these rules through the grievance procedure. Furthermore, when new work rules are established, the union must frequently be notified before the rules can be implemented.

Figure 15-4 Sample discipline rules

Offense	Discipline
Minor	
Absence without notification as per existing absentee and lateness policy.	1st offense—written warning.
	2nd offense—one-day suspension.
Horseplay.	3rd offense—two-day suspension.
Minor	
Possession of, drinking, smoking, or being under the influence of intoxicants or narcotics on company property.	1st offense—written warning that may result in suspension of up to 3 days without pay.
Sleeping on the job.	2nd offense—treated as an intolerable offense.
Gambling on company property.	
Intolerable	
Stealing company or personal property.	1st offense—subject to discharge.
Fighting on company property.	

Source: Adapted from the labor agreement between Babcock and Wilcox Company and the Laborers International Union of North America.

The following statements summarize the provisions concerning discipline that are contained in most collective bargaining agreements:

1. Several steps are outlined which must be followed by management in administering discipline.
2. Management usually reserves the right to discipline and discharge employees for just cause and to make reasonable rules that are not in conflict with the union contract.
3. Specific offenses and the corresponding disciplinary actions are spelled out in writing.
4. Specific appeals procedures (grievance procedures) are established, with steps outlined that are to be followed in the event an employee or the union challenges some managerial action.
5. Time limits are specified for each step in the grievance procedure.
6. A clause establishes arbitration as the final step in the grievance procedure; a neutral third party is designated to make a final and binding decision with regard to the grievance.
7. Probationary employees are generally not given access to the established grievance procedure.

THE GRIEVANCE PROCEDURE

Nonunionized as well as unionized organizations often have grievance procedures. However, the main emphasis of this section concerns grievance procedures in unionized organizations. In this context, grievance procedures are a systematic means of resolving disagreements over the collective bargaining agreement and providing assurance that the terms and conditions agreed to in negotiations are properly implemented. Grievance procedures outline the steps that are to be taken by an employee in appealing any management action which he or she feels violates the union contract. Grievance procedures are used not only to appeal disciplinary actions but also to resolve matters concerning contract interpretation.

In general, the grievance process is initiated by an employee who has a complaint regarding some action that he or she perceives to be inconsistent with the terms of the union contract. While it is highly unlikely that the organization would initiate a grievance, it can do so. Initially, the grievance (aggrieved employee) contacts the union representative (usually called a union steward) in his or her department, and they discuss the events causing the grievance. The grievant and the union steward then meet with the grievant's supervisor. If a mutually agreeable settlement cannot be reached at this meeting, the grievance is then put into writing. Generally, in the next step, the union steward discusses the grievance with the department manager or another appropriate management representative. Management's reaction is then presented, usually in writing. If the grievance is not resolved at this point, the next step generally involves the human resource or labor relations manager and higher officials of the union, such as the business agent or international representative. After fully investigating and discussing the grievance, the human resource department usually issues the final company decision. In the event that the grievance is still unresolved, the party initiating the grievance can request arbitration. Arbitration, which is discussed later in this chapter, is a process whereby the employer and union agree to settle a dispute through an independent third party. Because of the expenses to both the union and management, every attempt should be made to resolve grievances in the stages before arbitration. Figure 15–5 summarizes the steps involved in the grievance procedure. Figure 15–6 illustrates a grievance procedure as outlined in an actual union contract.

Just cause

Most union contracts recognize the right of management to discipline or discharge employees for just cause. In fact, in most discipline or discharge cases, the basic issue is whether or not management acted with just cause. In general, just cause is concerned with the burden and degree of proof of wrongdoing and with the severity of punishment.

It is generally agreed that the initial burden of proof in matters of discipline and discharge lies with the company. However, once the

Figure 15–5   The general process followed in a union grievance procedure

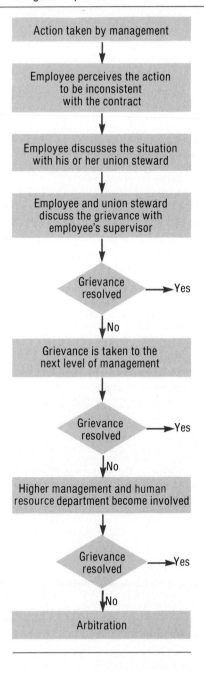

Figure 15–6   Typical union grievance procedure

Purpose

(53) The procedure under this article is available to the union for the presentation and settlement of grievances arising under the interpretation or application of the terms of this agreement as they relate to wages, hours of work, and working conditions and all other conditions of employment including discharge cases.

Foreman and superintendent's step

(54) a An employee or group of employees, having a question, dispute, or alleged grievance arising under the terms of this agreement shall present the matter verbally to his or her supervisor in person or in company with his or her departmental steward. The supervisor and the steward shall use their best efforts to resolve the matter.

b If deemed necessary by the supervisor or the departmental steward, the departmental head and a grievance committee may be requested to participate in reaching a satisfactory settlement.

c If the grievance cannot be settled satisfactorily within the foregoing step within three working days, it may be reduced to writing on forms provided by the company. The grievance shall be signed by the aggrieved employee or employees, and the departmental steward. The departmental supervisor shall have two working days thereafter to submit a decision in writing. The grievance shall be considered abandoned or settled if it is not appealed to the next step within five working days.

Industrial relations manager's step

(55) If the disposition in the foregoing step has not satisfactorily settled the grievance, it may be appealed to the industrial relations manager's step not later than five working days from the time of receiving the foreman's disposition. The industrial relations manager shall review and investigate the grievance conferring with a member of the grievance committee and such other persons essential to resolving the issue. The company's disposition shall be given to the union within three working days following such conference. The grievance shall be considered abandoned or settled if it is not appealed to the next step within 10 working days.

President and general manager's step

(56) If the industrial relations manager's disposition has not satisfactorily settled the employee grievance, it may then be appealed by the union grievance committee to the general manager (or designated representative) within 10 working days in a further effort to adjust the grievance. An international union staff representative shall participate in all general manager appeal step meetings. Any grievance not appealed within the time limit shall be automatically closed on the basis of the previous decision and shall not be subject to further appeal. The general manager shall issue the company's final disposition of the grievance within five working days after the appeal meeting is held. Any grievance not appealed in writing to arbitration as hereinafter provided within 21 working days after the issuance of the general manager's decision shall automatically be closed on the basis of such decision and shall not be subject to further appeal.

Arbitration

(57) If a grievance shall not be satisfactorily disposed of under the preceding steps, it may be submitted to arbitration upon proper notification by the union. Notice of appeal of a grievance by the union to arbitration shall be given in writing to the company not later than 21 working days following the date of the written decision of the general manager. This time limit may be extended by mutual agreement.

Source: Agreement between Powermatic Houdaille, Inc. and United Steelworkers of America. Used with permission.

case has been established by the company, the burden of proof shifts to the union to disprove or discredit the company's contention.

Once an organization proves that an employee was guilty of wrongdoing, the second area of concern in determining just cause relates to the severity of the punishment. Just cause results when the severity of the punishment coincides with the seriousness of the wrongdoing. The following general guidelines are frequently used by arbitrators for determining just cause as it relates to the severity of punishment:

1. The past performance of the employee should be considered.
2. Previous disciplinary actions taken against other employees in similar situations should be considered.
3. Any unusual circumstances surrounding the alleged offense should be considered.[10]

Due process

Due process refers to the employee's right to be dealt with fairly and justly during the investigation of the alleged offense and the administration of discipline. Due process typically guarantees that the employee will be notified of the allegations and have them explained, that an impartial investigation will be held prior to the imposition of discipline, and that the employee can present his or her version of the incident.[11] As was discussed earlier, in the disciplinary interview, unionized employees have the right to union representation if they request it and if disciplinary actions might reasonably be expected to result.

A breach of due process during the grievance procedure can result in either a modification or complete reversal of a disciplinary action. Procedural requirements are often spelled out in the grievance procedures of the contract. Failure to follow such provisions may constitute a breach of due process. In general, to ensure that an employee is afforded due process, all contract terms should be followed; adequate warning should be given prior to the discipline; explicit statements should be made to the employee and the union about possible disciplinary action being taken if the employee's actions do not change; and a full and fair investigation should be conducted immediately after the offense.

Fair representation

The National Labor Relations Act of 1935 gives the union the authority to decide whether a grievance has merit and, as a result, the authority to determine whether or not to pursue it through the formal grievance process. Under this act, the union has a statutory duty to fairly represent all employees in the bargaining unit, whether or not they are union members. This duty has been termed the doctrine of fair representation.

The rationale underlying the doctrine of fair representation is that the union is the exclusive representative of all employees in the bargaining unit. The extent of the union's duty to represent fairly its members and other employees was defined in a landmark case, *Vaca v. Sipes,* in 1967.[12] In this case, an employee who had a history of high blood pressure returned to work after six months of sick leave. Although his personal physician and another doctor had certified his fitness to resume work, the company doctor concluded that his blood pressure was too high to permit his reinstatement and, as a result, he was permanently discharged. The employee filed a grievance and the union took the grievance through the steps leading up to arbitration. The employee was then sent to a new doctor at the union's expense. When this examination did not support the employee's contention that he could safely return to work, the union decided not to take the grievance to arbitration, even though the employee demanded it. The employee sued the officers and representatives of the union for breach of their duty of fair representation. The case ultimately went to the Supreme Court, which held that (1) an individual does not have the absolute right to have his or her grievance taken to arbitration; (2) a union must make decisions as to the merits of particular grievances in good faith and nonarbitrarily; and (3) if a union decides in good faith and in a nonarbitrary manner that a grievance is not meritorious, a breach of fair representation does not exist, even if it is proved that the grievance was, in fact, meritorious.[13]

An exception to this court ruling is included in a provision of the Taft-Hartley Act, which states that an individual employee may present a grievance to his/her employer without the aid of the union. However, this is contingent on the fact that any resulting adjustments must be consistent with the terms of the contract and must be conveyed to the union. In recent court decisions, this has been interpreted as meaning that the employer is under no obligation to consider such grievances.[14] However, if a grievance is presented to the employer by the union, the employer is obligated to consider it and submit it to arbitration (if this is provided for in the contract), when the grievance has not been resolved in the earlier stages of the grievance process.

In addition, an individual cannot take the case into his or her own hands if the employee thinks that it is not being effectively handled. Courts have held that the employee must thoroughly exhaust the grievance procedure before taking individual action, and then such action is contingent upon proof of a breach of the duty of fair representation.[15]

A recent Supreme Court decision, *Bowen v. United States Postal Ser-*

vice, has established the proposition that an employee may be entitled to recover damages from both the union and the employer in cases where the employer has violated the labor agreement and the union has breached its duty of fair representation.[16]

Time delays in grievance procedures

Perhaps the greatest criticism of the grievance procedure is that a great deal of time may be necessary to resolve a grievance that goes through the entire process. Often, the internal stages of appeal may take several months to complete. If the case goes to arbitration, the parties usually request a list of potential arbitrators from an arbitration service. The parties must contact the arbitrator and must agree upon an acceptable date for the hearing—one that coincides with the schedules of the union representatives, the company representatives, and the arbitrator. Furthermore, after the hearing has taken place, the parties may desire to submit further briefs which can take several additional weeks. When the hearing is closed upon receipt of all briefs, the arbitrator is usually given 30 to 60 days to render a decision. Thus, many months and sometimes a year or more may elapse before a final decision is reached. An argument could be made that this time delay in itself denies the grievant due process.

ARBITRATION

Arbitration is the process whereby the parties voluntarily agree to settle a dispute through the use of an independent third party. In the United States, arbitration evolves from the voluntary agreement by two parties to submit their unresolved disputes to a privately selected neutral third party (arbitrator). Both parties agree in advance to abide by the arbitrator's decision. The arbitrator, who functions in a quasijudicial role, must work within the framework that the parties have negotiated in their collective bargaining agreement. Arbitrators have no legal power to subpoena witnesses or records and are not required to conform to legal rules of hearing procedures other than that of giving all parties the opportunity to present evidence.

Grievance arbitration attempts to settle unresolved disputes arising during the term of the collective bargaining agreement that involves questions of its interpretation or application. Provision for grievance arbitration is not, in general, mandated by law. However, most labor contracts provide an arbitration clause as the final step in the grievance process. This is considered to be the quid pro quo for the union's agreement to a no-strike clause.

An arbitrator may serve either on a temporary (ad hoc) or permanent basis. In ad hoc arbitration, an arbitrator is selected by the parties to hear a single case. Permanent arbitrators settle all grievance disputes arising between the parties for a period of time. An arbitrator charges for his or her services. Normally, the arbitrator's charges are paid on a 50-50 basis by the company and the union.

Both the Federal Mediation and Conciliation Service (FMCS) and the American Arbitration Association (AAA) provide lists of qualified arbitrators to the parties upon request. The role of the FMCS in collective bargaining is further described in Chapter 17. FMCS's services are available to both the private and public sector. AAA is a private, non-profit organization that also provides lists of arbitrators to both the private and public sectors.

Generally, court reviews of arbitration awards have been extremely narrow in scope. The attitude of the U.S. Supreme Court was expressed in the *Enterprise Wheel* case as follows: "It is the arbitrator's interpretation which was bargained for, and so far as the arbitrator's decision concerns interpretation of the contract, the courts have no business overruling him because their interpretation of the contract is different from his."[17] In spite of this opinion, some arbitration awards in discharge cases have been overruled by the courts.[18] However, the tendency of the courts has been, for the most part, to defer to the arbitrator's decision.

DISCIPLINE IN NONUNIONIZED ORGANIZATIONS

Until recently, management decisions on discipline or discharge in nonunionized organizations have been relatively free of judicial interference. Courts previously intervened in these organizations to prevent discipline or discharges which violated public policy concerning racial, sex, or age discrimination. However it had been rather firmly established in the United States that when an employer hired an individual, this was employment at will that could be terminated at any time by either party for any reason, or for no reason at all.[19] This situation has been gradually changing as the courts have begun to hear discharge cases in nonunionized organizations involving allegations of capricious or unfair treatment.[20] In some cases, the courts have ruled in favor of the discharged employees when the employee had been guaranteed due process under company procedures.[21] Basically, the courts seem to be moving toward requiring nonunionized organizations to show just cause and due process in disciplining or discharging employees. Of course, both of these requirements have long been the practice in unionized organizations.

In light of these developments, many organizations have established appeal procedures for disciplinary actions taken by management. The most common types of nonunion appeal procedures are open-door policies and step systems that allow employees to bring appeals to successively higher levels of management. An open-door policy gives an employee the right to appeal a disciplinary action taken against him or her to the manager's superior. Step systems in nonunionized organizations are very similar to the grievance procedure in unionized organizations. The only significant difference being that most non-union organizations do not include arbitration as the final step.[22]

SUMMARY

Organizational discipline is action that is taken against an employee when the employee has violated an organizational rule or when the employee's performance has deteriorated to the point where corrective action is needed. The ultimate form of discipline is discharge. Organizations should use discharge in cases of repeated offenses, or when the act committed is such that discharge is believed to be the only reasonable alternative.

The discipline process calls for the management of an organization to establish performance requirements and work rules and to communicate them to employees. Management then evaluates employees against the performance requirements and work rules and takes disciplinary action when necessary.

In conducting an interview with an employee concerning possible disciplinary actions, unionized employees are allowed to have a union representative present. Applying discipline should be analogous to the burn received when touching a hot stove. Often referred to as the "hot stove" rule, this approach emphasizes that discipline should be directed against the act rather than the person. The Civil Rights Act of 1964 and the Age Discrimination in Employment Act of 1967 as amended in 1978 gave employees the right to appeal to the Equal Employment Opportunity Commission (EEOC) and the courts any disciplinary action that is considered discriminatory toward a protected group.

A grievance procedure is a systematic means of resolving disagreements over the collective bargaining agreement and providing assurance that the terms and conditions agreed to in negotiations are properly implemented. Nonunionized organizations can also have grievance procedures.

Just cause requires that management initially bears the burden of proof of wrongdoing and that the severity of the punishment must coincide with the seriousness of the wrong doing. Due process refers to an employee's right to be dealt with fairly and justly during the investigation of the alleged offense and the administration of discipline. Fair representation refers to a union's duty to represent all employees in the bargaining unit fairly and without discrimination, regardless of their union membership.

Arbitration is the process whereby the parties agree to settle a dispute judicially but outside the normal judicial system through the use of an independent third party.

REVIEW QUESTIONS

1. What is organizational discipline?
2. What are the three types of conduct that normally result in the disciplining of an employee?
3. Outline the steps in the disciplinary process.
4. What was the significance of the decision in the *NLRB* v. *Weingarten* case?
5. What are the key points of the "hot stove" rule?
6. What was the significance of the decision in the *Alexander* v. *Gardner-Denver* case?
7. What are grievance procedures?
8. Define just cause, due process, and fair representation.
9. What is arbitration?

DISCUSSION QUESTIONS

1. "You simply can't discipline employees the same way you could 20 years ago." Do you agree or disagree? Discuss.
2. Two employees violate the same work rule. One is above average in performance and has been with your company for eight years. The other employee is an average performer who has been with your company for a little over a year. Should these employees receive the same discipline?
3. Under the doctrine of fair representation, unions are required to represent both members and nonmembers in the bargaining unit. Do you think that unions should be required to represent nonmembers?
4. If you were starting your own company, what type of grievance procedure would you establish for your employees?

REFERENCES AND ADDITIONAL READINGS

1. See Chapter 16 for a description of the NLRB.
2. *NLRB* v. *202 NLRB* 446 (1975).
3. *Baton Rouge Water Works,* 246 NLRB 161 (1980).
4. *Weingarth,* E. L. Harrison, "Legal Restrictions on the Employer's Authority to Discipline," *Personnel Journal,* February 1982, p. 138.
5. For a more in-depth discussion of the use of discharge and discipline procedures, see the *Grievance Guide,* 4th ed. (Washington, D.C.: *Bureau of National Affairs,* 1972), pp. 6–16.
6. *Alexander* v. *Gardner-Denver,* 415 U.S. 36, 7 FEP 81 (1974).
7. R. L. Greenman and E. J. Schwartz, *Personnel Administration and the Law* (Washington, D.C.: Bureau of National Affairs, 1979), p. 67.
8. Prima facie is a legal term which means evidence to raise a presumption of fact or establish the fact in question unless rebutted.
9. *McDonnell Douglas Corporation* v. *Green,* 5 FEP 965 (1973).
10. F. Elkouri and E. A. Elkouri, *How Arbitration Works* 3d ed. (Washington, D.C.: Bureau of National Affairs, 1973), pp. 621–53.
11. R. L. Hogler, "Industrial Due Process and Judicial Review of Arbitration Awards," *Labor Law Journal,* September 1980, p. 570.

12. *Vaca* v. *Sipes* 386 U.S. 171, 87 Sup. CT. 903, 17 L. Ed 2d 842 (1967).

13. Ibid.

14. A. R. Marchione, "A Case for Individual Rights Under the Collective Bargaining Agreement," *Labor Law Journal*, December 1976, p. 738.

15. Ibid.

16. *Bowen* v. *United States Postal Service*, 81 U.S. (1983).

17. *United Steelworkers of America* v. *Enterprise Wheel and Car Corporation*, 46 LRRM 2423 S. CT. (1960).

18. For a review of these cases see R. L. Hogler, "Industrial Due Process and Judicial Review of Arbitration Awards," *Labor Law Journal*, September 1980, pp. 570–76.

19. A. T. Oliver, "The Disappearing Right to Terminate Employees at Will," *Personnel Journal*, December 1982, p. 911.

20. B. P. Heshizer and H. Graham, "Discipline in the Nonunion Company," *Personnel*, March–April 1982, p. 72.

21. For a discussion of some of these cases, see T. A. Olsen, "Wrongful Discharge Claims Raised by At Will Employees: A New Legal Concern for Employers," *Labor Law Journal*, May 1981, pp. 265–97.

22. Heshizer and Graham "Discipline in the Nonunion Company," p. 73.

Case 15–1	**TARDY TOM**

On September 30, 1982, Tom Holland was hired as a mechanic for a large national automobile leasing firm in Columbus, Ohio. Tom, the only mechanic employed by the firm in Columbus, was to do routine preventive maintenance on the cars. When he first began his job, he was scheduled to punch in on the time clock at 7 A.M. On October 30, 1982, Tom's supervisor, Russ Brown, called him to his office and said, "Tom, I've noticed during October that you've been late for work seven times. What can I do to help you get here on time?"

Tom replied, "It would be awfully nice if I could start work at 8 instead of 7 A.M."

Russ then stated, "Tom, I'm very pleased with your overall work performance, so it's OK with me if your workday begins at 8 A.M."

During the month of November 1982, Tom was late eight times. Another conversation occurred similar to the one at the end of October. As a result of it, Tom's starting time was changed to 9 A.M.

On January 11, 1983, Russ Brown posted the following notice on the bulletin board:

Any employee late for work more than two times in any one particular pay period is subject to termination.

On January 20, 1982, Russ called Tom into his office and gave him a letter that read, "During this pay period you have been late for work more than two times. If this behavior continues, you are subject to termination." Tom signed the letter to acknowledge that he had received it.

During February 1983, Tom was late eight times and between March 1 and March 11, five times. On March 11, 1983, Russ notified Tom that he had been fired for his tardiness.

On March 12, 1983, Tom came in with his union representative and demanded that he get his job back. Tom alleged that there was another employee in the company, a woman, who had been late as many times as he was or more. Tom further charged that Russ was punching the time clock for this woman because Russ was having an affair with her. The union representative then stated that three other people in the company had agreed to testify, under oath, to these facts. The union representative then said, "Russ, rules are for everyone. You can't let one person break a rule and penalize someone else for breaking the same rule. Therefore, Tom should have his job back."

1. *What is your position with regard to this case?*
2. *What would you do if you were an arbitrator in the dispute?*

Case 15–2   **KEYS TO THE DRUG CABINET**

John Brown, a 22-year-old black, had been employed for only two-and-a-half weeks as a licensed practical nurse in the section under security at a local hospital's alcohol and drug treatment center. John worked the 11 P.M. to 7 A.M. shift. His responsibilities included having charge of the keys to the drug cabinet.

One morning at 1 A.M., he became ill. He requested and received permission from the night supervisor, Margaret Handley, to go home. A short time later, the supervisor realized that John had failed to leave the keys when he signed out. She immediately tried to reach him by telephoning his home.

More than a dozen attempts to call John proved futile; each time, Margaret got a busy signal. Finally, at 3 A.M., a man answered but refused to call John to the phone, saying that he was too ill to talk. She became frantic and decided to call the police to retrieve the keys.

The police arrived at John's home at 6:30 A.M. They found him preparing to leave to return the keys to the hospital. The police took the keys and returned them.

Later that day, John reported to work on his assigned shift, apologized for not returning the keys, and questioned the necessity of calling the police.

Two days later, however, the director of the unit, Marcus Webb, informed John that he had been terminated. The reason cited for the discharge was that he had failed to leave the drug cabinet keys before leaving the hospital and that the keys had been in his possession from 1 A.M. until 7 A.M. the following day. John learned that Margaret Handley had been verbally reprimanded for her handling of the case.

John filed an appeal regarding his dismissal with the human resource director of the hospital. However, the unit director's recommendation was upheld.

Following this decision, John immediately filed charges with the EEOC that he had been discriminated against because of his race. Both the night supervisor and the unit director were white. He requested full reinstatement with back pay. He also requested that his personnel file be purged of any damaging records that alluded to the incident.

1. *What would your decision be if you were asked to decide this case?*
2. *Should a supervisor and an employee be disciplined equally?*

FACT OR FICTION

Rosemary Toomey, an employee in the Service Department of the Caldwell Radiator Company, was on her way to the company cafeteria during her lunch break at 12:00 on May 24, 1983. While descending the stairs between the fourth and third floors of the building, she claimed to have slipped and fallen down three steps leading to the first landing of the stairwell. No outward evidence of injury was evident and she proceeded to have lunch.

Immediately upon returning to her work station at 1:00, she reported her accident to her supervisor and complained of severe back pains. Her supervisor insisted that Rosemary report immediately to the company infirmary as a precaution against serious injury.

At 1:15 Rosemary saw Dr. Barnes, the company physician, who checked her thoroughly and rendered the following diagnosis: "obvious lower back sprain, X rays negative for fracture, rib cage pain, mild tenderness." He prescribed a muscle relaxant, medication for pain, and a rib support. Rosemary was sent home on sick leave and told to report back to the infirmary the following day. On May 25, about 2:00 P.M., Rosemary was again seen by Dr. Barnes. She complained of pain and tenderness in her lower back. Dr. Barnes renewed her supply of pain tablets, prescribed moist heat applied to the lower back region several times during the day for about 20 minutes per application, and told Rosemary to remain inactive and to come back for another examination in three or four days. She failed to keep this appointment and did not contact either the infirmary or Dr. Barnes.

On June 10, while making a routine examination of the medical records, the appointment clerk discovered that Rosemary had not been heard from since May 25 and that as the result of an oversight, the Human Resource Department had not been informed of the incident. Action was initiated immediately to provide a complete report to the Human Resource Department and to contact Rosemary. Rosemary informed the infirmary that she had consulted her personal physician and thus did not see the need to check back with the infirmary. She was asked to have her physician send the company a report of his findings.

A review of the private physician's report on June 16 disclosed that after extensive tests, including a myelogram on May 31, there was no evidence of injury. The infirmary therefore informed Rosemary's department and the Human Resource Department that there seemed to be no reason why Rosemary could not come back to work. The Human Resource Department immediately called Rosemary and informed her that she was expected to return to work at the regular time on Monday morning, June 20. When Rosemary failed to report on Monday morning, the Service Department notified the Human Resource Department. A Human Resource Department clerk called Rosemary at 9:45 that morning and found her home. Rosemary said she still did not feel well and would come back to work as soon as she was physically able to do so. When she did report to work on Wednesday morning, June 22, at 8:00 A.M., she was informed that she had been terminated as of June 20 and should stop by the Human Resource Department to fill out the necessary papers.

Rosemary was visibly quite upset. She stormed into the Human Resource Department Manager's office and demanded an account of her employment status. She had understood that she was entitled to sick leave as a result of a work-related accident and had felt unable to return to work until now.

The Human Resource Department Manager explained to Rosemary that the Service Department Manager contended there was no medical evidence that her accident had resulted in an injury, and even if the alleged injury was sustained, the accident occurred during off-duty time (during the lunch hour), for which the company was not liable. Rosemary cited the company doctor's report, in which he mentioned "obvious lower back strain and rib cage pain, mild tenderness" as evidence to support her claim of a job-related disabling accident. The Human Resource Direcor pointed out, however, that a Memorandum for the Record, filed by the Service Department on June 1, documented the following facts:

1. There were no witnesses to the alleged accident.
2. Rosemary consistently had used the elevator between floors in the past. In fact, no one had ever seen her use the stairs before.
3. There was no outward evidence of bruises or fractures and the X-rays showed no fractures.
4. On May 25 the Service Department Manager observed Rosemary walking in a normal manner with no apparent difficulty.
5. Rosemary had an extensive history of back problems dating back to 1949, when she had missed one year of work because of an injury to her lower back. Subsequent to that, her medical records included:
    a. August 1967—10-day absence from work due to lower back pain (one year after starting with Caldwell Radiator Company).
    b. July 1973—22-day absence from work due to bronchitis and lumbar strain.
    c. April 1974—struck in the back by a door in the company building—lost 14 days of work.
    d. June 1974—91-day absence attributable to a variety of complaints, including back trouble, injured back while in hospital, off-duty accident.
    e. September 1974—Rosemary's personal physician diagnosed

lumbar strain, but said her complaints were only subjective. Possible diagnosis of conversion hysteria.

f. October 1974—company physician recorded the opinion that Rosemary was psychoneurotic and would probably be irregular in attendance because of this problem and lack of economic motivation.

g. June 1975—Rosemary fell at her mother's home, causing her arm to become numb—another off-duty accident.

Because of Rosemary's hostile attitude and implied threat of appeal, the Human Resource Manager requested a written statement from the infirmary as to whether Dr. Barnes felt the alleged accident qualified Rosemary to receive sick benefits under the company's benefit plan. On June 23, the infirmary wrote a memorandum to the Human Resource Department stating that, in Dr. Barnes' opinion, Rosemary should be covered by the company's sick benefits provisions for the period of May 24 through June 19, 1983. Since the Service Department Manager had requested that the Human Resource Department not recognize the incident as an on-the-job accident and since a controversy seemed to be in the making, the Human Resource Manager requested that the infirmary prepare a detailed evaluation of the alleged disability. This report was prepared and sent to the Human Resource Manager on June 27.

So as not to fall into a legal trap, the Human Resource Manager sent Rosemary's entire personnel file to the Legal Department for review. Since the company had been paying sick benefits to Rosemary, effective from the date of her alleged accident, the Human Resource Manager did not think it appropriate for the company to deny the incident. The primary question referred to the Legal Department was whether or not the alleged accident was job related, since it had occurred during an authorized break period. A copy of the Legal Department's reply is appended at the end of this case as Exhibit 1.

In summary, the company had paid Rosemary full salary and sick benefits from the time of her accident (May 24, 1983) until the date she failed to return to work as directed (June 20, 1983). On July 8, 1983, Rosemary filed a grievance with her union on the basis of being discharged without proper cause.

The Benefit Review Committee, a standing committee that had been functioning for several years within the company under the overall guidance and direction of the Human Resource Department, was asked to review the Toomey case. The committee agreed with the attorney's opinion that the alleged accident was not job related and with the medical reports that no specific event could be related to the current back problem. The committee members were charged, however, with recommending a course of action that would be equitable to all involved in this incident.

Exhibit 1

CALDWELL RADIATOR COMPANY
LEGAL DEPARTMENT
Philadelphia, Pa. 19105

July 6, 1983

M. K. Edwards
Attorney

Memorandum

To: Personnel Office

Re: Rosemary Toomey

   The Human Resource Department would be justified in denying Ms. Rosemary Toomey's alleged fall on May 21, 1983 as an on-duty accident for the purposes of worker's compensation so long as there is no question that Ms. Toomey was on her lunch break at the time she allegedly fell.
   As you know, Pennsylvania law is quite uniform in denying compensation for accidents occurring on scheduled breaks. Exceptions to this rule of law are made when the employee remains on call during break, is on an unscheduled break, is still conducting the employer's business during break, or is making preparations to return from break. Assuming Ms. Toomey's activities did not fall within one of the exceptions, the company is under no legal obligation to treat this as a work-related injury. Of course, a formal denial must be filed with the board.
   The opinion expressed herein deals solely with the company's obligation under the worker's compensation law and does not purport to assess the company's obligation under the benefit plan.
   If you have further questions, please call.

Sincerely,

M. K. Edwards

M. K. Edwards

Understanding unions and improving employee welfare

Chapter 16

Development and structure of labor unions

Objectives

1. To describe legislation that has influenced labor-management relations.
2. To discuss union organizational structures.
3. To present trends in union membership.
4. To outline current developments in the labor movement.

Outline

History of labor-management
    legislation
  Sherman Antitrust Act
  Yellow dog contracts
  Clayton Act
  Railway Labor Act
  Norris-LaGuardia Act
  National Labor Relations (Wagner)
      Act
  Labor-Management Relations (Taft-
      Hartley) Act
  Labor-Management Reporting and
      Disclosure (Landrum-Griffin) Act
  Civil Service Reform Act
Structural aspects of unions
  AFL–CIO
  National and international unions
  City and state federations
  Local unions
Union membership trends
Current developments in the labor
    movement

Absorption Union merger that involves the merging of one union into a considerably larger one.

Amalgamation Union merger that involves two or more unions, usually of approximately the same size, forming a new union.

American Federation of Labor–Congress of Industrial Organizations (AFL–CIO) A combination of national, international, and local unions joined together to promote the interests of unions and workers. The AFL–CIO was formed in 1955 by the amalgamation of the American Federation of Labor (AFL) and the Congress of Industrial Organizations (CIO)

Civil Service Reform Act of 1978 Act regulating labor-management relations for federal government employees.

Commonwealth **v.** *Hunt* Landmark court decision in 1842 which declared that unions were not illegal per se.

Craft union Union that has only skilled workers as members. Most craft unions have members from several related trades (e.g., Bricklayers, Masons, and Plasterers' International Union).

Executive orders Orders issued by the President of the United States for managing and operating federal government agencies.

Industrial union Union that has as members both skilled and unskilled workers in a particular industry or group of industries.

Injunction Court order to stop an action that could result in irreparable damage to property when the situation is such that no other adequate remedy is available to protect the interests of the injunction-seeking party.

Landrum-Griffin Act of 1959 (Labor-Management Reporting and Disclosure Act) Act regulating labor unions and requiring disclosure of union financial information to the government.

National Labor Relations Board (NLRB) A five-member panel appointed by the President of the United States with the advice and consent of the Senate and with the authority to administer the Wagner Act.

Norris-LaGuardia Act of 1932 Prolabor act that eliminated the use of yellow-dog contracts and severely restricted the use of injunctions.

Philadelphia Cordwainers case of 1806 Case in which the jury ruled that combinations of workers to raise their wages constituted a conspiracy in restraint of trade.

Right-to-work laws Laws passed by individual states prohibiting compulsory union membership.

Taft-Hartley Act of 1947 (Labor-Management Relations Act) Act which placed the federal government in a watchdog position to ensure that union-management relations are conducted fairly by both parties.

Wagner Act of 1935 (National Labor Relations Act) Prolabor act that gave workers the right to organize, obligated the management of organizations to bargain in good faith with unions, defined illegal management practices relating to unions, and created the National Labor Relations Board (NLRB) to administer the act.

Yellow-dog contract Term coined by unions to describe an agreement between a worker and employer that, as a condition of employment, the worker would not join a labor union. Yellow-dog contracts were made illegal by the Norris-LaGuardia Act of 1932.

Every single area of union activity is inevitably a management area whether it be working hours or working conditions, job definitions, job assignments, hiring and firing policies, supervisory authority, or seniority provisions. Even if a union were to abandon all these areas and confine itself entirely to the problems of cash income, it would have to set against profitability and productivity the needs of the worker for a predictable wage and predictable employment.

Peter F. Drucker *

Labor unions are an important environmental force affecting organizations. When an organization is unionized, wages, hours, and working conditions are negotiated between its union and management. Even when it is not unionized, an organization's wages, hours, and working conditions are influenced by those of other unionized firms.

The human resource department normally serves as the primary contact between the management of an organization and the union. Conducting a union election campaign, negotiating the union contract, and administering the union contract are typical functions handled by the human resource department. Thus, understanding the historical development and organizational structure of labor unions is an important aspect of the human resource manager's job.

HISTORY OF LABOR-MANAGEMENT LEGISLATION

The first unions in America appeared between 1790 and 1820. These were local organizations of skilled craftsmen, e.g., shoemakers in Philadelphia, printers in New York, tailors in Baltimore, and other similar groups. No unions existed among factory employees during this time.

The demands of these unions were similar to those of today. They wanted higher wages and shorter working hours. When union demands were not agreed to by management, these early unions resorted to strikes or "turn outs," as they were then called. A strike is the collective refusal of employees to work.

To offset the pressures of these unions, employers formed associations and took legal action against the unions. In the *Philadelphia Cordwainers* (shoemakers) case of 1806, the jury ruled that combinations of workers to raise their wages constituted a conspiracy in restraint of trade. The conspiracy doctrine is based on the idea that a combination of persons has power to inflict harm that an individual does not possess and that an action which is legal when taken by an individual may be illegal when performed by a group.

Over the next 35 years, unions ran up against the conspiracy doctrine on numerous occasions. Some courts continued to rule that labor unions were illegal per se. Others ruled that the means used by unions (e.g., strikes) in achieving their demands were illegal or that the ends

---

*P. F. Drucker, *The New Society* (New York: Harper & Row, 1962), p. 107.

sought (e.g., closed shops) were illegal.[1] A closed shop prohibits an employer from hiring anyone other than a union member.[2]

In 1842, in the landmark Massachusetts case of *Commonwealth* v. *Hunt,* the Supreme Court of Massachusetts rejected the doctrine that the actions of labor unions were illegal per se. The court noted that the power of a labor union could be used not only for illegal purposes but also for legal purposes. This decision, of course, left open the door for legal actions questioning the means used and ends sought by labor unions. Thus, even after 1842, the legal environment for unions remained vague and uncertain. Some courts held that a closed shop was a lawful objective and, thus, strikes for a closed shop were legal. Other courts reached an opposite conclusion. During this time, the legality of union activities depended to a large extent on the court jurisdiction in which the cases occurred.[3]

By the 1880s most courts had moved away from the use of the conspiracy doctrine, and the injunction became a favorite technique used by the courts for controlling union activities. An injunction is a court order to stop an action that could result in irreparable damage to property when the situation is such that no other adequate remedy is available to protect the interests of the injunction-seeking party. During this time, the normal procedure used in seeking an injunction in a labor dispute was as follows:

1. The complainant (normally the employer) went to court, filed a complaint stating the nature of the property threat, and requested relief.
2. The judge normally issued a temporary restraining order halting the threatened action until the case could be heard.
3. Shortly thereafter, a preliminary hearing was held so the judge could decide whether to issue a temporary injunction.
4. Finally, after a trial, a decision was made as to whether a permanent injunction should be issued.

Injunctions had three effects. First, failure of the union to abide by the temporary restraining order or the temporary injunction meant risking contempt of court charges. Second, compliance meant a waiting period of many months before the matter came to trial. Often this waiting period was enough to destroy the effectiveness of the union. Third, the courts placed a broad interpretation on the term property. Historically, injunctions had been issued to prevent damage to property where an award of money damages would be an inadequate remedy. However, during this time, the courts held that an employer's property included the right to operate the business and make a profit. Thus, the expectation of making a profit became a property right. Any strike, even though it might be peaceful, could be alleged to be injurious to the expectation of making a profit and could be stopped by an injunction. Injunctions were generally granted by the courts upon request and were frequently used to control union activities until the 1930s. The attitude of the courts over this time seems to have been that management had the right to do business without the interference of unions.

Sherman Antitrust Act

The Sherman Antitrust Act was signed into law in 1890. The law made trusts and conspiracies that restrain interstate commerce illegal and forbids persons from monopolizing or attempting to monopolize interstate trade or commerce. Furthermore, any person who believes that he or she has been injured by violations of the act has the right to sue for triple the amount of damages sustained and the costs of the suit, including a reasonable attorney's fee.

It is unclear as to whether Congress originally intended the act to apply to labor unions. Generally, it was thought that the primary purpose was to protect the public from the abuses of corporate monopolies. However, in 1908, in a landmark decision referred to as the *Danbury Hatters* case, the Supreme Court decided that the Sherman Antitrust Act applied to unions.[4] In this case, the United Hatters union, while attempting to unionize Loewe & Company of Danbury, Connecticut, called a strike and initiated a national boycott against the company's products. The boycott was successful and Loewe filed a suit against the union alleging violation of the Sherman Antitrust Act. In 1915, the Supreme Court sustained a judgment against the union and its members, ruling that the boycott was illegal because it restrained trade within the meaning of the Sherman Antitrust Act. The court further held that the individual members of the union were jointly liable for the money damages awarded.[5]

Yellow-dog contracts

Another device used by employers to control unions during this time was the "yellow-dog" contract. The name was coined by labor unions to describe an agreement between a worker and employer that, as a condition of employment, the worker would not join a labor union. These contracts could be oral or written or both.

In 1917, the Supreme Court upheld the legality of yellow-dog contracts in *Hitchman Coal & Coke Co.* v. *Mitchell.*[6] This case involved the management of the Hitchman Coal and Coke Company, whose employees had been unionized in 1903, and the United Mine Workers (UMW) in West Virginia. In 1906, a strike was called by the union against the company. However, management defeated the union and resumed operations as a nonunionized company. To ensure that it remained nonunionized, management required all of its employees, as a condition of employment, to sign an agreement saying that they would not join a union as long as they were employed by Hitchman.

Later, the United Mine Workers sent an organizer back into West Virginia. The organizer secretly contacted and signed up the employees of Hitchman Coal. When enough employees signed up, a strike was called and the mine was closed. However, the management of Hitchman brought suit against the union alleging that the organizer had deliberately induced the employees to break their agreements with the company. The Supreme Court ruled in favor of management, and thus upheld the enforceability of the yellow-dog contract. Yellow-dog contracts were used until they were declared illegal by the Norris-La Guardia Act of 1932. This act is discussed later in this chapter.

Clayton Act

In 1914, labor unions rejoiced at the passage of the Clayton Act. In fact, it was even called "labor's Magna Carta." Sections 6 and 20 were of particular importance to labor. Parts of both are summarized below:

> Section 6: The labor of a human being is not a commodity or article of commerce. Nothing contained in the antitrust laws shall be construed to forbid the existence and operating of labor . . . organizations . . . or to forbid or restrain individual members of such organizations from lawfully carrying out the legitimate objects thereof; nor shall such organizations, or the members thereof be held or construed to be illegal combinations or conspiracies in restraint of trade under the antitrust laws.

> Section 20: No restraining order or injunction shall be granted by any court of the United States . . . in any case between an employer and employees, or between employees, or between persons employed and persons seeking employment, involving or growing out of a dispute concerning terms or conditions of employment, unless necessary to prevent irreparable injury to property, or to a property right, of the party making the application, for which injury there is no adequate remedy at law.

An important interpretation of the wording of these two provisions of the Clayton Act was made in a case involving the International Association of Machinists and the Duplex Printing Press Company.[7] At the time, Duplex was the only nonunionized company manufacturing printing presses. The union attempted to organize the company requesting customers not to purchase Duplex presses, requesting a trucking company not to transport Duplex presses, and requesting repair shops not to repair Duplex presses. The company asked for an injunction against the union, but was denied by both the United States District and Circuit Courts on the basis of section 20 of the Clayton Act. However, in a split decision, the Supreme Court overruled the lower courts by deciding that an injunction could be issued against the union. In this decision, the Court ruled that section 6 of the Clayton Act did not exempt unions from the control of the Sherman Act. Furthermore, the Court's decision meant that the issuance of injunctions was largely unchanged by the Clayton Act.

Railway Labor Act

The legislation and its interpretations by the courts was largely antiunion prior to the passage of the Railway Labor Act in 1926. This act, which set up the administrative machinery for handling labor relations within the railroad industry, was the first important piece of prolabor legislation in the United States. The act was extended to air transportation in 1936.

One provision established the National Mediation Board to administer the act. Another provision eliminated yellow-dog contracts for railroad industry employees. The act also established mechanisms for mediation and arbitration of disputes between employers and unions within the industry. However, it is important to note that the original act only applied to railroad employees and not to those employed in other industries.

Norris-LaGuardia Act

The Norris-LaGuardia Act of 1932 was of significant importance to labor unions because it made yellow-dog contracts unenforceable and severely restricted the use of injunctions. The law prohibited federal courts from issuing injunctions to keep unions from striking, paying strike benefits, picketing (unless the picketing involved fraud or violence), and peacefully assembling.

Other parts of the law further restricted the issuance of injunctions. For example, the employer was required to show that the regular police force was either unwilling or unable to protect his or her property before an injunction could be issued. Temporary restraining orders could not be issued for more than five days.

The Norris-LaGuardia Act changed the rules of the game in labor-management relations. Prior to its passage, the law as interpreted by the courts was largely in management's favor. However, this act clearly gave employees the right to organize, to bargain with employers on the terms and conditions of employment, and to be free from interference or coercion in the exercise of these rights. The major weakness of the act was that it established no administrative procedures to ensure the implementation of these rights. Furthermore, the act did not require management to recognize or bargain with a union. The net effect was to remove certain legal restrictions that had been used by management for controlling unions. Under this law, the federal government assumed basically a neutral role in labor-management relations.

National Labor
Relations (Wagner)
Act

The National Labor Relations Act, commonly known as the Wagner Act after its principal sponsor, Senator Robert Wagner, Sr. of New York, was passed in 1935. The bill signaled a change in the federal government's role in labor-management relations. As a result of this law, government took a much more active role. Overall, the act was highly favorable to unions.

The Wagner Act gave employees the right to organize unions, to bargain collectively with employers, and to engage in other concerted actions for the purpose of mutual protection. Of course, these rights had already been granted by the Norris-LaGuardia Act. However, the Wagner Act went further in requiring employers to recognize unions chosen by workers and to bargain with such unions in good faith. Furthermore, employers were prohibited from engaging in certain unfair labor practices, including: (1) interference with, restraint of, or coercion of employees in exercising their rights under the act; (2) domination of, interference with, or financial contributions to a union; (3) discrimination in regard to hiring, firing, or any term or condition of employment to encourage or discourage membership in a union; (4) discharge or discrimination against an employee for filing charges or giving testimony under the act; and (5) refusal to bargain "in good faith" with the legal representative of the employees.

Also, the act created the National Labor Relations Board (NLRB) to administer the act. The NLRB is a five-member panel that is appointed by the President of the United States with the advice and consent of the Senate. The NLRB has the authority to establish regulations, procedures, and rules necessary to carry out the provisions of the act. For example, the NLRB establishes procedures for conducting union organizing and election campagins. The NLRB also has the authority to investigate charges of unfair labor practices.

When such a charge is made against an employer, the board or its representative holds hearings to determine whether an unfair labor practice did, in fact, occur. If a violation did occur, the board can issue an order requiring the employer to cease and desist from such actions, or it can order the employer to take corrective actions. For example, an employer could be ordered to reinstate an employee with back pay if it was determined that the employee was terminated for union activities. One weakness is that the board does not have the power to enforce its orders. It must petition the United States circuit courts when legal enforcement becomes necessary.

Labor-Management
Relations (Taft-
Hartley) Act

After the passage of the Wagner Act, union membership grew from approximately 6 percent of the total work force to approximately 23 percent in 1947. Accompanying this growth was an increase in union militancy. Strikes became much more frequent and widespread. Corruption, racketeering, and communist involvement in a small number of unions helped to create a negative public opinion. In 1946, a record 4.6 million workers participated in strikes. A nationwide steel strike, an auto strike, two coal strikes, and a railroad strike negatively influenced scores of other industries, causing shortages and layoffs.[8]

It was against this background of events that the Labor-Management Relations (Taft-Hartley) Act was passed in 1947. This act marked another change in the legislative posture toward union-management relations. The Taft-Hartley act basically placed government in the role of referee to ensure that both unions and management dealt fairly with each other.

The act increased the size of the NLRB from three to five members. It also created the Office of General Counsel to the board. This office has authority to investigate and issue complaints of unfair labor practices.

Under the Taft-Hartley Act, employees have the right to organize a union, bargain collectively with an employer, and engage in other concerted activities for the purpose of collective bargaining. The act also spelled out unfair labor practices by employers. Most provisions are identical to those of the Wagner Act, but one unfair practice was changed in a significant respect. Under the Wagner Act, employers were prohibited from discriminating in regard to hiring, firing, or any term or condition of employment to encourage or discourage membership in a union. However, closed and preferential shop agreements were permitted. With a closed shop, only union members can be hired, and the preferential shop requires that union members be given preference in filling job vacancies. The Taft-Hartley Act made closed and preferential shops illegal. However, these types of shops continued in the construction industry and were, in effect, legaized in 1959 by the Landrum-Griffin Act, which is discussed later in this chapter.

Unlike the Wagner Act, the Taft-Hartley Act established a number of unfair union practices. In general, unions were forbidden from coercing employees who do not want to join, forcing employers to pressure employees to join a union, refusing to bargain in good faith with an employer, forcing an employer to pay for services not performed ("featherbedding"), engaging in certain types of secondary boycotts (taking action against an employer that is not directly engaged in a dispute with the union), and charging excessive initiation fees when union membership is required because of a union shop agreement. A union shop agreement requires employees to join the union and remain members as a condition of employment.

In addition, the Taft-Hartley Act contained an important provision, the so-called "free speech" clause. This clause stated that management has the right to express their opinion about unions or unionism to their employees, provided that they carry no threat of reprisal or force.

Section 14(b) of the Taft-Hartley Act is one of the most controversial sections of the law. It states:

> Nothing in this act shall be construed as authorizing the execution or application of agreements requiring membership in a labor organization as a condition of employment in any state of territory in which such execution or application is prohibited by state or territory law.

Thus, section 14(b) permits states and territories to pass laws prohibiting union shops and other arrangements for compulsory union membership. Laws passed by individual states prohibiting compulsory union membership are called right-to-work laws, and states that have passed such legislation are right-to-work states. Presently, 20 states have such laws.

The Taft-Hartley Act also established procedures that must be followed in terminating or modifying union contracts. Finally, procedures were established for use in so-called "national emergency" disputes. These procedures are described in more detail in Chapter 17.

Labor-Management Reporting and Disclosure (Landrum-Griffin) Act

Even after the passage of the Taft-Hartley Act, complaints of corruption and high-handed practices by union officials continued. As a result, in 1959 Congress passed the Labor-Management Reporting and Disclosure Act, usually called the LMRDA or the Landrum-Griffin Act. This act was aimed primarily at regulating internal union affairs and protecting the rights of individual union members.

The LMRDA covers a wide variety of subjects. The main provisions of the act are summarized below:

1. Union members are guaranteed the right to vote in union elections.
2. Union members are guaranteed the right to oppose their incumbent leadership both in union meetings and by nominating opposition candidates.
3. A majority affirmative vote of members in a secret ballot is required before union dues can be increased.
4. Reports covering most financial aspects of the union must be filed with the U.S. Department of Labor.
5. Officers and employees of unions are required to report any financial dealings with employers that might potentially influence the union members' interests.
6. Each union is required to have a constitution and bylaws filed with the U.S. Department of Labor.
7. Rigid formal requirements are established for conducting both national and local union elections.
8. Union members are allowed to bring suit against union officials for improper management of the union's funds and for conflict-of-interest situations.

9. Trusteeships which allow national or international unions to take over the management of a local union can be established only under provisions specified in the constitution and bylaws of the union and only to combat corruption or financial misconduct.

A major concern of unions at the time of passage of the LMRDA was the intrusion of the government into the day-to-day operations of unions. However, several studies have concluded that the act has had little, if any, impact in this area.[9] Furthermore, the same studies have concluded that additional reforms of the LMRDA are needed if it is to accomplish its aims of regulating internal union affairs and protecting the rights of individual union members.

Civil Service Reform Act

Prior to 1978, labor-management relations within the federal government were administered through executive orders. These orders are issued by the President of the United States and relate to the management and operation of federal government agencies. Executive Order 10988, issued by President Kennedy, gave federal employees the right to join unions and required good faith bargaining by both unions and federal agency management. Executive Order 11491, issued by President Nixon, defined more precisely the rights of federal employees in regard to unionization by establishing unfair labor practices for both unions and federal agency management. It also established procedures to safeguard these rights.

In 1978, the Civil Service Reform Act (CSRA) was passed.[10] It basically enacted into law the measures that had previously been adopted under Executive Orders 10988 and 11491. The act gave federal employees the right to organize and removes any threat of modification, refinement, or termination as a result of presidential displeasure or change.[11] Some of the provisions of the CSRA are as follows:

1. Established the Federal Labor Relations Authority (FLRA) to administer the act. The FLRA is an independent, neutral, bipartisan body headed by full-time executives who are appointed by the president for fixed terms. These executives have no other position within the federal government.
2. Created the Office of General Counsel within the FLRA to investigate and prosecute unfair labor-practice charges.
3. Authorized the Federal Services Impasses Panel (FSIP) to recommend procedures for resolving impasses in collective bargaining and to take whatever action may be necessary to resolve impasses.
4. Established unfair labor practices for both management and unions.
5. Restricted the items that unions and federal agency management could bargain over.

6. Required binding arbitration for all grievances that are not resolved in earlier stages of the grievance procedure.
7. Prohibited strikes in the federal sector.

The use of the provisions of CSRA in collective bargaining is described in more detail in Chapter 17.

STRUCTURAL ASPECTS OF UNIONS

As the previously described legislation was passed and court actions taken, organizational units were developed within the union movement to deal with problems and to take advantage of opportunities. Four main types of union organizational units exist.

1. Local unions.
2. City and state federations.
3. National or international unions.
4. Federations of local, national, and international unions (e.g., AFL–CIO).

Some important dates relating to the development of the different union organizational units are shown in Table 16–1.

AFL–CIO

Structurally speaking, the AFL–CIO is the largest organizational unit within the union movement. Its primary goal is to promote the interests of unions and workers. The AFL–CIO resulted from the merger of the American Federation of Labor (AFL) and the Congress of Industrial Organizations (CIO) in 1955. Formed in 1886, the AFL was primarily composed of craft unions, which have only skilled workers as members. Most such unions have members from several related trades (e.g., the Bricklayers, Masons, and Plasterers' International Union). The CIO formed in 1938, was developed to organize industrial unions, which have as members both skilled and unskilled workers in a particular industry or group of industries. (The United Automobile Workers is an industrial union.)

Table 16–1   Important dates in the labor movement

Year	Event
1792	First local union—Philadelphia Shoemaker's Union
1833	First city federation—New York, Philadelphia, Baltimore
1850	First national union—International Typographical Union
1869	Knights of Labor—First attempt to form a federation of unions
1886	Formation of American Federation of Labor (AFL)
1938	Formation of Congress of Industrial Organizations (CIO)
1955	Merger of the AFL and CIO

The organization structure of the AFL–CIO is shown in Figure 16–1. Basically, the AFL–CIO is composed of affiliated national and international unions, affiliated state and local bodies, local unions affiliated directly with the AFL–CIO, and eight trade and industrial departments.

The basic policies of the AFL–CIO are set and its executive council elected at a national convention which is held every two years. The executive council which is made up of the president, secretary-treasurer, and 33 vice presidents carries out the policies established at the convention. Each affiliated national and international union sends delegates to the convention. The number of delegates a particular union sends is determined by the size of its membership.

To deal with specific concerns, the AFL–CIO president appoints and supervises standing committees which work with staff departments to provide services to the union membership. The general board meets at the call of the president or the executive council and acts on matters referred to it by the executive council.

The trade and industrial departments primarily serve to coordinate the activities of unions whose interests overlap, to seek means of resolving jurisdictional disputes between unions, and to promote cooperation in collective bargaining between unions. For example, the union label department promotes the use of union labels on products. The department of organization and field services assists in union organizing campaigns and contract negotiations.

It is important to note that all national and international unions do not belong to the AFL–CIO. For example, presently the Teamsters, the United Automobile Workers, and the United Mine Workers do not belong. In fact, of the over 23 million union members, approximately 30 percent are in organizations not affiliated with the AFL–CIO.

National and international unions

The organization of most national and international unions is similar to that of the AFL–CIO. In general, they operate under a constitution and have a national convention with each local union represented in proportion to its membership. Usually, the convention elects an executive council which normally consists of a president, secretary-treasurer, and several vice presidents. Normally, the president appoints and manages a staff for handling matters such as organizing activities, research, and legal problems.

The field organization of a national or international union usually has several regional or district offices headed by a regional director. Under the regional director are field representatives who are responsible for conducting union organizing campaigns and assisting local unions in collective bargaining and in handling grievances.

Figure 16–1   Organization structure of the AFL-CIO

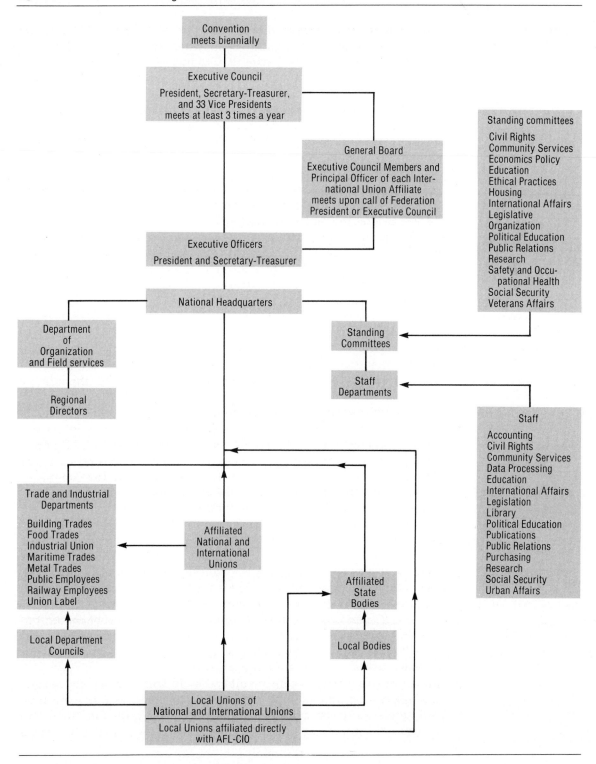

City and state federations

City federations receive their charter from the AFL–CIO and are composed of local unions within a specified area. Local unions send delegates to city federation meetings, which are generally held on a biweekly or monthly basis.

The primary function of city federations is to coordinate and focus the political efforts of local unions. During elections, city federations usually endorse a slate of candidates. Most city federations maintain an informal lobby at city hall and present labor's issues to legislative committees. City federations do not always focus their efforts only on labor issues. Other issues and activities frequently addressed by city federations include school board policies, community fund-raising drives, and public transportation problems.

State federations are also chartered by the AFL–CIO and are composed of local unions and city federations. The main goal of state federations is to influence political action favorable to unions. Efforts are made to deliver the labor vote to endorsed candidates. During state legislature sessions, the state federation actively lobbies for passage of bills that are endorsed by labor.

Local unions

Most local unions operate under the constitution of their national or international union. However, a number of local unions are independent in that they operate without a national affiliation. Furthermore, a local union can be affiliated directly with the AFL–CIO without being affiliated with a national or international union.

As a rule, the membership of a local union elects officers who carry out the union activities. In a typical local union, a president, vice president, and secretary-treasurer are elected. Several committees are also normally formed within a local. For example, a bargaining committee is usually appointed to negotiate the contract for the union. Similarly, a grievance committee is usually appointed to handle grievances for the membership. The latter committee is generally composed of a chief steward and several departmental stewards. The stewards recruit new employees into the union, listen to worker complaints, handle grievances, and observe management's administration of the union contract. Generally, most union officials work at a regular job but have some leeway in using working time to conduct union business. In large locals, most officials are full-time, paid employees of the union. The local usually depends heavily on the field representative of its national or international union for assistance in handling contract negotiations, strikes, and arbitration hearings.

In those industries where membership is scattered among several employers, local unions often have a business agent who is a full-time paid employee of the local union. This agent manages internal union activities, negotiates contracts, meets with company officials to resolve contract interpretation issues, handles grievances, and serves as an active participant in arbitration hearings.

**UNION
MEMBERSHIP
TRENDS**

Between 1935—the year the National Labor Relations Act (NLRA) was passed—and the end of World War II, union membership quadrupled. Membership was fairly constant during the second half of the 1940s, but picked up during the first half of the 1950s. However, between 1956 and 1964, union membership experienced a downward trend. From 1964 to the present, union membership has shown a steady increase. Figure 16–2 shows the membership of national and international unions from 1930 to 1981.

On the other hand, the proportion of the total labor force unionized has shown a steady decline since the mid 1950s. Furthermore, union membership as a proportion of nonagricultural employment (the sec-

Figure 16–2   Membership in national and international unions, 1930–1981

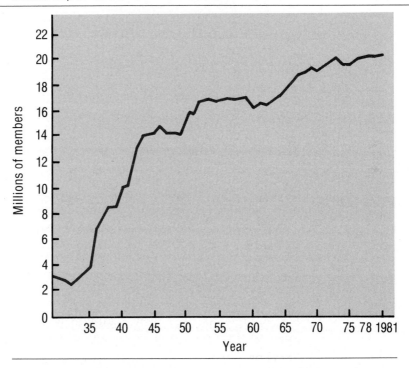

Source: *Directory of National Unions and Employee Associations* (Washington, D.C.: U.S. Department of Labor, 1981) p. 58.

Note: Excludes Canadian membership but includes members in other areas outside the United States. Members of AFL-CIO directly affiliated local unions are also included. Members of single-firm and local unaffiliated unions are excluded. For the years 1948–52, midpoints of membership estimates, which were expressed as ranges, were used.

Figure 16–3   Union membership as a percent of the total labor force and of
                      employees in nonagricultural establishments, 1930–1981

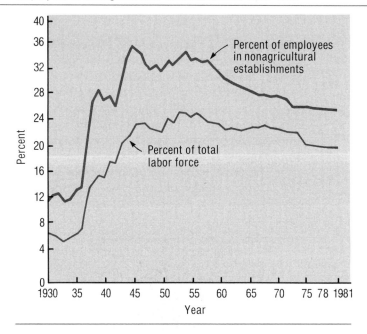

Source: *Directory of National Unions and Employee Associations* (Washington,
D.C., U.S. Department of Labor, 1981) p. 60.

Note: Employment in nonagricultural establishments excludes the armed forces,
self-employed and unemployed workers, agricultural workers, proprietors, unpaid
family workers, and domestic servants.

tor where most members are found) has also shown a steady decline
over the same time period. This is illustrated in Figure 16–3.

Historically, union membership has been concentrated in a small
number of large unions. This trend has continued through the early
1980s. For example, in 1982, 16 unions represented over 60 percent of
the total union membership. Another trend in union membership has
been a steady increase in the number of women union members and
in the proportion of women as a percent of total union membership.
For example, in 1981 over 5 million females were union members,
pushing the proportion of all union members who were women to
over 24 percent.

**CURRENT
DEVELOPMENTS IN
THE LABOR
MOVEMENT**

Several developments in the labor movement could have a significant influence on labor-management relations in the future. First, the
more successful unions in terms of growth have been increasingly
venturing out of their original jurisdictions into nonunion industries.

New path for labor relations

Unions, managers stress cooperation

Washington—Under the threat of slumping sales and tough foreign competition, some once-belligerent unions are taking a cooperative stance in their dealings with employers.

Management—no less concerned about dwindling profits than unions are about the loss of jobs—is increasingly inclined to meet workers at least half way by devising programs which give labor a voice in corporate decision-making.

"We've all become Japanese in recognition that we can no longer do business as usual," said Ray Marshall, Secretary of Labor in the Carter administration and now an economic consultant who commutes between Austin, Texas, and Washington.

Nowhere is the trend toward labor-management cooperation more pronounced than in the U.S. auto industry—an industry, which after many fat years, has fallen on lean times.

And, ironically, the search for new paths appears to be making the most headway at the Ford Motor Company, which had led the fight against unions during the depression under its tough-minded founder, Henry Ford.

Yet, like the rest of the auto manufacturers, Ford's domestic operations are suffering from a weak market and high interest rates. A new generation of managers at Ford is actutely aware that the Japanese produced 12 million cars in 1980, of which 8 million were exported.

Under that sort of pressure, the United Auto Workers has negotiated an unprecedented emergency contract with Ford—some eight months before the current three-year agreement is due to expire. The union won assurances of job security for its senior workers, while giving up future wages and benefits which could help restore the ailing company to profitability.

The 31-month tentative pact was overwhelmingly approved Wednesday by the UAW's 225-member Ford Council, which is made up of leaders of UAW locals, and now goes to the rank and file for a vote.

It is significant that the two top negotiators—Donald Ephlin of the UAW and Peter Pestillo of Ford—spent several weeks last summer touring Japanese auto plants together.

In Japan, long-term growth rather than quarterly profits are the central concern in corporate affairs. Unions are organized by company instead of by industry or trade. Hardly anyone is ever fired.

When Ephlin and Pestillo talked to reporters here Tuesday about their prospective pact, each of them emphasized that one of its most vital features was "a mutual commitment to work together."

"In the past, it might be said, all our contracts with the UAW were law driven," Pestillo noted. "But this contract is personnel driven."

What the Ford vice president had in mind was an approach largely based on mutual trust rather than the fine print of a detailed agreement. It is not unlike the approach which has worked so successfully for the Japanese.

Source: Andrew J. Glass, in *The Atlanta Constitution*, 18 February 1982, p. 1-C.

Banks, savings and loan associations, insurance companies, and the communications industry are likely targets for union organizing campaigns in the 1980s.

Another development that could influence the relationship between labor and management is the increase in union mergers. Such mergers take two basic forms. An amalgamation involves two or more unions, normally of roughly equal size, forming a new union. An absorption involves the merging of one union into a considerably larger one. The merger trend among unions accelerated substantially after 1955, and merger activity has remained relatively high.[12] Larger unions can, of course, bring much more pressure on management not only in negotiating collective bargaining agreements but also in union organizing campaigns.

In the 1980s unions are also expected to increase the use of financial pressure through its membership and its allies, in their organizing campaigns. For instance, unions can withdraw their business and money from banks and insurance companies that do business with companies vigorously resisting union organzing attempts. The Amalgamated Clothing and Textile Workers used this strategy with some success in its bitter organizing campaign with J. P. Stevens during the 1970s.

Furthermore, more unions are likely to demand a voice in investing the pension fund assets of union members. These funds are now largely administered by employers. Specifically, unions are likely to request that the funds not be invested in antiunion companies or companies that display "antiunion" conduct.[13]

SUMMARY

During the 1800s and early 1900s, the conspiracy doctrine, injunctions, the Sherman Antitrust Act, and yellow-dog contracts were used to inhibit the growth of labor unions. However, in 1932, legislative action began to be more favorable toward unions. Two prounion laws, the Norris-LaGuardia Act of 1932 and the Wagner Act of 1935, contributed greatly to the rapid development and expansion of labor unions.

The Taft-Hartley Act of 1947 attempted to place unions and management on an equal basis. This act put the federal government in the watchdog position of insuring that union-management relations were conducted fairly by both parties. The Landrum-Griffin Act of 1959 placed additional controls on unions, while at the same time affording additional rights to union members. The Civil Service Reform Act of 1978 gave federal government employees the right to organize and establish the framework for labor relations within the federal government.

The four main union organizational units are local unions, city and state federations, national or international unions, and federations of locals, national and international unions. The structure and operation of each of these units was described.

Between 1935 and the end of World War II, union membership quadrupled. Membership remained fairly constant during the second half of the 1940s, but picked up during the first half of the 1950s. Between 1956 and 1964, union membership experienced a downward trend. From 1964 to the present, union membership has shown a steady increase. However, the proportion of the total labor force unionized has shown a steady decline. Membership has continued to be concentrated in a small number of large unions. The number of women members and the proportion of women as a percent of total union membership have also shown a steady increase.

Banks, savings and loan associations, insurance companies, and the communications industry are likely targets for union organizing campaigns in the 1980s. Union merger activity is likely to continue at a high level in this decade. Unions are also expected to increase the use of financial pressures in their organizing campaigns and to demand a voice in investing of the pension fund assets of union members.

REVIEW QUESTIONS

1. What was the ruling in the *Philadelphia Cordwainers* case of 1806?
2. What was the decision in the *Commonwealth* v. *Hunt* case of 1842?
3. What is an injunction? How were injunctions used against labor unions?
4. What is a yellow-dog contract?
5. What major benefits were gained by unions with the passage of the Norris-LaGuardia Act of 1932?
6. What unfair employer practices were specified by the Wagner Act of 1935?
7. What unfair union practices were specified by the Taft-Hartley Act of 1947?
8. Outline the main areas covered by the Landrum-Griffin Act of 1959.
9. Outline the main areas covered by the Civil Service Reform Act of 1978.
10. Briefly describe the four main types of union organizational units.
11. What trends have occurred in labor union membership from 1935 to the present?
12. Briefly outline some current developments in the labor movement.

DISCUSSION QUESTIONS

1. What reasons can you give to explain why legislation took a prounion turn in the 1930s?
2. Discuss your feelings on the following statement: "Management should always fight hard to keep unions out of their organization."
3. Why do you think that white-collar workers should join unions?
4. Do you believe that college professors and nurses are good candidates for unionization? Why or why not?

REFERENCES AND ADDITIONAL READINGS

1. For a discussion of labor conspiracy cases see J. R. Commons, U. B. Phillips, E. A. Gilmore, H. L. Sumner, and J. B. Andrews, eds., *A Documentary History of American Industrial Society*, vol. III and IV (New York: Russell and Russell, 1958).

2. Closed shops were made illegal by the Labor-Management Relations (Taft-Hartley) Act of 1947.

3. For a summary of the varying theories involving the legality of union actions see E. E. Wittle, *The Government in Labor Disputes* (New York: McGraw-Hill, 1932), Chapter 3.

4. *Loewe v. Lawlor*, 208 U.S. 274 (1908).

5. *Lawlor v. Loewe*, 235 U.S. 522 (1915).

6. *Hitchman Coal & Coke Co. v. Mitchell*, 245 U.S. 229 (1917).

7. *Duplex v. Deering*, 254 U.S. 443 (1921).

8. "Big Labor's First Big Defeat: The Taft-Hartley Act," *Dun's Review*, October 1978, pp. 35, 38.

9. See, for instance, G. W. Bohlander and W. B. Werther, Jr., "The Labor-Management Reporting and Disclosure Act. Revisited," *Labor Law Journal*, September 1979, pp. 582–89, and B. A. Smith, "Landrum-Griffin After Twenty-One Years: Mature Legislation or Childish Fantasy," *Labor Law Journal*, May 1980, pp. 273–82.

10. For a more in-depth discussion of the Civil Service Reform Act, see C. J. Coleman, "The Civil Service Reform Act of 1978: Its Meaning and Its Roots," *Labor Law Journal*, April 1980, pp. 200–207.

11. H. B. Frazier, "Labor-Management Relations in the Federal Government," *Labor Law Journal*, March 1979, pp. 131–38.

12. G. N. Chaison, "A Note on Union Merger Trends, 1900–1978," *Industrial and Labor Relations Review* October 1980, p. 116.

13. A. V. Bradley, "Management and Labor in the Next Decade," *Personnel Journal*, December 1980, p. 981.

Case 16–1   **UNION POWER**

Example 1

    In late 1982, IAM Local 709 voted to end a strike against the Marietta Plant of the Lockheed-Georgia Company. The contract that was agreed upon contained a wage increase of about 13 percent and improved retirement, insurance, and other benefits. The company also agreed to pay employees for the seven days over the Christmas and the two days over the Thanksgiving holidays that were missed during the strike.

    As far as the Marietta workers were concerned, the main issue was their right to "bump" workers with less seniority from projects during times when there are not enough jobs to go around. Lockheed officials claimed that the bumping procedure, whereby a worker having at least one day's seniority over another could take his or her junior's job, would hurt production so badly that it could force the company to abandon projects. Lockheed's initial proposal had been that an employee not be allowed to bump unless he or she had at least three months' seniority over the junior employee. After the union rejected this proposal, the company proposed that employees not be allowed to bump unless they had at least one month's seniority over the junior employee. At that point, negotiations broke down.

The last Lockheed offer—which was accepted—was that the seniority system remain the same for all current Lockheed employees. However, anyone hired after January 1, 1978, would have to have at least one month's seniority before he or she could bump another worker.

Example 2

The Airline Pilots Association (ALPA) rejected the airline industry's proposal that the DC-9-55, also known as the Super 80, be flown with two-person crews. The DC-9-55 is a super-stretch version of the popular DC-9 airliner, which was first introduced in 1965. The original DC-9 had a capacity of 70 passengers, while the Super 80 can carry 172. The problem is that a third crew member is used in most larger jets. Even the Boeing 737, which is smaller in passenger capacity than the Super 80, is flown with three crew members by most airlines.

Since 1970, the ALPA has insisted on use of three crew members for all new jets. The management of the airlines contends that the Super 80 is merely an enlargement of an existing design, therefore, it should be exempt from requests. Management argues that the third crew member only adds to payroll costs. It is the ALPA's position that the third crew member is needed for safety.

1. *In light of these two examples, which rights of management do you think that a union should not be able to influence?*

2. *How do you feel about the influence of the union in these two examples? Do you think that the unions are correct?*

Case 16–2

FIRING AN EMPLOYEE

Sam Gunn was hired by the D-N Company on June 4, 1982. His employment record shows that he missed a great deal of work early in 1983 due to illness. Later that year, after Sam underwent an operation, he missed several months of work. Sam's surgeon authorized his return to work on December 15, 1983.

On December 14, 1983, Sam was hospitalized as a result of injuries suffered in an automobile accident. His wife called the company the next day to say that her husband would be unable to return to work. On December 18, Sam reported to George Crowson, the company's human resource director. He explained that although his surgeon had said he could return to work, he did not feel that he was ready. Sam also told Crowson that he was going to consult another doctor, an orthopedist, who had seen Sam in the hospital following the automobile accident.

Sam saw the orthopedist on December 26, 1983 and again on January 5, 1984. During the second visit, the orthopedist informed Sam that he could return to work on January 26. His doctor sent a notice to the company stating that Sam should be excused from work from December 24, 1983 through January 25, 1984. The company discharged Sam on January 5 for failure to return to work or to extend sick leave. The union filed a grievance on behalf of Sam on January 14, charging the company with violation of Article II, Section 2, Paragraph A-2: discharging an employee without just cause (see Exhibit I).

The parties have been unable to reach a settlement on this grievance.

Exhibit I
Pertinent Contract Provisions

Article II, Section 2, Paragraph A-2: The company shall have all the rights and functions of management not specifically and expressly restricted or limited under the terms of this agreement. Such management rights and functions shall include among others, but not limited to, the following:

(2) To promote, demote, transfer, classify, reclassify, make layoffs for lack of work or other legitimate reasons and for just cause to discharge, suspend or otherwise discipline employees. These rights are vested exclusively in the company provided, however, that in the exercise thereof the company shall not take any actions which violate the terms and provisions of this agreement.

Article VII, Section 3: Loss of Seniority. Seniority shall be lost only by the occurrence of any of the following:

A. Resignation.
B. Discharge for cause.
C. Layoff which continues for more than two years.
D. Absence without leave of absence as required, or failure to report for work on or before the termination of such leave.
E. Failure to report to work three consecutive work days without notification and reason satisfactory to the company.
F. Failure to notify the company of acceptance or rejection of recall within five workings days after posting of notice of recall by certified mail or by telegram to the most recent address shown on the company's personnel records or failure to return to work within

five working days after notifying the company of intention to report to work.

Article VIII, Section 2, Paragraph C: Leaves of Absence Leaves—to obtain a sick leave an employee must present a statement from a physician indicating the nature and approximate length of this disability. Such leaves shall be granted by the company for a period not exceeding 60 days which shall be extended upon advance written request by the employee, supported by the doctor's statement.

1. Employees returning from formal sick leave must, upon their return from such leave, submit to the company medical department a physician's statement certifying that the employee is authorized to return to work and the work restriction, if any, that should apply. The company's physician shall have the sole authority to determine whether said employee shall be returned to work and whether he or she shall be restricted or unrestricted.
2. Employees returning from informal leaves resulting from surgery, hospitalization, or contagious disease must also furnish the above statement.
3. The company shall attempt to place an employee who has been restricted from regular work in an available job he or she can do consistent with such restriction.
4. Should a dispute exist concerning the physical and/or mental condition of an employee, by agreement between the parties, the employee may be referred, at any time in the grievance procedure, to a reputable clinic or doctor chosen mutually by the parties. The fee shall be shared equally by the company and the union. The determination of the clinic or doctor shall be limited to medical findings concerning the disputed condition.

1. *Who do you agree with in this situation?*
2. *Discuss what you feel are the positive and negative implications of unions in organizations.*

C h a p t e r 17

The collective bargaining process

Objectives

1. To explore the reasons employees decide to join labor unions.
2. To outline the steps involved in a union organizing campaign.
3. To discuss the major participants involved in negotiating a contract.
4. To explain issues normally included in a collective bargaining agreement.

Outline

What is collective bargaining?
The union membership decision
The organizing campaign
  Determining the bargaining unit
  The election campaign
  Election, certification, and
    decertification
Good faith bargaining
Participants in negotiations
  The employer's role
  The union's role
  The role of third parties
    The National Labor Relations
     Board (NLRB)
    The Federal Labor Relations
     Council (FLRC)

    The Federal Services Impasses
     Panel (FSIP)
    The Federal Mediation and
     Conciliation Service (FMCS)
    Arbitrators
The collective bargaining agreement
Specific issues in collective
  bargaining agreements
  Management rights
  Union security
  Wages and benefits
  Individual security (seniority) rights
  Dispute resolution
Impasses in collective bargaining
Trends in collective bargaining

Glossary of Terms

Agency shop Provision in a contract which does not require employees to join the union, but requires them to pay the equivalent of union dues as a condition of employment.

Arbitration Process whereby the parties agree to settle a dispute through the use of an independent third party (called an arbitrator).

Bargaining unit Group of employees in a plant, firm, or industry recognized by the employer, agreed upon by the parties to a case, or designated by the National Labor

Relations Board (NLRB) as appropriate for the purposes of collective bargaining.

Checkoff Arrangement between an employer and union under which the employer agrees to withhold union dues, initiation fees, and assessments from the employees' paychecks and submit this money to the union.

Collective bargaining Process that involves the negotiation, drafting, administration, and interpretation of a written agreement between an employer and a union for a specific period of time.

Consent elections Union election in which the parties have agreed on the appropriate bargaining unit.

Cost-of-living adjustment (COLA) Contract provision which ties wage increases to rises in the Bureau of Labor Statistics Consumer Price Index (CPI).

Federal Labor Relations Council (FLRC) Organization authorized by the Civil Service Reform Act of 1978 to oversee the conduct of labor relations in the federal sector.

Federal Mediation and Conciliation Service (FMCS) Independent agency within the federal government that, as one of its responsibilities, provides mediators to assist in resolving contract negotiation impasses.

Federal Services Impasses Panel (FSIP) An entity within the FLRC whose function is to provide assistance in resolving negotiation impasses within the federal sector.

Good faith bargaining The sincere intention of both parties to negotiate differences and reach an agreement acceptable to both parties.

Informational picketing Patrolling at or near an employer's facility by individuals carrying signs to publicize the fact that the union is requesting an election to become the bargaining agent for the employees of the organization.

Lockout Refusal of an employer to let its employees work.

Maintenance of membership Provision in a contract which does not require an employee to join the union, but employees who do join the union are required to remain members for a stipulated period of time.

Mediation Process where both parties invite a neutral, third party (called a mediator) to help resolve contract impasses. The mediator, unlike an arbitrator, has no authority to impose a solution on the parties.

National Labor Relations Board (NLRB) Board created by the National Labor Relations Act to administer and enforce the act.

Right-to-work laws Legislation enacted by individual states under the authority of section 14(b) of the Taft-Hartley Act that can forbid various type of union security arrangements.

Seniority Refers to an employee's relative length of service with an employer.

Strike The collective refusal of employees to work.

Union shop Provision in a contract that requires all employees in a bargaining unit to join the union and retain membership as a condition of employment. Most right-to-work laws outlaw the union shop.

The lifeblood of trade unionism in the United States has always been the representation of members in negotiations with employers.*

Prior to the Industrial Revolution in the 19th century, an individual was normally born into a place in society with a predestined standard of living. Custom and tradition kept a person's position relatively stable. The Industrial Revolution saw the tradition of self-employment supplanted as large organizations evolved. In one sense, the Industrial Revolution gave individuals more control over their destiny. Although people were in a considerably weaker position relative to their employer, they were able to contract for employment by offering their skills and services for a wage. However, once people had been hired, they and their work output became the property of the employer.

It was not long before employees began to resort to joint action to gain some influence over the terms and conditions of their employment. These attempts, occurring as early as 1741, were initially frowned upon by the public and the courts. For the most part, the relationships existing between employees and management were unilateral: employees asking for higher wages approached their employers with a "take it or we'll strike" attitude, and employers usually refused or ignored their requests.[1] Rather than bargaining, what resulted was a trial of economic strength to determine whose wage decisions would prevail.[2] In most instances, employers prevailed. However, as time passed society became more aware of the plight of employees. Legislation was enacted which was much more favorable toward employees and unions. This legislation was described in detail in Chapter 16. The impact of this legislation on specific issues in the collective bargaining process is examined in this chapter.

WHAT IS COLLECTIVE BARGAINING?

Collective bargaining is a process that involves the negotiation, drafting, administration, and intepretation of a written agreement between an employer and a union for a specific period of time. The end result of collective bargaining is a contract which sets forth the joint understandings of the parties as to wages, hours, and other terms and conditions of employment. Contracts cover a variety of time periods, with the most common period being three years.

Traditionally, collective bargaining has been associated with the labor movement and unions. The basic tenets of a labor-management collective bargaining agreement are:

1. Recognition of a collective bargaining representative.
2. Negotiation in good faith over relevant issues.

Brief History of the American Labor Movement (Washington, D.C.: Department of Labor, Bureau of Labor Statistics, 1976, p. 55.

3. Incorporation of understandings into a written contract.
4. Administration of the working relationship according to the terms and conditions of employment that are specified in the contract.
5. Resolution of disputes in interpretation of the terms of the contract through established procedures.

Today, collective bargaining has moved beyond the traditional context of labor-management relations. For example, employee associations such as the National Education Association have become very similar in function to unions. Furthermore, several of the major tenets of labor-management collective bargaining have been used in resolving disputes between landlords and tenants, students and universities, prisoners and prison administrators, civil rights organizations and municipal governments, and physicians and health insurers.[3]

Understanding the collective bargaining process is an important part of human resource management. When a union organizing campaign occurs, the human resource department is directly involved in presenting management's view to employees, responding to statements made by the union, and representing management during the union certification election. If the organization becomes unionized, the human resource department is directly involved in the collective bargaining process.

THE UNION MEMBERSHIP DECISION

Today, over 23 million people, or approximately 20 percent of the U.S. work force, belong to unions or employee associations. One study reported that approximately one third of the nonorganized work force would prefer to unionize.[4] Understanding the reasons workers are attracted to unions is an important first step in understanding the collective bargaining process.

A variety of factors influence an employee's desire to join a union. Several empirical studies suggest that the most significant factor is dissatisfaction over the economic issues of wages, benefits, and working conditions.[5] Employees have the option of resolving these issues with their management without the aid of a union. It is only when employees perceive that they lack the ability or power to change the situation that they are motivated to join a union.[6]

While wages, benefits, and working conditions are the main issues contributing to the desire to join a union, other factors include a desire by employees for the following:

1. Better communication with management.
2. Higher quality of management and supervision.
3. Increased democracy in the workplace.
4. An opportunity for employees to belong to a group where they can share experiences and fellowship.

Of course, people in those states that do not have right-to-work laws join unions because union membership is required for them to keep their jobs.

Much speculation exists concerning the characteristics of people who join unions. A study by the Survey Research Center at the University of Michigan concluded that younger employees, women, and more highly educated workers are just as willing to join a union when their job conditions warrant it as are their older, male, or less educated counterparts.[7] Although it has been argued that southern employees are less likely to unionize than their northern counterparts, the same study found southern blue-collar employees just as willing to join unions when job conditions warranted it as northern employees. On the other hand, southern white-collar employees were not as willing to join unions as their northern counterparts.[8] Finally, this study found that employees in the smallest (fewer than 10 employees) and the largest (1,000 or more employees) organizations were least willing to join unions.[9]

Understanding why employees are against unionization is just as important as knowing why they are in favor of unionization. The previously cited University of Michigan study found that the major reason for not joining a union was that the job was satisfactory as it was.[10] In other words, satisfactory wages, benefits, and working conditions cause employees to be less interested in unionization. Some employees also have a negative image of labor unions, feeling that unions have too much political influence, require members to go along with decisions made by the union, and have leaders who promote their own self-interests. Other reasons include the belief that unions abuse their power by calling strikes, causing high prices, and misusing union dues and pension funds.[11]

Some employees identify with management and view unions as adversaries. This is especially true of professional employees such as engineers, nurses, and college professors. However, dissatisfaction with wages, benefits, and working conditions can quickly break down this negative attitude toward unions.

Obviously, many companies have avoided unionization. In most cases, the management of these organizations has provided satisfactory wages, benefits, and working conditions for their employees. Other management practices that decrease the likelihood of unionization include: creating a procedure for handling employee complaints; eliminating arbitrary and heavy-handed management and supervisory practices; establishing a meaningful system of two-way communication between management and the work force; eliminating threats to employees' job security; and making the employees feel like they are part of the organization.[12]

THE ORGANIZING CAMPAIGN

Most often, union organizing campaigns start with one or more employees requesting that the union begin an organizing campaign. However, in some instances, national and international unions contact employees in organizations that have been targeted for organizing campaigns. Typically, interested employees are given cards authorizing the union to represent them in bargaining with their employer. The interested employees and the union organizer then attempt to persuade other employees to sign the authorization cards.

Union organizers are given the right by law (the National Labor Relations Act of 1935) to solicit membership on an organization's premises, provided such activity does not disrupt the organization. Interpretations of the Taft-Hartley Act by the National Labor Relations Board and the courts have restricted this right and have resulted in companies usually prohibiting solicitation on company premises. For example, one interpretation used to prohibit solicitation is that if a company has previously prohibited all forms of solicitation, union organizers may not be permitted to recruit on the premises provided that, in the past, the policy has been strictly adhered to and not enforced in a discriminatory manner.[13] Furthermore, except in the case of retail organizations, company representatives can express their views about unions through speeches to employees on company premises and still prohibit union membership solicitation on the premises, if the union organizers have other reasonable means through which they can reach the employees.[14]

Employers are legally prohibited from interfering with an employee's freedom of choice concerning union membership. However, union organizers have complained for years that employers ignore this legal restriction because the consequences are minimal. One of the most frequently cited examples of an organization that has aggressively resisted union organizing attempts is the J. P. Stevens Company, a large textile manufacturer located in the southeast. Since 1963, the Amalgamated Clothing and Textile Workers Union (ACTWU), backed by the AFL–CIO, has waged a campaign to organize J. P. Stevens. The NLRB has found Stevens guilty of violating NLRB provisions in 15 separate cases since 1965. These NLRB decisions have been upheld by federal appeals courts, and by the U.S. Supreme Court eight times. More than $1.3 million in back pay has been awarded to 289 workers whose rights under the labor law were violated by Stevens.[15]

Determining the bargaining unit

When the union obtains signed authorization cards from at least 30 percent of the employees, either the union or the employer can petition the National Labor Relations Board (NLRB) to conduct a representation election. In the event that the union has signed authorization cards from more than 50 percent of the employees, the union can make a direct request to the employer to become the bargaining agent of the employees. When this happens, the employer normally refuses and the union then petitions the NLRB for an election.

After a petition is filed, a representative of the NLRB (called an examiner) verifies that the authorization requirement has been fulfilled and then makes a determination as to the appropriate bargaining unit. The bargaining unit (or election unit) is defined as "a group of employees in a plant, firm, or industry recognized by the employer, agreed upon by the parties to a case, or designated by the board or its regional director as appropriate for the purposes of collective bargaining."[16]

Although the NLRB is ultimately responsible for establishing an appropriate bargaining unit, the parties usually have a great deal of influence on this decision. Most elections are known as "consent elections" in which the parties have agreed on the appropriate bargaining unit. When this is not the case, the NLRB must make the bargaining unit decision, guided by a concept called "community of interest." Community of interest factors include elements such as: similar wages, hours, and working conditions; the employees' physical proximity to each other; common supervision; the amount of interchange of personnel within the proposed unit; and the degree of integration of the employer's production process or operation.[17]

The election campaign

During the election campaign, certain activities (called unfair labor practices) are illegal. These include: (1) physical interference, threats, or violent behavior by the employer toward union organizers; (2) employer interference with employees involved in the organizing drive; (3) discipline or discharge of employees for prounion activities; and (4) threatening or coercing employees by union organizers. After filing for an election with the NLRB, a union can picket an employer only if the employer is not presently unionized, the petition has been filed with the NLRB within the past 30 days, and a representation election has not been conducted during the preceding 12 months. Picketing of this type is called "informational picketing." Individuals patrol at or near the place of employment carrying signs to publicize the fact that the union is requesting an election to become the bargaining agent for the employees.

During the election campaign, management normally initiates a campaign against the union, emphasizing the costs of unionization and the loss of individual freedom that can result from collective representation. Management can legally state its opinion about the possible ramifications of unionization if its statements are based on fact and are not threatening. Management can also explain to employees the positive aspects of their current situation. However, promises to provide or withhold benefits in the future in the event of unionization or nonunionization are prohibited. An employer can conduct polls to verify union strength prior to an election, but it may not, in general, question employees individually about their preferences or otherwise threaten or intimidate them.

During the election campaign, unions emphasize their ability to help employees satisfy their needs and improve their working conditions. The ability of the union to sell these concepts to the employees is a most critical factor in determining the union's success in the election campaign. Employees must believe that the union cares about their problems, can help resolve them, and can assist in improving their wages, benefits, and working conditions. Unions are legally prohibited from coercing or threatening individual employees if they do not join the union.

The actual impact of an election campaign is unclear. The NLRB assumes that employees are likely to be influenced by the election campaign in deciding whether or not to vote for union representation.[18] However, a study of 31 elections found that the votes of 81 percent of the employees could have been predicted from their precampaign attitudes and intent.[19]

The campaign tactics of both management and the union are monitored by the NLRB. If the practices of either party are found to be unfair, the election results may be invalidated and a new election conducted. Furthermore, charges of unfair labor practices against management, if serious enough, can result in the NLRB ordering management to bargain with the union.[20]

Election, certification, and decertification

If management and the union agree to conduct the election as a "consent" election, balloting often occurs within a short period of time. However, if management does not agree to a consent election a long delay may occur. Delays in balloting often increase the likelihood that management will win the election.[21] As a result, fewer organizations are now agreeing to consent elections. For example, one study indicated that 46.1 percent of all NLRB elections in 1962 were consent elections; while only 8.6 percent of NLRB elections in 1977 were consent elections.[22]

When the exact date for the election is finally established, the NLRB then conducts a secret ballot election. If the union receives a majority of the ballots cast, it becomes certified as the exclusive bargaining representative of all employees in the unit. Exclusive bargaining representative means that the union represents all employees (both union members and nonmembers) in the bargaining unit in negotiating their wages, hours, and terms and conditions of employment. It is important to note that the union does not have to receive a positive vote from a majority of the employees in the bargaining unit. It only has to receive a majority of the votes cast.

After a union has been certified, it remains by law the exclusive bargaining agent for all employees unless the employees within the unit desire otherwise. In the event that the employees want to oust the union, they can file a petition with the NLRB for a decertification election. If 30 percent of the employees support the petition and a valid election to oust the union has not been held within the preceding year, a decertification election is conducted. If a majority of the voting employees vote to decertify the union, it no longer legally represents them. One study recently indicated that the number of decertification petitions and elections is increasing, and that the percentage of management victories in these elections is also increasing.[23]

Following a certification or decertification election, no elections can be held in that bargaining unit for one year. Even if a certification election fails to result in exclusive representative, another election cannot be held in that unit for one year. If a union is decertified, one year must elapse before another unionization election can be held. Figure 17–1 summarizes the steps involved in an organizing campaign.

GOOD FAITH BARGAINING

After a union is certified, the employer is required by law to bargain in good faith with the union. Of course, bargaining between an employer and the union also takes place before the expiration of an existing contract. The National Labor Relations Act stipulates the legal requirement of good faith bargaining for private enterprise organizations, whereas, the Civil Service Reform Act of 1978 makes the same requirement for federal agencies. Unfortunately, "good faith," or the lack of it, is not explicitly defined in either of these laws. Over the years, however, decisions of the NLRB, the Federal Labor Relations Authority (FLRA), and the courts have interpreted good faith bargaining to be the sincere intention of both parties to negotiate differences and to reach an agreement acceptable to both. Good faith bargaining does not require the parties to agree; it merely obligates them to make a "good faith" attempt to reach an agreement. Thus, the existence of good faith is generally determined by examining the total atmosphere in the collective bargaining process. The essential requirement is that a bona fide attempt is made to reach an agreement.

Several bargaining situations have been taken to the NLRB to determine the presence or lack of good faith bargaining. A key case involved the General Electric Company's use of *boulwarism*, which was named after a General Electric vice president, and means that management makes its best offer at the outset of bargaining and firmly ad-

Figure 17–1   Steps involved in a union organizing campaign

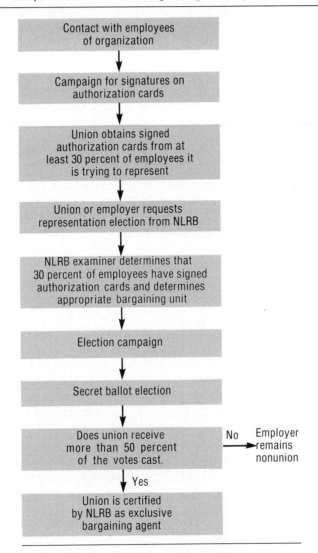

heres to the offer throughout the bargaining sessions. The NLRB has ruled that boulwarism is not good faith bargaining.[24] In its decision, the NLRB stated that management must fulfill the requirements by affirmatively demonstrating its willingness to resolve differences and reach common ground.[25] While the making of concessions is not required by law, a willingness to compromise is essential in establishing the existence of good faith.

PARTICIPANTS IN NEGOTIATIONS

Several participants may be either directly or indirectly involved in the collective bargaining process. The primary participants are, of course, the employer and union representatives. However, several third parties can play a significant role.

The employer's role

Participation of the employer in collective bargaining may take one of several different forms. The single-company agreement is most common. Under this approach, representatives of a single company meet with representatives of the union and negotiate a contract. Of course, it is entirely possible for one company to have several different unions representing different groups of employees within the company. In this situation, representatives of the company would negotiate a different contract with each union. Furthermore, it is entirely possible for one company and union to negotiate different contracts for each of the company's different facilities or plant locations.

In some industries, multiemployer agreements are common. Generally, individual employers in these industries are small and are in a weak position relative to the union. Employers then often pool together in an employer association. A single agreement is negotiated by the association for all involved employers. Multiemployer agreements may be on a local level (e.g., the construction industry within a city), a regional level (e.g., coal and mining), or at the national level (railroad industry). When multiemployer bargaining occurs on a regional or national basis, it is often referred to as industrywide bargaining.

In large organizations such as General Motors, master agreements are negotiated on wage and benefit issues between corporate officials and officials of the national or international union. However, in addition to the master agreement, local supplements are negotiated at the plant level. Local supplements deal with issues that are unique to each plant.

The union's role

Union participation in negotiations can also take several different forms. In single-company agreements, the size of the company determines the nature of union participation. For smaller companies, the local union normally works closely with a field representative of the international or national union in negotiations. In these instances, the international representative gives advice and counsel to the local union and frequently serves as the principal negotiator for the union.

In large companies with multiple plants, negotiations are conducted by the top officials of the national or international union. For example, the president of the United Automobile Workers (UAW) is normally a chief negotiator in negotiations with Ford, General Motors, and

Chrysler. Local union officials and a field representative of the national or international union negotiate local supplements to the master agreement for large companies.

In those industries with multiemployer agreements, union participation is normally directed by the president of the national or international union. However, in these types of negotiations, representatives of the local unions that are to be covered by the multiemployer agreement normally serve on the union's negotiating committee.

It is also possible for several unions to bargain jointly with a single employer. This type of negotiation is called coordinated bargaining. Although not commonly used, coordinated bargaining has been proposed as an approach for American unions in negotiating with multinational organizations.[26]

The role of third parties

Several third parties can and frequently do become involved in the collective bargaining process. Normally the services of third parties are not required unless one or both of the parties feels that the other party is not bargaining in good faith, or the parties reach an impasse in negotiat ons.

The National Labor Relations Board (NLRB) The NLRB was created by the National Labor Relations Act to administer and enforce the act. The act requires both unions and management to bargain in good faith. Refusal to bargain by either party can be overridden by an order of the NLRB. Furthermore, if the board's order has been properly issued, the United States Court of Appeals is required to order enforcement under the threat of contempt-of-court penalties.

Besides refusing to bargain, other kinds of behavior can be held to be unfair labor practices. Some of these were described earlier in this chapter. The NLRB has the authority to determine whether a particular behavior is unfair. If either party feels that an unfair labor practice has occurred during negotiations, a charge can be filed with the NLRB. An NLRB representative then investigates the charge and determines whether it is warranted. If the charge is held to be warranted, the parties are given the opportunity to reach an informal settlement before further action is taken by the NLRB. If an informal settlement cannot be reached, the NLRB issues a formal complaint against the accused party, and a formal hearing is then conducted by an NLRB trial examiner. Upon completion of the hearing, the examiner makes recommendations to the NLRB board. Either party may appeal the recommendations of the examiner to the board. If the board decides that the party named in the complaint has engaged in or is engaging in an unfair labor practice, it can order the party to cease from such practice and take appropriate corrective action. Either party can appeal decisions of the NLRB to the U.S. Circuit Court of Appeals and even to the U.S. Supreme Court. Thus, NLRB rulings and court decisions on appeals of these decisions play an important role in determining what parties can and cannot do in collective bargaining. [27]

The Federal Labor Relations Council (FLRC) The FLRC was given its authority by the Civil Service Reform Act of 1978 and serves as the counterpart to the NLRB for federal sector employees, unions, and agencies. Under procedures similar to those of the NLRB, the FLRC investigates unfair-labor-practice charges, conducts hearings on unfair labor practices, and can issue orders to cease from any such practices.

The Federal Services Impasses Panel (FSIP) If the parties in the federal sector reach an impasse in negotiations, either party may request the FSIP to consider the matter. The FSIP is an entity within the FLRC. The FSIP has the authority to recommend solutions to resolve an impasse and to take whatever action is necessary to resolve the dispute, as long as the actions are not inconsistent with the Civil Service Reform Act of 1978. In addition to the above, the parties may agree to adopt a procedure for binding arbitration of a negotiation impasse, but only if the procedure is approved by the FSIP. The FSIP is considered to be the legal alternative to a strike in the federal sector.

The Federal Mediation and Conciliation Service (FMCS) The FMCS, which was created by the National Labor Relations Act, exists as an independent agency within the executive branch of the federal government. The jurisdiction of the FMCS encompasses employees of private enterprise organizations engaged in interstate commerce, federal government employees, and employees in private, nonprofit hospitals and other allied medical facilities. [28]

One of the responsibilities of the FMCS is to provide mediators to assist in resolving negotiation impasses. Mediation (or conciliation, as it is often called) is a process whereby both parties invite a neutral, third party (called a mediator) to help resolve contract impasses. Mediators help the parties find common ground for continuing negotiations, develop factual data on issues over which the parties disagree, and set up joint study committees involving members of both parties to examine more difficult issues. In negotiations where the parties have become angry and/or antagonistic toward each other, the mediator often separates them and serves as a buffer carrying proposals and counterproposals between the parties. Mediators cannot impose decisions on the parties. Mediation services are also provided by various state agencies and private individuals such as lawyers, professors, and arbitrators.

Arbitrators Although arbitration is much more frequently used in the resolution of grievances during a contract period, it can be used to resolve impasses during collective bargaining. The use of arbitration to resolve negotiating impasses is called interest arbitration. Interest arbitration is rarely used in the private sector, but is common in the public sector. Such arbitration can take one of two forms: conventional and final offer. Under conventional interest arbitration, the arbitrator listens to arguments from both parties and makes a binding decision which can be identical to the position of either party or can be different from the position of both parties. In final-offer interest arbitration, the arbitrator is restricted to selecting the final offer of one of the parties. Furthermore, interest arbitration can be either voluntary or mandatory. Currently, 19 states have established mandatory interest arbitration laws as a final step in the process of resolving public-employee bargaining impasses.[29]

Both the FMCS and American Arbitration Association (AAA) provide lists of certified arbitrators.

THE COLLECTIVE BARGAINING AGREEMENT

The collective bargaining agreement (or union contract) results from the bargaining process and governs the daily relations between employer and employees for a specific period of time. The contract specifies in writing the mutual agreements reached by the parties during the negotiations. Under the Taft-Hartley Act, collective bargaining agreements are legally enforceable contracts. Suits charging violation of a contract between an employer and a union may be brought in any district court of the United States having jurisdiction over the parties.

As discussed earlier in this chapter, the National Labor Relations Act obligates employers and unions to bargain in good faith on wages, hours, and other terms and conditions of employment. These are called mandatory subjects of negotiation. However, as would be expected, controversy has developed over the subjects covered by the phrase "other terms and conditions of employment." Unions attempt to expand the mandatory area by giving a broad interpretation to the phrase. Employers, on the other hand, naturally resist this expansion. Numerous NLRB and court decisions have been rendered concerning this issue. For example, the Supreme Court ruled in one decision that all management decisions representing a departure from prior practice that significantly impair (1) job tenure, (2) employment security, and (3) reasonably anticipated work opportunities must be negotiated as mandatory subjects.[30] The number of mandatory bargaining items has definitely expanded over the years. Court and NLRB decisions have declared at least 70 basic items to be mandatory for bargaining purposes.[31] Figure 17–2 is a partial listing of mandatory bargaining issues.

Figure 17–2   Partial list of mandatory bargaining issues

Wages	Piece rates
Hours	Stock purchase plans
Discharge	Management-rights clause
Arbitration	Discount on company products
Holidays—paid	Shift differentials
Vacations—paid	Plant closing
Grievance procedure	Job posting procedures
Union security and checkoff	Employee physical examination
Work rules	Change in insurance carrier and benefits
Group insurance	Profit-sharing plans
Promotions	Overtime pay
Seniority	Sick leave
Layoffs	Company houses
Transfers	Subcontracting
Work loads	Duration of agreement
Severance pay	Merit wage increase
Plant rules	Retirement age
Safety	Price of meals provided by company
Lunch periods	Work assignments and transfers
Bonus payments	No-strike clause
Rest periods	Production ceiling imposed by union

Source: R. C. Richardson, *Collective Bargaining by Objectives* (Englewood Cliffs, N.J.: Prentice-Hall, 1977), pp. 114–15.

An issue on which the parties are not required to bargain is called a nonmandatory or permissive issue. During contract negotiations, the parties, if both agree, may bargain about permissive issues, but neither party is legally required to. Furthermore, it is an illegal labor practice for one party to insist upon bargaining about a permissive issue.[32]

The difficulties of establishing a group of mandatory and permissive issues for all organizations are great. Subjects in one industry or organization that are appropriately handled through collective bargaining may be inappropriate in another industry or organization. Ultimately, however, the courts and the NLRB decide whether an issue is mandatory or permissive.

In addition to mandatory and permissive issues, there is a small group of prohibited issues that cannot be included in a collective bargaining agreement. The leading examples are the closed shop and a hot-cargo clause. A closed shop requires employes to hire only people who are union members. A hot-cargo clause results when an employer agrees with a union not to handle or use the goods of another employer.

For the federal sector, the Civil Service Reform Act of 1978 makes it mandatory to bargain over "conditions of employment." The act defines conditions of employment as personnel policies, practices, and

Figure 17–3   Prohibited and permissive collective bargaining issues in the federal sector

Prohibited issues
    In general, wage rates cannot be negotiated.
    Mission, budget, or organization of the agency.
    Number of employees.
    Internal security practices of the agency.
    Hiring, assigning, directing, laying off, and retaining employees in the agency or sus-
        pending, removing, reducing in grade or pay, or taking other disciplinary action
        against such employees.
    Assigning work, making determinations with respect to contracting work, and deter-
        mining the personnel by which agency operations shall be conducted.
    Filling vacant positions from properly ranked and certified candidates.
    Taking whatever actions may be necessary to carry out the agency mission during
        emergencies.
Permissive issues
    Numbers, types, and grades of employees or positions assigned to any organizational
        subdivision, work project, or tour of duty.
    Technology, means, and methods of performing work.
    Procedures used by the management of the agency to exercise its authority in carry-
        ing out duties that cannot be negotiated.
    Arrangements for employees adversely affected by the exercise of management's au-
        thority in carrying out duties that cannot be negotiated.

matters affecting working conditions. Figure 17–3 summarizes the prohibited and permissive issues for federal government employees.

SPECIFIC ISSUES IN COLLECTIVE BARGAINING AGREEMENTS

While each contract is different, five issues are included in most
contracts. (1) management rights, (2) union security, (3) wages and
fringe benefits, (4) individual security (seniority) rights, and (5) dispute resolution.[33]

Management rights

The question of how many of their prerogatives can be retained in
the union-employer relationship is of great concern to most employers. Basically, two points of view exist among managers concerning
the management-rights clause. First, some managers feel that every
right which management has should be specifically spelled out in the
contract. On the other hand, some managers feel that the management-rights clause should be sparsely worded. Managers advocating
this position assume that the employer retains all rights except those
that are explicitly denied in the contract.

The primary purpose of the management-rights clause is retaining
for management the right to direct all business activities. Items that
are normally regarded as an integral part of management rights include the right to direct the work force, to determine the size of the
work force—including the number and class of employees to be em-

ployed or laid off—to set working hours, and to assign work. Generally, in the management-rights clause, the union insists on a sentence specifying that management will not discriminate against the union.

Union security

The issue of union security is the union equivalent of the management-rights issue. Union security clauses are concerned with the status of employee membership in the union and attempt to ensure that the union has continuous strength. Nearly all contracts provide some type of union security clause.

Union security is provided in several forms. A union shop requires that all employees in the bargaining unit join the union and retain membership as a condition of employment. A modified union shop requires all employees hired after the effective date of the agreement to acquire and retain union membership as a condition of employment. The inclusion of a "grandfather" clause enables employees who are not members of the union as of the effective date of the contract to remain nonmembers.

Under an agency shop provision, employees are not required to actually join the union, but they are required to pay the equivalent of union dues as a condition of employment. A maintenance of a membership provision does not require that an employee join the union, but employees who do join are required to remain members for a stipulated period of time as a condition of employment. Right-to-work laws, enacted by individual states under the authority of Section 14(b) of the Taft-Hartley Act, restrict the types of union security provisions that can be negotiated. For example, most right-to-work legislation outlaws the union shop. The Taft-Hartley Act also prohibits two additional forms of union security: the closed shop and the preferential shop. In a closed shop, only union members can be hired, whereas the preferential shop requires that union members be given preference in filling job vacancies. However, in certain industries such as contruction, exceptions to the Act's provisions are permitted.

In addition to providing a means for maintaining union membership, union security provisions often include checkoff procedures. A checkoff is an arrangement made with the company under which it agrees to withold union dues, initiation fees, and assessments from the employees' paychecks and submit this money to the union. Individual union members must sign cards authorizing the withholding before such arrangements can be made.

Wages and benefits

Traditionally, increased wages have been the primary economic goal of unions. Most contracts contain a provision for general wage increases during the life of the contract. Cost-of-living adjustments

(COLA) have become common in almost all industries. COLA clauses tie wage increases to rises in the Bureau of Labor Statistics Consumer Price Index (CPI). Most COLA clauses call for hourly increases in wages for each specified rise in the CPI. Adjustments can be made on a quarterly, semiannual, or annual basis.

Other wage issues specified in contracts include overtime pay and rates of pay for work on Saturdays, Sundays, holidays, and sixth or seventh consecutive days of work. Other employee compensation items normally contained in contracts include supplementary pay for shift differentials, reporting and call-in or call-back pay, temporary transfer pay, hazardous duty pay, and job-related expenses. Each of these terms is defined in Figure 17–4.

The benefits that are normally covered in union contracts include holidays, vacations, insurance, and pensions. Pay is normally required in union contracts for all recognized holidays. Eligibility for holiday pay is of one of two types: a length-of-service requirement or a work requirement. Normally, an employee must have worked a minimum of four weeks with the employer before being eligible for holiday pay. Furthermore, an employee generally must work the day before and the day after a holiday to receive holiday pay.

Vacation provisions are provided in most union contracts. Vacation entitlement is normally tied directly to the employee's length of service. One trend in contracts has been an increase in the amount of vacation time per year and a reduction in the amount of service required for receiving increased vacations.[34]

Most union contracts contain clauses providing health, accident, and life-insurance benefits. Major medical insurance, maternity care, accidental death and dismemberment benefits, dental insurance, and coverage for miscellaneous medical expenses such as prescription drugs, are also found in many union contracts.

Figure 17–4   Definitions of typical supplementary pay items

Shift differential pay—a bonus paid for working less desirable hours of work.

Reporting pay—pay given to employees who report for work as scheduled but find on arrival that no work is available.

Call-back or call-in pay—covers situations in which employees are called in or back to work at some time other than their regularly scheduled hours.

Temporary transfer pay—covers situations in which employees are temporarily transferred to another job. If the transfer is to a lower paying job, normally the employee continues to receive his old rate of pay. If the transfer is to a higher paying job, normally the employee is paid the higher rate of pay.

Hazardous duty pay—pay given for performing jobs that are considered to be more risky from a safety or health point of view.

Job-related expenses—covers travel expenses, work clothes, or tools required for the job.

The typical pension plan covered in union contracts provides for normal, early, and disability retirement. Vesting provisions, administrative procedures, and financing arrangements are also frequently outlined in the contract.

Individual security (seniority) rights

Seniority refers to an employee's relative length of service with an employer. Seniority may be measured on the basis of the employee's length of service in a job classification or a department, or on the individual's length of service with one plant, or with the company as a whole.

Job security for employees is a basic concern for unions. The seniority system is the method most commonly used to achieve job security. In general, union contract provisions specify that seniority is to be used within the bargaining unit for giving promotions, transfers, layoffs, recalls from layoffs, and choice of shifts of work and vacation periods.

Seniority systems are designed to benefit employees with greater length of service. Thus, women and minorities, who are generally the most recently hired employees, can be adversely affected by a seniority system. Title XII of the 1964 Civil Rights Act made it illegal to discriminate on the basis of race, sex, or religion. However, the act gave special treatment to seniority systems. It allows employees to be treated differently under a bona fide seniority system unless the system intentionally discriminates. Although the courts have sanctioned a wide variety of negotiated seniority system rules, employees are still free to legally pursue whether the rules were established in good faith (and, therefore, not entitled to the exemption for bona fide plans under Title VII).[35]

Dispute resolution

Inevitably, disputes arise during the life of a contract. Most contracts contain specific clauses describing how disputes are to be resolved.

A "no-strike" clause pledges the union to cooperate in preventing work stoppages. No-strike pledges can either be unconditional or conditional. Unconditional pledges ban any interference with production during the life of the contract. Conditional pledges permit strikes under certain circumstances. The no-strike ban most commonly is lifted after exhaustion of the grievance procedure or after an arbitration award has been violated.[36] In return for a no-strike pledge, the union normally asks for a promise on the part of the company not to engage in lockouts during the term of the contract. A lockout is a refusal of the employer to let employees work.

The grievance procedure provision is the most common method for resolving disputes arising during the term of the contract. The final step in the dispute resolution procedure is usually arbitration. Both grievance procedures and arbitration were discussed in Chapter 15.

IMPASSES IN COLLECTIVE BARGAINING

At the end of a contract period, if a new agreement has not reached, employees can continue working under the terms of the old contract until a new agreement is reached or a strike is called. Normally, union officials will not recommend that the employees continue working unless significant progress is being made in contract negotiations.

If no progress is being made and the contract expires, a strike is frequently called. A strike occurs when employees collectively refuse to work. Strikes are not permitted for most public employees. To strike, the union must first hold a vote among its members. Unless the vote is heavily (generally more than 80%) in favor of a strike, one will not be called. When a strike does occur, union members picket the employer. In picketing, individual members patrol at or near the place of employment to publicize the existence of the strike and to discourage the public from dealing with the employer. Frequently, members of other unions will refuse to cross the picket line of a striking union. For example, unionized truck drivers often refuse to deliver goods to an employer involved in a strike.

The purpose of a strike is to bring economic hardship to the employer, forcing the employer to agree to union demands. The success of a strike is determined by how well the union is able to interrupt the organization's operations. Employers often attempt to continue operations by using supervisory and management personnel, people not in the striking bargaining unit, or people within the bargaining unit who refuse to go on strike; or by hiring people to replace striking employees. Attempts to continue operations through these methods can increase the difficulty of reaching an agreement and often result in violence.

When the President of the United States feels that a strike may jeopardize the national health and safety, the emergency dispute provisions of the Taft-Hartley Act can be used. Under these provisions, the president is authorized to appoint a special board of inquiry which makes a preliminary investigation of the impasse prior to issuing an injunction to halt the strike. If the impasse is not resolved during this preliminary investigation, the president can issue an injunction prohibiting the strike action for 80 days, which is called a "cooling off" period. The parties then have 60 days to resolve the impasse, after which the NLRB is required to poll the employees to see whether they will accept the employer's last offer. If the employees do not agree to

Work-rule changes quietly spread as firms try to raise productivity

Until recently, United Rubber Workers union members at a B.F. Goodrich Company plant in Akron, Ohio, worked in two separate areas. Their contract specified that, under most conditions, workers in one area couldn't be required to do the same work in another area, regardless of how busy the plant was.

Now, the rule is gone.

The change is part of a quiet revolution in the nation's ailing industrial sector as labor and management agree to eliminate many long-standing and costly work rules in an effort to raise productivity and profits. Unlike the highly visible wage reductions or freezes agreed by union and corporate officials, most of the work-rule changes are being negotiated at the local level by plant managers and union locals.

During the past year, factory workers have given up seniority rules that govern the rehiring of laid-off workers and craft rules that limit management's flexibility to assign workers to different jobs; truck drivers have agreed to changes that eliminate the costly rehandling of certain freight; and airline pilots have extended the hours they will fly before being relieved.

Concern for efficiency

Some experts see such changes as part of a major change in the way corporations view their role as managers. "Top management is finally getting around to noticing that they better be concerned about how efficiently they produce things," says Audrey Freedman, chief labor economist for the Conference Board, a business research group.

During the last decade, she contends, managers focused on investment return and deemphasized operational management. "Now they're shocked that the Japanese and other competitors have out-Americanized us in production management," she says. "And we are rediscovering that it's terribly important how you manage what you produce."

At the same time, many industrial unions, reeling from layoffs and plant closings, have become more concerned about company profits. Paul Rusen, who as a district director of the United Steelworkers union has jurisdiction over some of the union's aluminum workers, says: "Our concerns are dominated by the economic condition of the aluminum industry. Right now, we are like the steel industry was 10 years ago. If we don't find more efficient utilization of our manpower, we're going to have the same problems in aluminum that we have in steel."

As a result, the union's local in Ravenswood, West Virginia, recently negotiated an agreement with Kaiser Aluminum Company that adds flexibility to the work force. Previously, workers at the plant were divided into 18 craft groups, such as electricians, carpenters, and certain maintenance workers. Workers in one craft couldn't do jobs in other crafts. If there wasn't specific work on a given day for, say, electricians, they remained idle but were paid. Now, the 18 crafts have been reduced to 12 broader units, expanding the types of jobs each worker may do.

Rusen, who helped negotiate the change, says that when the plant returns to full-time operations, it will require 600 fewer workers than the 3,400 it once employed. The local agreed to the change, he says, because the company said it would substantially reduce the Ravenswood operation if it couldn't be made more efficient.

Many of the work rules being eliminated have been preserved in union contracts for decades. Pan American World Airways recently abolished a rule dating from the early 1950s, when airlines began using jetliners. Under the change, the Airline Pilots Association agreed to expand the hours that Pan Am pilots may fly before being relieved to 9.5 hours, in most cases, from 9 hours. The company says the change, which means a third pilot doesn't have to be aboard the many flights that exceed 9 hours, will yield savings equal to salaries for about 150 pilots.

accept the employer's last offer, the injunction is dissolved and the president can refer the impasse to Congress and recommend a course of action.

TRENDS IN COLLECTIVE BARGAINING

Technological change and increased use of automation, changing government regulations, rising foreign competition, the decline in the percentage of blue-collar employees, and high rates of unemployment are just some of the variables that influence the collective bargaining process. These and other variables can change rapidly, making a contract provision negotiated two years earlier virtually useless. One form of collective bargaining that is evolving to cope with these rapidly changing variables involves the establishment of joint labor-management committees that meet regularly over the contract period to explore issues of common concern. Committees such as these already exist in industries such as retail food, over-the-road trucking, nuclear power plant construction, and men's garments.[37] The essential characteristics of this new form of collective bargaining are:

1. Meetings are held frequently during the life of the contract and are independent of its expiration.
2. Discussions examine external events and potential problem areas rather than internal complaints about current prectice.
3. Outside experts such as legal, economic, actuarial, medical, and industry specialists play a major role in making the final decision on some issues.
4. Participants in the meetings are encouraged to take a problem-solving, rather than an adversary approach.[38]

Another likely trend in collective bargaining within U.S. companies is productivity bargaining. Under productivity bargaining, unions and management develop a contract whereby the union agrees to scrap old work procedures and methods for new and more effective ones in exchange for gains in pay and working conditions. Productivity bargaining involves not only reaching an agreement, but also creating an atmosphere of ongoing cooperation in which the changes called for in the agreement can be implemented.[39]

A final trend that is likely to occur involves a significant increase in what has been called "take-back bargaining." This involves unions being asked to make concessions on wages and benefits.[40] This form of bargaining has already occurred in industries that have been especially hard hit by foreign competition.

SUMMARY

Collective bargaining is a process that involves the negotiation, drafting, administration, and interpretation of a written agreement between an employer and a union for a specific period of time. The end result of collective bargaining is a contract which sets forth the joint understandings of the parties as to wages, hours, and other terms and conditions of employment.

Several empirical studies suggest that the most significant factor contributing to the desire to join a union is dissatisfaction over the economic issues of wages, benefits, and working conditions. Other factors contributing to the desire to join unions are: the desire for better communication with management, the desire for an improved quality of management and supervision, the desire for increased democracy in the workplace, and the desire of employees to belong to a group in which they can share experiences and fellowship.

A union organizing campaign generally goes through the following steps: contacting employees, campaigning for signatures on authorization cards, obtaining signed authorization cards from at least 30 percent of the affected employees, the union or the employer requesting a representation election from the NLRB, determination by an NLRB examiner that 30 percent of the employees have signed authorization cards, determinination of the appropriate bargaining unit by an NLRB examiner, conducting of an election campaign, and conducting a secret ballot election. The union must receive more than 50 percent of the votes cast to become the exclusive bargaining agent for the employees in question.

Good faith bargaining is the sincere intention of both parties to negotiate differences and to reach an agreement acceptable to both. The participants in collective bargaining include the employer, union representatives, and sometimes independent third parties such as mediators and arbitrators.

The collective bargaining agreement results from the bargaining process and governes the daily relations between employees and employers for a specified period of time. Management rights, union security, wages and benefits, individual security (seniority) rights, and dispute resolution are five issues included in most contracts.

One approach to resolving impasses in collective bargaining is to strike. A strike occurs when employees collectively refuse to work. Mediation and arbitration can be used when an impasse has been reached.

REVIEW QUESTIONS

1. What is collective bargaining?
2. Describe some of the reasons employees join unions.
3. What is a bargaining unit?
4. Define some unfair labor practices that can occur during a union election campaign.
5. Define good faith bargaining.
6. What is a multiemployer agreement?
7. Describe the roles of the following third parties in the collective bargaining process:
   a. NLRB.
   b. FLRC.
   c. FSIP.
   d. FMCS.
   e. Mediators.
   f. Arbitrators.
8. Define the following union security clauses:
   a. Union shop.
   b. Agency shop.
   c. Maintenance of membership.
   d. Closed shop.
   e. Preferential shop.
9. What is the purpose of COLA clauses in a union contract?
10. Define seniority.
11. What is a strike?

DISCUSSION QUESTIONS

1. "Seniority provisions in a contract discriminate against women and minorities." Describe your opinion on this statement.

2. "Right-to-work laws should be rescinded." Discuss.

3. Identify several management rights that you believe should not be subject to collective bargaining.

4. Why do you think collective bargaining is increasing among white-collar employees?

REFERENCES AND ADDITIONAL READINGS

1. V. H. Jenson, "Notes on the Beginnings of Collective Bargaining," *Industrial and Labor Relations Review*, January 1956, pp. 225–34.
2. N. W. Chamberlain, *Collective Bargaining* (New York: McGraw-Hill, 1951), p. 7.

3. T. Bornstein, "Unions, Critics, and Collective Bargaining," *Labor Law Journal*, October 1976, p. 621.

4. T. A. Kochan, "How American Workers View Labor Unions," *Monthly Labor Review*, April 1979, p. 30.

5. Ibid., pp. 23–31. See also C. A. Schreisheim, "Job Satisfaction, Attitude Toward Unions, and Voting in a Union Representation Election," *Journal of Applied Psychology*, October 1978, pp. 548–52.

6. J. M. Brett, "Why Employees Want Unions," *Organizational Dynamics*, Spring 1980, pp. 47–59.

7. Kochan, "How American Workers View Labor Unions," p. 27–28.

8. Ibid., p. 26.

9. Ibid., p. 28.

10. Ibid., p. 28.

11. Brett, "Why Employees Want Unions," p. 52.

12. See, for instance M. S. Myers, *Managing Without Unions* (Reading, Mass.: Addison-Wesley Publishing, 1976), Chapters 1 through 13. Also see, W. Imberman, "Heading Off the Union Organizer," *Canadian Business*, August 1980, p. 34.

13. *NLRB* v. *Babcock and Wilcox*, 105 US 351 (1956).

14. *Marshall Field and Company*, 98 NLRB 88 (1952).

15. K. A. Kovach, "J. P. Stevens and the Struggle for Union Organization," *Labor Law Journal*, May 1978, p. 308.

16. 41 NLRB Ann. Rep. 203 (1976).

17. J. G. Kilgour, "Before the Union Knocks," *Personnel Journal*, April 1978, p. 188.

18. J. G. Getman, S. B. Goldberg, and J. B. Herman, *Union Representation Elections: Law and Reality* (New York: Russell Sage Foundation, 1976), p. 32.

19. Getman, Goldberg, and Herman, *Union Representation*, pp. 33, 72.

20. W. E. Fulmer, "Step by Step Through a Union Campaign," *Harvard Business Review*, July–August 1981, p. 101.

21. W. Prosten, "The Rise in NLRB Election Delays: Measuring Business' New Resistance," *Monthly Labor Review*, February 1979, p. 39.

22. Ibid., p. 39.

23. W. E. Fulmer, "Decertification: Is the Current Trend a Threat to Collective Bargaining?" *California Management Review*, Fall 1981, pp. 20–21.

24. *General Electric Company*, 150 NLRB 192 (1964).

25. L. G. Reynolds, *Labor Economics and Labor Relations*, 7th ed. (Englewood Cliffs, N.J.: Prentice-Hall, 1978), p. 569.

26. A. S. Leonard, "Coordinated Bargaining with Multinational Firms by American Labor Unions," *Labor Law Journal*, December 1974, pp. 746–59.

27. For a discussion of presenting cases before the NLRB, see K. C. McGuiness, *How to Take a Case Before the NLRB*, 4th ed. (Washington, D.C.: Bureau of National Affairs, 1976).

28. D. M. Kolb, "Roles Mediators Play: State and Federal Practice," *Industrial Relations*, Winter 1981, p. 3.

29. For a survey of the laws in all 19 states, see K. J. Corcoran and D. Kutell, "Binding Arbitration Laws for State and Municipal Workers," *Monthly Labor Review,* October 1978, pp. 36–40.

30. *Fiberboard Paper Products Corp.* v. *NLRB,* 379 U.S. 203 (1964).

31. R. C. Richardson, *Collective Bargaining by Objectives* (Englewood Cliffs, N.J.: Prentice-Hall, 1977), p. 114.

32. See *NLRB* v. *Wooster Division of Borg-Warner Corp.,* 356 U.S. 342 (1958).

33. For a discussion of most issues contained in a collective bargaining agreement, see L. Stessin and S. Smedresman, *The Encyclopedia of Collective Bargaining Contract Clauses* (New York: Business Research Publications, 1980).

34. *Basic Patterns in Union Contracts,* 9th ed. (Washington, D.C.: Bureau of National Affairs, 1979), p. 88–89.

35. G. J. Mounts, "Significant Decisions in Labor Cases," *Monthly Labor Review,* June 1980, p. 51.

36. *Basic Patterns in Union Contracts,* p. 78.

37. J. W. Driscoll, "A Behavioral—Science View of the Future of Collective Bargaining in the United States," *Labor Law Journal,* July 1979, pp. 434–35.

38. Ibid., p. 435.

39. J. M. Rosow, "Now Is the Time for Productivity Bargaining," *Harvard Business Review,* January–February 1972, p. 78.

40. J. Krislov and J. L. Silver "Current Challenges in Industrial Relations," *Labor Law Journal,* August 1981, p. 484.

Case 17–1   **AIRLINE BENEFITS**

Jim Woodbain grimaced as he heard the proposal. As chairman of the Airline Pilots Association's master executive council for Trans-States Airlines, Jim, along with two appointed negotiators, was responsible for bargaining with management on a new compensation agreement. He was conferring with his old and respected adversary, Lester Linkefeller, Trans-States' Vice President for Employee Relations.

Lester said, "You heard me right, Jim. All we can offer is 5 percent per year for the next two and a half years of the contract. That's a total of 12.5 percent over what you're now being paid."

"Lester, that stinks and you know it," said Jim, somewhat irked. "Your offer doesn't even begin to keep pace with inflation! We'd be losing over what we have now in terms of real wages and buying power if we accepted that proposal."

"Easy, Jim, not so fast," said Lester in a conciliatory tone. "You've heard only half of my proposal, and you're already rejecting it outright! Give me a chance! Now, here's the problem. As you know, our profits have fallen over the last few years. The stockholders are clamoring for an improvement, and Colonel Boringman is in a very tenuous position. How do you think he's going to justify a 35 percent raise to the investors? The answer is that he can't. However, we'd be willing to make some pretty sweet concessions in the area of fringe benefits."

"What kind of benefits are you talking about, Lester?" queried Jim. "Besides, aren't these benefits going to cost you money? How will Colonel Boringman justify *that* to the investors?"

"There's no doubt that it'll cost us money," replied Lester. "However, we can purchase things like life and health, dental, and disability insurance at considerably reduced rates over what you as individuals would pay for the same coverage. We can even beat what you get through the Airline Pilots Association. As an example of what this could mean to you and the other pilots, let's just take disability insurance. You pay about $500 a year for loss-of-license through ALPA, don't you?"

"Yeah, that's about right," said Jim.

"Correct me if I'm wrong," continued Lester, "but your maximum benefits under the ALPA plan would be around $69,000. If the company were to pick up the loss-of-license package with a plan that would give you 50 percent of your salary for the rest of your life in case of disability, that would be a pretty good deal, wouldn't it? And besides having a heck of a lot more protection than you now have, tax free, you'd also have an extra $500 to spend on something else."

"Sounds interesting, Lester, but how am I supposed to sell this to the membership?" asked Jim. "Twelve percent is a lot less than 35 percent, regardless of how you slice it."

"Well, you could sell it in terms of tax benefits," said Lester. "Suppose you assume that you have an average annual income of $60,000. Even with some pretty clever tax planning, you'd still be in a 40 percent marginal income tax bracket, maybe higher. And that's just for the feds. The same thing would apply for state, county, and city income taxes, ALPA dues, Pilot's Mutual Aid assessment, the whole ball of wax. . . ."

"OK, suppose we granted that 35 percent raise," said Lester. "That would up your gross income to $81,000 a year. However, it would also kick you into a marginal tax rate bracket of 56 percent, assuming your deductions stayed fairly constant. That means that your old tax bill was approximately $12,000, with $30,000 in deductions for the current year. With the raise, though, your tax bill would be $28,000. That means your net after-tax income with the present salary would be about $48,000. With the raise, it would go up to $53,000. How far in front of inflation does that put you?"

"Not very far," admitted Jim.

1. *Do you think Jim can sell this package to the airline pilots?*
2. *What differences do you believe exist between this negotiation and other contract negotiations?*

Case 17–2

DEFIANT UNION MEMBERS

The International Association of Machinists and Aerospace Workers has just concluded a lawful, 18-day strike against the Axel Aircraft Company over a new contract. The agreed-upon contract includes a maintenance-of-membership clause that requires all new employees to decide within 40 days after their hiring whether or not to join the union. It also requires union members to retain their membership during the contract term.

During the strike, about 150 production workers, who were represented by the union, crossed the picket line and reported to work. One fourth of these employees made no attempt to leave the union during the strike. Of the remainder, about 60 resigned from the union before crossing the picket line and the rest afterward.

After settlement of the strike, the union notified the people who had crossed the picket line that charges had been preferred against them under the union constitution for "improper conduct of a member" in accepting employment from a company in which a strike existed. For those found guilty of this charge, the union constitution permitted such disciplinary measures as a reprimand, fines, suspensions or expulsion from the union, or any combination of these actions. The people were told the date of the trial and that they had the right to be represented by counsel.

As a result of the trial, disciplinary actions were imposed on all individuals who had worked during the strike. No distinction was made between those members who had resigned from the union and those who had remained in it. Employees who did not appear for the trial or who appeared but were found guilty were fined $450 in addition to being barred from holding a union office for five years. About 30 employees appeared for trial, apologized, and pledged loyalty to the union, their fines were reduced to 50 percent of the earnings they had received during the strike period. The union then notified these people that in the event of nonpayment of fines, the union attorney would be empowered to collect these. Suit was filed against nine people asking for the full $450 plus attorney's fees.

To counter the union's actions, the company filed charges with the National Labor Relations Board stating that it was an unfair labor practice for the union to violate the workers' right to refrain from engaging in strike activities. The company believed that the levy of the fine in this situation was designed to force the members to engage in conduct against their will in the future. Furthermore, the fines would force employees to forego their rights not to honor the union's picket lines and to exercise free judgment over their own work and lives. The company asked that the union be found guilty of an unfair labor practice and that it be barred from such activity in the future. The company further requested that the fines and disciplinary actions be declared illegal.

The union, of course, argued that its actions were legal and appropriate under the law and under the union contract. It said that fining and discipline of members was an internal matter that it should handle.

1. *Which party do you agree with, the company or the union?*
2. *What specific laws relate to this case?*

Chapter 18

Employee safety and health

Objectives

1. To develop an appreciation for the importance of employee health and safety.
2. To present and discuss the major provisions of the Occupational Safety and Health Act (OSHA).
3. To explore what organizations are doing and can do to reduce the costs of work-related accidents and diseases.

Outline

The Occupational Safety and Health Act (OSHA)
  OSHA standards
    Establishment of standards
    Workplace inspections
    Inspection priorities
    Inspection procedures
    Citations
  Penalties
  Record-keeping/reporting requirements
  Reactions to OSHA
The causes of accidents
  Personal acts
  Physical environment
  Accident proneness
How to measure safety
Organizational safety programs
  Promoting safety
Employee health
  Occupational health hazards
  Cancer and the workplace
  Stress in the workplace
  Alcoholism and drug abuse
    Alcoholism
    Other drugs

Employee assistance programs
  Cost of personal problems
  Organization involvement
  Types of EAPs
  Features of a successful EAP
Physical fitness programs

Glossary of terms

Disabling injuries Work-related injuries which cause an employee to miss one or more days of work.

Employee assistance program Company-sponsored program designed to help employees with personal problems such as alcohol and drug abuse, depression, anxiety, domestic trauma, financial problems, and other psychiatric/medical problems.

Frequency rate Ratio that indicates the frequency with which disabling injuries occur.

Occupational Safety and Health Act (OSHA) Federal law passed in 1970 to ensure safe and healthful working conditions for every working person.

OSHA Form 200 (Log and Summary of Occupational Injuries and Illness A form for recording all occupational injuries and illness. Each occupational injury and illness must be recorded on Form 200 within six working days from the time the employer learns of the accident or illness.

OSHA Form 101 (Supplementary Record of Occupational Injuries and Illness) Form that requires detailed information about each occupational injury or illness. Form 101 must be completed within six working days from the time the employer learns of an occupational injury or illness.

Severity rate Ratio that indicates the length of time that injured employees are out of work.

Toxic Substances Control Act Federal law passed in 1976 requiring the pretesting for safety of all new chemicals marketed each year.

Employee safety and health are important concerns in today's organizations. On an average yearly basis in the United States, over 10,000 deaths and 6 million lesser injuries result from occupational accidents.[1] In addition, each year, approximately 400,000 new incidences of occupational disease result in as many as 100,000 deaths. The National Safety Council estimates the annual cost of occupational accidents to be $20 billion, and $15 billion for occupational diseases.[2] Employee safety and health are important concerns for all managers. However, the primary responsibility for designing employee safety and health programs generally lies with the human resource department. The purpose of this chapter is to explore actions and activities that can be undertaken to ensure a safe and healthy work environment.

THE OCCUPATIONAL SAFETY AND HEALTH ACT (OSHA)

The Occupational Safety and Health Act (OSHA) became effective on April 28, 1971.[3] The act established federal regulations relating to employee safety and health. OSHA applies to all businesses with one or more employees. (There are certain exceptions such as self-employed persons.) Its stated purpose is "to assure so far as possible every working man and woman in the nation safe and healthful working conditions and to preserve our human resources."[4] The act contains a "general duty" clause to cover to those situations not addressed by specific standards. This clause states that each employer "shall furnish . . . a place of employment which is free from recognized hazards that are causing or are likely to cause death or serious physical harm to . . . employees." In essence, the general duty clause requires employers to comply with the intent of the act.

The Occupational Safety and Health Administration of the U.S. Department of Labor enforces the act and is authorized to:

Encourage employers and employees to reduce workplace hazards and to implement new or improved existing safety and health programs.

Provide for research in occupational safety and health and develop innovative ways of dealing with occupational safety and health problems.

Establish "separate but dependent responsibilities and rights" for employers and employees for the achievement of better safety and health conditions.

Maintain a reporting and record-keeping system to monitor job-related injuries and illnesses.

Establish training programs to increase the number and competence of occupational safety and health personnel.

Develop mandatory job safety and health standards and enforce them effectively.

Provide for the development, analysis, evaluation, and approval of state occupational safety and health programs.[5]

OSHA standards

OSHA establishes legally enforceable standards relating to employee health and safety. Usually, the human resource department is responsible for being familiar with these standards and ensuring that the organization is complying with them.

Currently, OSHA publishes six different volumes of standards (see Figure 18–1) covering four major categories—general industry, maritime, construction, and agriculture. The *Federal Register* also regularly publishes all OSHA standards and amendments. The *Federal Register* is available in many public and college libraries. Annual subscriptions can be purchased from the Superintendent of Documents, U.S. Government Printing Office, Washington, D.C. 20402. OSHA also offers a subscription service through the Superintendent of Documents. In addition to providing all standards, interpretations, and regulations the OSHA subscription service periodically sends out notices of changes and additions.

Establishment of standards OSHA can initiate standards on its own or on petitions from other parties, including the U.S. Secretary of Health and Human Services (HHS); the National Institute for Occupational Safety and Health (NIOSH); state and local governments; any nationally recognized standards-producing organization; employers; labor organizations; or any other interested party. NIOSH, which was established by the act as an agency under HHS, conducts research on various safety and health problems. NIOSH recommends most of the standards that are adopted by OSHA.

Workplace inspections OSHA compliance officers (inspectors) are authorized under the act to conduct workplace inspections. Originally, employers were not given advance notice of inspection and could not refuse to admit OSHA inspectors. However, a 1978 Supreme Court decision, *Marshall* v. *Barlow's, Inc.*,[6] ruled that employers are not required to admit OSHA inspectors onto their premises without a search

Figure 18–1   Standards manuals published by OSHA

Volume I	General Industry Standards and Interpretations (includes agriculture)
Volume II	Maritime Standards and Interpretations
Volume III	Construction Standards and Interpretations
Volume IV	Other Regulations and Procedures
Volume V	Field Operations Manual
Volume VI	Industrial Hygiene Field Operations Manual

warrant. At the same time, however, the court also ruled that an OSHA inspector does not have to prove probable cause to obtain a search warrant.

Inspection priorities Because OSHA does not have the resources to inspect all workplaces covered by the act, a system of inspection priorities has been established:

1. Those situations involving imminent danger.
2. Investigation of fatalities and catastrophies resulting in the hospitalization of five or more employees.
3. Employee complaints of alleged violation of standards or of unsafe or unhealthful working conditions.
4. Programs of inspection aimed at specific high-hazard industries, occupations, or health substances.
5. Reinspection of organizations previously cited for alleged serious violations.

Inspection procedures Upon arrival, the representatives of the employer should first ask to see the OSHA inspector's credentials. Normally, the inspector then conducts a preliminary meeting with the top management of the organization. The manager of the human resource department is usually present at this meeting. At this time, the inspector explains the purpose of the visit, the scope of the inspection, and the standards that apply. The inspector then normally requests an employer representative (often someone from the human resource department), an employee representative, and a union representative (where applicable) to accompany him or her during an inspection tour of the facility. The inspector then proceeds with the inspection tour, which may cover part or all of the facilities. After the inspection tour has been completed, the inspector meets again with the employer or the employer's representatives. During this meeting, the inspector discusses what has been found and indicates all apparent violations for which a citation may be issued or recommended.

Citations In some cases, the inspector has authority to issue citations at the work site immediately following the closing conference. This occurs only in cases where immediate protection is necessary. Normally, citations are issued by the OSHA area director and sent by certified mail. Once the citation is received, the employer is required to post a copy at or near the place where the violation occurred for three days or until the violation is corrected whichever is longer.

Penalties

Figure 18–2 summarizes the five major types of violations which may be cited and the respective penalties that may be proposed. Under

Figure 18–2   Types of OSHA violations

Other than Serious Violation—A violation that has a direct relationship to job safety and health, but probably would not cause death or serious physical harm. A proposed penalty of up to $1,000 for each violation is discretionary.

Serious Violation—A violation where there is substantial probability that death or serious physical harm could result, and that the employer knew, or should have known of the hazard. A mandatory proposed penalty ranging from $300 to $1,000 for each violation is assessed.

Imminent Danger—A situation where there is reasonable certainty that a danger exists that can be expected to cause death or serious physical harm immediately, or before the danger can be eliminated through normal enforcement procedures. An imminent danger may be cited and penalized as a serious violation.

Willful Violation—A violation that the employer intentionally and knowingly commits. The employer either knows that what he or she is doing constitutes a violation, or is aware that a hazardous condition existed and made no reasonable effort to eliminate it. Penalties of up to $10,000 may be proposed for each willful violation. If an employer is convicted of a willful violation of a standard that has resulted in the death of an employee, the offense is punishable by a court-imposed fine of not more than $10,000, or by imprisonment for up to six months, or both. A second conviction doubles these maximum penalties.

Repeated Violation—A violation of any standard, regulation, rule, or order where, upon reinspection, another violation of the same previously cited section is found. Repeated violations can bring a fine of up to $10,000 for each such violation.

Source: *All About OSHA*, rev. ed. (Washington, D.C.: U.S. Department of Labor, 1982), pp. 29–30.

certain conditions, some of the proposed penalties can be adjusted downward. Additional penalties may be imposed for such things as falsifying records and assaulting an inspector.

Record-keeping/reporting requirements

Employers of 11 or more persons must maintain records of occupational injuries and illnesses as they occur. This includes all occupational illnesses, regardless of severity, and all occupational injuries resulting in death, one or more lost workdays, restriction of work or motion, loss of consciousness, transfer to another job, or medical treatment other than first aid.

Many OSHA standards have special record-keeping and reporting requirements, but all employers covered by the act must maintain two forms. OSHA Form 200 (Log and Summary of Occupational Injuries and Illnesses) requires that each occupational injury and illness be recorded within six working days from the time the employer learns of the accident or illness. OSHA Form 101 (Supplementary Record of Occupational Injuries and Illnesses) requires much more detail about each injury or illness. It also must be completed within six working days from the time the employer learns of the work-related injury or illness. Both Form 200 and Form 101 are maintained on a calendar-year basis. These forms must be retained for five years by the organization and must be available for inspection.

Reactions to OSHA

Few laws have evoked as much negative reaction as OSHA. While not many people would question the intent of OSHA, many have criticized the manner in which the act has been implemented. The sheer volume of regulations is immense. A second criticism concerns the costs of complying with and keeping OSHA-related records. Another frequent criticism is the vague wording of many OSHA regulations.. As an example, the Occupational Safety and Health Administration developed the following 39-word definition of "exit":

> That portion of a means of egress which is separated from all other spaces of the building or structure by construction or equipment as required in this subpart to provide a protected way of travel to the exit discharge.[7]

OSHA has also been criticized for issuing standards that seem trite and petty. For example, one standard states: "Where working clothes are provided by the employer and become wet or are washed between shifts, provision shall be made to insure that such clothing is dry before reuse."

THE CAUSES OF ACCIDENTS

Accidents are caused by a combination of circumstances and events, usually resulting from unsafe work acts, an unsafe work environment, or both.

Personal acts

It is generally believed that unsafe personal acts cause the bulk of organizational accidents, an estimated 80 percent of all such accidents.[8] Unsafe personal acts include such things as taking unnecessary risks, horseplay, failing to wear protective eqiipment, using improper tools and equipment, and taking unsafe shortcuts.

It is difficult to determine why employees commit unsafe personal acts. Fatigue, haste, boredom, stress, poor eyesight, and daydreaming, are all potential reasons. However, these reasons do not totally explain why employees intentionally neglect to wear prescribed equipment or don't follow procedures. Most employees think of accidents as always happening to someone else. Such an attitude can easily lead to carelessness or a lack of respect for what can happen. It is also true that some people get a kick out of taking chances and showing off.

Research studies have also shown that employees with low morale tend to have more accidents than employees with high morale. This is not surprising when one considers that low morale is likely to be related to employee carelessness.

Physical environment

Accidents can and do happen in all types of environments, such as offices, parking lots, and factories. There are, however, certain work

Figure 18–3   Unsafe conditions in the work environment

Unguarded or improperly guarded machines (such as an unguarded belt).
Poor housekeeping (such as congested aisles, dirty or wet floors, loose carpeting, and improper stacking of materials).
Defective equipment and tools.
Poor lighting.
Poor or improper ventilation.
Improper dress (such as wearing clothes with loose and floppy sleeves when working on a machine that has rotating parts).
Sharp edges.

conditions which seem to result in more accidents. Figure 18–3 presents a list of commonly encountered unsafe work conditions.

Accident proneness

A third reason often given for accidents is that certain people are accident prone. Some employees, due to their physical and mental makeup, are more susceptible to accidents. This condition may result from inborn traits, but often it develops as a result of an individual's environment. However, this tendency should not be used to justify an accident. Given the right set of circumstances, anyone can have an accident. For example, an employee who was up all night with a sick child might very well be accident prone the next day.

HOW TO MEASURE SAFETY

Accident frequency and accident severity are the two most widely accepted methods for measuring an organization's safety record. A frequency rate is used to indicate how often disabling injuries occur. Disabling injuries cause an employee to miss one or more days of work following the accident. Disabling injuries are also known as lost-time injuries. A severity rate indicates how severe the accidents were by indicating the length of time injured employees were out of work. Only disabling injuries are used in determining frequency and severity rates. Figure 18–4 gives the formulas for calculating an organization's frequency rate and severity rate.

Figure 18–4   Formulas for computing accident frequency rate and severity rate

$$\text{Frequency rate} = \frac{\text{Number of disabling injuries} \times 1 \text{ million}}{\text{Total number of labor-hours worked each year}}$$

$$\text{Severity rate} = \frac{\text{Days lost* due to injury} \times 1 \text{ million}}{\text{Total number of labor-hours worked each year}}$$

*The American National Standards Institute has developed tables for determining the number of lost days for different types of accidents. To illustrate, an accident resulting in death or permanent total disability is charged with 6,000 days (approximately 25 working years).

Neither the frequency rate nor the severity rate mean much until they are compared with similar figures for other departments or divisions within the organization, for the previous year, or for other organizations. It is through these comparisons that an organization's safety record can be objectively evaluated.

**ORGANIZATIONAL
SAFETY
PROGRAMS**

The heart of any organizational safety program is accident prevention. It is obviously much better to prevent accidents than to react to them. A major objective of any safety program is to get the employees to "think safety." Therefore, most programs are designed to keep safety and accident prevention on the employee's mind. Many different and varied approaches are used to make employees more aware of safety. However, four basic elements are present in most successful safety programs. First, it must have the support of top and middle management. This support must be genuine and not casual. If upper management takes an unenthusiastic approach to safety, employees are quick to pick up on this. Second, it must be clearly established that safety is a responsibility of operating managers. All operating managers should consider safety to be an integral part of their job. Furthermore, operating employees should feel a responsibility for working safely. Third, a positive attitude toward safety must exist and be maintained. The employees must believe that the safety program is worthwhile and that it produces results. Finally, one person or department should be in charge of the safety program and responsible for its operation. Often the human resource manager or a member of his or her staff has primary responsibility for the safety program.

Promoting safety

Many things can be done to promote safety. Some suggestions include:

1. Make the work interesting. Uninteresting work often leads to boredom, fatigue, and stress, which can all cause accidents. Job enrichment, which was discussed in Chapter 9, can be used in many instances to make the work more interesting. Often, simple changes can be made to make the work more meaningful. Job enrichment attempts are usually successful if they add responsibility, challenge, and other similar factors—which increase the employee's satisfaction with the job.
2. Establish a safety committee composed of operative employees and representatives of management. The safety committee provides a means of getting employees directly involved in the operation of the safety program. A rotating membership is desirable. The size should range from 5 to 12 members. Normal duties for the safety

committee include inspecting, observing work practices, investigating accidents, and making recommendations. Committee meetings should be held at least once a month and attendance should be mandatory.

3. Feature employee safety contests. Give prizes to the work group or worker having the best safety record for a given period. Contests can also be held to test safety knowledge. Prizes can be awarded periodically to employees who submit good accident prevention ideas.

4. Publicize safety statistics. Monthly accident reports should be posted. Ideas should be solicited as to how these accidents can be avoided.

5. Periodically hold safety meetings. Have employees participate in these meetings as role players or instructors. Use themes such as "Get the shock (electric) out of your life." Audiovisual aids such as movies and slides might also be used.

6. Use bulletin boards throughout the organization. Pictures, sketches, and cartoons can be effective if properly presented. One thing to remember when using bulletin boards is to change them frequently.

EMPLOYEE HEALTH   Until relatively recent times, safety and accident prevention received far more attention than did employee health. However, this has changed. As the statistics presented at the beginning of this chapter reflect, occupational diseases cost industry almost as much as occupational accidents. Other estimates show the cost of occupational diseases to be much higher.[9] In addition, there are many diseases and health-related problems that are not necessarily job related but which may affect job performance. Many organizations now not only attempt to remove health hazards from the workplace but also have instigated programs to improve health.

Occupational health hazards   "A coal miner in West Virginia can't breathe. A pesticide plant worker in Texas can't walk. A hospital anesthesiologist in Chicago suffers a miscarriage."[10] These people, along with hundreds of thousands of other employees, are victims of occupational diseases. Increased awareness of occupational disease was one factor that contributed to the passage of the Occupational Safety and Health Act (OSHA). In addition, the Toxic Substance Control Act of 1976 requires the pretesting of the approximately 700 new chemicals marketed each year.[11] A 1980 rule issued by OSHA requires organizations to measure for safety and record employee exposure to certain potentially harmful substances. These medical records must be made available to employees, their designated representatives, and OSHA. Furthermore, these records must be maintained for 30 years, even if the employee leaves the job.[12]

Cancer and the workplace

Society has been aware of certain occupational diseases, such as black lung disease, for years. However, it has only been in recent years that the potential extent of occupational diseases has been realized. Figure 18–5 lists 10 of the major substances that have been linked to occupational diseases. It should be noted that 7 of the 10 can produce some form of cancer. One government study estimates that between 20 and 38 percent of all cancer in this country is occupationally related.[13] In October 1977, OSHA issued a policy aimed at regulating carcinogens (substances that have been identified as causing cancer) in the work-

Figure 18–5	Ten suspected hazards in the workplace	
Potential dangers	Diseases that may result	Workers exposed
Arsenic	Lung cancer, lymphona	Smelter, chemical, oil-refinery workers; insecticide makers and sprayers—estimated 660,000 exposed
Asbestos	White-lung disease (asbestosis); cancer of lungs and lining of lungs; cancer of other organs	Miners; millers; textile, insulation and shipyard workers—estimated 1.6 million exposed
Benzene	Leukemia; asplastic anemia	Petrochemical and oil-refinery workers; dye users; distillers; painters; shoemakers—estimated 600,000 exposed
Bischloromethylether . . (BCME)	Lung cancer	Industrial chemical workers
Coal dust	Black-lung disease	Coal miners—estimated 208,000 exposed
Coke oven emissions . .	Cancer of lungs, kidneys	Coke-oven workers—estimated 30,000 exposed
Cotton dust	Brown-lung disease (byssinosis); chronic bronchitis; emphysema	Textile workers—estimated 600,000 exposed
Lead	Kidney disease; anemia; central-nervous-system damage, sterility; birth defects	Metal grinders; lead-smelter workers; lead-storage-battery workers—estimated 835,000 exposed
Radiation	Cancer of thyroid, lungs and bone; leukemia; reproductive effects (spontaneous abortion, genetic damage)	Medical technicians; uranium miners; nuclear-power and atomic workers
Vinyl chloride	Cancer of liver, brain	Plastic-industry workers—estimated 10,000 directly exposed

place. In January 1980, OSHA issued additional rules designed to clarify precisely how to identify and classify carcinogens in the workplace. However, because of problems in applying and interpreting these rules, many people feel that the entire OSHA cancer policy has been ineffective.[14]

Stress in the workplace

Stress manifests itself among employees in several ways: increased absenteeism, job turnover, lower productivity, mistakes on the job, low-key employees, and even death.[15] The potential for stress exists when an environmental situation presents a demand threatening to exceed a person's capabilities and resources for meeting it, under conditions in which the person expects a substantial difference in the rewards and costs resulting from meeting the demand versus not meeting it.[16] Certainly, organizational life presents numerous such situations. Figure 18–6 lists some of the more common sources affecting employees.

The cost of stress to organizations has been estimated to exceed $100 billion annually.[17] Recently, employees have even began to sue employers for psychiatric injury caused by job stress.[18] In an effort to combat stress, many organizations have recently instigated training programs designed to help reduce employee stress.

Alcoholism and drug abuse

A recent survey by the Federal Alcohol, Drug Abuse, and Mental Health Association reported that as many as 6 million employees were abusing drugs.[19] Even more disturbing is the apparent growth rate in the use of drugs by employees. The work-related consequences of drug abuse range from simple absenteeism and low productivity to outright theft to pay for drug habits.[20]

Alcohol is the most commonly abused drug. However, prescription drugs, marijuana, quaaludes, amphetamines, heroin, and cocaine have recently become more prevalent in the workplace.

Alcoholism The U.S. Department of Health and Human Services (HHS) estimates that alcoholism costs the nation more than $50 billion

Figure 18–6	Common sources of employee stress

Job or task stress (e.g., job or task is too difficult).
Role stress (e.g., ambiguities in the description of a particular job).
Stress from human environment (e.g., overcrowding or understaffing).
Stress from physical environment (e.g., extreme cold or heat or poor ventilation).
Stress from social environment (e.g., interpersonal conflict).
Stress from within an individual (e.g., intrapersonal conflict).

Many executives complain of stress, but few want less-pressured jobs

If you hate stress, steer clear of small businesses. People who own one complain of stress more than twice as frequently as those who run giant corporations.

Over 40 percent of top executives sometimes or often lie awake at night thinking about business problems. But fewer than one in five thinks he or she would be happier in a less stressful job.

Those are some of the findings of a Gallup Organization poll of business leaders conducted for *The Wall Street Journal.* It shows that highly placed executives and business owners commonly feel stress—and that they have developed a great range of techniques to cope with it.

"I exercise and run around with wild women," says the chairman of a big textile concern. "I scream at my employees and play golf," says the chairman of a large manufacturer. "After work, I go boating in the river, drink a double martini, jump in the pool and eat dinner," says a hardware store owner. And the chairman of a big company who owns a ranch in Oklahoma says he likes to "look at the cows and drink Dr Pepper."

Gallup found that 49 percent of the small-business proprietors it polled consider stress either a major problem or somewhat of a problem, compared with only 33 percent of the executives who headed medium-sized companies and only 19 percent of those who led big corporations.

Complaining the least

Of course, the disparity could partly reflect the ability of larger-company chiefs to handle stress rather than the degree of stress involved in the work itself. But even within the big-company group, the chiefs of the largest companies complained least about stress.

In telephone interviews last month, Gallup talked with top officers, almost always chief executives, of 327 companies drawn at random from *Fortune* magazine's lists of the 1,350 biggest U.S. concerns. Among the companies ranking in the biggest 200, only 8 percent of the chiefs polled consider stress a problem, compared with 24 percent of the chiefs whose companies rank between 500 and 1,350 in size.

Gallup also interviewed 312 chief executives of medium-sized companies (generally with annual sales of more than $20 million) and 206 proprietors of small businesses (usually with sales between $250,000 and $19.9 million a year). In polls like this, relying on a sample can result in errors of as much as six or seven percentage points either way, Gallup says.

For all the discussion of pressure on executives, 35 percent of the chiefs of the 1,350 largest companies say stress is "no problem." This compares with 25 percent of the medium-sized-company chiefs and 23 percent of the small-business proprietors.

"People who get to my position have the stomach of a goat; stress occurs in middle management," says the chairman of a medium-sized electronics concern. The chairman of a large company adds: "Most corporate executives are well staffed—secretaries, chauffeur-driven limousines. The person is either stress oriented or he isn't."

Of executives who do complain of stress, a disproportionate number are young. In medium-sized companies, for instance, 48 percent of the chiefs under age 45 find stress a problem, compared with only 29 percent among those aged 45 or more. "As you grow older, you learn to handle stress and don't feel it," says the chairman of a manufacturing concern. The president of a beverage concern adds, "I'm less strained at 54 than I was at 35—I've had to work on it."

annually.[21] Companies incur a significant portion of these costs in terms of impaired job performance, accidents, absenteeism, and turnover. In spite of these costs, organizations have only recently undertaken widespread efforts to combat employee alcoholism. For example, a 1973 survey reported that only 400 major U.S. companies had any type of program designed to help overcome employee alcoholism.[22] A similar survey in 1982 reported that the number had grown to over 5,000.[23] Most of the companies that have implemented such programs reported impressive results.[24] Programs for combating alcoholism are normally administered as part of an employee assistance program (EAP). EAPs are discussed at length in a later section of this chapter.

Other drugs The use of drugs, other than alcohol, is a relatively new phenomenon. Other drug usage usually falls into one of three categories: marijuana abuse, prescription-drug abuse, and hard-drug abuse. Although most drug users are young employees, they are not all blue-collar workers. Employees on drugs are often much more difficult to detect than are drinking employees. Alcohol can usually be smelled, where drugs can't. Also, it is relatively easy to pop a pill at lunch or on a break. As with alcoholism, many organizations are fighting drug abuse through employee assistance programs (EAPs).

Employee assistance programs

Many large organizations and a growing number of smaller organizations are attempting to help employees with personal problems. These problems include such things as alcohol and drug abuse, depression, anxiety, domestic trauma, financial problems, and other psychiatric/medical problems. This help is not purely altruistic, but is largely based on cost savings. The help is generally referred to as employee assistance programs (EAPs).

Cost of personal problems A primary result of personal problems brought to the workplace is reduced productivity. Absenteeism and tardiness also tend to increase. Increased costs of insurance programs, including sickness and accident benefits, are a direct result of personal problems brought to the workplace. Lower morale, more friction among employees, more friction between supervisors and employees, and more grievances also result from troubled employees. Permanent loss of trained employees due to disability, retirement, and death are also associated with troubled employees. Difficult to measure, but a very real cost associated with troubled employees, is the loss of business and damaged public image.

Organization involvement Until recently, organizations attempted to avoid an employee's non-job-related problems. Although aware of the existence of these problems, organizations did not believe that they should interfere with employees' personal life. In the past, organizations tended to get rid of troubled employees. In recent years, however, cost considerations, unions, and government legislation have altered this approach. The accepted viewpoint now is that an employee's personal problems are private until they began affecting his or her job performance. When and if that happens, personal problems become a matter of concern for the organization.

Studies have shown that absenteeism can be significantly reduced by employee assistance programs. It has also been found that EAPs help to reduce on-the-job accidents and grievances. Workers compensation premiums, sickness and accident benefits, and trips to the infirmary also tend to decrease with an EAP. For example, Kennecott Copper Corporation reported a 52 percent improvement in attendance, a 75 percent decrease in nonindustrial health and accident insurance, and a 55 percent reduction in hospital medical and surgical costs for the 150 employees who participated in their EAP.[25]

Types of EAPs There are several types of employee assistance programs. In one type, which is rarely used, diagnosis and treatment of the problem are provided directly by the organization. In a second type of program, the organization hires a qualified person to diagnose the employee's problem, then the employee is referred to the proper agency or clinic. The third and most common type of program employs a coordinator who evelutes the employee's problem only sufficiently to make a proper referral to the right agency or clinic. Sometimes the coordinator serves only as a consultant to the organization and is not a full-time employee.

Features of a successful EAP[26] Experience has shown that certain elements are essential to the success of an EAP. A recent survey reported "The most common ingredients, characterizing more than 75 percent of the programs in 1979, were assurance of confidentiality, written policies and procedures, and health insurance coverage for both inpatient and outpatient treatment.[27] Figure 18–7 further elaborates elements that are critical to the success of an EAP.

Dr. William Mayer, administrator of the federal Alcohol, Drug Abuse, and Mental Health Administration has estimated that EAPs return $8 for every $1 invested.[28] Because of the obvious benefits to both employees and employers, it is estimated that EAPs will continue to grow in popularity.

Physical fitness programs

According to the National Industrial Recreation Association (NIRA), as of 1980, about 50,000 organizations had established physical fitness programs (PFPs).[29] PFPs differ widely among organizations. For ex-

Figure 18–7   Ten critical elements of an EAP

Management backing—without this at the highest level, key ingredients and overall effect are seriously limited.

Labor support—the EAP cannot be meaningful if it is not backed by the employees' labor unit.

Confidentiality—anonymity and trust are crucial if employees are to use an EAP.

Easy access—for maximum use and benefit.

Supervisor training—is crucial to employees needing understanding and support during receipt of assistance.

Labor steward training—a critical variable is employees' contact with labor—the steward.

Insurance involvement—occasionally assistance alternatives are costly and insurance support is a must.

Breadth of service components—availability of assistance for a wide variety of problems (e.g., alcohol, family, personal, financial, grief, medical, etc.)

Professional leadership—from a skilled professional with expertise in helping. This person must have credibility in the eyes of the employee.

Follow-up and evaluation—to measure program effectiveness and overall improvement.

Source: F. Dickman and W. G. Emener, "Employee Assistance Programs: Basic Concepts, Attributes, and An Evaluation," *Personnel Administrator*, August 1982, p. 56.

ample, PFPs can be after-hours, company-sponsored athletic teams or very sophisticated physical fitness centers staffed by full-time company personnel.

While there has been little research on the overall effects of PFPs as they relate to organizational benefits, there is evidence that PFPs can produce positive personal benefits such as reduced heart disease, reduced obesity, improved psychological well-being, and decreased back problems.[30] Surely these personal benefits result in certain organizational benefits, such as reduced absenteeism and decreased health claims. However, some people have questioned whether the benefits offset the cost of these programs. Many organizations have justified PFPs by pointing out that many nonfinancial benefits such as contributing to employee well-being and community visibility, can be gained.

SUMMARY

On an average yearly basis in the United States, over 10,000 deaths and 6 million lesser injuries result from occupational accidents. In addition, there are approximately 400,000 new incidences of occupational disease each year.

The Occupational Safety and Health Act (OSHA) became effective in 1971. Its stated purpose is "to assure so far as possible every working man and woman in the nation safe and healthful working conditions and to preserve our human resources." OSHA covers all businesses with one or more employees. (There are certain exceptions, such as self-employed persons.) Many OSHA standards involve special re-cord-keeping and reporting requirements, but all employers covered by OSHA must maintain OSHA Form 200 (Log and Summary of Oc-cupational Injuries and Illness) and OSHA Form 101 (Supplementary Record of Occupational Injuries and Illness). OSHA has been harshly criticized for the manner in which its standards have been imple-mented.

Accidents are the result of unsafe personal acts, an unsafe physical environment, or both. It is generally agreed that unsafe personal acts cause the bulk of organizational accidents. Accident frequency and ac-cident severity are the two most widely accepted methods for meas-uring an organization's safety record. A frequency rate indicates how often disabling injuries occur. A severity rate indicates how severe the accidents were.

The heart of any organizational safety program is accident preven-tion. Many organizations have implemented safety programs and most are based on the concept of getting the employees to "think safety." Until relatively recent times, safety and accident prevention received far more organizational attention than did employee health. However, this has changed and the issue of employee health is now receiving substantial attention.

Organizational health hazards include all substances found in orga-nizational environments that may be hazardous to employee health. Asbestos, lead, cotton dust, and benzene represent some of the health hazards that have been identified, many of which have been linked to cancer. Another health-related problem that can be caused and/or ag-gravated by the work environment is stress.

Alcoholism and drug abuse cost industry billions of dollars each year. In spite of these huge costs, organizations have only recently under-taken any widespread effort to help employees with these and other personal problems. Employee assistance program (EAPs) have been implemented by over 5,000 organizations to aid employees with se-vere personal problems. Many organizations have reported impressive benefits from the use of EAPs. Another trend related to employee health has been the implementation of organization-sponsored physical fit-ness programs (PFPs).

REVIEW QUESTIONS

1. What is the Occupational Safety and Health Administration (OSHA) au-thorized to do?
2. What is the "general duty" clause as related to OSHA?
3. What are the inspection priorities established by OSHA?
4. What is the usual inspection procedure followed by OSHA?
5. Name and discuss the three primary causes of accidents.

6. How do organizations measure their safety record?

7. What four basic elements are present in most successful safety programs?

8. What can be done to promote safety in organizations?

9. What are the three general types of employee assistance programs (EAPs)?

DISCUSSION QUESTIONS

1. Express your personal philosophy on the responsibilities of management, especially human resource managers, for the well-being of employees.

2. Why do you think that OSHA has not been totally successful? What approaches to employee safety do you favor?

3. Do you think that an organization has any responsibility to help employees who have health problems that are totally unrelated to their work environment?

REFERENCES AND ADDITIONAL READINGS

1. R. S. Schuler, "Occupational Health in Organizations: Strategies for Personnel Effectiveness," *Personnel Administrator*, January 1982, pp. 47–48.

2. Ibid., p. 48.

3. Much of this section is drawn from *All About OSHA*, rev. ed. (Washington, D.C.: U.S. Department of Labor, 1982).

4. Ibid., p. 1.

5. Ibid., p. 2.

6. *Marshall* v. *Barlow's, Inc.*, 76-1143 (1978).

7. H. Sidney, "Trying to Regulate the Regulations," *Time*, 5 December 1977, p. 33.

8. G. R. Terry and L. W. Rue, *A Guide to Supervision* (Homewood, Ill., Learning Systems Company, 1982), p. 131.

9. "Is Your Job Dangerous to Your Health?" *U.S. News & World Report*, 5 February 1979, p. 41.

10. Ibid., p. 39.

11. Ibid.

12. *Nation's Business*, May 1982, pp. 19–20.

13. M. C. Anderson, R. N. Isom, K. Williams, and L. J. Zimmerman,eds., *The Proceeding of a Conference for Workers on Job-Related Cancer*, (Houston, Texas, March 30, 1981), p. 29.

14. W. W. Stead and J. G. Stead, "OSHA's Cancer Prevention Policy: Where Did it Come From and Where Is It Going," *Personnel Journal*, January 1983, p. 54.

15. R. Weigel and S. Pinsky, "Managing Stress: A Model for the Human Resource Staff," *Personnel Administrator*, February 1982, p. 56.

16. J. E. McGarth, "Stress and Behavior in Organizations," in *Handbook of Industrial and Organizational Psychology*, ed. M. D. Dunnette (Skokie, Ill.: Rand McNally, 1976), p. 1352.

17. M. T. Matteson and J. M. Ivancevich, "The How, What, and Why of Stress Management Training," *Personnel Journal,* October 1982, p. 770.

18. B. Rice, "Can Companies Kill?" *Personnel Administrator,* December 1981, pp. 54–59.

19. "On-the-Job Drugs Costly for Business," *Data Management,* December 1981, p. 19.

20. Ibid.

21. "Battling Employee Alcoholism," *Dun's Business Monthly,* June 1982, p. 48.

22. Ibid.

23. Ibid.

24. E. Norris, "Alcohol: Companies are Learning it Pays to Help Workers Beat the Bottle," *Business Insurance,* 16 November 1981, p. 53.

25. Ibid., p. 1. This article also reports similar success stories from several other companies.

26. Much of this section is drawn from F. Dickman and W. G. Emener, "Employee Assistance Programs: Basic Concepts, Attributes, and an Evaluation," *Personnel Administrator,* August 1982, pp. 55–62.

27. P. M. Roman, "Corporate Pacesetters Making EAP Progress," *Alcoholism,* 1, no. 4 (1981), pp. 37–41.

28. M. Tuthill, "Joining the War on Drug Abuse," *Nation's Business,* June 1982, p. 64.

29. J. Kondrasuk, "Company Physical Fitness Programs; Salvation or Fad, "*Personnel Administrator,* November 1980, p. 47.

30. Ibid., pp. 47–50., and R. W. Driver and R. A. Ratcliff, "Employees" Perceptions of Benefits Accrued From Physical Fitness Programs," *Personnel Administrator,* August 1982, pp. 21–26.

Case 18–1

SAFETY PROBLEMS AT BLAKELY

Several severe accidents have recently occurred in the 12-employee assembly department of Blakely company which has a total work force of 65 employees. The supervisor of this department, Joe Benson, is quite perturbed and in response to questions by the general manager and part owner of the company, claims that the employees do not listen to him. He has warned them about not taking safety precautions, but explains that he can't police their every move. The general manager countered with, "Accidents cost us money for repairs, lost time, medical expenses, human suffering, and what not. It's important that you to stop it. Your department has a bad safety record—the worst in the company. You are going to have to correct it."

Joe felt he had taken the necessary precautions but that he was not getting satisfactory results. He also believed there were more possibilities of accidents occurring in his department than in any other department of the company. He decided to talk it over with the human resource manager, Fay Thomas. From Fay, he got the idea of scheduling a 10-minute safety talk each week by a different employee. The first subject would be, "Using Machine Guards." Joe felt that "Good Housekeeping and Safety" and "No Smoking" would also be good subsequent subjects.

Fay suggested that Joe schedule part of his time to review his department periodically. Furthermore she suggested that any unsafe act he discovered should result in an immediate two-day suspension for the offender. "You have to get tough when it comes to safety. Your people are taking safety much too lightly. Of course, you start by making an announcement of what you are going to do. Put a notice to that effect on the bulletin board. Then enforce it to the letter."

Joe believed that by simply talking personally to each of his employees and urging them to work safely might get better results. However, he really felt that some type of incentive was needed. As a result, he evolved a plan in which the employee with the fewest safety violations over the next three months would be given a day off with pay. Joe's plan was approved by his boss.

1. *What is Joe's problem?*
2. *In your opinion, how did this problem develop? What were its main causes? Discuss.*
3. *What actions do you recommend Joe take? Why?*

Case 18–2   **CREDIBILITY AT OSHA**

Time magazine reported the following two situations involving OSHA:*

> OSHA inspectors have turned up in the most unlikely places with the most implausible demands. Michael Armstrong, manager of In-Line, Inc., a North Carolina construction firm, recalls the investigator who insisted that he provide a portable toilet for his crew while they were digging a tunnel under a highway. In vain did Armstrong argue that his men never complained about using the bathroom at a filling station 50 yards away. OSHA was even determined to give cowboys a new king of home on the range, complete with a portable flush toilet within five-minutes walking distance. Ranch hands who felt that nature provided ample resources for their needs hooted the proposal down. "Can you imagine a cowboy carrying his own rest room on the back of his horse?" scoffed Doug Huddleston, president of the Colorado Cattlemen's Association.

> The contradictions can be incredible and infuriating, as shown by just two conflicts between OSHA and the Department of Agriculture. OSHA

---

*"Rage Over Rising Regulation," *Time*, 2 January 1978, p. 49.

demands grated floors in butcher shops to reduce the risk of employees' slipping. The Department of Agriculture declares that the same floors must be smooth because grates increase the hazards of contamination. Last year, OSHA also directed that the Made-Rite Sausage Company of Sacramento, California, place protective guards on its meat-blending machine to keep employees' hands out of it, even though the machine is too high for workers to reach. But such a guard would have violated Agriculture Department regulations because it would have made the machine too difficult to clean. The company did the only sensible thing: nothing.

1. *With situations like the above occurring, can OSHA ever hope to be accepted by the business community as something other than a "bad guy"?*

2. *As human resource manager of a large organization, what are some actions you might take to encourage employees to pay attention to and abide by OSHA rules?*

CLOSING A PLANT

The Renegade Corporation, a manufacturer of nondurable goods, has been in business since 1921. The production process at Renegade has always been labor intensive because of the scarcity and cost of capital equipment. Historically, the work force has consisted of women. Most of the line supervisors and foremen are also women who began on the line and had superior work records. The average education level of the workers is high school or below.

The management of Renegade has always been very cost conscious. Renegade's product is mass marketed at such a low profit margin that any decreases in productivity or increases in cost directly affect profitability. For the same reasons, Renegade cannot afford any shutdowns or slowdowns. At the same time, however, Renegade cannot afford to increase wages or other production costs.

About 10 years ago, technological advances began to affect the industry. The greatest impact resulted from a machine developed as an offshoot of the space program. This piece of equipment could do the work of about 15 to 25 percent of the work force. The cost of the equipment at that time was prohibitive for Renegade, and management was forced to delay any purchase. All indications were that the cost of the machine would drop within a few years. In effect, Renegade's management decided to wait and let other purchasers pay for the research and development of the machine.

A number of employees became aware that the machine that had just been developed posed a threat to employment security in the future. Even though the employees had previously been satisfied to work at low wages, they suddenly realized that even their meager earnings were being threatened. Most of the women were married and their income afforded their families a considerably higher standard of living than was possible if they didn't work.

Because most of the women's husbands were blue-collar workers, several were aware of unionization and its potential benefits. Through the efforts of these few women, an organizing campaign by the Teamsters Union got under way.

Renegade's management was in a quandary. On the one hand, they could not afford to purchase the high-priced technological machinery. On the other hand, they felt that unionization would deal a crippling blow to profit margins with a possibility that they would be forced out of business.

A bitter antiunion campaign was waged, but the employees were adamant in their desire to maintain job security. The employees felt that they were better off with a union than with no jobs at all. In addition, they felt that the union would be as cost conscious as man-

459

agement was. After all, if the union demands forced the closing of the plant, the union would also be out of business.

The union secured more than the minimum number of employee signatures, and petitioned the National Labor Relations Board to designate the appropriate bargaining unit and conduct an election. The NLRB deemed the entire company (300 employees) to be a single bargaining unit. An election was held, and the union won more than 50 percent of the votes cast. Thus, the Teamsters Union was designated as the exclusive bargaining representative for the company.

Real difficulties followed the union election. The union went to the collective bargaining table knowing that it had to act fast to preserve employees' jobs and maintain its power base. A firm demand was made concerning employment security, and the union wanted to negotiate many points in the hiring, firing, and promotion procedures. Management looked upon these requests with indignant disdain, claiming that these procedures were management rights that were not negotiable. The management of Renegade then offered a firm but fair offer and refused to budge through negotiation.

Charging management with an unfair labor practice, the union filed a complaint with the NLRB on the grounds that collective bargaining was not being conducted in good faith. At almost the same time, a drastic price drop in the new machinery was announced. Within only a few days, the decision was made to purchase the machinery and begin installation as soon as possible.

The union members were incensed. Because of the refusal to bargain, no contract provisions concerning employee security had been negotiated and as a result the company was free to purchase the machine. Rumors of a strike began to abound. However, although the women desired union protection, they were reluctant to go on strike for fear they would lose their jobs altogether. The union also pondered the question of just how strong the security issue was with the employees.

Renegade's management was likewise upset. They had always thought that they should be able to manage the work force as they saw fit. They also perceived the importance that the employees placed on their job security. They knew that the only training most of the women had was unique to Renegade's production system. Thus, for the great majority of employees, the job skills they had obtained could only be applied in the Renegade corporation and were not easily transferable to other firms or jobs. However, the one problem that management did not foresee was a decrease in productivity by the employees as a result of the uncertain environment. The subsequent drop in productivity resulted in lower profit margins. This, combined with the additional costs of investing in new machinery and fighting the union, was rapidly pushing the company toward financial disaster.

Financial resources became scarce as Renegade's lines of credit began to tighten and dry up. The truth soon became apparent. A strike would send the company under. Union leaders knew this as well, but they were still pushing for a strike as a means of bringing the company to the bargaining table. In light of the fact that management could always exercise appeals procedures as an effective delay device, the union realized that the NLRB could not be relied upon to make management capitulate.

The strike vote never materialized, frustrating the union. Renegade went ahead and installed the machinery and eliminated 18 percent of the jobs. Management's feelings of victory were short lived, however. The cost of raw materials began to rise. Investor confidence began to drop because of the questionable management practices. In addition, it appeared as if the court of appeals was going to uphold enforcement of an NLRB decision that had been issued against the company. An unfavorable decision could result in a heavy fine against the company for willful violations of the NLRB. On top of all this, productivity continued to remain low.

Nine short months after the strike crisis, the company was forced to close its doors. The closing had the primary effect of displacing both production and management employees. The community also lost a good taxpayer.

APPENDIXES

Preemployment inquiry guide

This guide is *not* a complete definition of what can and cannot be asked of applicants. It is illustrative and attempts to answer the questions most frequently asked about equal employment opportunity law. It is hoped that in most cases the given rules either directly or by analogy, will guide all personnel involved in the preemployment processes of recruiting, interviewing, and selection. This guide pertains only to inquiries, advertisements, etc., directed to all applicants prior to employment. Information required for records such as race, sex, and number of dependents may be requested after the applicant is on the payroll provided such information is not used for any subsequent discrimination, as in upgrading or layoff.

These laws are not intended to prohibit employers from obtaining sufficient job-related information about applicants, as long as the questions do not elicit information which could be used for discriminatory purposes. Applicants should not be encouraged to volunteer potentially prejudicial information. The laws do not restrict the rights of employers to define qualifications necessary for satisfactory job performance, but require that the same standard of qualifications used for hiring be applied to all persons considered for employment.

It is recognized that the mere routine adherence to these laws will not accomplish the results intended by the courts and Congress. Employment discrimination can be eliminated only if the laws and regulations are followed in the spirit in which they were conceived.

Subject	Permissible inquiries	Inquiries to be avoided
Name	Have you worked for this company under a different name? Is any additional information relative to change of name, use of an assumed name or nickname necessary to enable a check on your work and educational record? If yes, explain.	Inquiries about name which would indicate applicant's lineage, ancestry, national origin, or descent. Inquiry into previous name of applicant where it has been changed by court order or otherwise. Inquiries about preferred courtesy title: Miss, Mrs., Ms.

(continued)

Subject	Permissible inquiries	Inquiries to be avoided
Marital and family status	Whether applicant can meet specified work schedules or has activities, commitments, or responsibilities that may hinder the meeting of work attendance requirements. Inquiries as to a duration of stay on job or anticipated absences which are made to males and females alike.	Any inquiry indicating whether an applicant is married, single, divorced, or engaged, etc. Number and age of children. Information on child-care arrangements. Any questions concerning pregnancy. Any such questions which directly or indirectly result in limitation of job opportunities.
Age	Requiring proof of age in the form of a work permit or a certificate of age—if a minor Requiring proof of age by birth certificate after being hired. Inquiry as to whether or not the applicant met the minimum age requirements as set by law, and requirement that upon hire proof of age must be submitted in the form of a birth certificate or other forms of proof of age. If age is a legal requirement, "if hired, can you furnish proof of age?," or statement that hire is subject to verification of age. Inquiry as to whether or not an applicant is younger than the employer's regular retirement age.	Requirement that applicant state age or date of birth. Requirement that applicant produce proof of age in the form of a birth certificate or baptismal record. The Age Discrimination in Employment Act of 1967 forbids discrimination against persons between the ages of 40 and 70.
Handicaps	For employers subject to the provisions of the Rehabilitation Act of 1973, applicants may be "invited" to indicate how and to what extent they are handicapped. The employer must indicate that: (1) compliance with the invitation is voluntary; (2) the information is being sought only to remedy discrimination or provide opportunities for the handicapped; (3) the information will be kept confidential; and (4) refusing to provide the information will not result in adverse treatment. All applicants can be asked if they are able to carry out all necessary job assignments and perform them in a safe manner.	An employer must be prepared to prove that any physical and mental requirements for a job are due to "business necessity" and the safe performance of the job. Except in cases where undue hardship can be proved, employers must make "reasonable accommodations" for the physical and mental limitations of an employee or applicant. "Reasonable accommodation" includes alteration of duties, alteration of work schedule, alteration of physical setting, and provision of aids. The Rehabilitation Act of 1973 forbids employers from asking job applicants general questions about whether they are handicapped or asking them about the nature and severity of their handicaps.

(continued)	Subject	Permissible inquiries	Inquiries to be avoided
	Sex	Inquiry or restriction of employment is permissible only where a bona fide occupational qualification exists. (This BFOQ exception is interpreted very narrowly by the courts and the EEOC.) The burden of proof rests on the employer to prove that the BFOQ does exist and that *all* members of the affected class are incapable of performing the job. Sex of applicant may be requested (preferably not on the employment application) for affirmative action purposes but may not be used as an employment criterion.	Sex of applicant. Any other inquiry which would indicate sex. Sex is *not* a BFOQ because a job involves physical labor (such as heavy lifting) beyond the capacity of *some* women and employment cannot be restricted just because the job is traditionally labeled "men's work" or "women's work." Applicant's sex cannot be used as a factor for determining whether or not an applicant will be satisfied in a particular job. Questions about an applicant's height or weight, unless demonstrably necessary as requirements for the job.
	Race or color	General distinguishing physical characteristics such as scars, etc., to be used for identification purposes. Race may be requested (preferably not on the employment application) for affirmative action purposes, but may not be used as an employment criterion.	Applicant's race. Color of applicant's skin, eyes, hair, etc., or other questions directly or indirectly indicating race or color.
	Address or duration of residence	Applicant's address. Inquiry into length of stay at current and previous addresses. "How long a resident of this state or city?"	Specific inquiry into foreign address which would indicate national origin. Names and relationship of persons with whom applicant resides. Whether applicant owns or rents home.
	Birthplace	Can you after employment submit a birth certificate or other proof of U.S. citizenship.	Birthplace of applicant. Birthplace of applicant's parents, spouse, or other relatives. Requirement that applicant submit a birth certificate before employment. Any other inquiry into national origin.
	Religion	An applicant may be advised concerning normal hours and days of work required by the job to avoid possible conflict with religious or other personal conviction. However, except in cases where undue hardship can be proven, employers and unions must make "reasonable accom-	Applicant's religious denomination or affiliation, church, parish, pastor, or religious holidays observed. Any inquiry to indicate or identify religious denomination or customs.

(continued)	Subject	Permissible inquiries	Inquiries to be avoided
		modation" for religious practices of an employee or prospective employee. "Reasonable accommodation" may include voluntary substitutes, flexible scheduling, lateral transfer, change of job assignments, or the use of an alternative to payment of union dues.	Applicants may not be told that any particular religious groups are required to work on their religious holidays.
	Military record	Type of education and experience in service as it relates to a particular job.	Type of discharge.
	Photograph	May be required for identification after hiring.	Requirement that applicant affix a photograph to his or her application.
			Request that applicant, at his or her option, submit photograph.
			Requirement of photograph after interview but before hiring.
	Citizenship	Are you a citizen of the United States?	Of what country are you a citizen?
		Do you intend to remain permanently in the U.S.?	Whether applicant or his parents or spouse are naturalized or native-born U.S. citizens.
		If not a citizen, are you prevented from becoming lawfully employed because of visa or immigration status? Statement that, if hired, applicant may be required to submit proof of citizenship.	Date when applicant or parents or spouse acquired U.S. citizenship.
			Requirement that applicant produce naturalization papers. Whether applicant's parents or spouse are citizens of the United States.
	Ancestry or national origin	Languages applicant reads, speaks, or writes fluently, (if another language is necessary to perform the job.)	Inquiries into applicant's lineage, ancestry, national origin, descent, birthplace, or native language.
			National origin of applicant's parents or spouse.
	Education	Applicant's academic, vocational, or professional education; school attended.	Any inquiry asking specifically the nationality, racial, or religious affiliation of a school.
		Inquiry into language skills such as reading, speaking, and writing foreign languages.	Inquiry as to how foreign language ability was acquired.
	Experience	Applicant's work experience, including names and addresses of previous employers, dates of employment, reasons for leaving, salary history.	
		Other countries visited.	

(concluded)	Subject	Permissible inquiries	Inquiries to be avoided
	Conviction, arrest, and court record	Inquiry into actual *convictions* which relate reasonably to fitness to perform a particular job. (A conviction is a court ruling where the party is found guilty as charged. An arrest is merely the apprehending or detaining of the person to answer the alleged crime.)	Any inquiry relating to arrests. Any inquiry into or request for a person's arrest, court, or conviction record if not *substantially related* to functions and responsibilities of the particular job in question.
	Relatives	Names of applicant's relatives already employed by this company. Names and address of parents or guardian (if applicant is a minor).	Name or address of any relative of adult applicant.
	Notify in case of emergency	Name and address of persons to be notified in case of accident or emergency.	Name and address of *relatives* to be notified in case of accident or emergency.
	Organizations	Inquiry into any organizations which an applicant is a member of, providing the name or character of the organizations does not reveal the race, religion, color, or ancestry of the membership. "List all professional organizations to which you belong. What offices do you hold?"	"List all organizations, clubs, societies, and lodges to which you belong." The names of organizations to which the applicant belongs, if such information would indicate through character or name the race, religion, color, or ancestry of the membership.
	References	"By whom were you referred for a position here?" Names of persons willing to provide professional and/or character references for applicant.	Requiring the submission of a religious reference. Requesting reference from applicant's pastor.
	Credit rating	None	Any questions concerning credit rating, charge accounts, etc. Ownership of car.
	Miscellaneous	Notice to applicants that any misstatements or omissions of material facts in the application may be cause for dismissal.	Any inquiry should be avoided which, although not specifically listed among the above, is designed to elicit information concerning race, color, ancestry, age, sex, religion, handicap, or arrest and court record, unless based upon a bona fide occupational qualification.

Source: C. M. Koen, Jr., "The Pre-Employment Inquiry Guide," *Personnel Journal,* October 1980, pp. 826–28. Copyright *Personnel Journal,* reprinted with permission. All rights reserved.

Finding a job*

An important—and often overlooked—aspect of a successful job hunt is what occurs *before* you write your resume or prepare for your interviews, namely—research. You must become familiar with your options, including the typical entry-level assignments and the more advanced job assignments along the career ladder. Besides learning the current "buzz words" and job titles associated with various careers, you should become familiar with your personal priorities and with the skills or qualities that are important for success in a particular job or career path. To help you with this process, the following example of a typical job hunter, "Chris", is presented.

Descriptive traits

The following research is the beginning of Chris's successful career planning/job-hunting effort:

Who am I?

Do I prefer:
  Working alone or in a group?
  Working with people, data, things, or a combination of these?
  Working as a facilitator or as an instructor?
  Working with the genral public or with a targeted group?

Do I see myself as a:
  Facilitator? instructor? supervisor?
  Negotiator? organizer? persuader?
  Analyzer? designer? data gatherer?

How do I feel about:
  Helping the organization make money?
  Working under the pressure of daily deadlines?
  Making presentations to a group?
  Digging for answers?
  Motivating others?

What are my long-term/short-term career goals?

---

*By Ms. D. L. Wormley, Director, Corporate Associates Program, Graduate School of Business Administration, Atlanta University. The Corporate Associates Program coordinates college recruitment for the Graduate School of Business Administration at Atlanta University.

These are only a few of the key questions a job hunter should ask, answer, and analyze on the way toward a successful job hunt. There's an almost endless combination of descriptive traits you can uncover about yourself during this research phase. Let's look at Chris's first set of findings.

Finding	How do I know this?
Prefer group/team work	Tennis team: doubles rather than singles play
Enjoy evaluating people	Tennis team: determine how much the person has progressed and how to improve play
Enjoy presentations	Senior seminar: enjoyed making presentation to classmates and to faculty
Fairly persuasive	Tennis: able to convince athletic manager to expand practice time for tennis team
Good observer/prober	Dorm life: able to determine and anticipate problems between roommates
Good at handling pressure	Tennis: handle tournaments easily
Detail oriented	Worked summers at Bloomingdale's: good at maintaining complex inventory records

The combination of these traits and the following "functional skills" will help you focus on which career paths make the most sense for you in light of your interests and priorities.

Functional skills

Functional skills, unlike the more widely recognized vocational skills, are found in all aspects of your life and are easily transfered between job, extracurricular, and academic environments. As a result, even the job hunter with little paid work experience can demonstrate skills (and potential) related to the career field he or she wishes to enter. Functional skills in Chris's case have been italicized.

Hobby	Tennis team captain: responsible for *assisting* team manager with *scheduling* practice and matches; *instruct* new players for League A; *determine* best matchings of players for tournaments.
Job	Bloomingdales (summers): *sell* sports equipment, *answer* customer's inquiries; *maintain* inventory and *organize* displays.
Major	Business Administration: majoring in management. *Analyzed* the recruiting practices of several companies and *presented* findings to the class.
Dorm	Volunteer hall counselor: *advise* peers on social, academic, and personal issues; *train* other volunteers in basic counseling skills.

The functional skills which Chris has identified are important in any number of environments including business, academic, community, or political organizations. Take a look at most detailed job descriptions and you will find similar functional skills describing the job. For Chris, a look at the preferences and the functional skills may lead to a variety of careers, but Chris has settled on considering the broad areas of consumer research, teaching, personnel representative, and admissions counselor. Now Chris is in a better position to research these various career options through the use of informational interviews in which key questions are asked of people who are in these careers.

Informational interviews

The following is a partial list of key questions for Chris to ask to learn about specific careers.

Job duties
  What do you do on a daily basis? Are there duties which occur at specific times of the month or year?
  What is the career ladder like for this option? How long does it generally take to reach each step on the ladder?

Requirements
  What are the entrance requirements for this field in terms of education, experience, etc.?
  Is further study required? recommended?

Realities of the job
  What is the normal workweek?
  Are you expected to take work home and/or work late?
  What are some of the pressures associated with the field?
  What are some of the pluses? minuses?
  How has the field changed in the past 10 years?
  How does a recession affect this field?
  How much extended travel is required? overnight travel?
  Is geographic flexibility a requirement for success?
  What is the general salary range for entry-level and advanced jobs?

The answers to these and other questions are easily obtained by contacting professionals already in the field. Contacts can be made through your career planning/placement office, family friends, graduates of your school, professional associations, and current places of employment. Most professionals enjoy talking about their work and helping others obtain a realistic overview of their career, so don't hesitate to ask for help!

After the informational interviews, Chris made the following journal entries:

Option (source of interest)	Preferences met	Functional skills used	Key questions ratings A: Meets needs B: Moderately meets needs C: Does not meet needs	Comments
Consumer research (from selling job and psychology courses).	Evaluating people's responses; some team work. A few oral presentations	Evaluating, observing, analyzing, concluding, handling details.	Duties: B Requirements: C (need more courses) Realities: B	Doesn't seem to have enough variety. Too much statistical analysis.
Teaching (Introduction to Business) (from enjoyment of classes).	Group work. Plenty of presentations. Creative.	Analyze and evaluate. Develop classes. Oral presentations.	Duties: C Requirements: C Realities: C	Too much disciplining and not enough creative work. Too much interference from chairperson or department head.
Personnel representative (suggested at work).	Group and individual work. Plenty of evaluation and presentations.	Evaluate, document, interview, present findings, some travel.	Duties: A Requirements: B Realities: A	Tough to enter the field but good career path. Will require some additional courses once in job.
Admissions counselor (recommended by personal friend).	Group/individual work. Plenty of evaluation. Many presentations. Some analysis of numbers. Work with students.	Presentations. Evaluations. Persuasiveness selling (the school's program.) Advise applicants.	Duties: A Requirements: A Realities: A	Lots of pressure in two to three month spurts. Lots of travel. Plenty of interaction with students.

After this analysis and comparison of options and interests, Chris is prepared for the "nitty gritty" aspects of job hunting, including developing the specific strategy, identifying specific employers and jobs, preparing the resume, and practicing for interviews. Chris has found that the college/university placement office and the public library reference section are especially good sources of information on careers.

Option	Typical Employers	Specific employers	Resume	Interview
consumer research	Consumer product companies (used: College Placement Annual)	Procter & Gamble General Mills M & M Products Pillsbury Pepsi-Cola Company Coca-Cola Company		
Teaching	Junior colleges	No longer interested in this		
Personnel representative	Large and medium-sized companies (College Placement Annual)	Saks Fifth Avenue (enter through buyer trainee program) Mobil Oil Inland Steel TRW		
	Community organizations (large, United Way national listings)	National Red Cross National United Way		
	Labor organizations (national directory)	AFL–CIO		
Admissions counselor	Most colleges and universities (directory of colleges/universities; chronicle of higher education)	NYU, Columbia, UCLA, University of Chicago, Duke University, Emory University		

Government publications from the Department of Labor and magazines and professional journals supplement the usual directories associated with the job hunt. Chris's expanded journal entry now includes information on typical and specific employers. There is also room for indicating when the resume was mailed, when interviews were scheduled and the type of follow-up.

Preparing for
interviews

In preparing for interviews, Chris reviews the job descriptions and checks them against identified preferences and skills. Chris knows that the answers to the following (and similar) questions will be an important part of the job interview:

What are your long-term goals? short-term goals?

How do you plan to achieve them?

What are your plans for further study?

What makes you stand out from all of the other applicants?

What does it take to succeed in this career?

Discuss your skills.

What are your strengths? weaknesses?

In addition, Chris refers to the key questions list (page 473) in developing questions to ask the interviewer. Chris is especially interested in growth potential and movement up the career ladder, so questions focus on these topics, as well as whether the employer is a leader in the field, changes in the organization in recent years, etc.

In summary, the successful job hunter cannot afford to bypass the research stage. This research—looking at yourself and at your options—is critical. The process can be applied to all occupational areas and, with minor modification, can be used as the job hunter moves up the career ladder. The process is also appropriate for any person who is involved with a major career change.

APPENDIX C

Resume writing*

A great deal has been written about resumes and resume writing over the years. As every job hunter knows, a resume is used by employers to determine an applicant's potential for a specific job (and subsequent jobs along the career path).

The following example of how a typical job hunter, "Chris," prepares a resume is presented to help you learn the difference between an ineffective and an effective resume. Keep in mind that the writing of the resume is *not* the first step of the job hunt. Unless you have taken the time to analyze your specific career interests, skills and potential (as discussed in Appendix B) *before* you pick up your pen, resume writing will soon grind to a halt.

A "do/don't" approach is used to organize the following discussion and to critique Chris' resume.

	Do	*Don't*
Format	Provide a *complete index* to your experience and skills, but keep it short.	Omit the seemingly dull or "unrelated" job.
	Include an objective, which may be written as a job title or in functional skills terms.	Omit the objective for sake of "flexibility."
	Keep it to one page, if at all possible. (The second page may not be read.)	Forget that the representative has many resumes to skim.
	Use reverse chronological order (most recent first).	
	Experiment with a variety of formats—select the one which best presents your potential and skills.	

*By Ms. D. L. Wormley, Director, Corporate Associates Program, Graduate School of Business Administration, Atlanta University. The Corporate Associates Program coordinates college recruitment for the Graduate School of Business Administration of Atlanta University.

(concluded)	Education	Focus on any course work which would help you in your career (statistics; counseling; computer programming; etc.)	Forget that courses outside your major are important.
		Indicate independent study, advanced research, or special projects which support your career interests.	Assume that everyone will understand all the requirements of your specific degree.
		Give a full picture of undergraduate and graduate-level education.	Include high school unless it's to highlight particular skill areas.
		Spotlight quantitative, interpersonal, research, or other functional skills.	
	Employment	Select employment which demonstrates skills even though the job may be unrelated to your career goal.	Underestimate what you have learned from previous work experiences.
		Indicate if you worked part-time to pay for your education (e.g., 1981–84 worked approximately 30 hours/week to finance education).	Forget that being able to manage your time is an important skill.
		Use active words in highlighting your experience: researched, sold, organized, developed, taught, prepared, etc.	Use sentences in describing your work.
		Include volunteer experience (after all—you gained skills from it).	Assume you can give details at the interview—you may not get one!!
	Honors/ affiliations	Indicate academic scholarships, leadership awards, etc. (The J & J Leadership Award; The Primo Academic Scholarship).	Just give the name of the award or scholarship without indicating the type of scholarship. (The Elma Curtis Prize doesn't mean much to an outsider.)
		Show patterns of success (member 1980; president 1983)	
		Indicate skills (conducted meetings; handled budget of $1,000).	

In reviewing the comments on Chris' resume, we find that without an objective, it isn't clear what job Chris wants, therefore, it is very difficult to identify skills or potential. By adding an objective which reflects Chris's interests, the employment representative now knows what skills and potential to look for when skimming Chris' resume:

Objective: An admissions counselor position including recruiting, counseling, and evaluating applicants.

By including the job title and a few of the functional skills associated with the job, Chris has clarified the focus of the resume and has dem-

Chris's resume—draft one

How about permanent address?

CHRIS CHAPMAN
PO Box 2333
Berkeley, Ca. 94111
(415) 990-0099

Single
Excellent Health
5'7"   135 lbs.   *Not necessary*
DOB: 01-16-62

→ OBJECTIVE: *What's your goal/focus?*

Reverse Chronological Order

Education:	Oak Grove High School	1979
	New School for Social Research	1979 summer
	UC Berkeley	1979–1983 BA
	Business Administration/Management	

Most recent first

Employment:	Bloomingdale's	Summers 1980-83
	New York	
	Sales	
	Supervisor: JJ Thomas	
	Domino's Pizza	Current
	Kitchen Supervisor	*(Where? City)*
	Supervisor: Rick Haynes	
	UC Berkeley Library	Current
	Research Desk	
	Supervisor: M.K. Polk *(Where)*	

Provide details/SKILLS using active words

| Hobbies: | Tennis, Reading, Music |

Honors:	R.T. Gilbert Award
	Dean's List
	Dorm Council

(What kind? Where? Duties)

References:	Mr. M.P. Reynolds
	1333 Main Street
	Richmond, CA 94113
	Mrs. Jane Julian
	3233 Richmond Road
	Richmond, CA 94111

Furnished upon request (this gives you flexibility to select references for particular jobs) onstrated knowledge of the career field. Now the representative can look for skills which are important to success in the job: interpersonal skills, communication skills, experience in interviewing, researching, evaluating and/or analyzing.

It's up to Chris to make certain that some of these skills appear on the resume in support of the stated objective. To do this, let's review Chris's identified functional skills (from the research aspect of the job hunt):

Communicating	Spokesperson and liaison for tennis team between team/athletic department and between team and community.
	Explained new procedures to kitchen help at pizza restaurant.
Presenting	Presented research findings from senior seminar to departmental faculty and honors students.
Counseling	Provided personal and social counseling as dorm counselor.
Evaluating	Observed tennis team members (junior varsity) and determined skills/weaknesses.
	Recommended singles or doubles play, etc.

Chris decided that these skills were the most interesting and the ones desired in any future job.

Now Chris is ready to describe experiences (including, but not limited to, employment) which reflect the skills needed for the position of an admissions counselor. Chris also has determined which courses, both inside and outside of his major, should be emphasized, namely: statistics, psychology, and human resource management. As a result, Chris has developed the following resume:

Chris's resume now reflects not only the facts associated with education, employment, and activities, but it also provides an overview of some of the skills Chris has developed. These skills, including researching, presenting, writing, training, counseling, and selling, will be discussed further if Chris has an interview.

Since the job hunter cannot simply put a resume in an envelope and mail it to employers, we will now spend a few minutes on the cover letter which accompanies the resume.

The cover letter—
Letter of application

There are two primary purposes for developing a cover letter: (1) to get the employer to review your resume, and (2) to ignite a spark of interest in your qualifications and potential. In some cases, you will be applying for a specific job which has already been announced; in others, you will be seeking information.

CHRIS CHAPMAN

Present Address
P. O. Box 2333
University of California
Berkeley, CA 94111
(415) 990-0099

Permanent Address
100 Cliff Avenue
New York, NY 10019
(202) 903-2893

OBJECTIVE
An admissions counselor position including recruiting, counseling, and evaluating applicants.

EDUCATION
University of California at Berkeley 1979-83
Bachelor degree in Business Administration. Majored in management. Course work has included human resource management, communication skills, psychology, and organizational behavior. Will graduate June, 1983.

New School for Social Research Summer 1979
Completed advanced coursework in sociology and statistics.

EMPLOYMENT
University of California at Berkeley Library 1980-83
Research Assistant. Assisted doctoral candidates in locating literature and reference materials through use of computer-based reference system.

Self-employed 1982-83
Edited doctoral dissertations in marketing, finance, and management.

Domino's Pizza 1982-83
Kitchen Supervisor. Scheduled all employees; trained new employees; determined new procedures with manager; assisted opening and closing store. Worked approximately 30 hours per week.

Bloomingdale's Summers 1980-82
Sales Representative Assisted customers in selecting merchandise in men's and sports departments; assisted buyers with ordering tennis equipment; selected items for tennis displays.

HONORS
UC Berkeley Dean's List, 1979-83

ACTIVITIES
Halloran House Council 1982-83
Provided personal and social counseling for freshmen.

Tennis Team Captain 1982-83
Assisted in teaching new team members; acted as liaison between team and Athletic Department.

REFERENCES
Available upon request.

Do	Don't
Have each letter individually typed and signed.	Send form letters or xeroxed letters.
Use good-quality typing paper.	Use stilted phrases.
Use acceptable business format.	Mention salary requirements unless ad requests it.
Check spelling and grammatical construction.	Forget to sign the letter.
Keep the letter to one page.	Act passively.
Adapt the letter for each position or organization.	Forget to ask for suggestions and advice or other people to contact, as appropriate.
Take the initiative to request an appointment to discuss your qualifications and potential.	Forget to ask for the organization literature and a more detailed job description.
Indicate how you can be reached (evening number if you are a student).	Forget that you can contact more than one person in an organization.

The following samples show two kinds of cover letters. Use your own style to highlight your qualifications and potential. Keep in mind that if you don't know of a specific opening, you may ask to meet with the person for some advice and suggestions about the field and how to best prepare for and enter it! Sample one is usually used during the research stage of the job hunt, while sample two is most used when applying for a specific job.

P. O. Box 2333
University of California
Berkeley, CA 94111
January 2, 1983

Mrs. Alice Green
Director of Admissions
Manyard College
Woodstock, CA 94123

Dear Ms. Green:

I am a senior management major at UC Berkeley, and am very interested
in entering the field of student services, especially admissions.

While researching the field, I have learned that recent college
graduates with skills and interests in planning, evaluating, and making
presentations best qualify for positions as admissions counselors. My
experience in working with young people as a dorm counselor and as the
tennis team captain has been both challenging and satisfying, and has
provided me with a good background for this career choice. I would like
the opportunity to meet with you at your earliest convenience to discuss
the career field. Enclosed is a copy of my resume.

I will be calling your office next week to establish a meeting time that
is convenient for you. Thank you very much for your assistance.

Sincerely,

Chris P. Chapman

Chris P. Chapman

enclosure

P.O. BOX 2333
University of California
Berkeley, CA 94111
January 2, 1983

Mr. David S. Peters
Dean of Admissions
Loyola College
Loyola, CA 94233

Dear Mr. Peters:

I am writing to ask that my credentials   (identify position
be considered for the position of Admissions   and the way you
Recruiter which was listed in the December   heard of it)
27, 1983 issue of the Chronicle of Higher
Education.

I am currently a senior at UC Berkeley with   (provide basic
a major in Management. I have had extensive   information and
experience in working with young people ages   a sense of your
17-19 through my role as a dorm counselor   skills which are
and as captain of the tennis team. These   needed for the job)
experiences, and those in selling, researching,
and editing, have provided me with skills in
communicating, evaluating, presenting, organizing,
and coordinating.

In addition, due to my senior honors project,
I have just recently been asked to provide
academic counseling to new majors. My familiarity with curricula, such as that at Loyola, plus
my other skills and enthusiasm provide an excellent
background for admissions.

Enclosed is a copy of my resume which gives   (refer to resume)
details on my education and experience.

I plan on being in the Loyola area in the   (indicate interest
next three weeks and will be available for   in an interview;
an interview at your convenience. I will   be active-not passive)
contact your office to discuss an appropriate
meeting time.

Thank you very much for your consideration.

                              Sincerely,

                              Chris P. Chapman

                              Chris P. Chapman

enclosure

Journals related to human resource management

Bulletin on Training (monthly)
The Bureau of National
    Affairs, Inc.
1231 25th Street, N.W.
Washington, DC 20037

Compensation Review (quarterly)
American Management
    Association
135 W. 50th Street
New York, NY 10020

Employee Benefits Journal
    (quarterly)
International Foundation of
    Employee Benefit Plans
18700 W. Bluemound Rd., Box
    69
Brookfield, WI 53005

*Industrial and Labor Relations
    Review* (quarterly)
New York State School of
    Industrial and Labor
    Relations
Cornell University
Ithaca, NY 14853

Industrial Relations (triannual)
Institute of Industrial
    Relations
University of California
Berkeley, CA 94720

Industrial Relations News
    (weekly)
Enterprise Publications
20 N. Wacker Drive
Chicago, IL 60606

Labor Law Journal (monthly)
Commerce Clearinghouse,
    Inc.
4025 W. Peterson Avenue
Chicago, IL 60646

Monthly Labor Review (monthly)
Bureau of Labor Statistics
U.S. Department of Labor
441 G Street, N.W.
Washington, DC 20212

Personnel (bimonthly)
American Management
    Association
135 W., 50th Street
New York, NY 10020

Personnel Administrator
    (monthly)
Society for Personnel
    Administration
30 Park Drive
Berea, OH 44017

Personnel Journal (monthly)
866 West 18th Street
Costa Mesa, CA 92627

Personnel Management (monthly)
  Business Publications Ltd.
  76 Shoe Lane
  London EC4A3JB England
Personnel Management Abstracts
  (quarterly)
  Graduate School of Business
    Administration
  University of Michigan
  Ann Arbor, MI 48104
Public Personnel Management
  (bimonthly)

International Personnel
  Management Association
  1850 K Street, N.W.
  Washington, DC 20006
Training and Development Journal
  (monthly)
  American Society for Training
    and Development
  600 Maryland Ave., S.W.
  Suite 305
  Washington, DC 20025

Important organizations and sources in human resource management

AFL–CIO
815 16th Street N.W.
Washington, DC 20006

American Arbitration
Association (AAA)
140 West 51 Street
New York, NY 10020

American Compensation
Association
P.O. Box 1176
Scottsdale, AZ 85252

American Management
Association (AMA)
135 West 50th Street
New York, NY 10020

American Psychological
Association (APA)
1200 17th St., N.W.
Washington, DC 20036

American Society for Personnel
Administration (ASPA)
30 Park Drive
Berea, OH 44017

American Society for Training
and Development (ASTD)
600 Maryland Avenue, S.W.
Suite 305
Washington, DC 20024

Association of Private Pension
and Welfare Plans

1725 K Street, N.W.
Suite 801
Washington, DC 20006

Bureau of Industrial Relations
University of Michigan
Ann Arbor, MI 48104

Bureau of Labor Statistics (BLS)
Department of Labor
3rd Street and Constitution
Ave., N.W.
Washington, DC 20210

Bureau of National Affairs (BNA)
1231 25th Street, N.W.
Washington, DC 20037

Department of Labor
3rd Street and Constitution
Ave., N.W.
Washington, DC 20210

Equal Employment Opportunity
Commission (EEOC)
2401 E. Street, N.W.
Washington, DC 20506

Federal Mediation and
Conciliation Service
Washington, DC 20427

Human Resource Planning
Society
P.O. Box 2553
Grand Central Station
New York, NY 10163

Industrial Relations Research
Association
7226 Social Science Building
University of Wisconsin
Madison, WI 53706

International Association for
Personnel Women
211 E. 43rd St.
Suite 1601
New York, NY 10017

International Personnel
Management Association
(IPMA)
1850 K Street, N.W.
Suite 870
Washington, DC 20006

National Association of
Manufacturers (NAM)
1776 F Street
Washington, DC 20006

National Labor-Management
Foundation (NLMF)

1901 L Street, N.W.
Suite 711
Washington, DC 20036

Occupational Safety and Health
Administration (OSHA)
200 Constitution Ave., N.W.
Washington, DC 20210

Office of Federal Contract
Compliance (OFCC)
200 Constitution Ave., N.W.
Washington, DC 20210

Prentice-Hall Personnel Service
Prentice-Hall, Inc.
Sylvan Avenue
Englewood Cliffs, NJ 07632

The Conference Board
845 Third Avenue
New York, NY 10022

U.S. Chamber of Commerce
1615 H Street, N.W.
Washington, D.C. 20062

Name index

Subject index